Model City Blues

Model City Blues

Urban Space and Organized Resistance in New Haven

MANDI ISAACS JACKSON

TEMPLE UNIVERSITY PRESS
Philadelphia

TEMPLE UNIVERSITY PRESS
1601 North Broad Street
Philadelphia PA 19122
www.temple.edu/tempress

∞ The paper used in this publication meets the requirements of the American National Standard for Information Sciences—Permanence of Paper for Printed Library Materials, ANSI Z39.48-1992

Library of Congress Cataloging-in-Publication Data

Jackson, Mandi Isaacs, 1977–
   Model city blues : urban space and organized resistance in New Haven / Mandi Isaacs Jackson.
      p. cm.
   Includes bibliographical references and index.
   ISBN-13: 978-1-59213-603-2   ISBN-10: 1-59213-603-6 (cloth : alk. paper)
   ISBN-13: 978-1-59213-604-9   ISBN-10: 1-59213-604-4 (pbk. : alk. paper)
   1. Urban renewal—Connecticut—New Haven—History.   2. City and town life—Connecticut—New Haven—History.   I. Title.

HT177.N47J33   2008
307.3'416097468—dc22   2007038122

2 4 6 8 9 7 5 3 1

For Scott

Contents

Acknowledgments

It is true what authors say in their acknowledgments about how their books were finished only because of a long list of other people. My list is long because I'm both very lucky and very prone to crises, so I've leaned on many extraordinary people in the past few years. This project began as my dissertation in the American Studies Program at Yale University, and I would like to thank Michael Denning and Matt Jacobson for their help along the way, their astute readings of overly long drafts, and their infinite patience. I would also like to thank Jennifer Klein, who read early versions of this project, and Amanda Seligman, whose students are lucky to have a great scholar and conscientious teacher in their corner. Many of my colleagues read pieces of this project and helped shape it over the years, including Amanda Ciafone, Daniel Gilbert, Sarah Haley, Brandi Hughes, Jana Lipman, Shana Redmond, Mary Reynolds, Anita Seth, and Melissa Stuckey.

Thanks to all of the people who took the time to tell me about their experiences in New Haven. Photographer Virginia Blaisdell generously offered both her time and her photographs. Amy Kesselman, whose important work on the women's movement in New Haven shares significant archival footsteps with this project, also lent me a large box of papers that proved invaluable, and her generosity is much appreciated. Joan Stone talked with me for hours despite her incredibly busy schedule as a dancer, choreographer, and teacher. I can't thank her enough for the use of the sketches drawn by her husband, Harris, and I hope this book does his memory justice. Thanks also to Charlotte Simms, Harriet Cohen, Bob and Karin Cook, Richard Wolff, David Dickson, Nina Adams, Betsy Gilbertson, and John Wilhelm, as well as a group of longtime New Haven residents who joined me for a Friday afternoon discussion at the New Haven People's Center in 2005.

Thank you to Yohuru Williams, the New Haven Oral History Project, the archivists and staff at Yale University's Manuscripts and Archives collection, the staff of the New Haven Free Public Library, and Amy Trout, photography curator at the New Haven Museum and Historical Society. Thank you to everyone in the union office at 425 College Street (and outside in the surrounding streets), where I received my formal education in collective action. I owe a great debt to UNITE-HERE locals 34 and 35, CCNE, CORD, and especially the Graduate Employees and Students Organization (GESO), the union for graduate teachers and researchers at Yale. Without the support and solidarity of the union—not to mention the gains won by academic organizers a generation before me—I would not have had the resources or the will to complete this project while teaching, organizing, and parenting.

Shortly after I started graduate school, my mother, who spent her childhood living above the small grocery store that her parents owned in Newark, New Jersey, decided she was going to open up a coffee shop. Her alternative model for a local business was more about the exchange of culture and the creation of a collective neighborhood space than it was about making a profit, which was unfortunate for her since she didn't actually start (or finish) with any money. She continues to inspire me, even though she has since had to sell Java Jane's. I hope she understands how much I learned from her vision, courage, and commitment through that process, and how much of her is in this book. Thank you also to my father, Ron Isaacs, and to my brothers, Seth, Josh, and Matt, for their support and encouragement. To my stepfather, Michael Maine, I owe a debt of thanks for his help in creating the maps for this book, and for teaching me about persistence and creativity over the past twenty years.

My son, Max, was born just as I was finishing a first draft of this project, and quite frankly makes it look like an insignificant piece of work. Although right now he prefers a book entitled *Goodnight Gorilla* by Peggy Rathmann, I hope one day he'll read this one and find it just as interesting. Betty Jackson enabled me to write this book not only by taking care of her grandson every day, but also by sharing her stories about New Haven, and inspiring me with her own sense of history. Thank you, finally, to Scott D. Jackson, the gentleman in the suit who bears a striking resemblance to my son, who has managed to serve the people of Hamden, Connecticut, while fixing all of my computer problems, cooking and cleaning, changing lots of diapers, getting things down from high shelves, and putting to use his own talents as a writer and reader—and as an expert in government and politics—to offer feedback and suggestions on my work.

List of Abbreviations

AIM	American Independent Movement
AWC	Area-Wide Council
CAC	Citizens Action Commission
CAP	Community Action Program
CBA	Community Benefits Agreement
CCC	Coalition of Concerned Citizens
CEO	Commission on Equal Opportunities
CORD	Community Organized for Responsible Development
CORE	Congress of Racial Equality
CPI	Community Progress, Inc.
DAG	Draft Action Group
DCMDA	Demonstration Cities and Metropolitan Development Act of 1966
DNI	Department of Neighborhood Improvement
EOA	Economic Opportunity Act of 1964
ERAP	Economic Research Action Project
FSA	Farm Security Administration
HCH	Hill Cooperative Housing
HECB	Hill Executive Coordinating Board
HERE	Hotel Employees and Restaurant Employees Union

HHFA	Housing and Home Finance Administration
HNC	Hill Neighborhood Corporation
HNU	Hill Neighborhood Union
HPA	Hill Parents' Association
HUD	Department of Housing and Urban Development
IBM	International Business Machines Corporation
MFDP	Mississippi Freedom Democratic Party
NAACP	National Association for the Advancement of Colored People
NEC	Neighborhood Employment Center
NHPD	New Haven Police Department
NOW	Neighborhood Organization Workers
OEO	Office of Economic Opportunity
PAG	People Against the Garage
PTA	Parent-Teacher Association
RA	Redevelopment Agency
SCLC	Southern Christian Leadership Conference
SDS	Students for a Democratic Society
SOS	Save Our Stores
SRO	Single Room Occupancy
TUP	Trade Union Plaza
UMIS	Urban Management Information System
WPA	Works Progress Administration

Model City Blues

Introduction

There's a place we all know
Where we all love to go
Where unity's heart is beating
On Thursday nights
We discuss our rights
At Community Union Meeting.

Let's strengthen the arteries of Unity's heart
And all pitch in and do our part.
Your suggestions and ideas are worth repeating
And the time and the place is
Community Union Meeting.

—Delores Maxwell, untitled poem on the cover
of *ERAP Newsletter*, published by Economic
Research and Action Project, Students for a
Democratic Society (SDS), October 5, 1965

Delores Maxwell was not a famous person. The story of her life is not evident from the words she assembled into poetry in October of 1965, but her call to a particular time and place—Thursday nights at the Community Union—articulates the essential components of both history and action. Her poetics encircle her demand with metaphor, giving "unity" both a heartbeat and arteries in an attempt to make a poem out of it all, but this voice from the grass roots, calling on readers to "all pitch in and do our part," is less about poetry than it is about collective action. This is not to diminish the poet, who is equally unknown as an activist, but to celebrate the fact that an individual who was probably many things in the world—perhaps a mother, a worker, a tenant, a daughter, or, to borrow a term from feminist scholar Karen Brodkin Sacks, a "center woman," whose social networks constituted a rich political life—took to heart the task of solving the problems in her city, and understood the importance of this particular time and place in doing so. She tells her readers not only to show up, but also to speak. She demands not only that they show up once, but also that they show up each week. On Thursday nights they discussed their rights at the community union meeting; that much we know.

It was nothing new in the summer of 1965 for people in a neighborhood to gather, share ideas, and plan campaigns for better streets, schools, and housing, but there was new faith and more widespread acceptance in the notion, at that particular time, that people like Maxwell and her neighbors had "suggestions and ideas worth repeating." The previous summer, Congress had signed into law the Economic Opportunity Act of 1964, calling for the "maximum feasible participation" of the poor in the project of eradicating poverty. This phrase prompted little debate in Congress, tucked away as it was in one clause of one section of the legislation. But in the years to follow, as community groups seized on that notion in their struggle for a new kind of urban democracy, and civil rights, community control, and black power activists demanded real structural changes to have more say in the physical, social, and economic landscape of their cities, a heated debate emerged. It took the form of legislation, policy, and scholarship, but also the form of petitions, marches, mass meetings, protests, and community and tenant unions like the one that Delores Maxwell attended each Thursday night on Chicago's South Side.

By 1965, when Maxwell penned her poem, cities large and small—from Chicago to New Haven, Connecticut—were rocked at the grass roots by the convergence of three forces: the idea and the practice of citizen participation, the rising tide of social movements, and massive reconfigurations of urban space. As city officials and national policy makers came face-to-face with the repercussions of vague mandates for citizen involvement, and community leaders grasped at the opportunity for a new kind of urban democracy, civil rights activists stormed the South registering black voters, culminating in the passage of the Voting Rights Act of 1965. That year, activists organized the first antiwar teach-in at the University of Michigan following the deployment of more than 3,500 combat troops to Vietnam. Shortly before Maxwell called on her neighbors to discuss their rights on Thursday nights, riots erupted in the Watts section of Los Angeles, ushering in the second round of an annual cycle of summer violence that had started in Harlem the previous year.

As the weather turned hot, newspaper maps accompanying images of broken glass and crowded streets delineated the sections of cities that were "volatile," "dangerous," "poor," and "black." But contrary to the chaotic images of these urban blocks, often outlined in dark lines and shaded and labeled on front-page, two-tone riot maps, these were also the places where community unions met, where citizens gathered to discuss their rights, and where some of the most promising grassroots models for urban renewal and the War on Poverty were constructed door-to-door, enacted on community playgrounds, and pushed by organized neighborhoods as an alternative to the city's model. Such alternative notions of what the "model city" should be are visible only in portraits drawn from street level, and legible only in accounts written from the grass roots.

What emerges from such an account is the significance of particular spaces—like the community union office—in mounting resistance movements, and how changes in the urban landscape circumscribe the possibility for organized dissent. Through an analysis of the different proposals and visions for both urban forms and modes of citizen participation during a time of "urban crisis," "urban management," and movements for social change, this story of one model city asserts the importance of particular everyday places and the viability of alternative models for revitalizing the city. The story of these particular times and places in New Haven, Connecticut, from the mid-1950s through the early 1970s reveals the extent to which the physical transformation of the city affects social movements, and organized movements can affect the physical shape of the city.

All of the sites excavated here came to serve as catalysts for the local fronts of national social movements for civil rights, black power, women's liberation, welfare rights, and draft resistance, to name a few. A rich and fascinating body of scholarship on these movements—including Frances Fox Piven and Richard A. Cloward's *Poor People's Movements* (1977), Robert Fisher's *Let the People Decide* (1984), and, more recently, David S. Meyer's *Politics and Protest* (2006)—offers useful histories and analyses of movement strategies and their relationships to national politics. However, they tend to understand movements in relative isolation from one another, and in relation to the national rather than the local, their histories and consciousness rarely intersecting, and judgments of success or failure continent on national political consequences. What this look at the "movement culture" of one small city reveals is that, in these spaces of resistance, different movements for change all manifested themselves locally somewhat outside their organizational structures. Individuals and families came together to push for alternative visions of how the city (if not the country or the world) should be economically, socially, and spatially organized.

Today the important questions raised by this historical moment remain not only relevant, but essential, as institutions expand into poor neighborhoods and postindustrial spaces, as the Supreme Court expands the power of eminent domain, while big boxes remake the suburban landscape and Wal-Mart elbows its way into resistant communities. These questions take on added importance as the working poor—largely unprotected by union contracts and increasingly concentrated in low-wage service-sector jobs, just as they are concentrated in low-rent, under-resourced neighborhoods—struggle to build collective power while carving out a sustainable life in cities and towns that were not necessarily designed with their needs in mind. What role do people have in shaping the physical spaces in which they live? Who controls the plan and vision for a particular place? What happens when the people who work and live in that place challenge those plans and visions?

How do they overcome the obstacles to organizing their communities around their own alternative plans—obstacles such as a lack of neighborhood cohesiveness, lack of financial resources, the overworked and overwhelming nature of daily life for the poor and working class, not to mention the complexity of urban development, and the difficulty in seeing and explaining how the segmented pieces of a particular "master plan" fit together?

The remapping, reimagining, and redesigning of the urban landscape inevitably call attention to the meanings of different spaces. The sites examined here include an intersection in the heart of a black community slated for redevelopment, where, in 1961, hundreds sat down in the middle of the street to protest the city's plans. They include a neighborhood union office, a children's park, a movement-run coffee shop, and a half-mile stretch of a downtown street that was slated for demolition to build a 5,000-car parking garage. They also include a downtown residency motel where residents refused to move out, even as the city pushed ahead with its plans for a new modern city center.

Each of these sites was a space of organized resistance in its own way, each with a particular geographical, political, and cultural significance. None holds great historical weight and most have since disappeared, but each was—for a time—a collective space given meaning through particular actions and ideas, and a point of resistance to plans to redesign the city around highways, shopping centers, and parking garages. As spatial, street-level anchors for organized resistance, each facilitated the convergence of time and place—of a "community union" in one form or another—and each was both predicated on and a catalyst for collective action. Recounting this story of how "movement people" in New Haven, Connecticut, staked a claim on physical, political, and cultural spaces forces a reimagining of the role of space—both physical and cultural—in our understanding of social movements in the postwar period, during which an increasingly suburbanized geography and a repeatedly "scattered" and "displaced" poor population posed a significant challenge to the potential for all kinds of collective action. The size, scope, complexity, and ambition of New Haven's urban renewal scheme focused the city's civil rights movement on the fight for affordable housing and galvanized antiwar activists around a fight against a particularly militarized domestic colonialism. Early studies of the city's predominantly black Hill neighborhood by city agencies were referred to in internal communications as "Hill Reconnaissance." Weapons of a war in Southeast Asia were tested along Columbus Avenue in that neighborhood as police and National Guardsmen in riot gear barricaded the streets.

At the level of the street—with its police barricades, neighborhood parks, and endangered storefronts—history and geography are intricately linked. Street names can articulate a timeline, as do Goffe Street and Whalley and Dixwell avenues, which converge at the edge of Yale University's campus, now a sort of unofficial gateway to the Dixwell neighborhood, but tied to a moment in the distant past, when each of those streets was named after one of the three judges who fled England in 1661 after signing the death warrant of King Charles II. Cemeteries in the center of town mark what once were its edges, the arrangement and ethnicity of names etched in stone calling out past inhabitants. Other historical geographies have a more persistent legacy, such as the red lines drawn by the Home Owners' Loan Corporation on insurance maps of hundreds of American cities in 1935. The practice, which came to be known as "redlining," designated predominantly black neighborhoods as high risk for mortgage lenders, exacerbating existing racial segregation and concretizing the links connecting race, place, and poverty.[1] But other histories have a more precarious connection to the landscape, anchored as they are to the lives and spaces of people who lack wealth and power. Whereas a passionate preservationist lobby is able to save some "historic places" and green and wooded sanctuaries from the wrecking ball or the bulldozer, the everyday places, homes, and histories of poor and working people are less likely to make headlines when they are under threat. Indeed, these blocks, acres, or square feet are worth more money as something else than they are as everyday places, homes, and histories, but so is the land that is now New York City's Central Park. Clearly, the predominant corporate logic of urban development is not completely impervious to the human spirit.

Writing about New York City in the 1980s, Neil Smith asserted that gentrification "scrub[s] the city clean of its working class history and geography."[2] His theory of the "revanchist" city shows how a middle-class, corporate, and private interest attack on the poor and working class replaces the social and geographic history of the city with a "mythical past." Urban renewal projects of the 1950s and 1960s—much studied and roundly condemned—had a similar aim, but rather than replace the social and geographic history with a "mythical past," they sought to replace it with a mythical future. Highways, parking garages, convention centers, and luxury hotels would eradicate slums, eliminate poverty, and save the city from the rise of the suburb.

This mythical future formed the basis of "master plans" for urban centers, the perceived needs and possibilities for which were reinforced by postwar corporate and suburban ideals, Watts-era anxieties about urban unrest, and Vietnam-era technologies for militarized control of the urban poor. In New Haven, residents suddenly found themselves living in what the city's Redevelopment Agency (RA) called the "*New* New Haven." This was a construction of the agency's publicity arm, and figment of that mythical future, in which an increasingly divided, impoverished, and decaying urban center would rise up out of "urban crisis" on the shoulders of a generation of experts, dressed in new high-speed roadways and thousands of parking spaces. As New Haven basked in the title of "model city," many residents organized and mobilized not so much to tear down the claim of that title as to revise the meaning of that model. The Demonstration Cities and Metropolitan

Development Act of 1966 (better known as the Model Cities program), a centralization and redesign of Johnson's antipoverty programs, intended to show—through concentrations of funding in "demonstration areas"—what effect a coordinated attack on urban problems could have on struggling cities. The legislation inadvertently called the question of what a city should demonstrate, and how, and to what extent the demonstrations of its inhabitants could shape its form and its content.

The Interstate and the Demonstration City: Master Planning and Maximum Feasible Participation

A master plan [is] . . . a flexible set of guidelines for a city's growth, in which patterns and trends of work, housing, transportation and population, and location of services and facilities for the city's functions and requirements are figured in broad but carefully calculated predictions of future needs.
—Ada Louise Huxtable, *New York Times* architectural critic, *New York Times*, July 13, 1964, p. 24

This story unfolds between 1954, when a thirty-seven-year-old New Haven newspaperman, Richard C. Lee, narrowly won the city's forty-fourth mayoral race on his third attempt, and 1970, when he ended his eight-term reign. This story isn't about Mayor Lee (although many have written extensively on that topic).[3] Nonetheless, his rise to national prominence in what became known as the nation's first model city, and his slow descent following the defeat of his master plan for a complex urban highway network, parking garage hub, and shopping mecca, offer artificial bookends to a story that continues, in many respects, into the present day. When Lee took office, a new interstate highway, I-95, had just opened, and was the only major artery connecting New Haven to its most prominent neighbors, Boston and New York, where the Central Artery and the Cross Bronx Expressway were, respectively, drawing a mix of excitement and criticism in advance of the traffic.[4] The inner-city conditions that would precipitate national debate about an "urban crisis" were just beginning to come into view: across the country, the urban poor crowded into aging structures while the more affluent began moving out to an ever-expanding ring of suburbs.

Mayor Lee took office months before the U.S. Supreme Court announced its decision in *Brown v. Board of Education*, and just as the Army-McCarthy hearings played out on national television, finally beginning the demise of Wisconsin senator Joseph McCarthy's anticommunist witch hunts. Republican Dwight D. Eisenhower was president and a close ally of big business. His cabinet was famously described in the press as "composed of eight millionaires and a plumber."[5] General Motors president Charles Wilson reportedly told a crowd of U.S. senators during the process of his nomination for secretary of defense, "What was good for our country was good for General Motors, and vice-versa."[6]

For the purposes of this historical sketch, Wilson's adage more or less summed up the priorities of the Eisenhower presidency. The country was embarking on an era in many ways defined by and catering to the automobile industry. In 1956, Eisenhower sailed into his second term with the signing of the Federal Highway Act, which called for a $25 billion highway-building project, enabling the construction of 40,000 miles of interstate highways over the next ten years. That was going to be "good for General Motors." It was also going to be good for Mayor Richard C. Lee, who envisioned the impending highway network not only as New Haven's ticket to modernity and efficiency, and its point of access to new pockets of suburban affluence, but also as the solution to urban decline—the remedy for the "slum cancer" that ate away at the city's center. Slums could be replaced by highways and highway access ramps. Federal highway funds could foot the bill. Urban life could be revitalized by suburban shoppers and culture seekers who could come in their cars on new, convenient high-speed roadways.

Faced with both decaying inner cities and a burgeoning national highway system, postwar policy makers and city governments resorted to the bulldozer, clearing slums to build highways, highway ramps, and the parking lots and shopping centers that this new network both demanded and facilitated. These included the Oak Street Connector, which replaced New Haven's densest "slum neighborhood," Boston's Central Artery, which eliminated densely populated communities in the middle of the city, and the Cross Bronx Expressway, which necessitated extensive demolition in the South Bronx. As massive displacements of the urban poor bared the human cost of the city's problems, Lyndon B. Johnson's "War on Poverty" attempted to address complex social needs (jobs, training, education, public health) through a more participatory process. Organized groups of the urban poor took to heart vague provisions for "citizen participation" and demanded more decision-making power in antipoverty programs, as they did in New Haven's Hill neighborhood in the late 1960s.

Meanwhile, mayors across the country began to voice their concerns, complaints, and outright protests about federal money flowing directly into the hands of community organizations. Federal aid that at one time was funneled through city hall no longer necessarily took that route. By the summer of 1964, waves of looting and violence were called "race riots" in the press and on the streets, a classification that in some cases concealed the realities on the ground, and on a national level challenged strategies both for policing and for the administration of existing poverty programs. The Demonstration Cities and Metropolitan Development Act of 1966 responded to these fears and challenges, scaling back expectations for citizen involvement and placing more control back in the hands of city administrators, while attempting to develop a more comprehensive approach to "urban management." By this time, urban programs faced two obstacles: a war in Southeast Asia siphoned off sorely needed funding, and the Nixon administration's policies and priorities were friendly to neither the poor nor the cities in which they lived.

Although the city of the 1960s is often characterized by the riots, poverty, and crime that constituted an urban crisis, it was also a time of urban redefinition during which both the landscape and the nature of city spaces were up for grabs. Urban renewal's bulldozers leveled many streets into a blank canvas, citizen participation requirements raised questions about the decision-making structures, and the Model Cities program offered the opportunity (taken to differing degrees by different groups) to question the nature of "models," their replication and design, and the notion of "urban management" in a time of war, at home and abroad. Whereas national policy makers saw this moment as an opportunity to devise more comprehensive methods of designing, controlling, and solving the problems of the city, at the grassroots level the moment raised questions about the power of working people to control the social and physical landscape of their own cities. For many, the words of a Los Angeles radio disc jockey—"Burn, baby, burn"—captured the inner city of the mid- to late-1960s, but another phrase emerging from the New Left around the same time—"Let the people decide"—captured the time's more important, if less photogenic, imperative.

Demands from the New Left and from organized communities of the poor to let the people decide were somewhat incongruous with the dominant cultural and political norms. Thick bureaucracies staffed with teams of college-educated "experts" tinkered with policies and plans under the influence of an expanding and evolving corporate ethos. The political and legislative impulse in response to a burgeoning urban crisis was to apply the practices of corporate management to the "management" of cities. Nowhere in the cultural realm was this proposal—this particular urban model—more brilliantly and disturbingly illustrated than in the planning, design, and execution of the 1964 New York World's Fair. The fairgrounds were designed and managed by the country's most famous and infamous urban planner, Robert Moses. According to historian Morris Dickstein, Moses "seemed to take an almost perverse pleasure in plowing through people's homes, even in decimating whole neighborhoods—for their own benefit, of course." As Dickstein notes, by the late 1960s, Moses' methods and ideas were "increasingly under siege. The Fair," he wrote, "would be their last monument, and their Waterloo."[7] The vision that Moses directed for the 1964 fair—his love of highways and garages and his celebration of corporate culture—was written with a heavy hand into the highway ramps, parking lots, and broad demolition strokes of cities like New Haven.

The World's Fair, like a city's master plan, offers a unique window into dominant mass culture and design since it is a self-conscious attempt to articulate and celebrate both, and its architects and boosters usually provided unabashed artistic and verbal gushings about their intentions, allegiances, and imaginations. As a deliberate mantle of its own kind of master plan—one invested in defining cultural norms and celebrating commercial enterprise—the fair was a significant and highly visible site of protest for the Congress of Racial Equality (CORE) and other groups eager to call attention to both the labor exploitation and discriminatory practices of the Fair Corporation and its exhibitors, and the vision of corporate dominance, segregation, and suburbanization it celebrated.

This was a dramatic shift in emphasis from the fair's traditional (albeit problematic) spotlight on world cultures and places. Taking a corporate form and content, Moses and his team insisted that the celebrated space be arranged not only on the structure of the corporation, but literally around the corporations themselves, which laid mammoth architectural "products" on a blank canvas in Queens, New York, just as urban renewal projects unfolded in a disturbingly similar manner in city centers across the country. Absent the intrusion of civil rights protests, the fair would have been a particularly strange projection of mid-1960s America. It celebrated affluence and "free enterprise" in a time and place of severe poverty. It celebrated "peace" and "understanding" in a time of war and fear, and it celebrated a neat, round world crafted of steel—which it called the "Unisphere," suggesting unity and balance—in a society segregated and soon to be shaken by "race riots" in Harlem, Watts, Detroit, Newark, Chicago, and New Haven, to name just a few. But it spoke to one particular take on this moment in time and suggested—commandingly if not deliberately—a certain kind of "model city."

The influence of this model's form (if not its content) was evident in a 1965 memo to President Lyndon Johnson from United Auto Workers president Walter Reuther, who proposed the creation of a task force to consider what he called "The 'World's Fair' of American civic, social production, and design." Taking up the challenge of redefining the urban model, this lifelong adversary of management devised a plan to create "research laboratories for the war against poverty" by establishing "prototype" communities—"full and complete organic neighborhoods" of 50,000 people in six major American cities. Reuther himself was not from the city. He was born in West Virginia in 1907 and moved to Detroit at the age of twenty to work on Henry Ford's assembly line. He rose to prominence in 1937 following a sit-down strike against General Motors in Flint, Michigan, and a violent clash at Ford's Rouge River Plant.[8] By the 1960s, he was a powerful voice in the Democratic Party, an outspoken advocate of both civil rights and expanded social programs, and a close advisor to President Johnson. Evaluating the challenges and goals of federal antipoverty initiatives, Reuther asserted that

by showing, in detail, "the interrelationship of the home, the school, the social services to the young and old, the cultural, the religious, and the recreational facilities" necessary to redesign the city, the nation could understand
more comprehensively what it would take to create what he called "architecturally beautiful and socially meaningful communities."[9]

Reuther's proposal formed the basis for Johnson's 1966 Demonstration
Cities and Metropolitan Development Act, which called for the concentration of resources and programs on compact "demonstration areas" to show
the most effective means of solving urban problems. The program originally
intended to provide competitive grants for a small number of municipalities
to fund coordinated programs for urban renewal, employment, housing, and
public health. The act envisioned a sort of "citizen participation filtered
through local government" and rejected the direct democracy model of the
1964 Economic Opportunity Act.[10] As demonstrations across the country
turned violent, the name "Demonstration Cities" began to strike a sour
chord. The less-controversial title "Model Cities program" quickly became
more prevalent, perhaps aiding in the bill's passage, "by a cat's whisker," in
November of 1966. Charles M. Haar, a member of the president's original
task force and author of a book-length study of the program, called the
Model Cities program "a realistic response to the shortage of money for new
domestic programs" during the Vietnam War. "Experiments, prototypes,
and models are fine ways for an administration . . . to economize," explained Haar.[11] But as applications to the program poured into the new office of Housing and Urban Development (HUD), and as the politicized
process of "awarding" Model Cities grants unfolded, it became clear that
the program would be anything but economical.

Of 193 original applications received in May of 1966, 112 "demonstration area" grants were awarded in a competition that Haar described as a
"variation on the Miss America contest."[12] Every American city with a population of more than 1 million people received a grant, with the exception of
Los Angeles, a city still scarred physically and politically by the 1965 riots,
whose mayor, Sam Yorty, failed to impress the committee in Washington.
New Haven, Connecticut, fell in the category of "mid-range city," and its
population placed it among the smallest in that group. Unlike Yorty, Lee's
name would be an asset in the political beauty pageant that governed the distribution of "demonstration area" funds, and New Haven would become a
"demonstration city" in more than one sense.

By the summer of 1967, New Haven's Model Cities Task Force was final-
izing its "Demonstration Cities" proposal, calling for the creation of a computerized Urban Management Information System (UMIS) in partnership
with IBM. UMIS would revolutionize the city's policing, planning, and management by streamlining the process of gathering, storing, and accessing information about all of the people in the Hill neighborhood, the city's largest
and poorest concentration of African Americans and Puerto Ricans. The

"Model Neighborhood" on which New Haven focused its proposal for computerized surveillance would be the same neighborhood that would capture national headlines with its own civil unrest later that summer, and the same community that would organize at the grass roots to take control of Model Cities funding, calling into question both the form and the content of this particular urban model. By the spring of 1968, when Martin Luther King, Jr., fell to an assassin's bullet in Memphis, prompting an early start to summer unrest in cities across the country, New Haven activists finally won control over Model Cities funds. It was a dramatic local victory eclipsed by national defeat as poor people nationwide scrambled for dwindling resources in a nation increasingly divided by race and class.

That same spring, on fifteen acres of West Potomac Park, between the Reflecting Pool and the foot of the Lincoln Memorial, a different kind of demonstration city took shape. Between May 14 and June 24, 1968, an estimated 3,000 people lived in A-frame tents in what became known as "Resurrection City," the first stage of Dr. King's final civil rights proposal, the Poor People's Movement. The temporary residents of Resurrection City, organized by the Southern Christian Leadership Conference (SCLC) into several "caravans," traveled from nearby slums, from the hills of Appalachia, from the Deep South, and from cities across the Northeast, Midwest, and Mid-Atlantic to set up a multiracial shantytown of the nation's poor. The campaign would culminate in a mass march, mass arrests, and then a national boycott of the country's most powerful corporations, in response to the failure of antipoverty programs and the exploitations of corporate America.

Ultimately, the Poor People's Movement failed to bring about either racial harmony or massive economic restructuring, but its explicit choice of model—a city built from scratch, populated only by the poor, and formulated around a social movement—offers another take on both the master plan and the urban form. Designed by a professor of architecture and built by its inhabitants, the camp included a city hall, a dining tent, a Poor People's University, a psychiatrist, and a cultural center. Entire families lived, worked, learned, and interacted on those fifteen acres for forty-two days, twenty-eight of which brought pouring rain, turning the "urban landscape" into a muddy swamp. Within Resurrection City, groups segregated themselves racially and geographically, contrary to King's vision of a cross-racial alliance of the poor, but on Solidarity Day, June 19, 1968, the crowed gathered and swelled to 50,000 people for a march on Washington. Speaking before the Solidarity Day crowd, Walter Reuther called on the government to close tax loopholes for rich corporations to fund programs for the urban poor. He called for new national fiscal policies to help the unemployed, raise wages, and lift families out of poverty.[13]

These demands, issued from the muddy town square of a "demonstration area," suggested the shortcomings of the federal Model Cities program that had grown out of Reuther's original proposal. Back in New Haven, the community fought to shape that model through collective action. It was a fight played out in many forms in cities across the country as poor neighborhoods organized around alternative plans to fight poverty and revitalize their cities. When President Richard Nixon took office in January of 1969, these grassroots struggles were just beginning to gain ground. That ground crumbled in the months that followed, as federal urban programs were reshaped by the Nixon administration's preference for centralized control, its political allegiances to the "silent majority," and its commitment to "law and order" in the management of cities. These federal responses to the urban crisis of the 1960s precluded the more democratic, participatory forms of urban planning and governance that emerged out of community movements. In many cases— as in New Haven—these community-grown alternative plans were ultimately supported by local elected officials compelled by the full force of an organized neighborhood in a politically and socially turbulent time and place.

Contested Spaces in a Model City

New Haven was once a playground for social scientists. For the policy wonks, sociologists, and political scientists of the 1960s and 1970s, this little city was fodder for plentiful scholarship.[14] Despite its small size and relative obscurity in comparison to its nearest well-known neighbors, New York and Boston, New Haven is home to a prestigious and wealthy university and has been the birthplace of many celebrated innovations that, before too long—like the forty-third president of the United States, who tries hard to hide the fact that he was born in New Haven—became terrible liabilities. These include an urban shopping mall (since gutted and turned into vacant high-rise condominiums), mammoth downtown parking garages that now interrupt the frayed urban fabric, and more recently, urban biotech industrial parks—supposed saviors of a struggling postindustrial economy—that remain vacant and obtrusive in the middle of residential spaces.

In New Haven, the fabulously rich live alongside the terribly poor, and all of the physical symbols of white American affluence and imperialism are within spitting distance of its street-level subjects.[15] It seems that New Haven was to the political scientists of the 1960s and 1970s what Chicago was to the sociologists of the first half of the twentieth century. A large, powerful, prolific research institution in the heart of an impoverished city made for fruitful scholarship. In the case of New Haven, many scholars commented on the extent to which the city was first a guinea pig, and soon after, a "demonstration" for poverty programs and community "involvement." So while Chicago's sociologists of the 1940s saw urban communities as their living laboratory and sought to understand the lives of working people, New Haven's social scientists, prompted by Robert Dahl's *Who Governs* (1961), examined a power struggle, asking over and over again in many different ways, "Who's running this place?"

The range of possible responses to that question, by 1960, seemed limited to politicians, political parties, business leaders, and possibly—in a way that was unique to this small city with an increasingly powerful university—the Yale Corporation, the aptly named governing board of the wealthy nonprofit institution. In the years that followed, organized citizens would throw that question wide open and insist on a new range of grassroots possibilities through a seemingly continuous set of battles over urban spaces and models that unfolded against a backdrop of national political change, large-scale racial reconfigurations, and local and national strategies for urban management and Watts-era policing. For his 1970 book-length study of New Haven, *Model City: A Test of American Liberalism; One Town's Efforts to Rebuild Itself*, journalist Fred Powledge interviewed customers and eavesdropped on conversations at Lindy's, a local (and now extinct) downtown lunch counter. "What made New Haven exciting was none of these usual [urban] excitements," wrote Powledge, "but the knowledge . . . that New Haven had the talent, the money, the leadership, and the energy—and therefore the potential—to become the Model City." It was this sense that a new and energetic generation of urban "experts" was setting out to "make a new town out of a very old, decayed, dying, or—as some said—already dead one" that captured the national (and at key moments, international) imagination of what a city could be.[16]

In June of 1957, the cover of *Time* magazine celebrated "Roadbuilders—on the New Highway Network." At the center of this story, in which old industrial urban centers were being eclipsed by more orderly, engineered, and exclusive spaces off highway exits, was this small city, where a powerful and ambitious young newspaper reporter–turned–mayor was foisting a would-be narrative of urban decline into the national and international spotlight, skillfully recasting it as one of innovation and rebirth. "In five years," Lee told *Time*, "families will be moving into the city instead of out to the suburbs."[17] His predictions proved to be quite inaccurate. Five years later, with a number of ambitious urban renewal projects in varied stages of completion, New Haven's population was in decline.

Once a major manufacturing center for firearms, carriages, corsets, and clocks, New Haven benefited from its position along a densely rail-connected coastline and a string of active ports. Today its distance from either New York or Boston is most commonly measured in car travel time along I-95—about ninety minutes and two hours, respectively. But the small city of just over 120,000 was once an industrial and commercial center in its own right. In the mid- to late nineteenth century, its own Little Italy, Wooster Square, flourished. Immigrants from Ireland and eastern Europe flooded into the Oak Street neighborhood, New Haven's most dense and vibrant immigrant community, where they walked to work in nearby factories, in offices, or at Yale University, just blocks away.

New Haven was originally mapped out in nine squares with a marketplace at the center. In the surrounding squares, the city's most prominent

planters set up shop, and the remainder of the city's original 120 families settled in outlying areas. This early settlement was given the Native American
name Quinnipiac when the first families arrived in the spring of 1638. Most
inhabitants came from other parts of Connecticut until the first wave of immigrants arrived from Ireland in the 1830s. With the Industrial Revolution
came the familiar list of immigrant settlers. Between 1839 and 1860, they
came from Germany, Italy, and eastern Europe, quadrupling the population
to 40,000. It was a walking city until a horse-drawn trolley connected the
Italian enclaves of Wooster Square to the Irish and German areas in the Hill,
and to Oak Street's Jewish sections shortly after the Civil War. By the 1870s,
New Haven became part of a regional network, connected by train to Hartford and New York City. By 1900, the city was home to more than 100,000
people in a handful of increasingly dense and diverse neighborhoods connected by electric and horse-drawn trolleys.[18]

This urban fabric flourished to differing degrees—weathering depression, racial and ethnic discord, and the transformation of the city's industrial
landscape—until the 1960s, when the growth of the suburbs combined with
the flight of industry challenged the city's tax base just as the most recent influx of African Americans from the South showed up in search of the manufacturing jobs that had just disappeared. By then, the city had been effectively
dismantled, gutted, and rearranged by a generation of experts, using unprecedented levels of federal and state funding. As New Haven architect and activist Harris Stone explained, "Within a few years, 140 acres of land were
totally cleared, thousands of units of housing for low-income families were
demolished. Hundreds of small businesses and dozens of dense, varied
streets disappeared."[19]

Much of this dramatic transformation was accomplished through the completion of Lee's touchstone urban renewal project, the Oak Street Connector,
a mile-long stretch of Connecticut's Route 34 in the heart of downtown,
charted in Figure Intro.1. The project was an ingenious marriage of highway
construction and slum clearance in that it demolished the city's "worst slum"
(and most dense and diverse center of population) to make way for four lanes
of highway traffic. The connector was intended to eventually extend ten miles
to the west but never made it any farther than the dead end that stumped highway watchers at the time of its completion in 1959. Nonetheless, its construction was celebrated then as much as it is reviled now. Images of the downtown
in ruins graced the front pages, not as stories of disaster, but as tales of
progress and rebirth.

By contrast, plans for a project uncovered nearly a decade later, which
called for a six-lane high-speed "inner circumferential loop highway" encircling the downtown area and Yale University, were greeted with outright
rage by many community groups. The plan for this "Ring Road," as it came
to be known, involved widening some outer downtown local streets, eliminating thousands of low-income residential units and small businesses, and

Figure Intro.1

The Redevelopment Agency charts the elimination of the Oak Street neighborhood with the dotted-line highways drawn on this aerial photograph of downtown New Haven. *(New Haven Redevelopment Agency, c. 1955.)*

significantly disrupting the daily lives and lived geography of New Haven's poor and low-income families in the Dixwell, Dwight, Hill, and State Street areas. This plan initially also promised significant disruption for the outer edges of Yale University's campus. After a series of very private meetings between Mayor Lee and the university's president, Kingman Brewster, the Ring Road plan was altered such that a small stretch of the road—the part that would have impacted campus—would tunnel underground. Brewster subsequently agreed to endorse the city's plan.

The significance of this loop of highway, for the construction of which the city sought federal funds, was not only the homes and small businesses that would be destroyed by the widening of these local urban streets to six-lane highways, but also the extent to which its construction would literally amputate Dixwell, Dwight, and the Hill from downtown, while insulating Yale from the rest of the city. By 1967, the year that violence erupted in the very neighborhoods that the Ring Road promised to isolate, the people of the Hill, Dixwell, and Dwight, along with residents and small-business owners on State Street, were beginning to see where they figured in the diagrams and scale models displayed at public meetings, and in the local press.

The difference between the Oak Street Connector's completion and the Ring Road's suppression was—on the most superficial level—the difference between the 1950s and the 1960s. The intervening years brought the civil rights, black power, antiwar, and women's liberation movements to a head in the Elm City, and saw the emergence—on a national scale—of racial unrest, coupled with War on Poverty "mandates" for citizen participation that challenged people and their governments to redefine, reshape, or reify the city's existing decision-making processes. But beyond this somewhat clunky and often ill-fitting decade splice, it is important to understand that many of the people moved from Oak Street were also the same people threatened by the constellation of urban renewal plans that would enable the construction of a Ring Road. By the time an activist organization's inside man at the RA leaked the confidential plans to organizers, and subsequently to the press, many of the individuals who showed up to protests, testified at public hearings, and signed petitions had already been moved two, three, or four times to accommodate the city's master plan.

Neighborhoods and Movement Spaces on the Ring Road Map

To ascribe boundaries to particular neighborhoods within a city—or even across municipal lines—is to make a particular argument about social constructions of space, political identities, and local culture. Add to this the passage of time, and the extent to which particular events can alter these boundaries, and the whole project of identifying, naming, and outlining "neighborhoods" starts to seem more like an act of historiography than one of cartography. But scholars do it all the time because people require intelligible units of space to understand a story or an argument. The unit of "neighborhood" is one with which we all tend to be familiar (although increasingly less so), despite the fact that this "unit" might mean entirely different things to any two readers. The boundaries of these units must take into account the social, political, cultural, and in some cases even topographical. The neighborhoods described here have been constructed with a view to 1960. Their boundaries take into account the city's designated "project areas," the spaces of resistance claimed by citizens and organizations opposing renewal, and personal accounts of spatial boundaries. None of these designations is any more authentic or reliable than another. But to simply take the city's official neighborhood boundaries or to rely on present-day boundaries, wards, or census tracts would obscure important elements of the stories and erase crucial connections and relationships.[20]

The Ring Road is important to this story because, as one of the centerpieces of the city's 1953 master plan, and as a useful and salient symbol of that plan's intention to remake the city in service of the automobile while isolating the poorest people from the city's center, it is also a road that was never built. As such, it constitutes one of history's often overlooked grass-roots victories, and suggests disquieting possibilities for what this still-segregated, heavily gentrified, and painstakingly remapped city would have looked like today if the road had been built. Economist Rick Wolff, an activist in the American Independent Movement (AIM), which fought many battles with the Lee administration, Yale University, and New Haven's other corporate powers, imagined that, had the project been completed, the city would be divided in three "stark" areas: a walled hospital and university complex accessed through a "safe, white" corridor down scenic Prospect Street, an isolated "black and Hispanic ghetto" comprised of the Hill, Dixwell, Newhallville, and Westville areas, and—across the Mill River—the "Hispanic ghetto" of Fair Haven. Taking the police as a fourth group, there would be "four distinct armed camps," suggested Wolff, adding, "And I mean *armed*."[21]

The city's proposal for an "inner circumferential loop" included the widening and recasting of four distinct urban streets as stretches of or spokes on a high-speed, multilane loop: Dixwell Avenue, a popular strip in the heart of New Haven's oldest African American community adjacent to Yale University; an extension of a state highway, Route 34, through local roads in the Hill and Dwight communities; a downtown stretch of small businesses and residences along State Street; and a section of Trumbull Street that would tunnel under Yale University's campus, as shown in Figure Intro.2.

Each of these pieces was centered on an extensive urban renewal plan and involved the construction of not only widened higher-speed roadways and highway extensions, but also parking garages and city spaces redesigned to meet the needs of the increased automobile traffic that a highway network would bring.

Mapping the Story

The following chapters are organized both chronologically and geographically. They loosely trace both the path of the proposed Ring Road and the footsteps of the city's redevelopment plans, while charting the historical trajectory of national policy in addressing an evolving set of "urban problems" alongside the alternative models and proposals put forward by organized communities.

Oak Street

Chapter 1, " 'The Ghosts of Oak Street's Paved Ravines': The Oak Street Project, the Construction of Public Consensus, and the Birth of a Slumless City," chronicles the clearance of the Oak Street neighborhood for the construction of the Oak Street Connector, during which the city developed an extensive

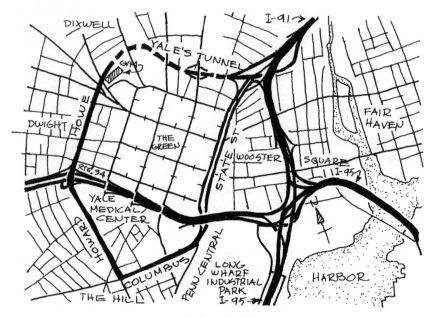

Figure Intro.2

Map of the proposed Ring Road as drawn and published by the Urban Renewal
Committee of the American Independent Movement in 1967. *(Published in Harris Stone,*
Workbook of an Unsuccessful Architect *[New York: Monthly Review Press, 1974].)*

public relations apparatus to push through urban renewal projects on an
unprecedented scale. It examines the city's public hearing strategies and a variety of other public relations mechanisms devised to preclude traces of dissent
from both the process and the record of slum clearance and redevelopment.

The Oak Street Connector was a short stretch of highway that would reconfigure the city and the highway system such that two important roadways, I-91 and I-95, would meet in the heart of the city rather than passing
through its perimeter, directing highway traffic to a downtown shopping
(and parking) oasis. It served another purpose as well in that it would eradicate an existing slum neighborhood. Until the late 1950s, Oak Street was the
city's most densely populated area, crowded with open-air markets, mom-
and-pop shops of every variety, restaurants, tenements, and ethnic and cultural organizations. The neighborhood once called Oak Street is now a
collection of extinct street names. In its place are a broad and somewhat use-
less highway connector and a few very large, architecturally prominent, and
visually underwhelming parking garages. A group of families who once lived
in the area still meet annually to remember it, as if it was a deceased relative
in danger of being forgotten. This is a ritual the members of the city's RA
could never have imagined as they drew thick lines on their aerial photos of

the Oak Street area to delineate the "project area" and help both their proponents and their detractors visualize where this new modern highway connector would be.

Between the "before" and "after" photos of Oak Street, nearly 900 households and 250 businesses were forced out of the area.[22] Many white households, comprising 56 percent of those displaced, ended up in nearby suburbs and in other New Haven neighborhoods (many of which would also soon face renewal). African Americans, about 40 percent of those displaced from Oak Street, were more likely to be sent by the city to "relocation areas" in other slums, largely in the increasingly overcrowded Hill neighborhood. Others found themselves—at rates far higher than whites—in public housing, such as the large and increasingly "troublesome" Elm Haven project in the Dixwell neighborhood.[23]

Dixwell

Chapter 2, "On Dixwell Avenue: Civil Rights and the Street," takes place on Dixwell Avenue, where a controversial sit-out in 1961 brought the local civil rights movement into the fight to resist urban renewal. Lower Dixwell Avenue was the heart of black New Haven, directly bordering not only the Elm Haven housing project, but also the edge of Yale University's campus. This chapter explores the competing visions for this stretch of road, the ways in which the city hoped to facilitate its transformation, and the role of the civil rights movement in resisting a suburban plan for Dixwell.

Dixwell's redevelopment was more disruptive than the much-publicized and celebrated Oak Street project. More than 1,100 households and close to 200 businesses were forcibly relocated, and nearly 30 percent of the housing units in the area were completely demolished.[24] The avenue defined the neighborhood, with the housing and small businesses along Dixwell serving as the heart of what was once called "New Haven's Harlem." The neighborhood's official boundaries stretched northward to Munson Street, marking the southern boundary of Newhallville, west to Winchester Street, where Winchester Repeating Arms employed hundreds of Dixwell residents, south to the campus of Yale University and Whalley Avenue, and east to Sherman Avenue, which roughly marked the start of the Beaver Hills neighborhood, one of the areas oldest planned suburban subdivisions.

In 1960, as the city unveiled its intention to make Dixwell its fifth renewal project area, the neighborhood was home to more than 10,000 people, 70 percent of whom were African American. Dixwell had its "old settlers" and its newcomers—the former a long-standing, established, black lower middle class, connected to large prominent churches and organizations such as the NAACP, and the latter largely displacees from Oak Street or new migrants from the South who had arrived just in time to witness the disappearance of the manufacturing jobs they had come to fill. Before the destruction of the Oak Street neighborhood in the late 1950s, Dixwell was known as home to New Haven's established black community, a mix of poor, working-class, and lower-middle-class families, and a rich collection of black- and white-owned small businesses. The neighborhood carried many of the social and economic markings of poverty, despite its long-standing network of black churches and institutions. With a median annual family income of less than $4,000, and total unemployment levels exceeding 10 percent, the neighborhood showed no signs of benefiting from the economic retail boom downtown. The bulk of Dixwell workers were employed in unskilled, low-wage manufacturing jobs, clustered primarily around the metal industries, such as those available at Winchester Repeating Arms, where war production had boosted the demand for labor and attracted new migrants. The neighborhood's pedestrian scale was written into the everyday lives of its working people, and daily routines were entwined with its sidewalks and street corners. Most worked close to home, driving a short distance. More than half walked or took the bus.[25] It was a neighborhood challenged by economic inequalities and poor housing conditions, but it was a highly organized community with deep institutional and residential roots, and a vibrant businesses community. This was not the case in the Hill, home to the city's other large concentration of African Americans.

The Hill

Chapters 3, 4, and 5 move to the Hill neighborhood to chart the involvement of first the New Left, and later an increasingly militant grassroots neighborhood movement, in the struggle to win community control of urban planning and antipoverty funds. The Hill, quite counterintuitively, is a peninsula reaching out into Long Island Sound. The "Hill Project Area" as designated by the RA included a five-block section stretching from Congress Avenue to Columbus Avenue, and from Hallock Street to West Street, an area that was home to a mix of ethnic whites, blacks, and Puerto Ricans. The Hill was inhabited primarily by Italian and eastern European immigrants and their children, until the demolition of Oak Street relocated hundreds of African American and Puerto Rican families to the Hill neighborhood in what quickly became a disorganized, overcrowded, and underemployed ghetto.

In 1960, the city declared the neighborhood a "middle ground" area, which meant it was tagged for rehabilitation and conservation. Just a few years later, it was marked for "large-scale demolition."[26] Urban renewal "will increasingly become the crucial issue," wrote Yale sociologist, activist, and soon-to-be congressional candidate Robert Cook in a document assessing the problems facing the Hill in the early 1960s. The housing stock was old, social and institutional networks nearly nonexistent, and the schools crowded and dilapidated. Through community organizing and mass mobilizations for improved housing, schools, and community control, a neighborhood that initially lacked institutional networks of support would become a mobilized "model" in ways the city hadn't expected.

Chapter 3, "The Hill Neighborhood Union and Freedom Summer North: Citizen Participation and Movement Spaces in a 'Project Area,' " starts with a series of rent strikes on Ann Street, through which a door-to-door, New Left-initiated community-organizing campaign was concretized in the formation of the Hill Neighborhood Union (HNU). Across the street from the HNU office, Hallock Street Park was the site of a small neighborhood playground, the result of a hard-fought battle by the youngest members of the HNU. The fight for the park, in which children from the Hill's Freedom School engaged city officials and local War on Poverty officials, claimed an important neighborhood space while teaching collective action and neighborhood identity.

The park and the HNU office provided safe, familiar places to meet, organize, and develop a collective voice and political confidence. This chapter follows the significance of these neighborhood spaces—where organizers met to plan rent strikes, pickets, and welfare office sit-ins—from the summer of 1965, when the language of civil rights dominated the organizing, to the summer of 1967, when the more militant Hill Parents' Association (HPA) emerged as the dominant community organization in the Hill, meeting the needs of the neighborhood that the city's antipoverty programs failed to address. The HPA's summer camp and breakfast programs predated similar (more widely known) initiatives by the Black Panther Party (BPP). Before the establishment of a BPP chapter in New Haven, the HPA asserted considerable political power as a militant community organization, demanding a seat at the table in the allocation of Model Cities money.

Chapter 4, "Maximum Feasible Urban Management: The 'Automatic' City and the Hill Parents' Association," deals with grassroots attempts to define citizen participation and challenge official antipoverty programs in the era of urban management, and Chapter 5, "Renewal, Riot, and Resistance: Reclaiming 'Model Cities,' " begins with New Haven's civil disorder in the summer of 1967 and its aftermath, concluding with the subsequent takeover of the city's Model Cities grant. These events marked both a more aggressive era in community organizing and a more oppressive response to a newly organized black community.

To a large extent, the neighborhood's identity was formed around opposition to "downtown"—meaning both the physical space that was New Haven's central business district and center of government, and the officials and institutions (such as the mayor, the RA, and particularly the police) with which that area was associated. The Hill was physically and socially separated from downtown by the construction of two wide frontage roads, and the city's renewal plans would exacerbate that situation by fully amputating the Hill from centers of business and government with the construction of the Ring Road. The redevelopment of the Hill would ultimately force the relocation of more than 1,000 families and about eighty businesses. Many of those displaced were experiencing urban renewal the hard way for the second, third, or even fourth time.

But in between what the Hill *used* to be and what it is now—a hotly contested space scarred with empty lots, parking garages, medical buildings, and poverty, but enlivened by a wave of neighborhood organizing and activism rooted in a labor-community coalition similar to the one that fought to save community spaces forty years ago—was a community-grown alternative plan for those five project blocks. It was not a plan devised by the RA, but rather one imagined by neighbors in conversation with one another. It included a cooperative housing project that started with an architect interviewing the future inhabitants, it included jobs, day-care, and food-assistance programs run by the community, and it provided a playground designed by the children who would use it, built up out of a vacant lot with discarded tires, lumber, and iron, the waste materials of urban renewal. A host of persistent "urban problems" make it easy to define this neighborhood by the 1967 "riots" or the media frenzy surrounding the murder trial of members of the BPP in 1971. However, the emergence of a new and promising community movement for responsible development around Yale–New Haven Hospital is further evidence that the Hill is an organized community fighting for an alternative urban model.

State Street

Two competing visions for the form and future of downtown came to blows on a half-mile stretch of State Street, which the RA hoped to widen from two lanes to six lanes and replace all of its occupants with an eight-block, six-story parking garage. This half-mile section of State Street is the subject of Chapter 6, "The City and the Six-Lane Highway: Bread and Roses and Parking Garages." It was home to more than 100 small businesses and light manufacturing firms, including Trio Plastics, Brown Clothing Manufacturers, and the General Sewing Machine Company, and more than a dozen restaurants, including John's, the Ship Shape Sandwich Shop, a number of bars and taverns, and Chef's Corner Restaurant, a popular hangout for local activists.[27] Despite the city's occasional assertion that the area was not heavily residential, these few blocks on State Street were home to some of the city's ever-decreasing stock of low-rent apartments, including three or four buildings with between twelve and sixteen units each, as well as J. W. Faugno's Furnished Rooms, one of the city's few remaining single-occupancy buildings.

State Street was once the city's Main Street, through the seventeenth and eighteenth centuries, when its position along the Farmington Canal attracted—in the words of architectural historian Elizabeth Mills Brown—

"wharves, shops, and well-to-do merchants' houses." In the 1840s, the railroad was built on the site of the canal, driving away many of the shops and homes, and attracting wholesalers. When Brown surveyed the area for her study of New Haven neighborhoods, she called twentieth-century State Street "a place of sooty buildings, secondhand furniture stores, and a paradise of Italian markets." But by 1976, she noted, it was "mostly demolished," with plans for the massive parking garage still looming (see Figure Intro.3).[28]

Before State Street was "renewed," foot traffic was common, and the existing small businesses survived on a combination of local reputation, longevity, and low rent. With the completion of I-91 in 1966, State Street businesses—located right near a highway ramp—may have had the potential to reach some suburban customers, but the city's plans for that stretch of road reflected different intentions. The proposed parking garage would obliterate the pedestrian scale and dominate the landscape. In 1969, as the controversy surrounding the State Street Redevelopment and Renewal Plan captured local headlines, a new business opened on one of the low-rent downtown blocks in the proposed shadow of that half-mile, six-story garage. Bread and Roses, a movement-run coffee shop at 536 State Street, was the project of an antiwar, anticorporate, left organization called the American Independent Movement (AIM), which emerged in 1965 when a group of New Left activists and a Yale-affiliated socialist club merged in response to the bombs dropping in Southeast Asia. They quickly tripled in number, tackling not only the Vietnam War, but also a wide array of local issues, including urban renewal.

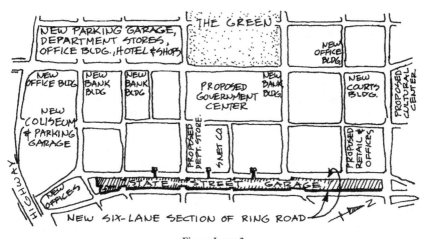

Figure Intro.3

Map of proposed State Street parking garage. *(Drawn by Harris Stone for his* Workbook of an Unsuccessful Architect *[New York: Monthly Review Press, 1974].)*

The idea for a coffeehouse emerged just as AIM's Urban Renewal Committee stepped up its fight against the State Street Garage, the Ring Road, and other highway plans throughout the city. Both AIM and its organizational ally, the Draft Action Group (DAG), sought a comfortable and relaxed space to bring people into the movement, hold meetings and cultural activities, distribute literature, and generally give people a place to meet and talk. Bread and Roses operated at cost, off of donated labor and supplies, and made the space into a living and thriving physical site of resistance to the RA's plans for State Street. By 1972, the State Street plan was all but abandoned, but the coffeehouse was gone, along with nearly 100 other businesses, homes, restaurants, and services occupying six blocks of downtown State Street. Another eighty were left vacant, in many cases awaiting demolition, in others, simply victims of the insecurities wrought by renewal.[29] But the massive garage was never built, and the plans for the Ring Road seemed to recede out of possibility as plans for its different six-lane legs were stalled or otherwise undone by a combination of collective actions and shifting priorities, locally and nationally.

Downtown

Somewhere between the downtown of the distant past—with its walking scale, mixed use, open-air markets, and mom-and-pop shops—and today's downtown—where luxury apartments are carved into the abandoned fossils of a one-time urban shopping mall—was the downtown of the 1960s: a scattering of the very old and the very new, scarred with construction sites, laced with scaffolding, in a seemingly constant state of "renewal" that looked to some like progress and to others like Armageddon. The final chapter—and the final site—is the Strand, a five-story downtown residential hotel that, by the late 1960s, housed about fifty residents. Chapter 7, "Downtown Lives and Palaces: From 'A Space of Freedom' to 'A Space of Exclusion,'" narrates the transformation of downtown, taking the Strand Hotel as its point of departure. Contrary to conventional misunderstandings about hotel living, most of the residents of the Strand were permanent—some had lived there more than twenty years—and nearly all chose initially to stay and fight their eviction, which they saw as part of a larger fight to keep New Haven accessible and livable for working people.

By the spring of 1969, when the city issued eviction orders to all of the tenants, it was one of only two residential hotels remaining in a city that once had nearly twenty of them. The city's central business district before urban renewal, the constellation of spaces in which Strand residents had made their lives, was a patchwork of businesses, residences, theaters, restaurants, bars, social services, and small hotels and motels, surrounding a classic New England town green. In an effort to separate uses, expedite and prioritize parking, and reimagine the city as a regional center for shopping, the Lee administration devised a massive government center, with police station, city hall, and federal building, to be dropped down upon the footprint of a number of smaller properties, including many small shops, restaurants, and the Strand Hotel. Separate from this area, they planned an arts and cultural center. In another area still would be a massive high-rise luxury hotel, the Park Plaza, with easy access, via a raised and enclosed walkway, to both shopping and parking lots, sparing visitors and shoppers the trouble of using city streets.

For those who fit into the city's 1960 vision of what belonged in a modern downtown, the RA's "*New* New Haven" would certainly be preferable to the old. It would be cleaner, more compartmentalized, more car friendly, more white, more affluent, and more likely to host a convention or attract a new corporate headquarters. Assertions that such a transformation would make the city more "safe" were soon challenged by critics of urban renewal such as Jane Jacobs, who argued that it was the presence of people on and around the street that made for a safe urban environment. Plans for a Ring Road, which the RA claimed to the bitter end—despite plentiful evidence to the contrary—was never part of their overall scheme, would remove people from the street, and insulate downtown and Yale University from the city's poorer areas by cutting off the Hill, Dixwell, and parts of the nearby Dwight neighborhood with a six-lane high-speed road. It would provide quick and easy access to new highways for suburban drivers, and eliminate a deteriorating strip of small businesses (and a haven for activists) along State Street while justifying thousands of new parking spaces. It would complete Maurice Rotival's early designs of the model city and bring order to the perceived chaos of the city's side streets.

The Ring Road was never completed, although many people in New Haven lived in fear of its impending arrival from the day it was revealed in 1967 through the early 1970s, when it became abundantly clear that the city would be unable to secure state and federal money to complete the project. For some who have lived in the Elm City since the urban renewal period, publicly contested plans for new development at the ever-expanding Yale–New Haven Hospital are a reminder of the persistence of competing visions for city spaces, and the impact that such struggles have on the jobs, social networks, and homes of city people.

The importance of the fight for community control over the city's master plan is not just in its material outcomes. Central to this story is the importance of space and geography in the construction of what historian Lawrence Goodwyn calls "movement culture." Goodwyn was, ironically, writing about the populist movement at the turn of the century, and arguing that rural life was more conducive than the urban environment to the development of movements for social change. But his ideas about movement culture are helpful in articulating the importance of particular spaces to building movements in the city. Goodwyn asserts that America is "culturally progressive," imbued with a general sense that "the system works." Consequently, he argues, acts of resistance or demands for change require a unique environment—a "movement culture"—that he asserts is possible only through collective political experiences, or a "collective self-confidence" that enables individuals to see their personal struggles and obstacles as collective problems with collective solutions.[30]

Sarah Evans and Harry Boyte have similarly argued that communal settings and structures of community participation allow working people to both identify with one another and collectively distinguish themselves from "the elite," enabling mobilizations for change.[31] Many organizations and individuals in New Haven in the 1960s imagined, designed, and fought for residential, political, and cultural spaces of working-class urban life that not only provided for all of the material and social needs of low-income people, but also allowed for the "collective self-confidence" that Goodwyn asserts is necessary for the establishment of a strong movement. These sites enabled regular people to intervene in the city's efforts to define the model city, and their physical and social forms helped define a collective alternative model.

All of these sites were meeting places, collective spaces, and points of contention in the struggle over what the model city would be. Each was an assertion of occupancy, a claim on space in and access to downtown, and an attempt to register dissent during a redevelopment campaign bent on broadcasting consensus. Each enabled an extended web of organizing and mobilizing beyond its own walls or fence posts. The Strand, the coffeehouse, the HNU office, and Hallock Street Park all served as meeting and gathering places for actions throughout the city and beyond. Buses coordinated at the HNU and AIM offices left for city hall, Washington, D.C., New York, and Hartford to protest the war, demand fair treatment for welfare recipients, walk picket lines, or attend public hearings. It was from these primary meeting places that groups of mobilized citizens gathered and drove to the state house, not just to testify before the State Highway Commission about the Ring Road plans, but to ask to see these plans and figure out how the state decided which highway should go where. In this way, many of these spaces of resistance are prerequisites for other such spaces.

No space for collective action exists in a vacuum. Lower Dixwell was powerful as a site of protest only to the extent that Goin Park, a block or so to the west, provided a space for the sit-out protesters to gather, hear speeches from local civil rights leaders, and resolidify their conviction to sit out in front of oncoming traffic. The catch (and the crux) is that it took a movement to preserve those spaces, and without those spaces, there cannot be movements. In order to "move," the movement must have a place to live, meet, grow, and claim. These are not utopian spaces—they are merely street corners, coffee shops, apartment buildings, and playgrounds. But these everyday spaces are what enable culture and collectivity—provided, of course, that they are actually in neighborhoods where people can afford to live. So this is why a story that seeks, in the end, to clarify the meaning of bodies sitting in the middle of the street must start with a highway in the middle of somebody's kitchen.

1

"The Ghosts of Oak Street's Paved Ravines"

The Oak Street Project, the Construction of Public Consensus, and the Birth of a Slumless City

> And that pair of One Way signs
> Whose directions collide
> In the middle of Columbus Avenue:
> Is it to keep August traffic from turning
> Onto Cedar Street some Saturday night?
> Detour, and fear not the ghosts
> Of Oak Street's paved ravines.
>
> —Elizabeth Rose, excerpt from untitled poem, *AIM Newsletter,*
> *Special Riot Edition,* August 31, 1967

"The model you see before you will be a model for all America," explained Mayor Richard C. Lee's disembodied voice through a state-of-the-art speaker mounted above a detailed three-dimensional model of the Dixwell Urban Renewal and Redevelopment Plan. This exhibit was one of the most popular at New Haven's Progress Pavilion, a temporary structure erected by volunteer labor in the heart of downtown in 1960 to house rotating exhibits about the city's many redevelopment projects. The pavilion educated New Haven's citizens and visitors on the notion of the "model" and its many meanings more than six years before the introduction of President Lyndon B. Johnson's Model Cities program. In a squat structure—a collection of beveled concrete rectangles overlooking the town green that seemed to sprout from the dirt almost instantaneously—the mayor and the Redevelopment Agency (RA) tested their notion of the model city, and their means of achieving it, on the throngs of locals and visitors who walked through the pavilion each day. From the time of its own "opening ceremony," the city celebrated the fact that it would soon be torn down to make room for bigger and better things. But in the meantime, the mayor and his redevelopment

Figure 1.1

Visitors to the Progress Pavilion look at a three-dimensional scale model of the city. The real Chapel Street is visible outside the pavilion's narrow window. *(New Haven Museum and Historical Society Redevelopment Agency photograph collection.)*

staff took the opportunity to teach the masses a new way of looking at these "project areas"—to school them in seeing what *would*, *should*, or *could* be there. Visitors were educated on how to translate a three-dimensional model, like the Dixwell project model, into real-life scale, and to focus on these new hypothetical views of the modern city, rather than the realities—the problems, but also the communities, the homes, and the people—a few blocks away. One such person was Victoria Thomas, and nearly a decade before the Progress Pavilion rose up out of the ground, her life—and her home—collided with Mayor Lee's particular model.

For twelve years, Victoria Thomas had lived in a modest apartment at 115 York Street, which is now a jumble of dentists' and doctors' offices near Yale–New Haven Hospital. She worked downtown as a buyer at Hamilton and Co., Inc., and adored her "lovely" three-room apartment. She took great pride in the fact that her neighbors were all "businesspeople. Very respectable." So it was unsettling to Miss Thomas when she heard rumblings about the city's plan to put a highway connector through her kitchen. She immediately went to put her name on a relocation list, but this didn't seem to put her at ease. "There are thousands of names ahead of mine," she wrote in her letter to the mayor, on Hamilton and Co. letterhead. She wrote at the suggestion of the mayor's wife, Ellen, who happened to come into the store one November afternoon. Miss Thomas considered herself a friend of the mayor's wife, and thought perhaps this connection might facilitate some resolution to her problem. "What are people like me going to do, or what are we to expect?" she asked, disquieted by the thought of highway traffic replacing not just her home, but also her neighborhood. "I'm hoping that the city is making plans for us—and that I can hope for a comparable apartment and not with *mixed* races." She sealed the envelope and wrote the word "personal" across the outside (perhaps at Mrs. Lee's suggestion), then dropped it the mail on November 2, 1955.[1]

The letter was, in fact, personal, as Miss Thomas had indicated. She was a working single woman in a walking city, emboldened by her social connections and working status to write to the mayor when she felt her familiar spaces and routines threatened. The city considered her neighborhood a "slum," a designation that city representatives often supported with intensely racialized and gendered descriptions of street life, disease, and sexual behaviors. This particular white working woman—about whom one can admittedly only infer or assume experiences, personality, and preferences from a single letter to the mayor—articulated claims on this particular network of urban spaces, palpable racial fears and prejudices, and a willingness to transcend usual gender boundaries in order to have a say in the shape of her city. Clearly, resistance to urban renewal was intensely personal, complex, and multilayered, and it manifested itself in many different forms. Was this letter a form of "citizen participation"? What did it mean for the city to have a master plan, or even a particular redevelopment scheme, without any real obligation to account for all of the Victoria Thomases who occupied the exact square feet of space depicted in the city's commissioned scale models and blueprints of the Oak Street Connector?

The mayor did eventually respond to Victoria Thomas' letter, along with a note of apology for his late response (perhaps also at Mrs. Lee's request). In fact, Miss Thomas could hope for a comfortable apartment, and probably did get one—the city erected thousands of middle-income units over the next decade. And, most likely, this new apartment also allowed her to live in a building without much proximity to the city's African American population, per her request, as most of these former Oak Street inhabitants wound up in Elm Haven, the city's largest public housing project, or in the African American areas of Newhallville, Dixwell, and the Hill.

New Haven's Oak Street neighborhood was once the most densely populated part of the city. In a few years' time, those forty-two acres were transformed by the nation's most ambitious and (per capita) costly redevelopment project into a tangle of parking garages and highway ramps, interrupted by the occasional high-rise and department store. In the early to mid-1950s, this transformation was fueled by federal dollars dependent on hard-fought (and, at times, carefully constructed) public consensus over what should be done to solve urban problems such as overcrowding, substandard housing, traffic congestion, and crime. This consensus, it seemed, was that the slums should be torn down and replaced by highways and downtown shopping and parking garages to serve the needs of the surrounding suburbs, thus providing New Haven with an influx of tax revenue and retail business while eliminating areas concentrated with "troubled and troublesome families."[2]

This was the predominant view of solutions to urban problems in America before waves of violence transformed the debate into one about an "urban crisis."[3] In the mid- to late 1950s, the question facing Mayor Lee and his counterparts across the country was whether cities could continue to thrive in an increasingly suburban nation. The mayor's plan would, in his words, "give New Haven . . . the kind of access highways that are required if the downtown area is to grow and prosper instead of continue to decline." To save the city, they had to make it much easier for people to drive in and out of it. Mayor Lee also added that he thought new highways and parking garages were essential to serving the city's "neighbors living in our suburban communities."[4] This push for growth and prosperity, in which the desire to see the city rise up and fortify itself against the troubles of the slums—to create elevated, protected spaces away from the street where gentle suburban shopping women could walk and safely spend their husbands' money—offered a striking foil for the urban problems that were gendered female. Overcrowded, fatherless households spilled out onto the streets, pushing private lives into public places, fostering crime, disease, and vice. Plans for a cleansed, elevated, protected city would allow suburban people to have an "urban" life separate from the living, breathing, walking city.

The Planning Tableau and the Experts' Dilemma

Like all innovations, this new urban vision came from an earlier time, influenced significantly by the "towers in the park" designs of Le Corbusier, born Charles-Edouard Jeanneret in 1887, a pioneer in modernist architectural design. They were merely high-rises of the mind in the 1930s when Le Corbusier wrote his most influential works, *The City for Three Million* and *Radiant City*. In 1935, he described his urban ideal, skyscrapers shooting into the sky out of a predictable and symmetrical pattern of parks and highways. The dominant features of his design were silence and blank space. "Surfaced with solemn marble, shining with clear mirrors mounted in stainless steel frames. Silence," wrote Le Corbusier. "Corridors and vast spaces; doors open automatically: they are the silent elevators unloading passengers.

No windows anywhere . . . silent walls. 'Conditioned' air throughout, pure, clean, at a constant temperature. Am I on the fifth floor or the fortieth?" The ideological framework of New Haven's master plan came from this placeless and noiseless vision of what urban scholar Daniel Solomon described as "a matrix of undifferentiated space."

As Solomon argued in *Global City Blues* (2003), the postwar urban vision of a "tabula rasa of Cartesian space"—like the vision of Le Corbusier—was a blank slate onto which urban renewal projects were written. These slates were not blank, of course; Victoria Thomas could attest to that. So could the families interviewed for one proposed movement-run housing cooperative, some of whom had also been displaced from Oak Street. They were offered fresh, clean accommodations in new "developments," often set off of the street, sometimes set down outside the city and away from public transportation and jobs, as well as "noise" and "houses and stores." They expressed a clear preference for close proximity to the sounds and experiences of the street. But it was on this ideal of rational design imposed upon empty space that the city planners and redevelopment agencies of the 1950s and 1960s built, to quote Solomon, "the elevated highways that wrecked urban neighborhoods."[5]

Le Corbusier's vision was compelling for the armies of social science and city planning experts who descended upon New Haven during the Lee administration. They, too, built Cartesian scale models of highway ramps encircling high-rises and blank urban space, pointing with pencils at monochromatic, three-dimensional renderings of buttresses and widened throughway lanes. They did this at closed meetings in city hall, at public meetings in school auditoriums, and in large black-and-white photographs on the front pages of the local papers. They were invariably white men in dark suits, their hair often greased back in a promising shine that mirrored the order imposed upon their urban vision. This print culture of expertise and progress was central to the development of consensus around New Haven's master plan. In RA promotional materials, and in stories in the local and national press, a proliferation of planning-room propaganda took shape. The visual trope was centered around the image of these white men in suits—sometimes two or three of them; at times one was sufficient—sitting around a set of blueprints or a scale model of a neighborhood, a city, or a new development.

They often pointed at the plans in a way that was reminiscent of Michelangelo's *Creation of Man*, white-collared deities hovering above the plans for the little worlds they would create. In 1955, when the *New Haven Journal-Courier* published one such image of five men looming over a three-dimensional model of Oak Street with the caption "Development Chief Explains Oak St. Connector," the Oak Street residents and business owners who picked up the morning paper saw themselves rendered in near-invisible black and white within the shadowed recesses of this desk model, held to cardboard with glue, constructed of flat, blank surfaces. It was with this

Figure 1.2

Members of the Mt. Vernon, New York, redevelopment agency view a scale model of New Haven's master plan, October 2, 1963. *(Photographer unknown, New Haven Museum and Historical Society Redevelopment Agency photograph collection.)*

model, and these five "experts" (actually revealed lower in the text to be the "management club of Olin Mathieson Chemical Corporation"), that the city purported to "explain" the highway connector that would replace their neighborhood. But only for the city's corporate giants would the planning chief do this in person. Only the men in suits were able to view and interrogate the 3-D model up close.[6]

A strikingly similar photograph had appeared in a *Journal-Courier* article about the state's approval to fund New Haven's urban highway construction in August of 1953.[7] By that time, the RA was able to report that, "after years of planning and study of blue prints and maps, which, pieced together, would above cover that Central Green, the [Oak Street] project is gaining momentum."[8] The proliferation of blueprints and maps seemed to speak for itself, and in doing so, encouraged public support and legitimized a generation of young experts. It was with the assurance of this public consent that the city secured state and federal funding to demolish its densest neighborhood and build the Oak Street Connector.

The city's drive to remake itself was fueled by more than vision. Local business leaders, including Yale University and the Southern New England

Telephone Company, exerted considerable pressure on the Lee administration to push the Oak Street project through to completion. While business and industry pressured city hall for progress on the highway connector, public uncertainty mounted. "People are fed up with our telling them we do not know when the highways are coming," one internal RA memo cautioned. "They believe we are holding back."[9] This belief wasn't completely unfounded. From the earliest planning stages of the Oak Street project, the RA worked covertly to prevent the growth of some Oak Street neighborhood businesses they secretly planned to destroy. In 1953, one Spruce Street business, Elm City Sales, asked the zoning board for permission to build an addition. An internal city hall memo alerted Edward Logue, the city's redevelopment director, of the zoning board hearing, suggesting that since the property was located within the "project boundaries," he should attend the hearing and appeal the request. Rather than tell the business owner that his property was slated to be demolished for construction of the highway connector, the RA instead chose to stop him from expanding.[10]

Residential spaces in the project area were also left to languish, revealing the city's dual dilemma of the early redevelopment period: they had a severe housing shortage and were simultaneously embarking upon a comprehensive plan to remake the city's landscape, access points, and traffic flow by destroying more housing. This promised a considerable public relations crisis. By skillfully and comprehensively dealing with the latter, they proved—for a short time, at least—that they could avoid dealing with the former. Throughout the mid-1950s, the shortage of affordable housing did not go unnoticed by city hall. The New Haven Human Relations Council Housing Committee wrote to the U.S. Senate Appropriations Committee in 1955 demanding 35,000 new units of public housing, citing a recent article in *Business Week* that suggested slum clearance would be jeopardized without the allocation of public housing funding to house those displaced by redevelopment.[11] But these calls went unheeded. Federal support for public housing dwindled while urban renewal continued, proving *Business Week*'s fears to be unfounded. Slum clearance would continue without much regard, it seemed, for the question of how to house the displaced.

This question had haunted the urban renewal debate since its inception. In a 1945 memo considering the "stages of exploration" for urban redevelopment in the city of Pittsburgh, the authors concluded with a concern for "the families which do not have incomes sufficient to pay an economic rent," asserting that they "will constitute a difficult phase of the problem."[12] The document refers to these families only as "the displaced," and asserts that they appear to be most suitably "the responsibility of a public housing agency than of any other type of agency." This was easy to argue in the 1940s, when public housing was more plentiful, but by the mid-1950s, when no new funding for construction of low-income public housing was on the horizon, it was a more problematic solution. Still, even in 1945, the architects of Pittsburgh's redevelopment plan concluded that "this subject, vitally important as it is," shouldn't deter plans for renewal, which they saw as in the "long term interest" of the municipality.

This was exactly what New Haven's RA wanted to hear, having met with "general pessimism" in initial discussions with governmental, community, and business leaders about their redevelopment plans. New Haven redevelopment administrator Samuel Spielvogel heard the Pittsburgh redevelopment team speak in 1954 about their initial difficulties in selling the idea of urban renewal to these constituencies. He wrote immediately to Pittsburgh's redevelopment office and requested a copy of their redevelopment plan, citing that the Pittsburgh team's written account would "greatly facilitate" New Haven's "constitutionality test" in the courts that would enable the city's first slum clearance project—the Oak Street Connector.[13] The test to which he referred was a 1954 Supreme Court case, *Berman v. Parker*, which established the constitutionality of clearing neighborhoods through a comprehensive redevelopment plan to make way for highways, schools, shopping centers, or other public uses.[14] By the time the parking garages and highway ramps of the "*New* New Haven" materialized out of a billow of dust and rubble, it would be hard to imagine that the very constitutionality of such a scheme had been challenged.

The RA recognized the housing shortage as a problem both for citizens in need of homes and for their own plans to mobilize state and federal resources (and, necessarily, public support) for massive urban renewal programs. Citizens had to be convinced that redevelopment meant "progress" and not destruction—after all, it was first visible as wrecking balls and scaffolding. Through the skillful public use of blueprints, maps, photos, and public relations campaigns in a new age of mass media, careful control and manipulation of all opportunities for public comment, and the cooperation of the local press, institutions, and business leaders, the RA and the mayor's office masterfully sold the notion of slum clearance and urban renewal to what was initially a skeptical and quite nervous public.

Creating Consensus and Illustrating Progress

Voices of dissent hardly register in the public record of Oak Street's redevelopment. A comprehensive public relations campaign in support of the Oak Street Connector carried Lee into the office of mayor and carried New Haven into the national spotlight—both in the press and in the political sphere. At the heart of New Haven's notoriety as an urban renewal success story was the almost too-constant assertion by the mayor and the RA that "the City of New Haven [was] together and not divided."[15]

In a new era of TV and mass media, visual documents held new and often intoxicating persuasive powers. In preparation for a lunch meeting with

Senator Prescott Bush at Mory's, an exclusive Yale dining club, Redevelopment Director Edward Logue asked one of his administrators to provide him with a one-page summary on the Oak Street project, concluding with "a summary of public support and lack of opposition." To support the memo, he asked for maps of the area illuminating, in quickly digestible visual form, "what the present uses are and what's wrong with that." In fact, Logue added, "they do not need to be maps at all, they can be sketches or photographs if they will do the trick." Logue's language here was telling. Whereas many parts of the city were very obviously in need of repair, reinvigoration, or even demolition, the RA needed to use photos, sketches, and maps to "trick" the public into accepting a wholesale demolition program for the city's most densely populated residential and business center. Logue had a particular tone in mind for the materials—he asked for "a happy blend of your HHFA-ese and [another staffer]'s TV-ese." "Certainly," he continued, "although we do not want to make the report public, it should be prepared with a recommendation that it might very well be made public at some time."[16]

In fact, many of these compiled materials were used at public hearings, and the law required in many cases that they be publicly accessible in government offices. Local press coverage of such meetings often noted the "two large maps pinned to the front and rear of the room to show the connector's path."[17] For those who attended, a map on the wall naturalized and legitimized the impending highway connector, and city officials were astutely aware of this. Knowing that the full written redevelopment plans could be more revealing and more jarring than a map of the future city, the RA revised one early press announcement about the availability of information to the public shortly before it went to press. The original draft stated that the written plans, "supporting documentation," and the maps would be on file and available to the public at the city clerk's office. The notice, as it appeared in November of 1955, mentioned only the maps.[18]

It was up to the RA to demonstrate to the public that its demolition and highway construction plans were intricately connected to improving the lives of all New Haven citizens. Through carefully crafted visual materials, including countless neighborhood maps crossed by the dotted lines that frequently indicated future highways, the RA asserted, as they did through the Citizens Action Commission's (CAC) *Annual Report and Development Guide of 1959*, that all of the city's neighborhoods were "mutually dependent." The report, which echoed the RA's own reports and statements for that year, but refashioned the prose and presentation to fill the CAC's commitment to the general public, asserted that "the needs of each area have been molded into a City-Wide Master Plan which contemplates a revitalized City free of slums and blight. . . . These pages," it continued, referencing the maps, photos, and diagrams of "citizen participation" intended to reassure those wary of the proliferating blank urban spaces and impending bulldozers, "illustrate that progress."[19] Maps and aerial photographs were superimposed with numbers labeling the projects in progress and the projects of the near future. Like a children's connect-the-dots game, these documents enabled the reader to imagine, once the pencil lines were drawn—once the RA's blueprints and scale models were transformed into three-dimensional life—that the city would be resurrected, this time free of slums, blight, and "dirty streets." Only "convenient urban living" would remain.[20]

Unattributed photographs of urban disorder, reminiscent of the progressive-era lantern-slide lectures of photojournalist Jacob Riis, occupied the pages as testimony to the fact that "only photographs and memories remain of the 42-acre Oak St. area which three years ago was Connecticut's worst slum."[21] The text mirrored the favored visual format: a "before and after" model, not unlike print ads of the time in which a dirty shirt collar was fantastically rendered clean by a new detergent, with side-by-side images providing the proof. "New Haven's most modern, well-planned area has replaced the squalor in which 886 families confronted a hopeless, miserable way of life," proclaimed the authors, and to prove it, they had photographs.[22] The "before" image contained a dirty sink and a dirty toilet against a crumbling wall. The caption read, "Depressing? Almost impossible to keep clean." The "after" picture was a well-groomed, modestly dressed white woman sitting on a couch with three children, all of them neat and well behaved. The frame was careful to include a shiny floor, television, new lamp, and curtains, a picture of domestic normalcy, provided we could assume that Dad was taking the photograph. To reassure readers of this missing piece, the caption stated, "The family relocation officer and staff found a clean, pleasant flat for this housewife and her family," careful to identify her as a housewife, rather than a working single mother, a welfare mother, or even the second working parent of a two-parent household.[23]

By positioning the evolving image of mother and children as the litmus for improvement, the RA reinforced the extent to which the problem—the slum—was feminized, whereas the solution—a physical reorganization and reassertion of the traditional family form—was masculinized. The "before and after" theme of redevelopment material predated the RA itself. A similar "before and after" image from the 1942 annual report for the New Haven Housing Authority illustrated the extent to which the Elm Haven housing project—which would, in the next twenty years, become its own "before" picture—transformed the Dixwell neighborhood's ghetto.

In the "before" image, the houses touch the sidewalk and connect with the street, but the structures lack uniformity and stability. A young girl stands out in front of the house, seemingly unsupervised, an early-stage woman-on-the-street, marking not only the connection between women's street presence and blight, but also the multigenerational reproduction of the problem, and the way in which it was tied to urban design. The "before" image shows no trees or lawns—necessary elements of the suburban ideal. The caption stretching across both images reads "New homes, new trees, new everything but the address," suggesting that the "after" image, in which homes are set back by small front lawns behind new trees, had neither disrupted, nor displaced, nor unsettled. The space appears completely unpopulated—presumably the women and children have been contained behind those new walls, protected (and blocked) from the street by new trees shooting skyward and a protective patch of green.

"This is truly a tale of two cities," wrote Mayor Lee in 1962, "New Haven *before* and *after*. The *after* began when this administration took office six years ago. I made promises then and since then—and kept them."[24] By the late 1960s, activists would begin to invoke this same "before and after" notion to challenge urban renewal and illuminate its failures, but throughout the 1950s and early 1960s, the city relied on the persuasive powers of photography, tested and proven through the Farm Security Administration's photography projects of the 1940s, to demonstrate the transformative powers brought to bear on slum areas by the combination of professional planners, comprehensive renewal plans, and state and federal support.

Despite the care and craftiness with which the RA assembled its own promotional literature, Edward Logue and his staff understood that they could not count on large segments of the New Haven public reading their annual reports, redevelopment guides, and promotional brochures. They could, however, count on most of the city's residents reading, or at least looking at, the city's two local papers, the morning *Journal-Courier* and the afternoon *Register*. Both were owned by the same man, John Day Jackson, and both took issue with the very concept of urban renewal, but in the words of Allan R. Talbot, one-time director of the city's anti-poverty agency, who wrote a 1967 book about the Lee administration, "the two papers provided the main formal link between the administration and the public."[25] As a former newspaperman, Lee understood both the power and the politics of the press. He maintained relationships with everyone from the managing editors to the "boys in the shipping department," who would hand him fresh copies right off the press. The editorial staff of the *Register* received daily calls from the mayor, during which he "plugged stories," offered professional journalistic advice, and exchanged gossip.

Despite their frequent criticisms of redevelopment, these news outlets deserved some credit for the success of the Oak Street project, and the lack of discernable public opposition to the clearance of the neighborhood. Following a series of feature articles on the project, which the *New Haven Register* ran in the early 1950s, the RA sent a thank-you note to the editor, Charles McQueeney, calling the piece a "splendid public service" that would allow the people of New Haven and "surrounding towns" to understand the "great potential" of urban renewal.[26] Eventually, the local newspapers' tacit support of the Oak Street project came in less explicit forms, through the way in which the project was covered. Headlines often naturalized the inevitability of the city's highway plans, as in "State Ready to Acquire Oak Street Connector Land," which suggested that this land—actually a dense urban neighborhood—had been waiting like an open frontier for the state to claim it. This story, from 1955, recounts a public meeting held by the highway commissioner at Mayor Lee's request, reporting that the audience of 300 was "mostly business people." The content of the meeting included some discussion of where displaced people would live, but the characterization of the audience suggested that none of the families to be displaced were so distraught by the prospect that they would show up to a public meeting. In fact, there were 866 families that the RA would, by 1959, take credit for successfully relocating.[27]

According to the *Register,* the entire area would be "cleared" by the following November, a word choice that downplayed the nature of what that "clearing" would entail, and focused the readers' attention on the blank canvas that would await the broad, flat lines of a highway connector.[28] According to the press, a total of about 100 property owners would be affected by the Oak Street project, but the city's own records indicated that about 125 individual residents would be displaced on just one small block of the forty-two-acre project.[29] Perhaps by counting "property owners" rather than residents, the press was able to make the disruption seem minimal—around 70 percent of Oak Street's residents were actually renters, as were many of its small-business owners.[30]

The city was careful to arrange public meetings in such a way as to minimize the possibility of dissent. The simplest strategies involved having as few public meetings as possible under the law, scheduling those meetings too late in the legislative or budgetary timeline to make significant changes, and scheduling them at times of the day (usually early afternoon) when most working people could not attend. State approval of and financial support for a redevelopment project required two weeks' public notice for two public hearings, one of which had to be before the board of aldermen.[31] Proof of notice had to be submitted to the state—a copy of a small notice in one of the local papers sufficed. The public notice of such meetings was often limited to that which was required by law, with little attempt made to get the word out beyond mainstream local press outlets and into the black community through the well-established network of churches, community service agencies, and community centers, or the long-standing chapter of the NAACP. Yet, beyond the announcements of public meetings sent to the *Register* and *Journal-Courier,* the city also reached out to neighboring towns through such publications as the *Branford Review, East Haven News, Hamden Chronicle,* and *West Haven Town Crier,* suggesting the extent to which it desired input (or, more likely, expected support for highway and parking plans) from its suburban neighbors.[32]

Despite the extent to which the residents of "slum" communities were uninformed about their legally mandated opportunities for public comment, chances are that many concerned citizens did know about the meetings, which at the time of the Oak Street project were often held in downtown city buildings, another deterring factor for many in the black community. In case vocal citizens with dissenting opinions about the city's redevelopment plans did show up, the RA employed a number of strategies to maintain the appearance of consensus. The three most common tactics were identifying the State Highway Department (rather than the city) as the responsible party for redevelopment concerns, arranging the agendas to frontload the city's experts, placing the opportunity for public comment at the very end of an extremely long meeting, and using the expert testimony—which often took up the bulk of the public meeting—to focus public attention on the "undesirable" elements in neighborhoods or blocks slated for demolition. This testimony often centered on public health and public safety risks, with particular emphasis on sexual deviance, crime rates, and juvenile delinquency, all of which were popular tropes in the visual materials intended to sell urban renewal to the general public.

The mayor and the RA took great care to emphasize that public meetings held about the plans for the Oak Street project were hosted by the State Highway Department, and not the city of New Haven. Announcements for the meetings listed the State Highway Department as the appropriate contact for people seeking additional information, and the mayor and Ed Logue explicitly instructed their staff to be clear that this was the State Highway Department's responsibility.[33] In October 1955, Mayor Lee suggested that the State Highway Department open a local office in the Oak Street neighborhood "for at least two days a week with a competent person in charge to answer questions for people." He suggested staffing the office with a retired local judge, a legal aid volunteer, or someone from the attorney general's office.[34] The mayor was unclear as to what this office should say to or do with concerned Oak Street residents, since the state was not legally obligated (nor was it willing) to take any responsibility for residents or business owners displaced by the highway connector, but he was clear about the need to give the office "widespread publicity."

Although the city claimed that public meetings were sponsored by the State Highway Department, and that they, as city officials, were simply accepting an invitation, RA executive director Ralph Taylor and the city's RA administrator Edward Logue designed an agenda that placed public comment at the end of a very long meeting, but made sure that there was time for a handful of citizens to speak, understanding that "it would be bad public relations for the various official agencies to utilize so much time that opponents could claim they were shut out." Taylor and Logue stacked the agenda with a string of experts, including prominent citizens from Lee-appointed committees, business leaders, and an array of city officials and department heads. Taylor suggested that open public comment could start after all of the experts finished, around ten o'clock in the evening, "late enough to have the audience restive if an opponent gets too long-winded, but not so late everyone couldn't be heard even if the hearing lasts until midnight."[35]

Before those "in the path of the highway" (as the local press identified them) who had waited out the agenda could speak their piece, they had to sit through this lengthy expert testimony, which Logue described to the mayor as "the positive side of the hearing." The scripts he crafted for the experts— included in his memo to the mayor—were anything but positive.[36] Categorized under the headings of "Law and Order," "Fire Hazard," "Health and Welfare," "Traffic Congestion," "Educational Facilities," "Recreation," and "Housing Standards," each piece of expert testimony was summarized for the "expert" on a small piece of paper, about the size of an index card. These sheets offered instructions, written by Logue and Taylor, on the content of the testimony. For example, the police chief's testimony outline suggested that he describe the Oak Street neighborhood as one that "attracts [the] worst kind of people." The city planning commissioner was instructed on his sheet to testify that the neighborhood was an example of the "spread of slum cancer."[37]

Transcripts of these expert testimonies reflect not only compliance with the RA's directives, but also a significant amount of dramatic flourish lending credence to the agency's plans to replace a neighborhood with a highway. In a public hearing on December 1, 1955, Chief of Police Francis V. McManus testified that Oak Street "attracts the worst elements. The bad eggs—the dope pushers—the vice rings—the numbers racket operators—the prostitutes—all gravitate toward the area." Focusing attention on sexual deviance and crime, and away from the plans to demolish homes and businesses, McManus offered vivid testimony on the pathology of criminals. "If you turn a flashlight on a rat, he'll run. The same is true of criminals and that's just what we'll do—we'll keep them on the run until they learn that New Haven is no longer a comfortable place for their kind."

City Court Judge Charles Henchel began his expert testimony by talking about prostitution. "Individual women who live in this area," he testified, "are constantly seeking to solicit persons who come to the area for such purpose. As a result, the area now houses a large contingent of persons who either live alone or with a person of the opposite sex without the benefit of marriage." He went on to cite the high levels of deviant sex crimes in the neighborhood, including charges of "lascivious carriage," a charge that amounted to a woman spending the night in a man's home, one that was disproportionately levied upon black women. In requesting and crafting this testimony, the RA sexualized the Oak Street neighborhood and used progressive-era moralities to justify the demolition of the city's most dense and diverse area. The expert testimony from the Department of Public Health, given by Dr. Clement F. Batelli, ignored issues such as malnutrition, lack of quality health care, and lack of access to medications, in favor of highlighting alcoholism, juvenile delinquency, and venereal disease. Even the expert testimony from the welfare office fixated on the high rates of sexually transmitted diseases in the neighborhood, citing that as a predominant reason for reliance on welfare.[38]

To the general public, and to the state and federal government, the RA and Mayor Lee referenced extensive expert studies of the Oak Street area, fact-finding investigations that uncovered both the devastating conditions in the neighborhood and the dire need for a highway connector in its place. At the required public hearings, however, rather than making a case for slum clearance and the need for (and existence of) a good highway construction plan, they orchestrated and unleashed an arsenal of expert testimony to vilify the neighborhood and its residents. Rather than demonstrate proof of any plan for relocation or rehousing, they dehumanized the neighborhood's inhabitants to detract from that question. The hearing put the neighborhood—rather than the urban renewal project—on trial, and allowed no witnesses for the defense. Ultimately, the RA's motives were clear from its instructions for the expert testimony from the Department of Public Works: "If [you] can say area costs more than similar areas with far less to show for it in terms of condition of streets, garbage, etc.—good." In other words, the fact that the neighborhood was run-down and neglected worked to the RA's advantage, because they sought not to find solutions to the problems that caused these conditions, but to cite those problems as reasons for demolition.

To Oak Street residents, the promise of new homes, cleaner streets, and safer blocks would certainly have discouraged vocal opposition to the agency's plans, but this "relocation question," as the city and state called it, was not what the experts talked about. From the perspective of any Oak Street resident attending the hearing, the experts testified to the delinquency, immorality, criminality, and unsanitary lifestyles of her family, her friends, and her neighbors. This makes it all the more suspicious that no record of public statements in opposition seems to exist. Either the residents were not present at these hearings, or they were not given the opportunity to speak. Or perhaps the omission suggests they were intimidated by the expert testimony, or even that their testimony was not recorded and reported to the press, or to the regional director of the Urban Renewal Administration (URA).

In compliance with federal law, five days after the public meeting, RA executive director Ralph Taylor sent a letter to the New York office of the regional director of the URA, Charles Horan. Enclosed was the required "proof of notice"—a clipping from the New Haven Journal-Courier announcing the meeting two weeks in advance, and a "full copy of the text" of a statement by Rev. Robert Frosberg, New Haven's Human Relations Council chairman and a "minister of a church located in the project area." This testimony was sent "as evidence that the relocation question was considered at the public hearing."[39] The Human Relations Council was the group responsible for developing the RA's public relations campaign to sell projects to the public. Frosberg's wife, incidentally, was hired by the RA's relocation office, and although his church was in the project area, his family's home was not "in the path of the highway." But it was this statement by Frosberg, along with notification of a unanimous board of aldermen vote, which met the legal requirement for public comment.

With the help of the local press, which reported on such proceedings as formalities in a predetermined and quite natural process of municipal land acquisition, the public record of hearings on the Oak Street project show very little in the way of questions, much less controversy or dissent. The state required a copy of the minutes of the public meetings, but these minutes were kept and submitted by an employee of the RA, and even a very cursory comparison between the official typed minutes and the personal notes kept by the city's redevelopment administrator, Edward Logue, reveal key omissions.[40] Whereas the submitted minutes read as though they could have been written before the meeting, or from a compilation of the administration's memos to various city agencies and experts about what they should be saying at the meeting, Logue's own personal notes reflect a palpable fear among city officials that a failure to convey consensus to both the state and the public could dash both New Haven's hopes of being the first "slumless city" and its plans to revitalize the urban core by attracting suburban shoppers. Names written along margins with underlines, asterisks, or question marks indicate possible pockets of dissent. At 9:35 p.m., Logue took down the name of a local real estate company treasurer, Louis Fraight, who questioned the Oak Street project's inclusion of the two blocks from George Street to Crown Street. This area included "17 parcels and 9 houses," noted Logue. "Protest those two blocks," he wrote.[41] No such protest ever materialized, however. Perhaps Logue was noting Fraight's testimony as a protest in and of itself, but the city's assertions to the State Highway Commissioner claimed otherwise.

"Once again," the mayor wrote to the state highway commissioner in May of 1954, "I wish to reiterate that the City of New Haven is altogether and not divided. We are going to forge ahead as rapidly as possible."[42] A month later, the mayor wrote to the highway commissioner again, stressing a "United City Position." "A great deal of work has gone into the effort of getting the city agencies . . . to speak with one voice," he asserted.[43] A unified voice was crucial, and when it came to the residents, quite hard to capture. Reading between the lines of the public record reveals a steady clamor of uncertainty among Oak Street's residents, as well as a few gaping holes of silence.

The Oak Street Redevelopment Plan was approved, funded, and carried out in a flurry of national attention for a mayor with innovative strategies for collecting federal funds and eliminating slums. "With a snapping of scissors, a burst of police flares, and launching of multi-colored balloons," reported the *New Haven Journal-Courier*, Connecticut governor Abraham Ribicoff and Mayor Richard Lee celebrated the official opening of the Oak Street Connector, a $15 million, one-mile-long highway ramp connecting New Haven to the Connecticut Turnpike. It was a chilly October afternoon in 1959, and more than 3,000 people watched a motorcade of 650 cars, four across, drive the length of the six-lane roadway. The dignitaries gathered under a 100-foot tent erected at the end of York Street, where they enjoyed a "buffet of hors-d'oeuvres, cocktails, and coffee," on a spot that was once a living room, a front stoop, or a sidewalk.[44] After the festivities, the governor's official Cadillac was not actually allowed to travel by way of the new connector to get back onto the turnpike, since he himself "promptly ordered [it] closed" on safety grounds.

When the traffic was finally flowing over the Oak Street Connector where there had once been only venereal disease and juvenile delinquency, the RA celebrated its success by scoping out new slums to eliminate. The demolition of nine stores on Church Street, not far from the Oak Street project, were to be the next "step towards New Haven's 'new look.' "[45] These were the words of New Haven's CAC, which in 1959 was celebrating its fifth anniversary. The CAC had rallied around the Oak Street plan, and celebrated the project's success in its annual report, proclaiming, "Here is evidence, in concrete and steel . . . that the city can be freed from slums and decay." Just as Oak Street had been transformed from a slum into "a super-highway, new office buildings, a commercial plaza, and high-rise apartments," Church Street would become a "modern downtown shopping center." So, too, would the rest of downtown, as the city remade itself to be "more convenient for downtown shoppers."[46]

The Progress Pavilion: "Watch the Picture Change!"

More than 100 private companies engaged in construction work, unions, citizen groups, and individuals gave freely of their time, energy, and money towards the construction of the Progress Pavilion . . . a unique example of citizen participation.

—Citizens Action Commission, *New New Haven: Progress Pavilion*, 1962

By 1960, with construction projects kicking up dust and disrupting the flow of traffic throughout the city, the RA began to worry that public frustration would overshadow public support of redevelopment projects. Although it would be a few years before condemnation of redevelopment on a national level would shift the focus of federal urban programs, the early start and unprecedented scope of New Haven's urban renewal programs prompted early criticisms. One headline in the *New Haven Register* announced that the city was "Making a Business of Being Destructive," citing the demolition of

Figure 1.3

Progress Pavilion. *(New Haven Museum and Historical Society Redevelopment Agency photograph collection.)*

more than 2,600 buildings. The front-page photograph showed piles of bricks and rubble, and the paper reported that nine city blocks had been leveled, "leaving a hole not far from the center of the city, not unlike the open areas found in many bomb ravaged cities of Europe after the last war."[47] The city's relocation office began to field criticisms from both the press and individual citizens.

The solution proposed by the public relations committee was a "campaign instituted to build-up and emphasize the positive aspects of the redevelopment program." This entailed "newspaper ads, billboards, and a radio jingle proclaiming 'Things are moving fast in the *New* New Haven!' "[48] The billboards and radio jingles took to the highways and airwaves, respectively, pleading with the people of New Haven to "Pardon our dust, we're pushing ahead." In giant letters against a scaffolding logo that seemed to blend in with the grid of scaffolding jutting up into the city's ever-changing skyline, a new CAC billboard read, "The *New* New Haven. Watch the Picture Change."

In a small invitation-only ceremony on a Friday morning in July of 1960, Mayor Lee welcomed dignitaries and a few select citizens to the official opening of the Progress Pavilion. A reporter for the *New Haven Register* couldn't resist a jab at the Lee administration for the persistence of down-town rubble and the slow pace of redevelopment, noting that the pavilion was, "appropriately enough, the first new structure to rise on Church St. Redevelopment Project land."[49] A welcome letter was enlarged for the purpose of display in the entryway of the small structure on the corner of Church and Chapel streets. "In a little more than a year, this handsome building will be removed to make way for another important element in our plan," the letter began, without revealing what that element might be. "In the meantime, however, this Pavilion will house a continuing, yet ever-changing series of exhibits oriented to specific parts of the program. I trust that every last person, young and old, will take the opportunity to visit the exhibits—not once, but many times." It was, in every respect, inspired by the spirit of world's fairs, and like the one that took place four years later in Queens, this small-scale celebration of the modern city was plagued by a considerable undercurrent of racial and economic tension. Like the 1964 World's Fair, which sparked a series of pickets and protests when it cele-brated free enterprise and corporate culture in a time of poverty and dis-crimination, the pavilion celebrated progress, as well as the powers and flourishes of city hall and industry, in a segregated city.[50] A last-minute memo to the mayor on the morning of the grand opening suggests the un-steady ground on which this extended celebration was erected by the free labor of Mayor Lee's citizen-admirers. "DICK—no ribbon cutting," it read.[51]

The material conception of the Progress Pavilion structure reflected an inherent tension in the Lee administration's liberal-democratic notion of civic responsibility. Al Jepson, chairman of the CAC, called the structure a "unique example of faith in America," referring to the fact that it was built entirely of donated labor and materials. The 2,500-square-foot structure was erected by seventy union workers. "As far as we know," wrote Jepson to a Boston U.S. Steel executive, "it is the only citizen built building of its type in the country. Most of its construction was accomplished in a single day by scores of volunteers. They were served lunch by the Girl Scouts and adjoining restaurants sent coffee and doughnuts. In short, it was a real 'barn-raising'—city style."[52]

The local implications of the term "barn raising" make it a somewhat in-accurate description of the process that was unfolding on one New Haven street corner. In both spirit and strategy, the Progress Pavilion was an inter-national event, intended to highlight the city's transformation on a global scale. The grand opening was attended by a dozen officials from Japan's Housing and Community Development Team before they sat down for a meeting with New Haven's redevelopment officials.[53] Many of the pavilion's maps, photographs, plans, and models were still on display at Paris' Petit Palais as part of a 1960 exhibit sponsored by the U.S. Information Service, called "Urbanisme et Collectivité—New Haven, ville pilote."[54]

Back in New Haven, Mayor Lee welcomed visitors to the Progress Pavilion. "The theme of the building, 'WATCH THE PICTURE CHANGE,' is indicative of the excitement and enthusiasm in the rebuilding of downtown," declared Lee's welcome letter. The building itself was an environmentally controlled assertion of this "excitement and enthusiasm," but it was also a carefully crafted gauge of those elements. The pavilion served as a sophisticated and heavily surveilled approval-o-meter to survey the public's responses to the RA's plans. It was also a propaganda outpost for the city's urban renewal programs, offering brochures, film screenings, fliers, and posters. A woman named Anita Palmer was hired to be the full-time caretaker/tour guide/plant waterer (and, it would seem, unbeknownst to her, secret agent) at the pavilion. She was instructed to file weekly narrative reports on the daily activities at the museum and supervise the pavilion's guest book, in which visitors from New Haven and around the world could scrawl their own personal reactions to the exhibit on the *new* New Haven.

Each week, Palmer dutifully reported the attendance numbers and the "type" of visitors (servicemen, out-of-towners, school groups, New Yorkers), developing an array of informal visitor classifications that would make for an interesting study in their own right. The week of September 26, 1960, she reported an impressive 1,200 visitors, and in response to the mayor's request for information about what people seemed to think of his plans for New Haven, she reported, "The majority of our citizens are very enthused and approve wholeheartedly of all of the projects." Still, her short list of commonly asked questions suggests mounting insecurities and even dissent. "Will anything be done to Chapel, Orange, and State St. area?" "Will there be new low[-income] housing?" With a hint of exasperation, Palmer's first cataloged report concludes, "They ask about completion dates on almost anything."

It was that last week in September that the pavilion unveiled what would become one of its most popular attractions, an intricate three-dimensional model of the Dixwell project, reflecting the extent to which the schedule of exhibits was determined by the agency's redevelopment timeline. The *Dixwell Redevelopment and Renewal Plan*, published jointly by the RA, the mayor's office, the City Plan Commission, and the CAC, with Maurice Rotival's consulting firm, came out in August of 1960. The Dixwell model was actually scheduled to go on display beginning August 22, and remain in the exhibit halls through mid-December, by which time it was expected that all public hearings and opportunities for public comment would have passed and demolition would be under way.[55] Although no specific reason for the exhibit's delay is outlined in the archival footprints of the Progress Pavilion, it is likely that the delay was due to the fact that the board of aldermen didn't approve the initial plans until September 7. (In fact, it wasn't until almost seven years later that the final redevelopment plan for Dixwell won aldermanic approval.)[56]

The following week, the pavilion welcomed another 1,200 visitors, and Palmer noted their "attitude" as "in generable favorable." But even in these brief accounts, which in some cases border on fan letters from Palmer to the mayor, the palpable nerves of individual visitors come through. What is summarized and characterized in the weekly reports as citizen suggestions on how to improve this "fine exhibit" or evidence of public curiosity about an "innovative" and "awe-inspiring" redevelopment scheme could easily be reread as drop-ins at a redevelopment crisis outpost (complete with Muzak and potted plants): "Many citizens came in to inquire about locations referring to their property, in reference to land acquisitions for new roads, industry, or housing," Palmer wrote on October 3. "People think we should have more maps," she added. A week later, her report included the popular suggestion that "more should be published in the paper about what is planned to date."[57] What was intended as a showplace became, for some, the only access to the RA—a group of anonymous men who made decisions in closed-door meetings about homes and small businesses they had often never visited.

Of course, these are the kinds of things the mayor expected to hear. He had no delusions that his massive redevelopment schemes would easily be swallowed and celebrated by all of the people who lived in and around the paths of the wrecking crews. But the weekly reports protected every rare criticism in a thick armor of personal flattery, none of which was particularly useful to the mayor or his redevelopment staff, who were clearly more interested in detecting possibilities of dissent. In mid-October, after a few months of Palmer's weekly updates, the mayor sent her a quick note, hastily written, asserting, "I'd be interested to know what percentage of people complaining are, in your opinion, negative in what they are complaining about."[58]

Palmer wrote back to report that the number of complaints was so small that it couldn't even be calculated as a percentage. She could recall "about two people" who said "all we are doing is tearing down buildings and not rebuilding fast enough."[59] But her weekly accounts continued to devote more attention to observations like "people use such adjectives as tremendous, fantastic, terrific, wonderful, and may I add they give our mayor all the credit."[60] Her memo dated November 21 did report an incident of vandalism in which Palmer caught an eight-year-old boy smashing one of the light fixtures outside the pavilion. She brought the incident to the attention of the police patrolman on a nearby corner, and he turned the offender over to the juvenile division. Yet her accounts of the public response inside the pavilion seemed to ignore the possibility that any hostility on the part of a neighborhood kid might be in some way connected to the particular form of "progress" that the pavilion celebrated. The day after the vandalism incident, the mayor wrote a note to Palmer, revealing both his exasperation and his paranoia. "Dear Anita," he began with an acknowledgment of her incessant flattery. "Your memos overwhelm me, and I am grateful to you. There must be some people critical, however. What are they critical about? What are they negative about? What do they believe is going to happen? Are they concerned about the timetable? Do they make any snide comments?"[61]

Winter approached, and attendance at the pavilion climbed as holiday shopping attracted more downtown foot traffic. The RA installed a state-of-the-art speaker system and recorded a welcome message from the mayor to pipe periodically through the ceiling and walls. "This is your mayor, Dick Lee," said a disembodied voice to whoever might be entering the pavilion at any given time. "You are now standing on one of the most important sites in the Church Street Redevelopment Project—the site of the dramatic new Sheraton Hotel which will open in 1963." Like the voice of a hypnotist, Lee was training visitors and citizens of the city to see urban space in a completely different way—to see a particular spot not as what it *was*, but as what it was *going to be*. This was a significant act of persuasion on the part of the mayor and the RA, and a significant leap of faith on the part of the public.

No matter how impressive the prerecorded voice of the mayor was, and no matter how vivid the scale models, photographs, sketches, and brochures might have been, many visitors clearly had trouble putting the actual lived city—the world outside the pavilion walls—out of their minds. The plans for I-91, which promised to be an impressive, ultramodern, high-speed artery, raised a lot of questions about the local streets on which people lived their daily lives. "Will it go through Temple St.?" "Will Humphrey St. be affected?" "What about George St.?"[62] But in their October report on the Progress Pavilion, the CAC and the RA cited as the most common concern among visitors the fact that the pavilion itself was only temporary. They reported to Mayor Lee that the citizens of New Haven saw the pavilion as a "useful information center," serving around 300 visitors a day, and eliciting a "very minimum" of negative comments.[63]

"Very Minimum" Dissent

Despite Anita Palmer's assertions, internal city hall correspondences, primarily those authored by CAC chairman Alan Jepson, admitted rumblings of anxiety and discontent. Jepson recommended, in September of 1961, that "at pre-announced and pre-publicized times on a given day (or days)" the mayor and his redevelopment staff "could be 'on duty' in the pavilion to answer questions" for a sort of a " 'The Public Meets the Redevelopers' " program.[64] By this time, the pavilion had attracted considerable attention from a newly organized New Haven chapter of the Congress of Racial Equality (CORE) and the local NAACP chapter, both of which were agitating for an end to housing discrimination in the city and the construction of more low-income housing.

James Gibbs, a local civil rights leader, headed up a coalition of local clergy, NAACP and CORE members, and concerned citizens, who had, that past spring, sent an open letter to the mayor's office calling for attention to what they saw as a "housing crisis" for the city's African American citizens. They demanded support for local fair-housing legislation. The mayor denied any such crisis, asserting that the city had successfully relocated more than 2,300 families, only 12 percent of whom ended up in public housing. Furthermore, he replied, the state of Connecticut already had fair-housing legislation that would go into effect that fall—legislation on the local level didn't seem necessary. Besides, he said, "discrimination is much more a suburban problem than an urban one."[65]

One could hardly disagree with the mayor's logic there. Discrimination *was* a problem exacerbated, reified, and written in concrete through the process of suburbanization. This was precisely why a "suburban" plan for the Dixwell neighborhood, erected in miniature for all to see and celebrate in the Progress Pavilion, awakened such ire in the more radical segments of New Haven's civil rights community. Understanding this, the mayor invited Gibbs to serve on his Special Housing Advisory Committee, at which—the mayor assured Gibbs—the issue of a fair-housing ordinance could be discussed. Gibbs refused.[66] But a handful of Dixwell notables agreed to join the committee, including Rev. Edwin Edmonds of the Dixwell Congregational Church, who had taken over the congregation of more than 300 after moving to New Haven from North Carolina in 1959. Edmonds had been the president of the Greensboro chapter of the NAACP, and upon moving north to flee the persecution of his family by white supremacists, he became an outspoken leader in the Dixwell community, helping to start preschool programs and housing developments in his neighborhood.[67] Edmonds would become one of Mayor Lee's key supporters in the process of redeveloping Dixwell, exemplifying the role black clergy—even those who had lived a life of radicalism and civil rights work—played in the project of selling redevelopment to the black community.

In his capacity as special housing advisor, Edmonds passed along some "interesting news" to Mayor Lee in late September of 1961. He reported that Gloster Current, national NAACP branch coordinator, had recently returned from California, where he had been fighting communist cells in the NAACP who had been doing "the same type of thing that Gibbs has been doing here in New Haven."[68] Gibbs had been pushing the NAACP to take a more militant stand against housing discrimination and the destruction of low-income housing. An aid informed the mayor that Gloster Current was pretty confident they could "get rid of Gibbs" at an upcoming NAACP chapter meeting, at which Gibbs—the chapter president—would propose a controversial "sit-out" protest. While tensions within the civil rights community revealed factions of Dick Lee loyalists and a new generation of more militant leadership, the RA, the Citizens Action Commission, and the office of the mayor scrambled to dodge charges of racism and assert redevelopment's intentions to improve housing for everyone.[69]

Attempting to defuse charges that the RA was a closed, secretive, and racist body, and finding itself in an increasingly fierce public relations battle, the agency refocused the pavilion's message. Scripted statements by the mayor took on an increasingly defensive tone. "We have pioneered in the fields of family relocation, of home rehabilitation, and of conservation," Lee stated at the opening of a housing exhibit in September of 1961. "Now, on Court Street and on East Shore, in the Hill and in Dixwell Avenue we are pioneering a new type of urban construction." This new "type" of urban construction was, by most accounts, a *suburban* type, in which expansive parking lots fronted widened streets, and horizontal shopping plazas interrupted formerly vertical mixed-use arrangements of apartment buildings, shops and offices, and single- and multifamily housing. "Working together as a united community," the mayor continued, "we have demolished whole streets which symbolized hopelessness, poverty, and despair. . . . Decaying buildings have become neighborhood showplaces."[70]

A project called "University Park Dixwell" was considered one such showplace, but it was certainly premature for Lee to boast about it in September of 1961, when the popular three-dimensional model at the Progress Pavilion was really all anyone had seen of this particular example of a "new type of urban construction." At that time, the "decaying buildings" still stood along Dixwell Avenue, many of them housing thriving businesses, multigenerational households, and long-standing community institutions. This was the case throughout the city. "Clustered around [new] expressways are four active redevelopment projects," claimed a Progress Pavilion publication, "where residential, commercial, and industrial slums are being replaced by bright new buildings of glass and steel."[71]

2

On Dixwell Avenue

Civil Rights and the Street

> *A street together with the buildings on either side of it forms a distinct cultural idea.*
> —Harris Stone, *Monuments and Main Streets* (1983), p. 243

The Mayor's Proposal

"Why not a sit-out to follow the sit-ins?" asked Mayor Richard C. Lee. It was a warm summer evening in 1960, and Lee was addressing the Seventeenth International Sunday School Convention of the Church of God in Christ. The topic of this talk was "The Civil Rights Movement," following a wave of lunch-counter sit-ins in the American South. Lee suggested that those who lived in the "slums," like those who lived under legally sanctioned segregation, should do something to call attention to their conditions. Noting the lack of response from the transfixed Sunday school crowd, he proceeded. "What is a sit-out? Just imagine if all the people who live in the slums of our great cities were to leave their tenements, take chairs into the middle of the street, and sit out under the stars some fine summer evening at 5:30."[1] He went on to explain that this sit-out would catch the bankers and the landlords in traffic, en route from their city offices to their suburban homes, and make them "late for supper." This, he suggested, would force them to take a look at the slums.

Slums were a particularly infuriating sight for Mayor Lee, as he had been elected on a campaign promise to eliminate them—to make New Haven the first "Slumless City."[2] Lee's sit-out proposal caught even city officials by surprise. Police officials questioned at the event said that anyone caught sitting in the street would be removed for obstructing traffic. Upon further reflection (or perhaps upon having his words read back to him by a *New York Times* reporter), Lee clarified. He meant to say that sit-outs were a good idea for cities like Detroit and New York, but really unnecessary in New Haven, where he was already solving the problem of the slums. Mayor Lee's quickly retracted sit-out proposal serves as an amusing allegory for the national liberal-democratic response to both poverty and civil rights in the early 1960s. He rhetorically embraced the sentiments and impulses of the civil rights movement, shaped his message for a moderate, northern, middle-class audience, and invoked a romanticized vision of direct action. However, when pressed on his proposal—when called upon to act, defend, and even expand upon it—he backed down, celebrated existing "improvements," and ignored pressing questions of housing access and equal rights in his own city.

The mayor of the model city provoked a national response when he uttered those words in front of all of those Sunday school teachers. The press took his proposal very seriously. An editorial in the *Hartford Times*, for example, criticized the effectiveness of such an action, calling a sit-out a mere "attention-getting gimmick" compared to lunch counter sit-ins. "At the lunch counters, the demonstrations ended when Negroes were served. . . . Would the people lying in the streets wait until a wrecker's hammer struck the first blow at some slum tenement?"[3] (It was, in fact, the construction of low-income housing—and not its destruction—that civil rights activists advocated.) Taking the mayor's suggestion as an earnest proposal, an analysis of the editorial's views revealed some of the problems facing the possibility of organized resistance to urban renewal plans. The public understood the need to improve housing conditions in poor neighborhoods, but people lacked comprehensive awareness of both the effects that urban renewal had on the low-income housing supply and the importance of demands within the black community for direct involvement in redevelopment planning.

The *Hartford Times* editorial praised the strategy of lunch-counter sit-ins, in which "Negroes sat quietly waiting to be served their coffee," but blasted the idea of a "sit-out" as an affront to "law and order" and a spectacular imposition on the "flow of traffic." One syndicated columnist called potential sit-out participants "exhibitionists" seeking "special privileges," and suggested they be dealt with using fire hoses. That is, of course, exactly how anti-integrationist police forces dealt with those seeking to desegregate the South. But commentary from the press in the enlightened North saw their condemnation of the potential "sit-outers" as something very different from southern oppression of the "sit-inners." The *Hartford Times* claimed to be defending the masses who would be inconvenienced by such an action. "What about the majority of decent, hard-working citizens who are attending to their own affairs?" asked the columnist. "What about the grocer whose doorway is blocked by the sitter-outers? What about the worker who is driving in a car to his or her place of work? What about the doctor or the ambulance, or for that matter, the funeral procession?"[4] A flood of letters to the mayor's office revealed the sentiments to be widespread. Evidently, the open-minded liberals of the North viewed the prospect of a "sit-out" to be very different from that of a sit-in, and reacted with outrage even before any action had taken place.[5] This dialogue revealed some interesting public sentiments about direct action. What passed for a civil rights movement in the South would not so easily be tolerated by northerners in their own backyards, particularly if it impeded the flow of their traffic. Although it had become safe if not popular in the mainstream northern press to suggest sympathy for an end to legal segregation, there was very little understanding about the direct links between segregation and urban renewal in the North.

A national spokesperson for the NAACP declined, at the time, to comment on Lee's sit-out proposal, but James Gibbs, president of the organization's New Haven chapter, told the *New York Times* that he planned to "study" the idea. He suggested that sit-outs might be an effective way to open up residential areas from which black home buyers and renters were being discriminated. It is ironic that Gibbs' initial thought was that sit-outs could be effective in calling attention to the exclusion of blacks from suburban areas, since the strategy would ultimately be used to stake a claim on a small stretch of urban space that had, for so long, been a black neighborhood. The Redevelopment Agency's (RA) plan for the city's long-standing center of black life was to fill it with middle-class white people by developing middle-income housing and replacing a dense, mixed-use street with a suburban-style shopping center. The Dixwell redevelopment project was the one site in which the city boasted a program for "integration," while resisting local fair-housing legislation for which civil rights leaders, such as Gibbs, had advocated.

Meanwhile, within blocks of six new proposed middle-income housing developments, a new suburban-style shopping center, and a new Dixwell Redevelopment Office, the city's first mosque opened its doors in the summer of 1961, announcing the presence of what the local papers referred to as a "negro anti-integration sect" in what Mayor Lee hoped would be New Haven's newest integrated project area. Malcolm X spoke at the mosque's dedication. "Integration is just a white man's technique to slow down Negro progress," he told a crowd of more than 150 men, women, and children packed into a large second-floor room at 142½ Dixwell Avenue, right where the city planned to put its "University Park Dixwell."[6]

Two Dixwells, One Corner

University Park Dixwell is a brand new neighborhood. . . . Shop and stroll in a sylvan setting. . . . A footbridge crossing over Dixwell Avenue traffic will take you from the shopping plaza to the new civic center.

—"The New University Park Dixwell," New Haven
Redevelopment Agency promotional brochure, c. 1960

In 1960, as the mayor delivered his Sunday school speech, this "University Park Dixwell" was an imaginary tree-lined place where a young, white family of four—the father in suit and tie, the mother at his side, the son dressed as a cowboy, and the daughter's blond locks blowing in a light breeze—could pass the day shopping and dining. From their home at one of the six new, modern, middle-income housing developments, they could cross over busy traffic on an elegant new footbridge to a new multimillion-dollar shopping plaza. Trees dominate the RA's footbridge rendering, and—as in the family tableau—the street itself is barely visible. Nothing in this depiction would indicate that the street shown was Dixwell Avenue, one of the densest, busiest thoroughfares in the heart of the city's black community.

Although the neighborhood depicted and sold in the city's 1960 brochure was an imaginary one, its location was the real home to more than 2,500 families, nearly 70 percent of whom were black. A 1958 survey found only thirty-six houses in the area to be "unfit," yet the redevelopment plan called for demolition of more than 200 buildings, forcing the relocation of about 500 families. Of these, more than 400 were African American, ac-

Figure 2.1

The New Haven Redevelopment Agency marketed its new University Park Dixwell development to white middle-class families with images such as this one, which appeared in a 1960 brochure.

Figure 2.2

The imagined Dixwell: A Redevelopment Agency sketch shows a footbridge stretching elegantly across Dixwell Avenue, framed in trees.

cording to the Housing Authority director, Robert Wolf, who predicted that nearly half of these displaced families would be eligible for low-rent housing, another 17 percent would qualify for moderate-rent housing, and the rest wouldn't qualify for any assistance at all. To meet the housing needs created by the redevelopment of the 250-acre Dixwell project, the city was proposing "the construction of 142 moderate-rent units." The math falls somewhat short, but the focus of the redevelopment proposal was less on housing and more on the elimination of the "worst two blocks" around the Elm Haven low-income housing project, where the RA blamed "mixed use" buildings for ruining "neighborhood coherence." Their solution to this problem was the construction of a new "commercial center" for Dixwell Avenue.[7]

Elm Haven was what existed just beyond the trees in the foreground of the RA's "Dixwell Plaza" sketch. It consisted of 855 units in forty buildings, ranging from two to nine stories. It was built in 1939, expanded in the mid-1950s, and by 1960 had become both the city's most pervasive "before" picture and a terrifying example for alarmist white New Haven of what a "black" city would look like. More than 600 of the project's 855 units housed black families—many of them considered "problem families" by New Haven's social service agencies. It was a pocket of concentrated poverty in the backyard of Yale University, and was seen as both an embarrassment to Mayor Lee and a threat to "Old Blue." The RA hoped to change the Dixwell area from one dominated by the image of Elm Haven to one dominated by new middle-income housing cooperatives such as the Florence Virtue townhouses, one of six new proposed developments that would cater to young middle-class families.

The RA first approved Maurice Rotival's "Redevelopment and Renewal" plan for the Dixwell neighborhood in August of 1960, stating that it would "contribute materially to the achievement of the long-range goals of New Haven's comprehensive development program."[8] The plan called for acquisition of "all properties necessary" in order to "eliminate unhealthful, unsanitary or unsafe conditions." The RA could legally seize any property considered "obsolete" or "noxious." Although the agency never clarified what would qualify as "obsolete," it did specify what would constitute a "noxious use"—in their words, "the emission of smoke, fumes, odors or other objectionable by-products, excessive noise, the generation of excessive truck traffic," and "adverse location of the particular use with respect to the general character of the area and its impact on immediately adjacent uses." Ironically, the RA's own definition of "noxious" seemed—to the letter—to describe a stretch of highway. It offered a very accurate description of what had replaced Oak Street's apartments and businesses, and a pretty clear picture of what it was like to live in many "redeveloped" sections of New Haven. The city's secret plan for a "Ring Road" would affect not only those properties that would be acquired and demolished to build the roadway, but also the surrounding homes and businesses that would suddenly find that they had a noxious high-speed roadway outside their front door or in their backyard.

Although city officials persistently denied the existence of any plan for a Ring Road, right up until the day they publicly stated that such a plan had been canceled, an August 1960 memo from the RA to the mayor's office explained that the clearance of eighteen structures on Lake Place, near the Dixwell project's border with Yale University, would facilitate "the extension of Howe and Dwight Streets from Whalley Avenue to Trumbull Street," which would be "an important segment of the inner circumferential to be constructed between the Oak Street Connector and Interstate 91."[9] Most of the structures in question were multifamily units with multiple housing-code violations, owned by absentee landlords from neighboring towns. The majority of the tenants were nurses, clerks, and "industrial workers," both black and white; more than ninety families would have to be relocated to construct that small stretch of the Ring Road, which would provide access to a new, modern shopping plaza.

The new $2 million commercial center, "Dixwell Plaza," would replace a total of twenty-two buildings, none of which had been identified as in need of "extensive repair," much less demolition. The net loss in housing would be about 500 units, nearly all of which were low-rent apartments.[10] Although the new shopping center was touted as the centerpiece for the Dixwell project, the true hope for the RA's plans to integrate the Dixwell neighborhood was the adjacent middle-income housing development, Florence Virtue, which they hoped would attract an influx of young white families. A promotional brochure promised "privacy and seclusion" in the "heart of New Haven's newest neighborhood."[11]

Brochures for Florence Virtue depicted white families in modern homes, walking to new schools and cultural attractions in what was—even at the moment that potential buyers read the promotional text—a completely imaginary space. The "University Park Dixwell" brochure boasted 129 living units with "private entrances, patios, off-street parking, and attractive landscaping." New residents would be surrounded by a flock of new middle-class neighbors in surrounding new developments, including the middle-income Martin de Porres townhouses, the Winter Garden moderate-income townhouses, garden-style elderly housing described as an "All-American neighborhood," and remodeled row houses that would trade in their drab

Figure 2.3

A brochure advertising the Florence Virtue townhouses promised private patios and modern kitchens, and pictured white nuclear families performing gender-specific tasks in neatly arranged boxes. Private and public spaces were depicted in strict separation, and noticeably absent from the promotional materials are any views of Dixwell Avenue itself.

Henry Street addresses for the name "University Row," which the RA compared to "the fashionable townhouses of Philadelphia and Georgetown."

A model apartment at Florence Virtue was furnished by New Haven's new Macy's department store. Promotional materials reminded prospective suburban buyers that the townhouses were "easy to reach" since the construction of the Oak Street Connector, the Connecticut Turnpike, and the Wilbur Cross Parkway. "Scheduled for construction three blocks away," said the brochure, "is a new connector linking I-91 to the Connecticut Turnpike." Mayor Lee's two-pronged plans for the city as a highway hub and the vision of a suburbanized, revitalized space came together in the selling of the Florence Virtue project, at the heart of the projected new University Park Dixwell.

The units were priced to meet the needs of "moderate income" families, and marketed to suburban and upwardly mobile white families from other redeveloped areas of the city. High rents and down payments enabled this exclusivity. "I would like to know why people with low income can't get into the co-ops," wrote one black resident, Lula Parker, in a letter to the mayor, just three weeks before she would have to vacate her low-rent apartment. "I thought the reason these co-ops are being built was so that people with low income could live in them." Parker was told by one co-op manager that she "wasn't making enough money" to live there, although she claimed she could save up enough to pay the down payment. The mayor's office responded two weeks later. "According to federal housing administration guidelines, co-op housing was designed for moderate-income families," wrote a RA relocation official.[12]

The creation of such middle-income housing developments, billed as a potential means of integration and revitalization, initiated what was intended as a slow but steady gentrifying process—one that never quite succeeded in that area of Dixwell, but that in the early 1960s struck a bitter chord with many Dixwell residents. A former assistant city planning director, Mary Hommann, said that the Dixwell project's success was indicated by the fact that "a white family chose a lot in the neighborhood on which to build a home."[13] She suggested that this model could turn out to be "an ideal prototype for urban renewal all over America," a model by which low-income black families were removed from a neighborhood to build housing for middle-income white families. It was this model to which local NAACP president James Gibbs referred when he charged that city officials were "using city agencies to express their prejudice." Gibbs spoke for a new generation of young civil rights leaders in New Haven's black community—and against the wishes of old-guard NAACP leadership—when he charged that racism was being written into redevelopment plans, celebrated in the Progress Pavilion, and implemented at the taxpayers' expense.

If Dixwell was going to be transformed from a "decaying slum" to a "showplace," there would be many obstacles for the mayor and the RA to overcome. The mayor's political opponents seized on the Dixwell project to criticize his redevelopment policies, and in the summer of 1961, three black Republican aldermanic candidates staged a "march for better housing" in the project area, which drew about thirty participants.[14] The New Haven Human Relations Council led a campaign to desegregate the city and was heavily critical of the Dixwell project, in particular, which council members said posed "relocation problems different from those incurred in other areas." A statement issued by the council said that displaced Dixwell families were "faced with widespread discrimination and the threat of exploitation in the neighborhoods which are open to them."[15] Plans to redevelop Dixwell enlivened a preexisting fight by the city's civil rights groups for local fair-housing legislation.

As organized opposition to redevelopment became more vocal, the city had to devise new strategies for surveillance and reconnaissance of project areas. In assessing public acceptance and detecting public dissent, the Progress Pavilion's weekly logs seemed to have failed as a means of man-on-the-street reconnaissance, despite the mayor's best efforts to coax something negative out of the Progress Pavilion hostess. As the Dixwell project progressed, the city would both refine its strategies for identifying exactly who and where the biggest obstacles to redevelopment would be, and develop a more sophisticated means of "involving" the community in order to defuse charges of secrecy and racism. The RA would venture for the first time into the project area and open a Dixwell Project Office, which—like the Progress Pavilion—would serve as both an information center and a point of contact for the community. It would be an information-gathering outpost and a site of organization for the distinctly political project of redevelopment in the community.

A New Kind of Project

The Dixwell Project Office responded to the challenge of organized dissent by developing an intricate battery of community programs—from a newsletter to a parade—aimed at rallying the black community around the excitement of urban renewal, even as the master plan for a whiter, suburbanized landscape threatened to dismantle the black community that had lived along this busy stretch of road for generations. By courting the very community that posed a potential organized threat—the established civil rights community, and "young black men on the street"—the Lee administration hoped to defuse possible dissent and pave the way for new plans for the Dixwell corridor.

As the RA went about the task of acquiring properties along the route of the Ring Road's access points in the Dixwell neighborhood, it kept a careful eye on signs of resistance. An agency memo to the mayor reported that families on Lake Place had the opportunity to comment on the plan at a meeting of the Dixwell Renewal Committee at nearby Winchester School, but that they had "not done so." Redevelopment administrator Charles Shannon told Mayor Lee, "A Mrs. Anne Timm of 25 Lake Place, whose home we are not buying, reported some unrest to me, but apparently there were no after effects. . . . I do not believe Lake Place will create any substantial difficulties during the public hearing stages." Central to the plans for Dixwell's renewal was the establishment of what the mayor's office called a "human relations project" aimed at mobilizing the community around renewal and minimizing dissent. The human relations office would work with what an internal memo called "some of the Negroes on the Avenue who could be considered 'natural leaders,' " people like "bartenders, barbers, ex-prize fighters, a poolroom operator, and 'just men on the street.' "[16] The city's human relations advisor told the mayor, "This kind of project has the potential for *getting to* the kind of people in the Dixwell Area who must be brought along if renewal is to have the hoped for results."

Although the decisions of the RA affected families, the agency imagined the arbiters of the street and leaders of the community as a collection of male figures, most of whom were vaguely associated with vice and sport. The "hoped-for results" for Lee's redevelopment staff and the "hoped-for results" for the black community in the Dixwell area seemed to be very different, making the "human relations" proposal all the more crucial. As civil rights activists began their push for a fair-housing ordinance and a seat at the redevelopment table, the RA developed a unique new strategy—they would have many tables, and they would set one up in the heart of the Dixwell neighborhood.

The mayor's office established a city-appointed group to represent the Dixwell community in matters related to urban renewal, the Dixwell Neighborhood Renewal Committee. This group held its inaugural public meeting at Dixwell's Winchester School on August 10, 1960, where Mayor Lee announced "the start of a new life for this fine old neighborhood."[17] Lee announced that $14 million in federal loans and grants would pay for the neighborhood's renewal plan, which promised the clearance of the "worst slums and blight in the center of the neighborhood," a new "central square," new private housing, the widening of a few streets, more parking lots, and new parks and playgrounds. The entire project was slated for completion sometime in 1966. "Just imagine . . . the fresh air and the sunlight which is going to pour into the heart of the Dixwell neighborhood after the bulldozers once and for all have removed the dank and degrading slums a short walk from this very auditorium," pontificated Mayor Lee.[18] Dixwell resident Charles Twyman, chairman of the new Dixwell Neighborhood Renewal Committee, also spoke at the meeting, calling his neighborhood a "Negro ghetto with fire hazards, rats attacking babies in cribs," and living conditions that attract " 'only the dregs of humanity.' "[19]

The public meeting at the Winchester School was hailed internally as a great success since nobody stood up to speak in protest, and nobody posed

Figure 2.4

Meeting of the Dixwell Neighborhood Renewal Committee at the Winchester School, August 1960, as published in the first issue of the RA's *Dixwell Renewal News*. Although the RA reported that the meeting was a success, and the plans for Dixwell were well received, the woman gesturing in the lower right-hand corner—looking directly at the camera as she speaks—could be read as a suggestion of dissent.

any difficult questions to the Dixwell Renewal Committee. Charles Shannon called a subsequent hearing on the Dixwell plan "a very good show," saying it was "far and away the best substantive solid support we've had."[20] But public criticism would boil to the surface as the plans for Dixwell touched a nerve with those who recognized the familiar patterns of urban renewal, and feared the loss of more affordable housing in a city that already faced a critical shortage.

In a letter sent to the *New Haven Register*, local attorney Sherman Drutman asked the mayor, "Where are the 500 families that will be forced to move from this area to go?" Drutman had read the Dixwell plan carefully, and—citing plans to build middle-income housing on either side of the avenue—asked if the current low-income residents of the area would be able to afford the new apartments and cooperatives that would replace the "slum." "When you told the audience assembled at the Winchester School that they stood 'at the threshold of creating a new and finer Dixwell neighborhood,'" asked Drutman, "did you also tell them how much it might cost them to live there?"[21] A member of the mayor's staff suggested that the letter simply be ignored, and that support for the Dixwell plan was, indeed, strong and widespread. The city's RA continued to insist that "Dixwell residents have supported the [redevelopment] plan, and are enthusiastic about the prospects of renewal in their neighborhood."[22] Aggressive picketing of the downtown Progress Pavilion, and of nearby city hall, by the newly formed New Haven chapter of the Congress of Racial Equality (CORE) suggested otherwise, and demonstrated the extent to which the increasingly militant civil rights movement had set its sights on the issue of urban renewal. With direct actions casting a shadow on the Lee administration's civil rights record, the mayor took great pains to strengthen his ties to black leadership both locally and nationally.

There was no eluding the fact that the city was continuing to destroy low-income units—displacing thousands—and replacing them with middle-income housing or parking lots. Persistently, Lee attempted to pass off his urban renewal program as a "civil rights" victory, asserting—as he did in a letter to Jackie Robinson, who wrote to the mayor to express concern over picketing at city hall—that "we have relocated close to 3,000 families . . . perhaps half of them Negro, from slums to decent housing in all parts of the city."[23] In addressing the board of aldermen's decision to vote down a fair-housing ordinance, Lee blamed CORE's picketing at the Progress Pavilion and city hall, and sit-ins at the private offices of city officials, saying the organization's tactics "alienated" many aldermen.

Such assertions by liberal mayors fueled the allegations of Black Nationalist leaders, such as the one made by Malcolm X at the dedication of the city's first mosque in July of 1961, that integration would never happen because "white men don't intend that it should." A reporter for the *New Haven Journal-Courier* explained that members of the group "were reluctant to discuss details of their organization here, other than to say meetings would be held every Thursday night."[24] The local press reported that Black Muslim leaders, such as Abdel Kurriem of the new Dixwell mosque, disquietingly referred to their group as a "movement" rather than a religion, and although they preached separatism, and remained closed and secretive, they claimed large and growing numbers of supporters and practitioners, all swearing off alcohol, drugs, pork, and "loose women" in an effort to uplift the black race, develop independent, self-sustaining black institutions, and resist calls from both the white liberal establishment and the civil rights movement to "integrate." "This is where we differ from the NAACP and CORE," Kurriem told a reporter for the *Journal-Courier*.[25] "In our movement, we just don't have room for whites. We have so much to do among our own people trying to make them responsible citizens."

The Black Muslim movement would continue to grow in the Dixwell neighborhood, never posing a significant challenge to either the increasingly militant civil rights leadership or the downtown power structure, but nonetheless claiming both a physical and cultural space in the Dixwell neighborhood, and posing an alternative model for solving both the problems of "the street" and the problems of the black community. This alternative model was very different from the one that city agencies had in mind, but it was not the threat that mainstream press accounts made it out to be, fixating on the group's perceived secrecy, militancy, and powers of manipulation.[26] "No white persons were present at last night's session," reported the *Journal-Courier*, "but one observer described the audience's reaction to Malcolm X as 'enraptured, as at a revival meeting.'" Alarmist descriptions of the Black Muslim community in the Dixwell neighborhood underscored the perceived urgency of reconfiguring and integrating these storefront spaces along the avenue to suburbanize and subdue a potentially volatile area.

Taking the Street

The struggle for a voice in urban renewal plans defined the civil rights movement in the urban North for nearly a decade, as sit-ins in the South captured the lion's share of press attention. In New Haven, as redevelopment schemes cut repeatedly and with increasing depth into the city's black communities, and as the RA grew more pervasive within the mostly black "project areas," an increasingly militant local civil rights movement underwent a significant transformation. The controversy surrounding plans for a 1961 Dixwell sit-out hastened what might have been a slow and steady transition.

On September 16, 1961, as the city announced the grand opening of its Dixwell exhibit at the Progress Pavilion, emphasizing the "positive aspects of the redevelopment program," James Gibbs, president of New Haven's NAACP chapter, called attention to its negative aspects, announcing that members would vote that evening on his proposal to stage a sit-out protest in the middle of Dixwell Avenue.[27] Willie Pritchett, the Nineteenth Ward aldermanic candidate, told the *New Haven Journal-Courier* that "Mayor Lee and his stooges are ignoring the human problems confronting New Haven's Negro population." When asked by the paper to comment on this allegation, and on the plans for a sit-out action, the mayor's staff reiterated their announcement about "an exciting new exhibition" in the Progress Pavilion unveiling "a comprehensive program to provide better housing for all its citizens."[28] This marked the first significant direct challenge to the RA's master plan and the beginning of a transformation in the local civil rights movement. It marked a moment in which the Lee administration, cornered by the realities of its urban renewal program, could point only to an already contested celebration of its master plans and promises.

The RA's proposed vision for Dixwell developed alongside the dissonant realities of poverty and discrimination, underscored by both the emergence of a Black Muslim voice and the radicalization of the neighborhood's civil rights leadership. By the early 1960s, the stories of lunch-counter sit-ins, department store boycotts, and other acts of organized protest shared pages of

New Haven's local papers with the constant barrage of RA headlines. The fight to desegregate the South raised questions for civil rights activists in New Haven, many of whom took arrests and risked violent reprisals in sit-ins in Baltimore, Washington, D.C., and points further south.[29] Many CORE members took direct nonviolent action in the South, but civil rights agitation at home in New Haven seemed limited to NAACP pressure through electoral and city hall politics, including unsuccessful pushes on the board of alder-men to pass fair-housing ordinances, enforce housing-code violations, and mandate the representation of African Americans on real estate boards and redevelopment projects.

However, as the housing crisis for black New Haven became more acute, national attention to direct action became more widespread, and the bravado of the RA became more pronounced, the largely middle-class, established leadership and strategies of the NAACP gave way to a new, younger, and more militant chapter of CORE, which immediately focused its activism on urban renewal. The NAACP operated primarily in middle-class circles, with many of its leaders maintaining strong ties to Mayor Lee, but CORE quickly became the organization for poor New Haven blacks, and for the next few years, posed a considerable threat to Lee's redevelopment schemes.[30]

The New Haven NAACP chapter was founded in 1917 and at its peak could list between 400 and 500 members. With the dramatic increase in the city's black population in the 1950s, the organization was able to leverage considerable electoral power, and its decision to back Richard Lee for mayor in 1953 may have been what brought him his narrow victory. In return, Lee promised an end to police brutality and more representation of African Americans on the police force, which was a key NAACP issue. At the urging of the mayor, Redevelopment Director Edward Logue joined the NAACP in 1955. By that time, a younger generation of members, also liberal and middle-class but radicalized by direct civil rights actions of the mid-1950s, constituted a growing group of young leaders who were less interested in maintaining cordial relationships with the mayor.[31]

One such leader was James Gibbs, elected president of the New Haven NAACP branch in 1959. He was a New Haven native and an employee at the Seamless Rubber Company, where he was an organizer for United Rubber Workers of America Local 338. Gibbs was active in the Dixwell branch of the Communist Party from 1953 to 1954, agitating for improvements in housing and workplace conditions, and in his five years as an NAACP member, he headed up the organization's youth council and political action committee. In taking the office of branch president, he attempted to transform it into a more radical organization.[32] It was on the issue of housing rights that Gibbs realized the NAACP would have to dramatically break from the mayor in or-der for real improvements to happen in the city's black neighborhoods.

From the moment Gibbs took over the branch presidency, the NAACP's national leadership, local old-guard NAACP leaders, and the mayor's office tried repeatedly to unseat him, but the events surrounding the sit-outs of 1961 enabled Gibbs to leave the NAACP—and not quietly—on his own volition, propelling the city's civil rights movement into a new more militant era. Despite early warnings from the NAACP national office, James Gibbs took the podium in the Winchester School auditorium in September of 1961, in front of more than 200 NAACP members, where he proposed a "sit-out for decent housing." His proposal lacked the mayor's romantic flourishes (like sitting under the stars in lawn chairs), and instead focused on the urgent need for decent low-income housing, desegregation, and fair-housing enforcement, as well as real black representation in the redevelopment process.

Following Gibbs' proposal, national branch director Gloster Current walked up to the podium and warned, "If you want to retain your charter you cannot have a sit-out at this time." The crowd responded with shouts of "Uncle Tom!" and "Sellout!"[33] Blyden Jackson, then a Democratic candidate for the board of aldermen and a local NAACP leader, spoke in response to Current's threat: "As long as the Negro has lived in New Haven, we have had a ghetto . . . promises . . . and no action!" Through a burst of applause and cheers, he continued, "We want an open occupancy law and we are going to sit-out so that black people can have decent housing!" A few voices from the crowd, mostly black clergy, spoke out against plans for a sit-out, claiming such an action would be "to slap our friends [in city hall] in the face." Even the local press didn't fail to note that it was their friends in city hall—the mayor in particular—who had initially suggested this plan. A somewhat flustered NAACP executive board called for adjournment. The membership voted down the proposal to adjourn, but the meeting ended anyway. The leadership decided to table the sit-out vote for another two weeks, and during that time, according to Gibbs, the local chapter's membership increased by more than 50 percent.[34]

Following that meeting, Blyden Jackson, a young Marine Corps veteran and milling machine operator, withdrew from the political arena to head up a local chapter of CORE.[35] Jackson announced that his organization would go forward with plans for a Dixwell sit-out, demanding a black appointment to the city's board of realtors and a public hearing on the Dixwell redevelopment plan. At midday on Monday, October 9, 1961, a small group picketed in front of city hall with signs that spoke to their demands for more say in redevelopment decisions, articulated their vision for what an urban neighborhood should look like, and called attention to the mayor's own hypocrisy. One sign read "No University Towers on Dixwell." Another simply contained a quote from the mayor: " 'I would take my chair and sit out in the street'—Dick Lee."[36]

The city hall pickets, although small and relatively nonconfrontational, provided an opportunity to announce the upcoming Dixwell sit-outs to the public through a press that generally paid more attention to what nine people did in front of city hall than what a hundred people did in the middle of Dixwell Avenue. These pickets coincided with CORE's Progress Pavilion pickets, which took over the corner of Church and Chapel streets, in the heart of downtown, each day that week from 4:45 p.m. to 5:15 p.m., a time that would offer the most visibility as the workday came to a close.[37] This timing enabled them to be seen by the "suburban neighbors" who commuted to work in New Haven and left around that time to drive back out of the city on new highway ramps. Press coverage of all these direct actions provided an opportunity to mention the sit-out that would take place that weekend, at the corner of Foote and Dixwell.[38]

On Saturday evening, nearly 300 protesters met in Goin Park, adjacent to the future site of the Florence Virtue townhouses. It was an unusually warm and sunny October day. As a light breeze made its way around the baseball diamond, the protesters heard James Gibbs, who had resigned from his position as NAACP chapter president, speak about the need for more low-income housing, an end to discrimination, and fair public hearings for redevelopment plans. As the sky darkened, about 100 of the protesters marched from the park, down Munson Street, to "the heart of the negro district," Dixwell Avenue, where they sat down, peacefully, for twenty minutes in the specter of what the city promised would soon be "Dixwell University Park."[39]

Understanding the Avenue

By the time CORE protesters blocked Dixwell Avenue, eight vacant stores and homes marked the stretch approaching and leaving this site of protest. The number of owner-occupied properties had been cut nearly in half since the 1940s, and many units that had previously held one family were doubled or tripled up with families displaced by the Oak Street Connector. The physical and social space of lower Dixwell Avenue, like the other everyday spaces examined in the following chapters, enabled a sense of collectivity. In the early 1960s, before the RA replaced a stretch of multifamily housing and small businesses with a "business and shopping plaza" set off from the street by a parking lot, people lived *on* Dixwell Avenue, in every sense of the word. From their front steps and bedroom windows, they could see and hear the avenue, shout up at a friend or family member from the sidewalk, walk by their grocer, barber, or pharmacist on the way home from work or school. The sidewalk was their "commute" and offered, in the words of urbanist Jane Jacobs, a "web of public respect and trust."[40]

Through the 1950s, this particular stretch of road was home to Zipoli's Barber Shop, Junction Liquors, Lutz's Restaurant, Paul's Shoe Store, and a drugstore called Garden Drug that was, at the time, a forty-year resident of the neighborhood. Nearly twenty small business and fifteen owner-occupied structures lined the few blocks north and south of the site of the sit-outs by

Figure 2.5

Redevelopment Agency photograph of Dixwell Avenue, the future "sylvan" site of University Park Dixwell. *(Courtesy of New Haven Museum and Historical Society.)*

the mid-1950s. It was around the time of CORE's sit-out action that Jane Jacobs published her well-known and influential tract, *The Death and Life of Great American Cities*. She responded to urban renewal projects, like the one that transformed Oak Street, by demanding that urban planners and policy makers look to everyday urban experiences and lessons from the mistakes of past projects, rather than suburban ideals, "imagined" cities (such as world's fairs), or theoretical models in deciding what was best for the modern city.

Jacobs was particularly outraged by the "garden city" ideal, based on the turn-of-the-century designs of British architect Ebenezer Howard, which she believed vilified the street, faced homes inward, and isolated residential sections from other uses of city space, such as businesses, recreation, and municipal buildings.[41] This model was the basis for the design of Florence Virtue and other Dixwell projects, as well as similar middle-income developments throughout the country. Jacobs asserted that it was the eyes of the city's inhabitants—strangers on the city sidewalks—that kept the city safe, and that the "street ballet" of everyday city life provided an ideal urban environment. She championed mixed-use design, in which small businesses thrived alongside residences, and everyone enjoyed immediate and direct access to the streets and sidewalks.[42]

Rarely did anyone charge city residents with the task of defining their own urban ideal, or with articulating their own vision for their living and working spaces, but at least one such experiment in New Haven illustrates the extent to which low-income families, the supposed beneficiaries of urban renewal, agreed with Jacobs' idea of the "great American city." When a progressive group of architects, academics, and organizers in New Haven set out to design and develop a housing cooperative for low-income families in the city's Hill neighborhood (see Chapter 3), they took great care to involve the future residents in every step of the project. This was not only an alternative model for urban planning, but also an alternative model for citizen participation. The design process began with a series of interviews. Architect Harris Stone interviewed the families for whom the project would be home, and reported that one family "hoped that the development would be on a noisy rather than a quiet street, because noisy streets that had houses and stores and lots of people were much safer and better to live on." Like Jacobs, all eight of the participating families demanded mixed-use designs that incorporated recreational, business, and community spaces within the residential area, and, according to Stone, "members of the group stated again and again that they wanted to live in a real city neighborhood, not in a suburban-type project."[43]

As Dixwell's neighborhood institutions faced relocation, many were adamant about their need to be on the street. Alphonso Tindall, executive director of the Dixwell Community House at 98 Dixwell Avenue, wrote to the mayor shortly after the redevelopment plans for the area were unveiled with the demand that the community center's new building "should front on Dixwell Avenue. The Dixwell Community House has always been identified with Dixwell Avenue. It has been and should remain a part of the main drag," wrote Tindall.[44] The Dixwell Community House served an urban population, which—like the families interviewed for the low-income housing experiment in the Hill—had no desire to live in the "suburban-type" ideal that the RA had in mind. When Dixwell residents sat in the street in October of 1961, it was this "suburban-type project" they resisted, and these same visions of a "real city neighborhood" that they demanded.

Mayor Richard C. Lee's Republican challenger for the 1961 mayoral race, James J. Valenti, saw potential resistance to the Dixwell redevelopment plan as his opponent's key vulnerability. Although he stood no chance of defeating Lee at the height of his popularity in a Democratic city, and had lost to Lee in the previous mayoral race, Valenti's campaign landed a critical analysis of urban renewal in the local press. Valenti called for an "immediate halt" to all demolition in the Dixwell neighborhood after reportedly visiting with 300 Dixwell-area families to "ask their opinion" about the city's redevelopment plans. He declared that those displaced from other redevelopment areas were finding it hard to find new housing at "comparable costs." Some tenants, claimed Valenti, were paying twice their former rents after relocation.[45] By summertime, Valenti and his volunteers had collected 600 signatures on a petition demanding a halt to all demolitions and a public hearing on both the Dixwell renewal plan and housing problems throughout the city. Brandishing fifteen pages of signatures on the front steps of his Livingston Street home in one of New Haven's finer neighborhoods, Valenti estimated that 95 percent of the signatories lived in the Dixwell neighborhood. "It's a clear cut mandate," he told the *Journal-Courier*.

"The Dixwell Project has already been the subject of 3 public hearings," the mayor's office responded.[46] A coalition of Lee-supporting Dixwell leaders, including Rev. Edwin Edmonds of the Dixwell Ministerial Alliance, charged that Valenti simply sought to "preserve a sort of 'Negro Ghetto' in the Dixwell area." As the election drew nearer, criticisms of Lee's redevelopment plans took the center of many political stages. Although Lee's victory in the mayoral race seemed clear, his administration was forced to respond to many claims about the housing crisis, and the effects of urban renewal on the city's poorer neighborhoods. In late October, U.S. senator Prescott Bush criticized the Lee administration at a GOP fund-raising dinner in Connecticut, calling redevelopment "overly ambitious." Bush said he was distressed by "vast areas which have been laid waste by the wrecker's ball and the bulldozer, and by the slowness with which rebuilding has taken place." As Lee sought his fifth term in the mayor's office, he was believed to be a potential challenger to Senator Bush in future races. Speaking in support of Republican Lee challenger Henry T. Townsend, Bush referenced the sit-out protest that had recently taken place in the middle of Dixwell Avenue, claiming it "indicate[s] either a failure on the part of the administration to plan in time to provide proper housing for the families who will be displaced by that project, or a failure to communicate those plans to the people whose lives are being affected and give sympathetic understanding to their problems."[47] These criticisms, as they unfolded, anticipated a national shift in sentiment, ushered in by the publication of Herbert Gans' *Urban Villagers* (1962), which showed the devastating human effects of urban renewal on displaced Italian immigrants in Boston's West End, and Martin Anderson's *Federal Bulldozer* (1964), which criticized redevelopment programs from the conservative perspective, asserting that private developers could do the job much more efficiently.[48]

In New Haven, criticism of urban renewal programs also came from both the Left and the Right, with civil rights organizations and Lee's Republican political opponents both calling for reforms. In the spring of 1962, Republican alderman Richard Belford wrote a letter to the RA (and many press releases to the local papers) demanding that the RA "confer closely with citizens . . . in renewal areas," emphasize rehabilitation over demolition, keep the public and press better informed of their plans, and "avoid 'high pressure glowing publicity' that contains 'unrealistic dreams' about redevelopment."[49] In response to mounting criticisms locally and beyond, Lee publicly announced the formation of an advisory committee—more formalized than the committee he had introduced at the neighborhood meeting in August of 1960—and charged it with "four specific tasks:" to "review" and "advance" his proposals for moderate-income housing, to make "specific program recommendations" for 500 new units of low-income housing, to make recommendations for elderly housing, and to "report" on ways to expand existing home-rehabilitation programs. All members of the committee would be appointed by Lee. Its members would, in fact, have no decision-making powers—only the power to advise and consent.[50] The appointed chairman of the committee, Charles Twyman, described its origins in a 2004 interview. "They needed a lay component, you know, a group of citizens who were supposed to sort of have oversight," said Twyman. "That's maybe too gracious a word, but I mean that's what it was supposed to have been."[51]

Twyman said that people on the renewal committee internally discussed their overall plans to use urban renewal as a way of "dispersing" the residents of this predominantly black neighborhood, and "moving people into areas that were not integrated." "We didn't go around preaching this," he recalled, "but within the inner circle this was what we were talking about, just a few of us. We didn't realize that we were sort of playing in the hands of another plan, a grander plan," Twyman explained. The Dixwell Renewal Committee organized community meetings during which the appointed representatives "pushed" people to support the city's plan, which—in the absence of clear alternatives and with the key community leaders speaking for the city—most people were willing to do. "I don't think that they were setting us up or anything," said Twyman. "I just think that it just worked this way and we weren't perceptive enough to understand all the inner workings of what was happening."

Voices of dissent came from marginalized places, but with increasing numbers and increasing volume. "We are interested in the plight of the black masses. The ones who are dissatisfied, impatient, and have become very angry," Malcolm X told a "standing-room only" crowd of 600 people in the auditorium of Dixwell's Winchester School in May of 1962, at the NAACP's annual Race Relations Forum. It was two years after the city celebrated consensus on the Dixwell renewal plan in that same auditorium, and nearly a year after the opening of the city's first mosque, about a block away from the future site of the Florence Virtue townhouses. Also appearing at the Winchester School that night was former NAACP leader Roger Williams, who had formed an organization called Action for Equality after he was "kicked out" of the NAACP for his participation in the pickets, sit-outs, and sit-ins of 1961. In a debate that pitted a radical civil rights leader—demanding swift action on integration—against a Black Nationalist in a "liberal" city, accusing the United States of practicing "20th century bondage," the *Open Gate News* reported that Malcolm X was interrupted seventeen times by cheers and applause during his thirty-minute speech. He criticized the "hypocrisy of the white world, the folly of integration, and 20th century 'Uncle Tom' preachers."[52] The paper declared him the overwhelming victor.

A block away from the packed auditorium, where Malcolm X drew a frenzied standing ovation as he exited the hall, the Dixwell Urban Renewal and Redevelopment Project opened a new office at 223 Dixwell Avenue. With a staff of six, each with annual salaries of between $4,000 and $7,000, the project's new director, Lloyd Davis, made as one of his first appeals to the mayor's office a request for significant salary increases—by around $2,000 per staff member—pushing Dixwell project staff salaries to more than twice the average annual income earned by Dixwell residents.[53] The New Haven Redevelopment Agency Dixwell Project Office was open to the public from 9 a.m. to 5 p.m. each weekday, and the new project director immediately secured funds for a new slide projector "to be used in giving talks on rehabilitation to area residents." The first edition of a new RA publication, *Dixwell Renewal News*, declared, "Clubs and organizations in Dixwell are invited to have members of the staff show these slides" at their meetings.[54] To reach out to the estimated 1,500 children in the neighborhood, the Dixwell Project Office created a fictional character, Freddy Fixer, "symbolizing the neighborhood's overall improvement efforts," and announced the "Freddy Fixer Art Contest."[55] "The children will be asked to create 'Freddy Fixer' as they think he ought to be, including his physical appearance, personality, dress, and outlook on life," said Charles Twyman, as chairman of the Dixwell Renewal Committee.[56] By age categories, children would be awarded donated cash prizes for coming up with the image and description of this fictional character, and shortly thereafter a battery of "neighborhood activities" would commence, all centered around this new neighborhood hero.

Throughout the community, young people joined Freddy Fixer Clubs, centered around neighborhood cleanup efforts and citizenship. Club members took a pledge to help those in need, clean up backyards and shovel snow in the winter, and dress, speak, and act appropriately.[57] The Freddy Fixer programs tied physical neighborhood improvements to self-improvement. In an article authored by the RA's Dixwell office staff and run in the *Open Gate News*, a black neighborhood publication, the text below a drawing of a dilapidated house read, "This house is sick because the family who lived in it didn't take care of it. This was once a new house . . . it was a happy house because it had good floors, and its roof provided protection from the rain."

The article went on to describe the house's decline due to neglect. "Now, this house is no longer a happy house. It has become sicker and sicker and sadder and sadder," wrote the RA. "A lot of houses in our Dixwell neighborhood have become sick houses and sad houses," the RA explained, "and so one day the people in the neighborhood decided to do something about it. They invited a friend by the name of Freddie Fixer to come and help them. . . . Freddie Fixer is really the City of New Haven and the Federal Government, but we like to think of Freddie Fixer as a real live person—a kind of helper who has come to Dixwell to work with us, to make our neighborhood a better place for us to live in." The RA was explicit with Dixwell's children about the real identity of Freddy Fixer, and transparent in its attempt to recast the city's redevelopment plans as not only benign, but also heroic.[58] They used the familiar rhetoric of sickness and disease to characterize the manner in which the neighborhood's physical structure had declined, and invoked the figure of the doctor in their characterization of the fictional Freddy Fixer that the children were called on to create. The RA quite ingeniously devised a means by which urban renewal could be born for the Dixwell community in the body of a cartoon figure created by the neighborhood's own children, and demands for citizen control over plans to build a shopping plaza, parking lots, and middle-income housing could be made moot by transforming these efforts into an image drawn by ten-year-olds, embodied by children's cleanup clubs, and—by that coming spring—celebrated in the streets with an annual "Freddy Fixer Parade."

Soon after the art contest was announced, the Dixwell Project Office's new director of community relations, James Mitchell, invited residents and community organizations to participate in a neighborhood cleanup day. Charles Twyman remembered the events of that cleanup day with some clarity—particularly the ways in which his committee worked with the city on that occasion to undermine dissent. He recalled in a 2004 interview, with some regret, that a group of Dixwell residents wanted to confront the chief of police about getting permits for some cleanup-related activity. "This was marching time," he recalled, and the people in the neighborhood wanted to march. Twyman met with Dixwell public relations director James Mitchell, who suggested that the two of them speak with the police chief in advance. "We had access," said Twyman. He and Mitchell, knowing of the people's plan, went to the chief and told him that a group of Dixwell residents were angry, and that they planned to march. "Look, they're going to march down here and it's just going to create a problem," Twyman told the chief. "It's going to be a confrontation between you. You're going to call out your officers and you're going to have a problem." In an attempt to undercut the angry group, he suggested, "Why don't you put out the red carpet and receive them?" The police chief agreed, and Twyman went back to Dixwell Avenue, where he told the agitated group that they should just go to the chief and feel out the situation, rather than march. Twyman didn't mention his meeting. The group was, indeed, met with a red-carpet welcome. "We took great pride in the fact that we had manipulated this thing," remembered Twyman. "This wasn't a good thing to do, it really wasn't. At the time it felt good," he recalled, "but then sooner or later they began to see through it. They would ask for this much [a lot], and they would get this much [a little], and they would be sort of satisfied because they got something." Twyman understood, in retrospect, the ways in which his actions as Dixwell Renewal Committee chairman undercut collective action in the Dixwell neighborhood. "What I feel now," he said in 2004, "is if they ask for this much, they should get this much."[59]

The acting president of New Haven's NAACP chapter, Earl I. Williams, was publicly skeptical of the Dixwell program, stating that Mayor Lee was using Dixwell's cleanup projects as "window dressing to cover up . . . neighborhood poverty and illiteracy."[60] Williams spoke to the press following a meeting of the Dixwell Peace Corps that was held at the home he shared with his aunt and uncle. He was shocked to see that all of the twenty-five young people who took part in the meeting (representing about half of the Peace Corps participants) were white. The corps drew from area schools, including Yale, nearby suburban high schools, and New Haven's Hillhouse High School. Williams charged that the program was a product of "white paternalism" and "white man's guilt." Although he claimed to be expressing only his own personal views, Williams suggested that he was in the process of drafting a statement for the NAACP.[61]

The mayor's office and the RA took Williams' public statements very seriously. Dixwell Redevelopment Director Lloyd Davis suggested to the mayor that James Mitchell carry out the "public counter-attack" against Williams, and after the public relations director had appeared on television and radio, and met at length with neighborhood leaders, "the tide began to swing." By the next morning, December 11, Mitchell reported that businesspeople and "just plain citizens" were flooding the Dixwell Project Office, "voicing their displeasure with Williams' action." With this one instance of response to public criticism, the Dixwell Project Office proved effective at, as Lloyd Davis boasted to the mayor, "clearly identif[ying] Earl Williams as a troublemaker (politically motivated)." Davis also reported the success of efforts to indoctrinate young people into the redevelopment program. "Our school children took their bikes and blanketed the Dixwell community with our newsletter. They have now been organized into a solid striking force for disseminating our publication."[62]

This "striking force" was never more evident than when the schoolchildren of the Dixwell area took to the streets for the first annual Freddy Fixer Parade. On May 11, 1963, they walked the route with trash bags in a pre-parade Clean-Up Day. Homes and businesses along the avenue hung red, white, and blue bunting from rooftops and porches. The following day, at 2 p.m., hundreds of marchers gathered at Beaver Pond Park and released fifty helium-filled balloons to kick off the event. Twenty-five floats, a fleet of convertibles, and some of the state's most impressive marching bands and bugle corps marched the route in step with hundreds of schoolchildren. An estimated 10,000 spectators lined Dixwell Avenue as the New Haven Police Department color guard led a procession that included Deborah Michie, Albert Griffin, and John Solomon—winners of the Freddy Fixer art contest—and

10,000 ENJOYED FIXER DAY PARADE

Figure 2.6

"An estimated 10,000 persons participated and watched excitedly the Freddy Fixer Day Parade as you can see by the youngsters in this photo who are taking their duties as seriously as soldiers marching." *(Open Gate News, 38th ed., May 24–June 6, 1963.)*

the Freddy Fixer Songster Float. "Riding atop," reported the *Open Gate News*, "were two large Litterbugs and 24 songsters who sang the 'Freddy Fixer Limbo Song.'" Hundreds of marchers carried signs that read, "Hi Freddy!" The Dixwell Community Council sponsored a float with the theme "Need Advice?—Ask Freddy Fixer!" The hour-and-a-half march ended at Basset Junior High School, where many of the young marchers would file into their classrooms on Monday morning.[63]

Remaking "New Haven's Harlem"

By the summer of 1964, the city was explicitly selling "University Park Dixwell" to the white middle-class public. "It is being advertised as 'a brand new neighborhood,'" reported the *Journal-Courier*, the explicit purpose of which, it said, was to desegregate the area. Six new apartment projects opened in quick succession, including Florence Virtue and Fred Smith houses, as well as a housing development for the elderly. Rents of between $100 and $200 per month ensured that the new units were out of reach of most black Dixwell families, who on average earned just over $250 per month.[64] Lloyd Davis, Dixwell Redevelopment Project director, told the *Journal-Courier* that the RA sought to "reverse the traditional image of the Dixwell area as New Haven's Harlem," and that it hoped to "attract a wide range of prospective tenants." The RA did this with new schools, a new library branch, new housing, and neighborhood beautification efforts. "While agency officials have not said so directly," reported the *Journal-Courier*, "the purpose of the campaign will be to sell the idea of the altered and remade neighborhood to families who would not otherwise consider living in the inner city."[65] This, of course, raised the question of why such magnificent amounts of redevelopment money—$22 million on the Dixwell project alone—were never spent in order to improve the neighborhood for those who already lived there, who not only "considered" living in the inner city, but in fact had attempted to do so—through repeated relocations and "slum conditions"—for decades.

One of the central selling points for the new University Park Dixwell was Yale University. Its close proximity to the project offered culture, prestige, and university people, which in 1964 meant a concentrated population of affluent white men. Yale's proximity and influence in the city's redevelopment plans complicated the project of integration, infusing the interests of an elite institution into the complex problem of ending segregation in "New England's Newest City." Yale's financial involvement in Dixwell's redevelopment raised legal questions in the fall of 1962, when the *Register* reported that the city had received between $1.5 and $4 million in federal aid to fund Yale University development within the boundaries of the "project area," particularly the construction of two college residence halls on the sites of what had previously been two public high schools.[66] Meanwhile, the push for integration—shared by prominent civil rights leaders and the liberal Democratic establishment—collided with the rights of black Americans to stay in their homes and neighborhoods and see them improved and maintained. This tension was intensified by the appeal of Black Nationalist leaders to resist integration, demand black institutions, and strengthen ties to a worldwide "nonwhite" majority. It was illuminated by the organized action of hundreds of protesters who sat down in the middle of the street one October day in 1961.

The particular form of the protest—placing seated bodies in the path of automobile traffic—shot directly through the center of the community's place in the urban renewal debate. The protesters wanted good urban neighborhoods and adequate affordable housing, and they wanted their vision of New Haven to be included in the city's blueprints and redevelopment schemes. This protest predated both the citizen participation debate ushered in by the War on Poverty and more widespread public criticism of urban renewal, but it came precisely as the civil rights movement was negotiating its terrain in the North. The cars in the street did, in many ways, embody the RA's vision of New Haven's future. The city's plan for lower Dixwell would quite literally remove the neighborhood from the street and eliminate (or at least reconfigure) a collective space. It would replace a street-level crossing with a footbridge and designate a formerly low-income space on either side of that crossing as a middle-income area through the construction of new housing, targeted at middle-income families and designed around middle-class ideals. In doing this, developers hoped, they could transform this spot from a black space to an "integrated" space, from a "slum" to a showcase for urban renewal nationwide.

This model would offer two disquieting lessons for redevelopment on a national scale. First, it would demonstrate that true renewal was accomplished by changing not just the physical structures of a neighborhood, but also the people who occupied them. In other words, the Dixwell project offered a disturbing take on what the mayor liked to call "human renewal," a concept for which New Haven would become famous with the development of the Ford Foundation "Gray Areas" program, a model for the Johnson administration's War on Poverty. The program involved a long list of social services, job training, educational and literacy initiatives, combined with the classification of neighborhoods and plans for physically "renewing" certain places through rehabilitation and slum clearance. But ultimately, the plan for achieving human renewal—written into the blueprints and watercolor renderings of physical redevelopment proposals—was to systematically replace one group of humans with another.

The second lesson offered up by Dixwell's redevelopment was the potential for a new kind of relationship with the public, one in which neighborhood interaction with (if not involvement in) the project could disarm criticisms—such as those inherent in the CORE protests—that poor black people were not being consulted in the redevelopment of their neighborhoods. It turned out, in fact, that the black community—if skillfully courted and plugged in to the redevelopment process—could be useful in providing information that would facilitate the city's plans, even if those plans were to demolish that community's homes and businesses.

The story of this stretch of road marked the intersection between the projected and the lived Dixwell, and laid bare both the transformation of the civil rights movement as it would take shape in northern ghettos and the cultural and political underpinnings of the War on Poverty that would capture both national policy and national sentiment. Although the media still focused its attention on the civil rights struggle of the American South, where sit-ins and marches took on the legal barriers to equal rights, the Kennedy administration was aware of the situation in northern cities, where the affluent were exiting for the suburbs, poor neighborhoods were becoming poorer, and black communities were beginning to articulate clear voices of dissent. In May of 1963, members of the Kennedy administration met secretly in New York City with a handful of black leaders to discuss the "racial problem" in northern cities, among them James Baldwin, who had recently published his widely read book about discrimination in America, *The Fire Next Time*. "The Negroes of this country may never be able to rise to power," wrote Baldwin, "but they are very well placed indeed to precipitate chaos and bring down the curtain on the American dream." Coming off of that meeting, Attorney General Robert Kennedy described the situation in black urban centers as "explosive."[67]

A month later, the Reverend Martin Luther King, Jr., announced a "March on Washington for Jobs and Freedom." President Kennedy feared a mass action would make passage of the Civil Rights Act more difficult. He pleaded unsuccessfully with organizers to call it off, and although the historic and widely celebrated protest was carried off successfully, both the militancy and the message of the event were compromised. Some estimated that as many as 500,000 people gathered at the Washington Monument for what Malcolm X later called "the farce on Washington." A large and diverse crowd gathered peacefully for a program of speeches, music, and poetry, not necessarily what authorities expected when they put 15,000 paratroopers on alert, shut down the sale of liquor, and ordered riot-trained suburban police forces at the ready. With demands redirected away from jobs and freedom and toward passage of civil rights legislation, "It ceased to be angry," declared Malcolm X to a Detroit crowd a few months later. "It even ceased to be a march. It became a picnic. A circus."[68]

Less than a month before President Kennedy's assassination, his Council of Economic Advisors proposed a program for a "Concerted Assault on Poverty," which listed a constellation of cyclical problems, including "cultural and environmental obstacles to motivation, poor health, poor education, poor jobs, and limited earning potential."[69] But many of the Kennedy administration's "New Frontier" proposals—particularly those concerning racial equality—were limited by his very narrow victory over Nixon in the 1960 election, and the demands of southern legislators. A vision for economic programs, in the absence of sweeping and enforceable civil rights legislation, would have severe limitations. Problems of poverty and problems of race tripped over each other in the halls of Congress, just as they did on one particular stretch of Dixwell Avenue, where calls for integration collided with demands for black community participation in the process of renewing their own neighborhoods, Black Nationalism, and comprehensive plans for slum clearance and "Negro removal."

Less than a year after the march on Washington, a fifteen-year-old African American, James Powell, was shot and killed by a white off-duty police officer in Harlem. CORE organized a protest that quickly turned violent, flaring for two nights before spreading to Brooklyn. It was an uneasy summer in cities across the country, and the fall brought little solace to those who feared more violence. Abdel Kurriem, leader of the Dixwell Avenue mosque, told a reporter shortly thereafter—just days after the assassination of Malcolm X—that his movement sought "to take our people off the street and then send them back better people—not send them back [with] guns." As the few blocks between Kurriem's mosque and the Dixwell Redevelopment Office began to bear the sights and sounds of demolition, the reporter ended his portrait of New Haven's growing Black Muslim movement by noting that Kurriem added, "But that doesn't mean we can't."[70]

3

The Hill Neighborhood Union and Freedom Summer North

Citizen Participation and Movement Spaces in a "Project Area"

> *Everything they do we want to know, and we want to be a part of it. That's number one.*
>
> —Mr. Durham, Hill Neighborhood Union (HNU), July 1965

Why I Like Freedom School

Freedom school is a place to learn
*   About your own kind and that's black.*
The reason why [I] am writing is because I'm
*   getting sick and tired of my people*
*   being not put in [the] big thing.*
And I'm getting tired of having my
*   People beate [sic] for the first*
*   little thing they do.*
The only time we[']re put in [the] big thing
*   Is sports.*

> —Calvin West, Jr., New Haven, Connecticut, July 1965[1]

alvin West, Jr., attended a Freedom School, not in the hot Mississippi Delta, but in New Haven, Connecticut, where the summer heat was less relentless, but where he was no less "sick and tired" of being excluded from the "big thing." The city's master plan for the Hill neighborhood, like the master plan for Oak Street, which had long since been executed, would turn twenty-two acres of dense, mixed-use, low-rent properties into a large blank canvas punctuated with a carefully landscaped high-rise, in Cartesian tradition, "standing free and unfettered in a matrix of undifferentiated space."[2]

This would, in the words of new urbanist scholar Daniel Solomon, "eradicate the messy, irrational layering of centuries that burdened cities and distorted their architecture." Calvin West and his family lived in

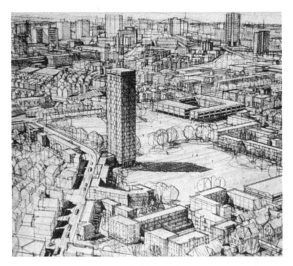

Figure 3.1

Master plan for the Hill neighborhood. *(New Haven City Plan Commission, 1942.)*

that messy, irrational layering of street corners, porches, markets, and sidewalks. The city's design, derived and more or less unchanged from a 1942 master sketch, called for the neighborhood's spaces to be compartmentalized by a wide roadway on which cars cut off pedestrian connections between the proposed institutional spaces at the center and residential sections beyond the highway. In the sketch, the Hill Project Area looks disconnected from the distant downtown, and all sense of neighborhood scale is obliterated by the high-rise near the center, which would provide fifteen stories of senior housing. The image seems to have been drawn from the sky, offering no pedestrian perspective or human scale. In the middle is an expansive patch of nothing, surrounded not by homes or businesses, but by large institutional structures. The image is populated not by people, but by big buildings, tiny cars, and a careful and symmetrical scattering of new trees.

Calvin may never have seen this particular sketch of the "big thing," but other images of his city's model future were more prevalent—images of the process itself—participation in which was still reserved for a select few. President Lyndon B. Johnson announced the War on Poverty in his State of the Union speech in January of 1964, and by that summer—following riots in Harlem—Congress passed the Economic Opportunity Act, which called for the "maximum feasible participation" of the poor in the administration of antipoverty programs across the country. The new Office of Economic Opportunity (OEO) asserted that the War on Poverty required a coordinated "network of anti-poverty attacks."[3] It called for the creation of Community Action Programs (CAPs) to provide federal assistance—both "technical and financial"—to fight poverty in urban and rural communities.

It was the "coordinated" nature of such programs—the oversight and tight fiscal control of city hall and the vague nature of requirements for citizen involvement—that enabled many CAPs to undercut community organizing while providing services for poor neighborhoods. As the recurring image of Mayor Lee and other dark-suited gentlemen tinkering with scale models saturated the public consciousness of the urban renewal process, Calvin West could see that, once again, as the city finally embarked on a plan to "fix" the problems of the Hill through redevelopment and antipoverty initiatives, he and his neighbors would have to fight to be "put in the big thing." Calvin's sentiments were shared by increasing numbers, and that summer—as the Harlem riots were repeated on a much larger scale in Los Angeles' Watts neighborhood—demands for jobs, housing, and community control over redevelopment plans and social programs intensified.

This chapter explores specific sites of resistance to the city's master plan in the Hill neighborhood, where a rich organizing fabric, woven out of interconnected neighborhood organizations, depended a great deal on a localized walking geography—the very type that was threatened both physically and ideologically by the city's Hill Redevelopment Plan. This fight unfolded just as New Left organizations across the country, such as Students for a Democratic Society's (SDS) Economic Research and Action Project (ERAP), set up their own "project areas" demanding that governments and institutions "let the people decide." It played out as American policy makers—stunned by waves of urban violence, and bent on solving the "urban crisis"—shifted from a policy of urban renewal to a War on Poverty with vague mandates for "citizen participation," and finally to a more comprehensive but more top-down "model cities" strategy, calling for innovative, far-reaching programs administered by city hall.

By the late-1960s, the idea of "urban management" would emerge, encompassing comprehensive programs for "law and order," municipal information gathering and record keeping, and a thick web of bureaucratic machineries. This urban management model, informed by corporate decision-making structures and war technologies, posed a significant challenge to the type of "citizen participation" that organized poor communities envisioned. New Haven's Hill neighborhood—like other poor communities of color in cities across the nation—was becoming increasingly organized, militant, and insistent upon its own plans for a "model city" just as top-down proposals for that model were taking on more centralized, managed, and even repressive forms. By 1965, the city's own antipoverty agency, Community Progress, Inc. (CPI), had only recently ventured into New Haven's poorest neighborhood, where the displaced black families of past redevelopment projects collected in an increasingly crowded and disorganized ghetto. Anchored only by a new and revolving cast of storefront churches, and connected only through family networks and occasionally their children's schools, the people in the Hill faced staggering unemployment, dilapidated housing, and a complicated and sometimes antagonistic web of social services—a concentrated dose of the problems facing all of the city's poor communities, and others like it across the country.

CPI was established in 1962 with a $2.5 million grant from the Ford Foundation. It predated Johnson's antipoverty legislation, and its innovative focus on "human renewal" (along with physical redevelopment) would serve as a model for programs nationwide. Using War on Poverty funds made available through the 1964 Economic Opportunity Act, similar CAPs sprung up across the country. Although their programs in remedial reading, job training, and homemaking were valuable to poor communities, all of the government's recommended CAP programs—following New Haven's CPI model—focused on self-improvement and were based on conventional pathologies of the poor. None of them "attacked" (to borrow the War on Poverty's own language) underlying structures of poverty, such as unemployment, low wages, unequal schools, housing and job discrimination, and the construction of luxury apartments and commercial developments that diminished the supply of affordable housing. For example, in articulating its support for adult literacy programs, the OEO astutely stated that "a remedial reading program . . . has little effect if there is no comparable course to permit the parent to guide and help his child," but this proposal ignored the underlying problem, addressed head-on by neighborhood groups like the Hill Parents' Association (HPA), of the overcrowded, segregated, and substandard schools that most poor children attended.

In order to receive antipoverty funds, a city was required by federal guidelines to "involve the poor themselves in developing and operating antipoverty programs."[4] However, the OEO's own suggestions as to how "the poor themselves" could be "used" were limited to positions such as "aides" and "assistants."[5] Never did the federal government suggest to municipalities seeking their antipoverty dollars that "the poor themselves" should serve in any decision-making or managerial capacity. In fact, the OEO's requirement for "maximum feasible participation" was left open for interpretation, and in many municipalities, as in New Haven, the mayor took that to mean he could *appoint* all community participants.

By this time, the fight for community involvement in the project of urban renewal, and the demand for access to more and better low-income housing, came to constitute the predominant civil rights fight in the North. In 1965, Rev. Martin Luther King, Jr., took the Southern Christian Leadership Conference (SCLC) to Chicago's West Side to take on housing discrimination and end slum conditions in the city in what would come to be known as the Chicago Freedom Movement. Both the Chicago movement and the concurrent movement in New Haven's Hill community offered an activist alternative to antipoverty programs proposed by both Mayor Lee and the federal government, suggesting an alternative vision of how to achieve a "slumless city" through civil rights and citizen control.[6] In New Haven, the fight would center on the fate of the Hill neighborhood, and the shape of federally mandated "citizen participation" in one of the nation's first, most famous, and most top-down antipoverty programs.[7]

The direct actions, vocal dissents, and activist culture of the Hill neighborhood charted new territory in community organizing, brought the city's poorest citizens into direct confrontation with both the mayor's office and the redevelopment staff, and developed not only grassroots leadership, but also neighborhood institutions and alternative community-bred models for urban design and citizen participation. The story of neighborhood organizing in the Hill also offers an alternative microhistory of the New Left. Although an infusion of young white activists who moved to the neighborhood in 1964 facilitated the establishment of a neighborhood union and a number of other community programs, the concurrent emergence of an organized group of black parents—demanding improvements at their children's school—laid the foundation for more comprehensive and radical community organizing in the years to come. The success of the HPA came not just out of the organizing work of New Left activists, but also out of community cooperation with them.

The Hill

There is more to New Haven than the beautiful buildings downtown. Ask the Mayor to show you the Hill, Dixwell Ave., Newhallville, and the projects. You may have to ask for directions. He might not know that they are there.

—"The Shame of Our City," Congress of Racial Equality document, 1965

What would become known as "the Hill" was, until the 1950s, a heavily Italian and eastern European working-class community. When the demolition of the Oak Street neighborhood began, displaced blacks and Puerto Ricans moved to this neighborhood in large numbers, joining the thousands of African Americans who traveled to the city from the South between 1940 and 1960. A significant number of white families still lived in the area, concentrated in the City Point section, which was both socially and geographically separate from the central Hill neighborhood. Some aging Italian couples, widows, and widowers still held on to their longtime homes in the Hill, which one resident said could often be identified by their well-tended tomato plants and flower boxes.[8]

Four spaces of resistance within the Hill community became gathering places, community spaces, and symbols of the neighborhood's fight for control over urban renewal plans, War on Poverty programs, Model Cities grants, and the notion of the model city. These spaces included the Hill Neighborhood Union (HNU), which opened its doors in February of 1965 on the corner of Congress Avenue and Hallock Street; a group of apartment buildings on nearby Ann and Liberty streets, which would become the sites of a coordinated rent strike; and a children's park, which took shape through the physical labor and door-to-door organizing of families involved in HNU, the children marching and picketing for a safe place to play, and the adults gathering materials and donating time and labor to build the park that the city refused to provide. The final planned space was one that never actually materialized, but even in its ideological form it offers both inspiration and insight. The Hill Cooperative Housing (HCH) project became an alternative model for urban design predicated not on just "citizen participation," but on citizen design and citizen imagination.

At a time when federally funded antipoverty programs called for community involvement while pouring large sums of money into top-down city agencies, a group of young organizers in New Haven's Hill area worked on a shoestring to develop leaders within the black community and help them establish neighborhood institutions, such as the HNU. Many organizers moved to the Hill from college campuses or other civil rights and community organizing projects with a somewhat naive vision, by their own accounts, of organizing "the poor themselves" to seize upon the opportunities presented by citizen participation requirements in the War on Poverty. Forms of neighborhood resistance in the urban North, and in New Haven in particular, were heavily influenced by and interwoven with concurrent civil rights organizing in the South.

In 1964, two Yale undergraduates, Jake Blum and John Wilhelm, ventured off of the campus and into the Hill neighborhood under the guise of a "sociology research paper." Wilhelm had been involved in some campus activism, and Blum had recently traveled to Hattiesburg, Mississippi, to register voters and volunteer at a Freedom School, but neither had any particular training or expertise in community organizing.[9] They were among ten or fifteen young activists who moved into the Hill community between 1964 and 1966, hoping to mobilize the poor to demand real "maximum feasible participation." The group was organized loosely and in name only (for the purposes of a grant application) as Neighborhood Organization Workers (NOW), a title that prompted two longtime "members" (John Wilhelm and Robert Cook, the faculty advisor) to reveal its irrelevance by asking, in recent interviews, "What was that?"[10] Hill organizers helped establish a Freedom School, a preschool, a neighborhood union, and tenant organizations by working with community members and developing leadership in the neighborhood. This model contrasted with the city antipoverty agency's tendency to work *around* or *in place of* community leaders in providing the "human renewal" services for which it became so nationally renowned. Hill organizers lived and worked in the neighborhood, and were a loose affiliation of student and civil rights activists united less by a plan or strategy than by a desire to aggressively take the government up on its request for citizen involvement. Their most important contribution to the movement in the Hill was the establishment of a neighborhood space and institution, the HNU, which would later be the headquarters of the HPA. A low-rent storefront office on Congress Avenue quickly became a meeting place, a base of operations, and point of interaction for a growing and varied network of activists.

The Hill Neighborhood Union

The [Hill Neighborhood] Union has nothing to do with C.P.I. or the City. It is run by the people who live in the neighborhood.
—First issue of *Hill Union News*, Issue 1, July 2, 1965, p. 1

People in the Hill can meet together, decide on a better way to deal with Redevelopment, and fight for that better way.
—HNU organizer Eddie Smith, July 1965

In February 1965, the HNU opened its doors with twenty-five dues-paying members. The dues gradually gave the HNU financial independence from the small grant that had supported the early organizing work of the young activists, and neighborhood leaders began to take over the responsibilities of organizing their neighbors, developing campaigns, running meetings, and writing the organizational newsletter, *The Hill Union News*.[11] Within a month, the new organization had succeeded—through door-to-door organizing, petitions, and visits to city hall—in winning repairs in a handful of buildings. A few property owners were fined or jailed, suggesting that bigger changes were possible.

Before the establishment of the HNU, the only organized group advocating for the rights of New Haven's poor black community was CORE, which had staged a number of direct actions demanding improvements in housing and enforcement of housing codes. But CORE's geographical focus had been the Dixwell and Newhallville neighborhoods, where more institutional networks facilitated organizing efforts. When organizers moved into the Hill, they discovered that the people there were just as angry and just as willing to fight, but lacked an institutional structure and a physical site of mobilization. The HNU and its Congress Avenue office offered both, and people living in the Hill responded immediately. "This whole notion of trying to expose the fallacy of the Model City drew a lot of people together," said

John Wilhelm. By July, the HNU had four people from the neighborhood working part-time as community organizers.[12] Many more worked full- or part-time on different programs and campaigns in the Hill, but funding limitations prevented the HNU from having a larger staff.

By contrast, the city's antipoverty agency, which—at its peak—employed more than 300 people, had an enormous budget, estimated at close to $8,000 for each low-income family it was intended to serve, an amount that was more than twice the average salary in the city's low-income neighborhoods.[13] CPI already had offices in Dixwell, Newhallville, and a few other neighborhoods when it opened its Hill area office in the Prince Street School. Prince Street was a dilapidated, substandard elementary school, and its condition would become the impetus for the city's most radical grassroots community organization, the HPA. By the time the CPI opened its Hill office, the HNU was already skeptical. "The law says people in the neighborhood have to have a big voice in deciding what CPI does. The rule says that people in the Hill and other neighborhoods should be able to elect people to the governing board of CPI," asserted the *Hill Union News*. But the authors claimed that CPI wasn't following that law, citing the fact that, of the nine members of CPI's board, five were handpicked by the mayor, and the others were chosen by Yale University and "three big organizations downtown."[14]

The HNU, in coordination with the local CORE chapter, was heavily critical of CPI for taking federal money—and continuing to apply for additional funds—while violating guidelines demanding community involvement. HNU organizers met with CPI officials in July of 1965 and informed them that they had written to the OEO demanding that the agency cease all funding of CPI until such time as the city allowed communities to popularly elect a majority of CPI board members. The OEO responded with a commitment to "send someone" to check up on CPI, and the HNU began contemplating a trip to Washington to push for more community control of antipoverty funds.[15] Despite the dire need for services in the Hill, residents were already growing very wary of official city programs to aid poor neighborhoods. Upon close reading, the HNU's description of the "problems" facing poor black communities like the Hill offers an interesting contrast to the manner in which they were stated by the Redevelopment Agency (RA). The HNU cited "bad housing and ridiculous rents, a hard time finding a decent job, bad treatment by the welfare department, prejudice and discrimination, old and crowded schools, not enough place for children to play," and "redevelopment, which often pushes people out and puts out houses they can't afford."[16]

The city, through CPI and the RA, set out to solve a slightly different categorization of urban problems (poverty, malnutrition, delinquency, crime) with a very different set of solutions, including "relocation, homemaking, education, and housing programs" that focused on "self-improvement" and individual uplift. "The people of our city will have the chance for much greater personal achievement," proclaimed *Opening Opportunities*, the founding document of CPI, published in 1962.[17] In the first few pages, Mayor Lee asserted that the goal of a "democratic society" was "the fullest possible development of individual potentialities." Further underscoring the relationship between human renewal and self-improvement, he concluded by declaring that the city's renewal programs would mean "the people of our city will have a chance for much greater personal achievement."[18]

By contrast, the programs that emerged out of community organizing in the Hill, anchored by the HNU and the HPA, and envisioned as legitimate alternatives as much as reactions to city hall programs, were centered on notions of collectivity, drawing from the civil rights and labor movements. The Hill's Freedom School was one obvious civil rights legacy, initiated by young organizers fresh off of Freedom Summer voter registration drives in the South. These Freedom Schools established first in the Hill, and soon thereafter in Dixwell's Elm Haven housing project and Newhallville, were grounded in the teaching of activism and spurned by ongoing local campaigns for not only school desegregation and the improvement of dilapidated inner-city schools, but also early movements for community control over teaching and curriculum. Despite CPI's national reputation as an "anti-poverty" agency and knack for sniffing out grant money, the HNU did not perceive it as a true advocacy group for the poor. The union's goal was to push "the Mayor, our aldermen, the redevelopment Agency, C.P.I., and the landlords to do what we want and need." The lines were clearly drawn.

The HNU office was both the physical site of community meetings and actions, and a space central to the neighborhood's identity. The union met at the Congress Street office at 8:30 p.m. on Tuesdays, but the office was open "all day every day." To the Hill community, the HNU office was, in the words of one organizer, "a symbol of the unity and strength poor people can have when they organize. To some extent," she explained, "it legitimize[d] and dignifie[d] the whole movement."[19] Besides the symbolic and logistical powers the office lent to community organizing efforts, it also illuminated the contrast between the RA's perception of physical neighborhood spaces and the view of the neighborhood held by community members: the RA painted its descriptions in broad strokes called "project areas" and characterized entire streets or sections as "gray" or "middle ground" areas, as either blighted, in need of improvement, or perhaps improving. For the people of the Hill, it was an individual street address that held particular significance. "Understand what happens when a Hill resident is able to say to another: 'Tonight we are having a meeting about the Prince St. School in our office at 605 Congress Ave," said an HNU letter to the organization's friends and supporters, both a monthly report and a plea for financial contributions.

The office required rent, supplies, and other expenses, but it was one of the most essential components of the organizing, perhaps second only to the organizers themselves. It was where the members of the community could go not only for support, communication, and resources, but also to make key decisions, such as "whether to march down to the board of education or to continue picketing the school."

Around the office, spaces of resistance and community-grown renewal emerged, including a Freedom School, neighborhood parks, and tenant union meeting rooms in cramped apartments. This web of spaces would not have mapped neatly onto an RA "project area" map; its points connected not by roads and highways, but by networks of family and neighborhood interaction. These were boundaries drawn by actions rather than blueprints, and the result, by the late-1960s, was a scattering of spaces defended by a network of organizing and activism, poised to not only defend against the agency's plans, but also push for an alternative to that model.

HNU organizers established activist networks among tenants, parents, the unemployed, the displaced, and even children, while bringing the people in direct contact with New Haven's power brokers and decision makers through walk-ins, sit-ins, petitions, and public meetings. One such event took place in the auditorium of the Hill's Prince Street School at a meeting called by the RA in July of 1965. HNU members turned out because they wanted to hear what the city was planning for their neighborhood, which officials had taken to calling "the Hill Project Area." RA staff members told the group that the city had received federal money for projects in the Hill, and that it would be used "to rent an office in the neighborhood and to find out about the housing conditions, the amount and condition of play space for children, and other things about the neighborhood."[20] At this first chance for public information and comment on the Hill Redevelopment Plan, community leaders sensed that crucial decisions had already been made without their input.

The meeting began with RA director Melvin Adams, who spoke at length about the successes of the Oak Street Redevelopment Project, and from time to time other city officials chimed in with their interpretations of these successes. One official, described by a Hill resident, Mr. Durham, as "the president of something," talked at length "about how much he'd been doing, for eight years. We asked him how come we never heard of anything," said Durham. "Must be because he was downtown all the time."[21] City officials continued to speak at length on the many ways in which projects like the Oak Street Connector had cleaned up New Haven, eliminated crime and blight, and paved the way for a modernized city. Some in attendance, like Durham, who had been displaced from Oak Street by the new stretch of highway, shifted in their seats, whispered to one another, and sighed. "At the meeting nobody would say nothing until we started talking—then everybody wanted to join up with us," explained Durham. He reminded RA officials that they were supposed to "send a paper around and guys around asking would we agree to the type of thing they'd drawn up. But we never got the paper." All they ever knew, asserted Durham, was that they would have to move.

Many shared Durham's experience and his opinions on the city's redevelopment program—and had for years—but few initially let their voices be heard. A brief comment, question, or allegation uttered by a member of the Hill community to the officials on the stage of Prince Street School auditorium was often the result of multiple conversations, during which, over time, an individual overcame very real fears (eviction, embarrassment, the power of city officials) and came to understand what kind of difference it would make for his or her own voice to be heard. For some, these close and intense conversations were necessary simply to get a neighbor to show up and sit in the auditorium seat.[22] Besides skepticism about the city's motives, fears of eviction, negative interactions with "downtown," and more general fears about "speaking up," many working people in the Hill were busy with jobs and family, or just more interested in their own day-to-day problems. It was only after many conversations with an organizer that people came to understand the urgency of such a public meeting, and its relationship to their daily lives. But to many people in the HNU, the urgency of the situation was indisputable. "We don't want them to get away this time with what they got away with last time," explained Durham. He was confident that history would not be repeated if people in the Hill spoke up. "The Hill Neighborhood Union really stands up for themselves," he said, "and nobody said a word to us until we got organized."[23]

Through door-to-door organizing and weekly Tuesday night neighborhood union meetings, Hill residents were becoming more educated about the process of urban renewal and the citizen participation guidelines put forth by the OEO. They were also becoming, collectively, more vigilant and savvy about opportunities to interact with public officials. "We don't mind going to meetings and making reports . . . we want to make sure we know what's happening all the time so the same thing won't happen in the Hill neighborhood as happened with the Oak St. Connector." The HNU's demands were simple. In the words of Mr. Durham, "Everything they do we want to know, and we want to be a part of it. That's number one." Whereas the city's definition of "citizen participation" seemed to be presentational or informational, the HNU's understanding was clearly more comprehensive.

HNU organizers understood the city's tactic of creating puppet organizations to rubber-stamp renewal plans. Beyond simply demanding a seat at the table, HNU organizers articulated the dangers of cooptation and the lengths to which the city would go in offering them seats at a table at which real decisions were not actually being made. "We don't want to join up with them, we want to keep to ourselves and work the way we've been working," wrote organizer Eddie Smith and Mr. Durham. "Every time they have a meeting, we like to be in the meeting, and if we have a meeting, they can be in our meeting. We don't want to keep nobody out of nothing." The neighborhood organizers asserted that the citizens of the Hill were going to push on their own terms for their own vision of their neighborhood, unlike residents of the Dixwell community, who had served—in some cases, regretfully—on the city's Dixwell Neighborhood Renewal Committee, undermining attempts at organized dissent and facilitating the city's plans.

Community demands caught Melvin Adams and the rest of the redevelopment staff off guard. "They didn't know we was going to be down there and come out with this," said Smith. Seeing an escalating vocal challenge to their time-honored process, the RA staff clumsily fielded a few questions, one of which was when the public would have a chance to meet with them again in the Hill. Adams said that a few of them were going on vacation, and others were doing "this or that," and that they would notify the community before the next meeting was to take place. It was clear to the HNU members and organizers that they had demonstrated their strength and put the city officials on notice. "It was a good meeting, an inspirational meeting," proclaimed Smith and Durham. The organizers decided that if they didn't receive notice soon about another meeting, they should "take action."

RA officials called upon the people of the Hill to "pick a committee" with which the RA could discuss their plans on a more regular basis. "The people from the Hill Neighborhood Union said that was no good," one organizer at the meeting explained, "because Redevelopment should go out and talk to all the people and listen to all the people."[24] Organizers, many of whom had experienced firsthand the tactics of the RA when they were moved out of their Oak Street homes, or who knew of the plans and practices in the Dixwell neighborhood, understood the purpose of that public meeting to be the formation of what was essentially the RA's "company union." As organizer Eddie Smith wrote in the *Hill Union News* days after the meeting, "The Hill Neighborhood Union can stop Mel Adams from setting up a committee that does what he tells it to." A puppet organization could fulfill the necessary citizen participation requirements while bypassing activist demands in the community. It could reinforce contested neighborhood boundaries and diminish the organized power of the black community. "People in the Hill can meet together, decide on a better way to deal with Redevelopment, and fight for that better way," said Smith, "and we should do it soon—in time for that [next] meeting in August. *Let the people decide!*" he concluded, employing one of the central slogans of the New Left, one that resonated in community union newsletters and at community union meetings in urban areas throughout the country.[25]

The Hill Rent Strikes

I believe they're trying to put the colored out of New Haven. It's not that people don't want things to be better, it's just that they're afraid of getting put out with no place to go.

—Mrs. Preston, 29 Ann Street, New Haven, "The Conditions in
My House," *Hill Union News*, July 2, 1965, p. 2

It was a hot June morning when the city shut off the water in Mrs. Preston's apartment building at 29 Ann Street. Her faucet was dry. That was about the last straw for Mrs. Preston, who had been calling her landlord for months to deal with a leak in the ceiling. After walking across the street with her four children to get water for the day, she called the health department. They already knew about the shutoff and claimed there was nothing they could do. They instead referred Mrs. Preston to the city's Department of Neighborhood Improvement (DNI), where she was informed that the landlord hadn't paid his water bill. "So I called my landlord," she explained. "He was furious because he said the water bill had been paid. Anyway, I said I had paid my rent, so it's not my responsibility. I asked what he was going to do." The landlord claimed to know nothing of the leak (despite Mrs. Preston's assertions that she had called every day), and said *he* wanted to know why Mrs. Preston had a broken window in her apartment. "I said there had been one," Mrs. Preston recalled, "but I had put it back with my own money, so it wasn't his business."

This exchange was typical of Mrs. Preston's dealings with her absentee landlord, and most were preceded or followed by the comings and goings of men in suits poking around the properties, noting the conditions of porches and doorways and sidings and stairwells—but never actually making repairs, and never responding to tenants' repeated calls to the city. That summer, Mrs. Preston had noticed a few men returning repeatedly to take photographs. When she asked the DNI about it, they told her they had, indeed, sent the men with the cameras, but would offer no information about why the pictures were taken. It was this combination of disregard and surveillance that intensified Mrs. Preston's anger as her calls for repairs were ignored, her questions about the city's mysterious interests in her building went unanswered, and water continued to drip from her ceiling while refusing to flow from her faucet.

The day after her calls to the health department, DNI, and her landlord regarding the water emergency, Mrs. Preston was awakened early by the familiar sounds of demolition. "They were out back," she recalled, "and tore down all the back porches that people used. . . . They didn't say why. They didn't say nothing, or tell anything. We still don't know what's happening." It was the lack of information and lack of responsiveness by the city and landlord, as much as her living conditions, that fueled Mrs. Preston's anger,

Figure 3.2

Photographs such as this one of a Hill neighborhood apartment, taken for the Redevelopment Agency, often filled the pages of city reports and publications, justifying the need for slum clearance and relocation. Rarely, however, did published images include within the frame the figure of the RA or DNI staff person, as in the image above. The woman appears impatient and uncomfortable with this investigative process, whereas her child seems excited by the presence of a photographer. This image was not published. *(Courtesy of New Haven Museum and Historical Society.)*

and the series of rent strikes that would formulate in the months to follow. What, after all, did "citizen participation" mean if demolition crews were going to show up early one summer morning to tear down the back porches on which people lived some significant part of their public and private lives?

Mrs. Preston was not the only angry tenant at 29 Ann Street. Her leaky apartment would soon become the meeting place for a new Tenants' Council aimed at pushing the city to enforce its existing housing codes in a neighborhood that was alternately neglected and accosted with prospectors eager to build institutions and highways through a residential space. The tenants were concerned not only with chipping paint and leaky roofs, but also with the lack of information from the city, the lack of transparency in the redevelopment and relocation process, and the discomfort of constantly having their homes sized up and photographed. The rent strikes of 1965—like others throughout the city and across the country in the mid-1960s—were about much more than housing conditions.[26] Tenants were well aware of this, and they organized themselves not only as a group of angry tenants, but also as a network of activists within a larger movement for neighborhood control in the Hill, in New Haven, and, for many at the time, within the national civil rights movement. "I believe they're trying to put the colored out of New Haven," Mrs. Preston wrote in the *Hill Union News*. She realized the racial context of urban renewal even if its architects downtown explicitly claimed its success as a civil rights victory. "Redevelopment comes into Dixwell and everywhere and moves us from one place to another. Where do they expect us to go? . . . If I had a place, I'd move tomorrow, but the way it is, I'm afraid they'll move us out and we won't have anyplace to go." Countering common criticisms of any public scrutiny of redevelopment, Mrs. Preston concluded, "It's not that people don't want things to be better, it's just that they're afraid of getting put out with no place to go."[27]

Mrs. Preston attended the weekly HNU meeting one Tuesday night in July to talk about the conditions in her house and the city's unwillingness to enforce existing housing codes. The next day, a neighborhood organizer and Yale chemistry graduate student, John Froines, went door-to-door with Mrs. Preston to talk with all of the building's other tenants—Mrs. Brown, Mrs. Henry, and Mrs. Wilkins. That accounted for all of the heads of households in the building—of the six apartments, two were vacant, and the rest were run by women who evidently shared Mrs. Preston's frustrations. Froines and the four women met that Thursday evening in Mrs. Preston's apartment as water continued to drip from the ceiling.

At the first meeting, they listed all of the existing housing-code violations and drafted a letter to the landlord, the mayor, and the DNI. "We hope to have the conditions of the building improved," said Mrs. Preston, "but we think that the city is going to have to do much more in the Hill if it is going to be a decent place to live."[28] The HNU's Housing Committee decided they would begin compiling a list of all empty apartments in the Hill area so that they could hand it over to the DNI along with their demands for repairs to the Ann Street apartments. They also decided at that meeting to elect a chairman, and talk with more tenants at 27 and 28 Ann Street.

HNU organizers from a neighboring Ann Street building held a meeting in their apartment that week with Mrs. Preston and a few of her neighbors. They decided the best course of action would be a rent strike. They also spoke with tenants in "five or ten buildings" in the surrounding area about joining HNU in fighting the "slumlords" who owned properties in the Hill.[29] One of the tenants, Eddie Smith, was new to organizing in the neighborhood, and was one of the first Hill residents to take on a concerted leadership role through the rent strike. "I am really interested in my work after having had a real long talk with [HNU organizers] John, Marianne, and Vicki, and hope to talk some more if they will listen," Smith wrote in the

Hill Union News, articulating the extent to which organizing relied upon close personal conversations and genuine relationships with friends and neighbors. He went on to say that he hoped if other people in the neighborhood had any problems, they would talk it over with someone from the HNU. "These words are from the bottom of my heart," he concluded.

Smith and the other organizers also mobilized tenants on nearby Liberty Street, where ten families in two buildings agreed to withhold rents to demand repairs.

As HNU organizers and law student and legal aid counsel to the Hill tenants, Brian Glick, entered through the front entrance at 147 Liberty Street, the landlord, Mr. Levine, stopped them in the doorway and asked if they were from CPI. "No," they all answered with a smile, as Mrs. Reed, a tenant, held the door for them. "Are you going along with this?" Levine asked her, waving his finger at the three men. "Yes," she told him. "We all have to stick together."[30]

Levine watched as the three continued down the hallway and disappeared into the apartment where one organizer's family lived. Eufizine Bethea was hosting the meeting that afternoon, and a handful of people had already gathered in the kitchen. "My mother left the door open in order for him to see the people in the apartment so he would know we were waiting on him," recalled Bethea. They watched from inside as Levine ran by the door and frantically barged into the apartment of their neighbor, Mrs. Taylor, slamming her door behind him. With his back pressed against her closed door, he asked Mrs. Taylor who the men were. "What in the hell did they want out of me?" he asked, catching his breath from his sprint down the dim hallway. Mrs. Taylor responded with a list of repairs that were in need of attention: a broken light socket, holes in the wall, leaky plumbing. "Do *you* go to all those *meetings*?" he asked her, gesturing toward Bethea's unit. "No," Mrs. Taylor responded calmly. "But the times I miss, my sister is there for me." Mr. Levine's face tightened with anger. "Did you sign up with them?" he asked, his voice growing louder and his face growing redder. "No," she responded. "My husband did." The story, as told by Bethea, was that "sweat was popping off his face as big as your thumb. [He was] scared stiff."

After just a few weeks of organizing, the tenants on Liberty Street had claimed their apartment building as their own space. Ten families who had never held any legal ownership over the small, dilapidated spaces they called home had—through organizing—transformed discrete, run-down units into a strong collective space, made stronger through the HNU by its alliance with the families on nearby Ann Street. Having orchestrated the withholding of rents at four Hill addresses, the tenants began planning direct actions. "We are thinking about picketing his office and home," said Bethea, putting Levine publicly on notice, and proposing similar pickets for the home and office of "Gold and Gold," the owners of the Ann Street apartments. "Everyone who thinks this is a good idea, join in and help us picket," announced

Bethea in an article for the ERAP newsletter. "The more people the better it is," she said. "We feel that we are not bums, why should we live in a slum?"

The strategy for the Hill rent strikes, as it had been for the Dixwell sit-outs, was to take the pickets, marches, and sit-ins out of the neighborhood and directly to the downtown centers of power, or to the suburban homes and offices of the landlords. Ultimately, city hall did intervene on behalf of the Hill tenants, forcing some repairs and taking the landlords to court for fines and damages. Although the ramifications were minor as far as the land-lords were concerned, and the living conditions for the Ann and Liberty Street families were not vastly improved, the rent strikes marked the emergence of an organizing network in the Hill, as well as the development of a handful of strong neighborhood leaders who had the experience of not only "speaking truth to power," but also of taking that truth downtown. The rent strikes created a culture of organizing that extended beyond emboldened, angry mothers into the experiences of the entire family.

The Freedom School

As HNU mobilized around the Ann and Liberty Street rent strikes, a younger generation of activists also saw themselves as part of the struggle between Hill families and the landlords, the DNI, CPI, and the RA. Activism surrounding the living conditions of Hill families in a few neglected buildings helped to concretize and animate the perceived relationship between the neighborhood and downtown, both undoing the "human relations" work of CPI as it tried to acquaint itself with the people of the Hill, and illuminating for multiple generations the power relationships at play. The rent strikes fundamentally changed the tenants' relationship with landlords, the DNI, and city hall by proposing an alternative model by which organized tenants could challenge the power imbalance that had—to that point—fostered hopelessness and anger. This was an important lesson for the children who lived in those apartments.

A drawing of Mrs. Preston's "leaky house" below her article about the strike in the *Hill Union News* suggested the involvement of children in the Ann Street apartments or surrounding buildings, many of whom attended the Hill's Freedom School or were involved in the activities of the HNU. The newsletter, like the Freedom School, became a space to teach resistance and develop a new generation of activists. Throughout the 1960s, parents and educators nationwide fought fierce battles not only to improve inner-city schools, but also to take decision-making powers away from downtown and put them in the hands of the community. As a movement flourished in the Hill around resistance to the RA and accountability for slumlords, this culture of resistance had a major influence on school reform activists, many of whom—in the tradition of the Freedom Schools in the South—set up their own alternative schools. Some were intended to take the place of public school classrooms, and others were intended to supplement the traditional school day with evening, summer, and weekend programs about black culture, citizen participation, the history of radical movements, music, arts, and ethnic dance.

The Freedom School in the Hill, and others like it in New Haven, were the youth component of a national movement of young people who were beginning to, in the words of one HNU organizer, "realize that they and most other people in the country, especially people with low incomes, are not allowed to decide what the government does with their city and in the country."[31] The Hill's Freedom School started in mid-June of 1965. It was one of many taking shape in northern cities, patterned after their southern predecessors, but focused on the issues of importance to poor black neighborhoods in the segregated North, such as redevelopment, housing, educational inequality, and the availability of safe recreational spaces.

Freedom Schools originated in Mississippi, where a coalition of civil rights groups organized Freedom Vote in the fall of 1962, a "mock vote" pitting actual balloted candidates against an interracial Freedom Party to demonstrate the potential power of a southern black electorate. With the help of about sixty white student activists from Yale and Stanford, Freedom Vote turned out 93,000 black Mississippi voters for their mock election. It was a solid victory for the Freedom Party and for the project of voter registration in Mississippi.[32] This project formed the basis of "Freedom Summer" voter registration drives for the 1964 presidential election, during which 800 college students signed up to take on the dangerous job of registering black voters in a racially hostile South. As part of this project, students of all ages flocked to makeshift classes—Freedom Schools—in churches, or under the shade of magnolia trees, to learn traditional subjects like reading and math, along with more radical topics like black history and civil rights.

In their northern form, Freedom Schools served similar aims of political education and basic educational support in urban communities that faced a kind of isolation similar—although not identical—to that of the rural South. Three of the New Haven project's ten summer staff organizers had taught classes and helped register voters in Hattiesburg, Mississippi, before making their way to the Hill neighborhood. By July, the Hill's Freedom School program involved about twenty children between the ages of six and eleven who came together every afternoon for classes, discussions, and activities. In the evening, about fifteen teenagers usually gathered for intense discussions on topics such as black history, the war in Vietnam, and the history of capitalism. Shortly thereafter, a smaller group of seventeen- to twenty-year-olds also started its own "advanced seminar" Freedom School group. Teachers helped with research papers, offered instruction in reading, writing, music, and math, led discussions on weekly film screenings, and engaged students in issues affecting their neighborhood.

There was a very loose national network of Freedom Schools through exchanges in the ERAP newsletter, and at national conferences and national actions. "It is . . . important that people in freedom schools are aware of what's going on in other places; that they meet other people and exchange experiences; that they begin to work together on solutions to the problems that they present and discuss," wrote Jake Blum, a Yale student and HNU organizer who served as one of the Hill Freedom School's teachers. Blum saw the project as an important means of educating and inspiring young neighborhood people, but was careful to note that it was not a "real substitute for direct action on a local level."[33] Freedom Schoolers often attended regular HNU weekly meetings, led their own campaigns (for parks, community control of schools, summer job programs, and recreational facilities), and contributed their drawings and writings to the *Hill Union News*. In July of 1965, students boarded a bus at the HNU office and traveled to Washington, D.C., to support lobbying efforts for the Mississippi Freedom Democratic Party (MFDP). Two students, one identifying himself only with the byline "Poochie," and the other identified as "Roy," documented their first trip to the nation's capital for the HNU's newsletter.

The group arrived in Washington late on a Monday night, and early the next morning they went to the offices of the MFDP, where they heard about a group of Mississippi blacks who had made a trip similar to their own, all the way to Washington, to talk with a court clerk named Ralph Robert. The Mississippi delegation was told to come back the next day, and they were given a written appointment for ten o'clock in the morning. When they returned the next day, the clerk's secretary told them he had to leave the office to attend a funeral. They decided to wait, sitting down in the reception area and refusing to leave. "They got arrested and we went to the trial," wrote Roy, noting his own intersection with the direct action of a group of Mississippi blacks he had never met.

As he sat and listened to the testimony of a "Mrs. Gray," who stood before a judge fielding questions about her participation in the alleged demonstration at the clerk's office, Poochie was captivated by her strength. "The judge, he was all right," Poochie recalled, "but he was just trying to bring out a point whether they were demonstrating or whether they were just trying to see the clerk, but he didn't seem too interested in it. He seemed as though he had had it solved already. He was going to sentence them to whatever he wanted to." Nonetheless, Poochie wrote, "Mrs. Gray still kept to that one thing." Poochie said the clerk's refusal to see the Mississippians was "one of the rudest things" he had ever heard of. After all, as Mrs. Gray's testimony asserted, they *did* have an appointment. This was familiar terrain for Poochie and Roy—old ladies and young mothers sitting defiantly outside of municipal buildings. It was scenes such as this one that captured the Hill's relationship to downtown New Haven. People from the Hill—Roy and Poochie's friends and neighbors—sat in at city hall for better housing, a better welfare system, and better schools. In Washington, DC, as Poochie watched and listened to Mrs. Gray's testimony, he admired her poise and strength, and was incensed by the unwillingness of both the clerk and the judge to hear her out.

The court took a ten-minute recess and some of the Freedom Schoolers went outside to watch the Shriners Parade make its way down Pennsylvania Avenue before they headed over to the offices of their congressman, Robert Giaimo. Roy felt a special connection to the congressman. "My mother works for his neighbor," he explained in his account of the trip. But ultimately, he—like Poochie—would be somewhat disappointed. When asked if he would vote in support of the MFDP's challenge to the Democratic slate of candidates, Giaimo told the group that he wasn't able to answer that. When one student, identified as "Coop," asked the congressman about "Negroes voting," Giaimo redirected the conversation by talking about "how he sold a house to a Negro in [nearby suburban] North Haven." The students were somewhat puzzled by the response, but persisted in their questions. What did Giaimo think about the crisis in Vietnam, and should black people go there to fight? "Giaimo replied by saying that Negro leaders said that Negroes should accept the duties of citizenship along with the privileges, like the duty of being killed," reported Roy. Editorializing, he added, "I think that Negroes shouldn't have to fight somebody else's battle."

They raised the issue of urban renewal, anxious to hear what their representative in Washington thought about the transformations taking place in their own neighborhood. "I didn't like what he said pertaining to urban renewal projects," reported Poochie. "He said poor people control urban redevelopment. Now if poor people control urban redevelopment, why can't they set up their own rates in housing?"[34] Poochie had internalized the notion of "Let the people decide," extending it so far as to challenge the for-profit real estate market. Although it may come off as naïveté in the retelling, it was the product of a rich organizing culture and explicit movement education in one New Haven neighborhood that naturalized, for Poochie, the idea that perhaps he could challenge existing economic structures on the basis of his own lived experiences.

The young men and women from the Freedom School, kids from Dixwell and the Hill, whose parents had moved from Oak Street to make way for the highway connector, and who had marched in their own streets for better parks and better schools, told the congressman what they thought about urban redevelopment. "He wasn't interested in what we had to say," said Poochie. "It seemed like he was a big man, which he is. He thinks he knows everything but he really knows nothing. All they know is things in the paper and junk like that, but the small problems around here, which are the most important problems, he don't know nothing about." It isn't clear from Poochie and Roy's account of their visit to Washington, or from the Freedom School's account of their activities and programs, exactly where they might have learned how government works, or how class and race operated in cities like their own, but Poochie did offer a keen hypothesis as to what the congressman from Connecticut might have been thinking as he fielded questions and comments from a group of Freedom Schoolers from the poorest neighborhood in his district. "In order to make good on himself," Poochie suggested, "he's going to try to stick with the higher class people and forget about the lower class. He act like if he helped somebody in the lower class, then somebody in the higher class would have something to say about it. They would be mad at him."

The reality was that the national political situation was complex, the MFDP was headed for defeat, and Representative Giaimo was not quite as blind to the street-level experiences in the Hill as he seemed in that moment. Following years of pressure from Hill organizers, and violence in the streets in the summer of 1967, Giaimo would conduct his own investigation of CPI. In 1968, he would criticize the agency before Congress, calling it an "overly centralized, paternalistic, big brother institution manned by 'planner-administrators,'" and charging that its administrators and staff "serve themselves rather than the poor."[35] The Freedom School students were by no means sophisticated scholars of national policy or Washington politics, but their explicit challenges to a very popular Democratic congressman, and their expectations of their federal government, speak to the extent to which their neighborhood union had claimed this "maximum feasible participation" as an individual and collective right.

Whatever the curriculum might have been at the Freedom School, there are a few clear lessons that Poochie and Roy took from their experiences that day. They saw a black woman stand trial for demanding to be heard by a clerk of the court. They saw her stand her ground and insist to a judge that the actions of the clerk, not her own actions, were the ones that deserved reprimand. They confronted their government face-to-face and didn't like the answers their government gave. They seemed baffled by the congressman's ignorance and—in an era of experts—uniquely confident in their own ideas and assessments of the problems facing the urban poor. And whereas a somewhat forced group discussion of On the Waterfront earlier that summer failed to awaken in them any sense of class consciousness, a four-minute conversation with their congressman certainly did.

The Children's Park

We are kids who live in the Hill area. The only park near our house is the Hallock Street Park, which is in bad condition. We want:

1. *A place to play baseball*
2. *More swings (baby and big ones)*
3. *More benches*
4. *Lights for playing at night*

5. *New basketball court lines*
6. *A place in the park for little kids to play*
7. *A gate for kids to get in from Arch Street*
8. *A merry-go-round*
9. *Fix the outside fence*
10. *Keep the park clean of glass and trash*
11. *A drinking fountain*

—Playground petition signed by more than 200 Hill children,
published in *Hill Union News*, Issue 1, July 2, 1965

In the summer of 1965, much like any other summer, kids flooded the Hill's streets throughout the daylight hours, taking the occasional time-out in their makeshift games for the passage of cars, fielding shouts from motorists, feeling the hot pavement under their feet. With apartments overcrowded, and air-conditioning (a new innovation fairly recently showcased in the Progress Pavilion) a conceptual impossibility in poor black neighborhoods, summer offered few choices for the young people of the Hill, pushed or propelled out their front doors at the start of the day. The Hill was "desperately short of open space," and only two small asphalt playgrounds provided an alternative to the street—one on Hallock Street and one on West Street. Both were in a sad state of disrepair, and neither offered trees for shade, water fountains, or trash cans.[36]

As their mothers, fathers, neighbors, and grandparents mobilized that summer to fight the "slumlords," CPI, and the RA, the children of the Hill—many of whom attended the Hill's Freedom School, as well as weekly HNU meetings with their families—began to see their own stake in collective action. A group of kids, ranging in age from around four to fifteen years old, gathered frequently at the run-down, ill-equipped Hallock Street Park. Sweating one morning, as usual, in the shadeless patch of crooked pavement that passed for a playground, they hatched an idea to force the city to make their park into the kind of space they wanted. That afternoon, transforming the park was the hot topic of conversation at the Freedom School. A petition was drafted by the students, with help from their teachers, demanding repairs, playground equipment, a water fountain, and regular maintenance. They made posters to articulate very specific demands, such as, "We need more swings and a trash can to put the papers and bottles in," and "They should have lines for the basketball court." The group then took to the streets of their neighborhood, collecting signatures from children and adults. They marched down Hallock Street to Columbus Avenue, then down Redfield, and back up Congress, collecting signatures along the way. When they returned to the HNU office, they regrouped and fanned out again to hang up their posters in the park and on surrounding streets.

The next day, the kids received a visit from the park commissioner. They gathered that afternoon as they usually did for the Freedom School, but a

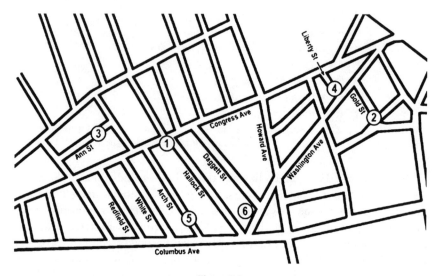

Figure 3.3

Map of the Hill neighborhood spaces in the 1960s.

1. HNU/HPA Office
2. Prince Street School
3. Ann Street rent strike apartments
4. Liberty rent strike apartments
5. Hill Freedom School
6. Children's Park

boost in attendance suggested that many neighborhood kids felt they had a lot at stake in the fight for a new playground. The park commissioner politely fielded questions and comments from the kids. "We need trees because it's too hot," was the first request. "And sand," another child added. The meeting was brief but effective. The following day, kids arrived at Hallock Street Park to find city Parks Department employees installing new swings and painting lines on the basketball court. One of the young organizers, Ruth Green, walked up to the man installing the new swings and asked when they could expect the new water fountain. Her boldness reflects the extent to which that first experience with successful collective action raised her expectations. The man told her there was no money for a new water fountain, but Ruth remained unfazed. "I think the demonstration did some good. I think they should have a merry-go-round for the little kids to play on and I think they should have a water fountain because you might get thirsty," she asserted.[37]

In their drawing entitled "Getting a Better Park," two young Hill children demonstrated their understanding of just how a neighborhood goes about "getting" something.[38] The simple drawing depicts a boy holding a sign that reads "Clean our park." The boy's mouth is open, suggesting the use of his voice, and the sign is raised, suggesting he has an audience. Below him on that page of the *Hill Union News*, another line drawing depicts a new set of swings beside a new trash can. Through the park protest and the successful acquisition of trash cans and swings, the youngest Hill activists learned the potentially direct relationship between collective action and the shape of the physical spaces in and around which they lived. As the depiction in the crudely executed comic strip narrated, an improved playground was predicated on a collective message, voice, and action, rather than on administrative generosity, an antipoverty agency, or a master plan.

The persistence of the Freedom School children in their park campaign inspired the older members of the HNU to initiate a concerted push on the city for more park space. Adults in the Hill also needed a safe outdoor space to meet and relax. But this push took on more urgency when, on July 29, a young girl was seriously injured by a car speeding down Hallock Street. The HNU identified a piece of unused land, littered with trash and broken glass, bordering a fifty-foot-wide unused railroad track that ran right through the middle of the neighborhood. Although it was, in the words of an HNU organizer, "unsightly and a hazard," it was also out of the path of automobile traffic, and very green, shady, and quiet. The HNU proposed the development of a triangular piece of land between Daggett Street and Washington Avenue for a park that would be "limited only by imagination and resources." They proposed benches, tables, walkways, shuffleboard, creative play equipment for the youngest children, and spaces for dancing, basketball, and relaxation for adults and older neighborhood youth. With resources from the city, they could also install lights so the park could be used after dark, and a stairway entering the park from the main intersection to provide better access. They proposed that the people of the neighborhood be involved in both the planning and construction stages, and that "much of the work could be done by resident teenagers" involved in the city's existing "Work-Study" programs.

That summer, the push for safe playground space was happening across the country. In Newark, Detroit, Harlem, Boston, and Chicago, children and their grown-up allies mounted similar playground campaigns. On July 2, in Cleveland, Ohio, a three-year-old boy was killed by a speeding car. "Had we had a playground area, that child would not have been dead today," said a Cleveland organizer. "And if people would cooperate we could have a playground area for our children—if we unite." Like the Hill, Cleveland's impoverished Fulton Street area had a five-block stretch, home to more than 200 kids, with no safe place to play. A vacant lot in the neighborhood—home only to a condemned house where rats scaled piles of trash and broken glass—offered some promise. "If we could possibly get the city to buy this lot, it would make the perfect playground."[39] Like the people of the Hill, the people who lived on and around Fulton Street had very clear and specific ideas about how to improve their neighborhood in critical ways, but found themselves up against those in control of redevelopment and antipoverty money. Like the members of the HNU, Cleveland's organized neighborhood people saw playground space not as something that would inevitably be given to them in the process of redevelopment, but as something for which they had to fight. In the words of one Cleveland resident, Leona Wilcox, from a poem she wrote entitled "Children Playing in the Street":

> *And where are the children to play?*
> *But in a street?*
> *Just because they have no place to play,*
> *Let's stop to think that we were once children ourselves.*
> *Let's not let someone*
> *Beat us out of this playground we need.*[40]

Wilcox was not explicit about the identity of this "someone," perhaps a reflection of the extent to which antipoverty and redevelopment officials were removed from the everyday lives of people in the community, but her urgency was evidence of the sense that she and her neighbors would have to take action if their children were to have a place to play. Across the country, there was consensus among neighborhood organizations that playgrounds would be born out of struggle, not out of planning or policy.

It was through their advocacy for a new park, and their work with the children of the Hill neighborhood, that the activists of the HNU first significantly raised the ire of city officials. Meeting with supervisors from the city's Parks Department at Mayor Lee's request, HNU organizers refused to "align themselves" with the city's Hill Community Council, Hill Recreation Committee, or "any other established neighborhood organization." This was, according to an interoffice memo copied to the mayor's office, "because they are CPI-dominated."[41] The head of the Parks Department reported that his supervisors found the organizers to be "evasive." He was able to ascertain (rather inaccurately) that the group consisted of "four or five white men, one white girl, and two or three Negro men, all of college age, who live in a rather dirty building at 35 Arch St." They were most likely referencing the address of the Freedom School, which at the time was 46 Arch Street. Moreover, the group had much wider community involvement by that point, and its members lived throughout the Hill neighborhood.

From what the parks supervisor could understand, the organizers ran a "'program'" (which he took great care to qualify in quotes) that served about a dozen children between the ages of seven and twelve. When he asked what went on at that program, one of the organizers responded, "The children decide." When asked about the source of their funding, they said they had a grant from the Norman Foundation, "whatever that is!" wrote the parks supervisor in his memo to the mayor's office. The mayor's staff was concerned that the HNU was "letting the children do whatever they want." However, they seemed more concerned about the broader implications of an organized neighborhood for their plans in the Hill. "I have my own ideas about this group and what their real aim and purpose is," wrote a Lee administration official to the mayor. "I imagine your reaction is similar to mine. By the way, do you know anything about this Norman Foundation?" These correspondences were forwarded by the mayor to the local FBI director, Charles Weeks, in hopes of gathering more information on both the HNU and the Norman Fund. "Are they perhaps on the Attorney General's list of subversive organizations?" asked Lee.[42]

The mayor also turned to his contact at the Ford Foundation in New York City. "An organization called the Hill Neighborhood Union has been formed in the Hill," he wrote, explaining that his enclosed memo would give the foundation insider "some idea of the problems they are creating." Lee stressed, again erroneously, that the leadership was made up of Yale undergraduates and that there was "no responsible adult guidance." City officials' insistence on believing that the HNU was entirely run by white Yale students was consistent with expert opinions at the time that "the poor themselves" couldn't actually be counted on to run antipoverty programs. In fact, poor people increasingly ran the bulk of HNU's programs, a reality that may have been even more troubling to Mayor Lee. He asked his contact to dig up any available dirt on "The Norman Fund."[43] Incorporated in 1935, the relatively small foundation was established to improve "inter-cultural and interracial relations" and protect civil liberties. It also funded projects that addressed the problems of "economically and socially disadvantaged youth," including programs offering experimental forms of education. Disqualified from receiving Norman Fund support were any organizations that had "broad public support"; the projects of the HNU seemed to fit the fund's goals quite well.[44] Unfortunately for Mayor Lee, there was no evidence that the federal government considered either the Norman Fund or the HNU to be "subversive."

In fact, much of the Norman Fund's support of the HNU was granted on the basis of the organization's head-on attack of CPI as a national model for antipoverty programs. "CPI is one of the most powerful and monolithic agencies of its kind, and has served in many ways as a pilot project for the 'War on Poverty,' " wrote Yale sociologist and eventual congressional candidate Robert Cook in a plea for Norman Fund support. "It has also been touted as one of the most successful. We think it is something less than that, and we see New Haven as a test case, i.e., in the face of this kind of power, can the poorer people of the city still exert meaningful control over their lives by creating independent community organizations which, while serving to keep the government agencies honest (e.g., get them to enforce their housing code, follow their own rules, etc.), will at the same time be transforming the very character of politics and urban existence?"[45] It was HNU's identity as an alternative to the city's antipoverty agency, and a corrective for its centralization of power, that formed the basis of the organization's appeal for foundational support. It was precisely because the Norman Fund—like President Johnson and Mayor Lee—saw New Haven as a model city that they felt the HNU's mission was so urgent, and it was their fight to revise the shape, structure, and form of that "model" that they hoped would enable them to affect the shape of antipoverty programs on a national level.

Hill Cooperative Housing

As the neighborhood union and its programs grew in size, scope, and vision, the people of the Hill—both its newer young white residents who had moved there to organize, and its preexisting black community (many of whom hadn't lived there too much longer)—began to recognize the HNU's capacity to develop viable alternatives to the programs put forth by CPI and the RA. Central to this capacity was a loose affiliation of experts committed to the idea that the city should "let the people decide," a group that rivaled the city's own cavalcade of young experts if not in number and resources, then in mastery, persistence, and vision.

One of the RA's most vocal and qualified critics was architect and activist Harris Stone, who—alongside his wife, Joan, a Yale-educated urban planner—fought vocally against the city's master plans in many New Haven neighborhoods. The Stones had both worked for the RA, and eventually left in protest after growing disillusioned with the policies and practices of the city's urban renewal projects. The problem with architecture, asserted Harris Stone, was that the client was always "a small group of rich and powerful men who control the institutions and businesses." Design, he argued, was generally limited to a small number of "monumental structures," leaving no room for experimentation. Moreover, most people had very little contact with architects and no influence on architecture. It was this isolation and imbalance of influence that caused problems with urban renewal, a concept that was inherently positive, but that, by most accounts, had gone terribly wrong. "These 'renewal areas' turned out to be physical and social disasters, because they had no relationship with the existing urban fabric," he explained in an unpublished 1966 document. Stone asserted that this was not how urban design and architecture had to be. He advocated an entirely different kind of urban planning in which architects could have "a direct client relationship with low and middle-income people, thereby creating the possibility for developing different programs, construction budgets, and techniques, and design objectives."[46]

Between June and September of 1966, after leaving his position with the city's RA, Stone collaborated with other likeminded experts, meeting face-to-face with groups of Hill residents, to design what they called "a new kind of housing project." Those who attended these meetings would be the future residents and cooperative owners of the project. There was a "bachelor," two couples, and four families, each of which had between four and seven children. There was a single father with seven children, and a single mother of two. Among the potential residents were both Fred and Rose Harris, who were vocal community leaders in the HPA, and John Wilhelm and Betsy Gilbertson, a young white couple who had been living and organizing in the Hill for nearly two years. It was a racially and socially diverse group, but every individual was a current Hill resident involved to some degree in the HNU. Through four months of intense conversation, they all decided what their vision for the urban model would look like.

The Hill Cooperative Housing (HCH) plan included stores as well as housing in order to "help two of the families get off welfare" and help other members of the group "make a better living doing something they really wanted to do"—run a store and serve customers. The community would include a day care, sports facilities, access to shared auto repair equipment, and arts resources, such as a kiln for firing pottery. One family stated they wanted to live on a "noisy street," rather than a quiet one, because "noisy streets that had houses and stores and lots of people were much safer and better to live on," and all of the families expressed a preference for "real urban" spaces over "suburban"-style living.[47] One family "wanted their apartment to have unfinished areas so that they could collect materials (like stone) and build things themselves over time."[48] Another requested "only one private space—a combination bedroom and study," but wanted the rest of the apartment to be "very open and public" so people "would feel free to drop in at any time."[49] In every respect, the desires and imaginations of these regular and quite diverse Hill families challenged familiar notions of the sanctity of private property, and the conventional middle-class ideal that dominated new urban designs of the time. The requests called for a complete reorientation of 1960s understandings of urban space, and a reconsideration of the impulse to compartmentalize groups, functions, and economies within the city.

After more than ten extensive interview and discussion groups, the team proposed a "low-cost, do-it-yourself housing development"—"a self-supporting cooperative residential and commercial development in the Hill."[50] The project would house eight to ten families, who could both live and work within the development. The families themselves would be in charge of every aspect, from design and construction to day-to-day management. Because there was no vacant land in the Hill suitable for new housing development, the HCH team knew they would have to plan their community on existing residential space. In contrast to the policies of the RA, the group decided to rehabilitate rather than demolish and rebuild, and they offered those living on the proposed site an opportunity to join them. "We all agreed that we had no desire to be a miniature redevelopment agency," Harris Stone and Robert Cook wrote in 1966, "pushing out and relocating one set of families so that another could move in." Drawings, models, and mock-ups of the development were a group project and reflected the styles, visions, and ranges of sophistication represented by all of the HCH families. The only qualification for participation at every level was a personal stake in the project and the willingness and creativity to contribute.

Perhaps the most extraordinary thing about HCH was that its originators and families saw it not as an isolated incident—a mirage of communalism and grassroots creation in a desert of top-down free enterprise—but as a viable alternative model. They imagined that their design could expand and serve the whole neighborhood, becoming not an aberration, but an anchor for the rest of the Hill community. Moreover, they predicted that others might "decide to undertake a similar project." Imagining a new way to build and rebuild cities, at the same time that President Johnson's "demonstration cities" task force was meeting in Washington, Hill organizers suggested that "eventually entire neighborhoods could be rehabilitated and renewed on this basis."[51]

Unfortunately, theirs was a model that was never to take full physical form. Harris Stone explained that the project was ultimately scrapped because of "the indifference, if not downright hostility, of the RA and [CPI]."[52] Stone applied for the position of architect for the Hill Redevelopment Plan but was turned down in favor of prominent and "monumental" architect Louis Kahn. The unfinished story of HCH offers a nearly concrete example of the often-ambiguous term "maximum feasible citizen participation." It was a project that could have come to fruition—could have been given the opportunity to actually succeed or fail—to reveal its lack of viability or perhaps provide a real model for alternative urban design. It offered a glimpse of what the Hill and other similar neighborhoods across the country could be like if the residents themselves were actually given the opportunity to decide how antipoverty and urban renewal money was to be spent.

In New Haven, as in many other cities, such decisions were the exclusive purview of the RA and CPI, who faced mounting pressure to show that they had some mechanism for citizen input. This pressure was magnified—in New Haven and throughout the country—by civil disorders in Watts, Harlem, Detroit, Newark, and eventually New Haven. But in 1966, while New Haven's image as the model city had not yet been tarnished by the familiar, persistent, and sometimes misleading images of urban unrest, the RA stepped up its attempts to ward off discontent by going straight to the community to announce its plans for their backyards, front steps, and corner stores. That summer, many residents and business owners in the Hill got a letter in the mail from the RA. Across the top, it read "The Hill: A Neighborhood Plans for the Future."

The wording struck an awkward chord for some, since the plans, maps, and sketches were all news to them. Nonetheless, the letter explained, "The plan outlined here is the product of a working relationship between the Hill community and the City," and readers were assured that the plans were a product of "your thoughts and suggestions combined with our techniques for putting them to work."[53] The map displayed a large portion of the densely populated Hill neighborhood transformed into a series of neatly arranged developments situated around a "large park-playground area," quite a stark contrast to the physical arrangement imagined by those involved in the HCH project. Conspicuously missing from the RA's designs were plans for housing—particularly affordable housing for the overcrowded residents of what had become New Haven's most dense "relocation area." This ignited some organized anger on the part of Hill residents, but it was not until the following summer that the federal government's own redevelopment road show—on its stop in the model city—would open up an opportunity for clear visible dissent.

The National Commission on Urban Problems: "Too Many People Are a Blighting Influence"

Why don't you let me go and walk around, so I can take my wife out once a week or something, and take her out to dinner? Let my kids go to a decent school, and wear shiny shoes, you know . . . I'm not asking for a million dollars. All I want is the little things out of life.
—Uninvited testimony of Hill resident Columbus Keinsler
before the National Commission on Urban Problems,
May 25, 1967, Conte School, New Haven, Connecticut

There are too many newly organized groups making their claims for registering their preferences on the political system.
—Invited testimony of Herbert Kaufman, Yale Professor of
Political Science, before the National Commission on Urban Problems,
May 25, 1967, Conte School, New Haven, Connecticut

In the 1960s, the laws that governed redevelopment were predicated on a fundamental misunderstanding about "public consent," or, more specifically, public opposition. The law required that hearings be held—that someone "hear" something—that the public have the opportunity to raise objections and register dissent, and then that these hearings be documented and sent along to the federal government agencies that funded redevelopment and antipoverty programs. But the federal government, like most individuals—history would suggest—seemed to misunderstand the nature of collective action. The fact that a room at city hall wasn't packed with citizens yelling, chanting, and carrying signs and banners did not mean that those people would like to have their kitchen cabinets replaced by a highway ramp. But in the absence of a feasible solution, unless people facing such dislocations saw that they could actually change the situation, or alter the city's plan, they were often not willing (because they worked and lived and had fears and in-securities and distrust or just general hopelessness) to do so much as sign a petition, much less show up at a meeting in a government building. Not to mention the fact that they were rarely asked to do either, and rarely even in-formed of existing opportunities to do so.

This was the misunderstanding under which Illinois senator Paul Douglas was operating when he appeared at New Haven's Conte School at one of many public hearings around the country organized by President Johnson's National Commission on Urban Problems. It was the spring of 1967, just months before the police would invade the Hill neighborhood following a vi-olent altercation between a Puerto Rican man and a white shop owner. It was also just months after the New Haven RA filed an application for HUD's new "Demonstration Cities" program, seeking federal funds to sup-port an "innovative" computerized neighborhood surveillance and policing system for the Hill, designed quite secretly in coordination with the Ad-vanced Systems Development Division of IBM. The proposed system would have "the ability to draw a street and property map of a redevelopment area and show the location of families with specific characteristics," to quote just one of many ominous passages.[54]

Senator Douglas' commission didn't actually travel to the Hill neighbor-hood that summer afternoon. Instead, Mayor Lee welcomed them to New Haven at the city's newest "showplace" school in its well-publicized "show-place" renewal project, Wooster Square, where row houses by the dozens had been rehabilitated from flophouses to the residences of an upwardly mo-bile middle class. It was at this meeting in the heart of the city's showplace renewal project that Senator Douglas told Fred Harris, president of the HPA, that the biggest problem facing cities was that people "like him" didn't "come out to meetings." Ironically, Harris and the HPA had not actually been invited. Harris responded to the senator by saying the federal govern-ment should "find out who they [the city] don't want you to talk to, and then go talk to them." He also suggested that the senator spend more than a few hours in each city, and that perhaps he would hear from people in the neigh-borhood if someone from the federal government took to the streets, talked to people, and actually brought them to meetings.[55] Harris was basically suggesting that the government needed to not just organize meetings, but go out and organize *for* them.

That's what the HPA had done. Despite its prominence by this time as the Hill's most far-reaching neighborhood organization, its leadership and members had not been notified about the commission's plans to stop in New Haven. Although they had no formal invitation, Harris explained that a friend in city hall had tipped him off, and the HPA set to work immediately mobilizing a group of neighborhood people to make their presence known at the meeting. That afternoon, Harris and eleven other HPA members piled into two cars to confront the mayor and his panel of experts about the city's plans for their neighborhood. "We knew . . . that Mayor Lee was going to be speaking for the people of New Haven," Harris later told photographer Richard Balzer. "Now ain't that a bitch? He lives in good housing and sure as hell didn't get us good housing, so how was he going to speak about housing for us?"[56] Recounting the events for Balzer's 1972 photo-essay on the HPA, *Street Time*, Harris said, "We sent one big guy in, I think it was a guy named Wade. He just walked in, walked down the aisle to the stage, looked at the people on the stage, looked at the audience, turned around without saying a word, and walked back out again. He came outside with a big smile and said 'I checked everything out and it's ok.' " At that point, the rest of the group filed in, and finding no seats available, they all sat down on the floor. It was from those seats, eye-level to the edge of the stage and barely visible to the rest of the crowd, that the members of the HPA took over the meeting, and ultimately tried to take over their model city. "We went to a lot of meetings this way," Harris recalled.[57]

The events at the commission's hearing in New Haven were illuminating in both form and content. In New Haven, as in the other cities on the commission's tour, an impressive lineup of experts and city officials were set to discuss the problems of the poor. But at the Conte School that Thursday morning in May, Fred Harris and the HPA inserted their voices into that dialogue by force, raising the possibility of a new kind of debate, and a new kind of citizen involvement. Following Mayor Lee's statements before the commission, Fred Harris rose from the auditorium, interrupting the proceedings. "You people have listened to the mayor. How about listening to us?" he asked, his words recorded alongside those of invited experts in the published transcripts of the 1967 hearings. "If this is supposed to be a public hearing, you should allow the people that are involved in all this redevelopment to speak their opinion, seeing that we are the ones who have to go through all this redevelopment, all these urban programs."[58]

CPI director Mitchell Sviridoff, one of the scheduled speakers, interrupted Harris. "I see no point in conducting a debate on this level," he insisted.

"You live in [suburban] Woodbridge, that's why," Harris responded.[59]

Harris introduced another Hill resident, Columbus Keinsler, whose criticism of Lee's redevelopment plans was intensely personal. "He's pushing us completely out," said Keinsler. "I want to know why he's pushing us all out of New Haven where nobody can see us." Keinsler—identified only by Harris' introduction as "my brother," and by his description in the hearing's transcripts as "a lifelong New Haven resident"—testified to the demographic ramifications of the city's renewal programs that neither the mayor nor the cavalcade of experts had raised. "Now he has us so far in three neighborhoods. You have the Newhallville section, you have the

Congress Avenue section, and the Washington Avenue section. You have got a few living out in Fair Haven. But now they're coming through Congress Ave., as I understand, with a new turnpike."[60] The "turnpike" to which Keinsler referred may have been a stretch of the Ring Road along Howard Avenue that would connect to Columbus Avenue and a widened State Street.

The HPA's disruption of the hearing's normal format opened up the space for others in New Haven who found themselves cut out of the redevelopment process. "I would much rather have been invited than to have to get to talk in this sort of way," said Stephen J. Papa, a white member of the Dwight Improvement Association who spoke not as a representative for that organization, but as a New Haven resident. "Usually in an investigation or story there are both sides. . . . Fortunately, one of the gentlemen in the early morning session got up and asked to be heard," said Papa, crediting Harris' insertion into the debate with opening up his own opportunity to speak. Papa testified that many of those who had left New Haven through the redevelopment process were the "backbone of the community, the middle class people, the man who brings home $125, $150 a week. Contrary to what you might think," he asserted, "there are many good houses, two- and three-family houses, with five and six rooms to a flat . . . these were torn down."[61]

The takeover of the hearings in May 1967 by not only "black radicals" in the Hill, but also uninvited guests from the white community, predicted the unique political and social movement that would formulate in the years to follow, as organized citizens took over control of the New Haven's Model Cities funds. Taking the story of the hearing back to people in the Hill neighborhood, organizers reported how the mayor had insisted to the commission that "too many people are a blighting influence," and that the city's population was declining "because of the usual kind of ethnic problem." In response to Fred Harris' testimony that New Haven had "more parking lots than apartment buildings," CPI director Mitchell Sviridoff responded by reporting that, "by *statistical* standards, New Haven has the highest level of housing integration in the state and even in the nation." Writing for the *AIM Newsletter*, Robert Cook explained, "Fred wasn't talking about statistics and integration, he was talking about real people, their houses, and their neighborhoods."[62]

Harris demanded a full and open public hearing on urban renewal. "It's unfortunate that we have to do this type of thing to be recognized as human beings," he told the commission. "All we want is a decent place to live, decent schools . . . and decent rent." The commission chairman told Harris that they would "try" to respond to his request for a hearing. "Try?" Harris responded. "You'll *try*? These are our lives you're dealing with." Then, in the "model city" on the commission's summer-long tour, where the mayor had time and again claimed consensus and enthusiasm for his urban programs to those who held the purse strings for his federal money, Fred Harris led a walkout. By four thirty in the afternoon, the day's proceedings were fizzling to an end. Closing out the commission's New Haven hearing, one city official turned to the chairman, concluding, "The nation looks forward to your report to provide insights as to how we get out of this jungle."

4

Maximum Feasible Urban Management

*The "Automatic" City and the
Hill Parents' Association*

> *They tell me I control everything. I punch these buttons on the
> intercom and talk to all these officials. But I can't sit down with
> that kid, whoever he is, and find out what he wants. One match,
> and my city—after 13 years of work—will be down with all the
> rest of them.*
>
>

—Mayor Lee, quoted in the *New York Times*,
September 3, 1967[1]

> *You can't take a guy with a white shirt and a tie, with a college
> degree, that doesn't understand the functioning of these people's
> minds, and comes down looking down his nose on us, when he
> lives in Woodbridge . . . and he's going to tell us, 'Clean yourself
> up. Pull yourself up by your bootstraps.'"*
>
>

—Fred Harris, testifying at New Haven hearing of the
National Commission on Urban Problems, June 1967, p. 148

Hill Reconnaissance

Howard Hallman came to New Haven in 1959 from a position
with the Philadelphia Redevelopment Agency. He was only
thirty years old at the time, and held a master's degree in political science from the University of Kansas—an archetype of the young
college-trained experts who tinkered with New Haven's many scale
models during the Lee administration. Working under Redevelopment
Director Edward Logue, Hallman immediately laid out a plan for what
he called "reconnaissance of the Hill," which included a survey of every
property and lot from Legion Avenue to City Point, and from the Boulevard to the boundary of the neighboring project area on Church Street.
The survey would take "40 man-days," Hallman estimated, and it would

serve to "demarcate sections that appear certain to remain as residential areas" and "locate problem areas for further study."

Here was the answer to Mrs. Preston's question about who was taking pictures of all of the backyards, porches, and front stoops in her neighborhood. Hallman proposed to Logue that the surveys be tallied using punchcard technology—an early form of computer. This reconnaissance plan, he suggested, would be only for "internal use." The survey that the redevelopment staff would take out to the Hill included questions about building materials, number of floors, census tracts, block numbers, and exterior conditions. None of the questions were intended to gather information about people. The instructions on the printed survey informed staff that it wasn't "necessary to inquire about occupancy, but rather to indicate what it appears to be."[2] The results of the survey were to be presented to and discussed by the Hill Community Council, an organization established and appointed by the Lee administration to serve as the representational body for the Hill community.

A more comprehensive proposal for neighborhood "reconnaissance" would emerge a decade later as the city—in a partnership with IBM—sought funds through Lyndon Johnson's 1966 Demonstration Cities and Metropolitan Development Act to fund a massive computer "data bank" to keep "detailed records" on the identities, histories, and known associations of all Hill residents, in order to facilitate policing, social services, and redevelopment. This component of New Haven's "Demonstration Cities" application was never widely publicized—particularly not in the Hill neighborhood—but it revealed both the racial fears and the form of "management" on which the Lee administration based its urban model. The proposal was written (although not yet finalized) before the outbreak of civil unrest in the summer of 1967, just as the city's massive antipoverty agency, Community Progress, Inc. (CPI), fielded growing criticism about its lack of citizen participation.

New Haven's master plan required the surveillance and control of the Hill, as well as its characterization as a disorganized, dangerous, and potentially revolutionary place. The "riots" posed a problem for the model city, but also a solution, as media attention to violence and disorder in the Hill Project Area provided the opportunity (albeit unwelcome) to institute a police state, cast neighborhood leaders as militant instigators, and convince those who criticized the city's antipoverty and urban renewal programs that direct citizen control was out of the question. Unlike the "maximum feasible participation" requirements mandated by the Office of Economic Opportunity in 1964, the Demonstration Cities Act explicitly proposed a top-down, "urban management" model. This was necessary for the bill's passage at a time when conservative voices in Congress were charging that rioters across the nation were simply using "social ills" as an excuse for "illegal behavior," and asserting that more programs, funds, and power for the poor would be interpreted as a reward for "criminal behavior." It was also in part a response to significant backlash from frustrated mayors who didn't like the idea that city hall could be bypassed in the allocation of antipoverty funds, placing money directly into the hands of increasingly militant community organizations.[3]

Critics winced at the word "demonstration" in the title of the legislation, fearing that its double meaning would further encourage insurrection. Senator Strom Thurmond spoke for many southern and conservative legislators when he said, "I wish to say here and now that if we pass this demonstration cities bill, it will not stop the demonstrations." Thurmond's indictment was directed not only at the urban poor, but also at the "outside agitator," a label commonly given to organized labor, New Left activists who moved into poor neighborhoods through projects like Students for a Democratic Society's (SDS) Economic Research and Action Project (ERAP) or the Hill Neighborhood Union (HNU), and Communist or Socialist Party–affiliated organizations that advocated for the poor. "There is evidence that some of these demonstrations are either communist inspired, communist directed, or communist controlled," charged Thurmond, underlying the need for both increased policing and surveillance of project areas, and centralized control of existing urban programs.[4]

Between the late 1950s, when reconnaissance-style urban renewal by young imported experts seemed plausible, and the late 1960s, when a new kind of citizen participation was not so much a legislative requirement as it was a popular mandate, a crucial question emerged: Would cities be something that could be "managed," like a corporation, a factory, or a corner grocery store, or would they be governed, designed, and sustained by the people who lived and worked there? Both complicating and illuminating this question were two wars, one on poverty in American cities and towns, and another in Vietnam. As one American Independent Movement (AIM) activist asserted, "The U.S. has taken upon itself the task of armed pacification both at home and abroad." Cataloguing the strategies and tools of repression used in Southeast Asia and Latin America throughout the 1950s and 1960s, he wrote, "All residents of our urban areas are subject to this same treatment."[5] And in the heat of summer unrest in America's city streets, when the technologies and strategies of an overseas war were turned inward on Newark, Detroit, New York, New Haven, and dozens of other U.S. cities, it became clear that "urban management" spelled trouble for the grassroots model of citizen participation.

This was the historical context of the "maximum feasible participation" debate. Many in power hoped to place much greater emphasis on their own definition of "feasible," while the poor seized and mobilized around their own sense of what "maximum" might mean. A wave of social scientific work in the late 1960s ranged from skeptical to critical of the policy and its implementation. In her 1969 study of citizen participation, Sherry Arnstein identified a "typology of eight levels of citizen participation," described in the form of a ladder. At the bottom rungs, she described an "illusory form of participation," central to which, she argued, were "neighborhood councils" or "neighborhood advisory groups" like the one Lee established in the Hill when the project was in its early "reconnaissance" stages. "These bodies frequently have no legitimate function or power," Arnstein argued. They were used to " 'prove' that 'grassroots people' are involved in the program."[6] By the late 1960s, mounting resistance to the city's skyscraper-in-the-park plans for the Hill community, and escalating demands for housing, jobs, and democratic structures, would reveal the limitations of this "reconnaissance"-style planning. Demands for community control by organizations like the Hill Parents' Association (HPA) forcibly reinserted the question of "occupancy" back into Hallman's proverbial questionnaire, while a national debate about "maximum feasible participation" clashed with a nationwide turn to a new urban model that was tested, contested, and rejected by organized citizens in the designated "demonstration area" of the model city.

A Particular Kind of "Model"

There is no reason why we cannot apply modern business methods to government, and this is what I propose to do in the next two years.

—Mayor Lee's personal notes concerning his ideas for his seventh term of office, December 1965

As Mayor Richard Lee prepared for his seventh term, jotting down notes to himself in preparation for a speech, he had in mind a particular model for New Haven. "I have held preliminary conversation with Dave Hacket of IBM," wrote Lee, setting the stage for a close municipal-corporate relationship in the years to come.[7] IBM and the city of New Haven were old friends. The company had long considered the city a "good IBM customer," noting that New Haven was the first "non-federal government body" to purchase and install IBM's Ramac 305 for municipal use. New Haven was—in the words of one employee of the company's Advanced Systems Division—"one of the most progressive cities in the US" and a "leader in urban renewal and human renewal."[8] One thing that IBM and New Haven had in common in the late 1960s was their remarkable ability to amass large amounts of federal money. As the war in Vietnam escalated, and IBM quickly became the driving force behind a sophisticated battery of computerized weaponry and war technology supported by astronomical research and development budgets, the computer giant was an obvious choice of partner for Mayor Lee in his endeavor to come up with a reliable model for "urban management."

In his February 1966 State of the City address, Lee announced the creation of a task force to modernize city government. In light of new and challenging urban problems, Lee asserted, "we must . . . continue to equip our government with the tools of modern business management." This task force would be drawn from "many sources," he announced, including "business leadership, labor and professional men, top city staff, and management specialists from academic life." Noticeably but unsurprisingly absent from that list were groups or individuals representing the Hill neighborhood, which would serve as the "Model Community" for this test program.

It seemed as though Lee's New Haven was interested in not only the tools of the corporation, but also its culture. In staking a claim on how the city of the future would look, feel, and operate, Lee chose to partner with IBM instead of grassroots citizens groups, a choice that was by no means inevitable. The mayor's nine-man committee, which became known as the Urban Management System Task Force, met periodically over the course of two years with representatives from the mayor's office and IBM. The city wasted no time in updating to a state-of-the-art IBM computer system capable of performing basic clerical and computational functions. The task force was quick to identify that the problems facing New Haven were largely caused by what they called "population mobility." Of course, no single force had caused more "population mobility" in New Haven than urban renewal, and the partnership between IBM and New Haven promised to smooth the increasingly rocky process of redevelopment projects in the face of rising citizen dissent.

With an eye toward a more "managed" city, Lee's new task force proposed a "complete information system—a so-called data bank—for all city departments and agencies." They proposed that "data on all property inspections, by whatever agency, would be automatically placed in the bank, for use in fire prevention, prosecution of slum landlords, studies by the city plan commission, or dozens of other purposes." The police, Lee reported, already had the beginnings of such a system, having "placed a substantial amount of information on computer tapes," including "descriptions of known criminals."[9]

This was not entirely new terrain for IBM, or for strategies of information management. In the summer of 1966, a special subcommittee of the U.S. House Operations Committee on the Invasion of Privacy held hearings in Washington after the federal budget bureau proposed a "national data center" through which more than twenty government agencies would share data using a central computer. According to the *New York Times*, this data bank would contain information on education, grades, credit rating, military service, employment, and "just about anything else." On the local level, a program for the city of Santa Clara, California, was already in the works. Like the New Haven proposal, Santa Clara's Local Government Information Control (LOGIC) was also a joint venture with IBM. It would record name, alias, social security number, birth record, driver's license, property holdings, employment status, and voter and jury status, along with any information from the welfare department and juvenile, district, criminal, or probate courts.

The *New York Times* quoted a Stanford graduate student, Clarence Wadleigh, who warned that "the toy could easily become a monster." Wadleigh told reporters it would "seem an almost irresistible temptation to 'record' more than is necessary. . . . there are too many people out there saying, 'we're going to have to build a case against this person in the future. Let's start building his history now.'" At the time, Santa Clara and IBM were still considering the question of whether to gather information on venereal disease. IBM argued that any risks associated with such a system would "depend on the decisions of the people who operate the computers." A spokesperson for the data-processing center said that the public should have nothing to fear if they "have no arrests, no outstanding warrants . . . if [they're] not on welfare, or if [they've] stayed out of the clutches of adult probation."[10]

One August 1967 report predicted the "end of privacy by the year 2000," by which time all Americans would have computers and robots in the home, pocket telephones, programmed dreams, and "artificial moons for lighting large areas at night." This report by the Commission on the Year 2000, supported by the Carnegie Corporation, also predicted that by that time, the entire U.S. population would live in three large "supercities": Boswash (Boston, New York, and Washington, DC), Chipitts (Chicago to Pittsburgh), and Sansan (San Francisco to San Diego).[11] The predicted elimination of small cities and the severe regionalization of the nation along superhighways went conceptually hand in hand with computerization and the loss of personal privacy. In August of 1967, Columbia University lawyer and political scientist Alan F. Westin published *Privacy and Freedom,* in which he warned that "electronic eavesdropping" by government and police was becoming more prevalent with the availability of new "undetectable technologies." He claimed that with microphones that could fit on a button "secretly sewn onto a coat," or "mounted in the victim's false teeth," any person could become a "wireless transmitter."[12]

Perhaps this is why, in a city fraught with overcrowding, dilapidated housing, poverty, and a host of other "urban problems," the Lee administration chose not to widely publicize this joint project with IBM. As organizers in the Hill had long since discovered (and aggressively asserted), information gathering was not the most urgent problem facing New Haven. These organizers had—without the assistance of a "computerized databank"—developed a long and detailed list of slumlords, housing-code violations, and necessary repairs throughout the Hill neighborhood. By mid-1966, when Mayor Lee's task force was initiating its outreach to the Advance Systems Development Division of IBM, Hill organizers were still fighting the Department of Neighborhood Improvement and city hall to get someone to pay attention to their list. The enforcement of existing housing codes didn't have the same potential to bring in federal Model Cities funds, nor did it promise to contribute to the rising national reputation of "New England's Newest City."

In April of 1967, the city and IBM completed the survey phase in the development of their proposal to the department of Housing and Urban Development (HUD). "All of the city's files will be put into computers to obtain a statistical profile of all New Haven residents," the proposal promised. They spelled out very explicitly some of the powers this would afford the city. "The Police Department would have available all the information about suspects known to have been in the area where the crime was committed," stated the proposal. Similarly, the fire department would be able to locate all convicted arsonists living within a certain vicinity of a fire. Less explicit were the advantages promised in facilitating renewal plans and thwarting organized dissent. The basic design of the Urban Management Information System (UMIS) involved a combination of individual and spatial identification files to be utilized in coordination with one another in order to keep track not only of who lived in the Hill, but also—quite significantly—where they lived, went, came from, and frequented, and with whom they associated. UMIS would contain information on every individual's name, phonetic spelling, social security number, address, date of birth, national origin, employment status, race, and gender. It would also keep files on "family relationship," "method of travel to work," "educational achievement," children's educational levels, "shopping preferences," "recreational preferences," number of automobiles, "years in present residence," and "areas moved from."

The computers would code "pre-determined geographic areas" defined by both census tracts and Redevelopment Agency (RA) project boundaries, which were themselves contested boundaries. By taking the RA's definition of New Haven's spatial arrangements, UMIS would reify the unilateral and controversial decisions the agency had made, and more important, embed them in this highly technological tool for municipal projections and decision making. Information would be collected on particular addresses, blocks, and buildings. "Grid coordinates" would allow for something UMIS's architects called "visual display routines and geographic inquiry," a perceived benefit that leaves much to imagination and nightmare.[13]

The system would be able to "correlate social, economic, and physical data" on the level of individual blocks, and even buildings, enabling authorities to track and target—for example—the HPA office and the surrounding network of community organizations and leaders.[14] Over the course of the few years leading up to the development of a UMIS plan, these activists and organizations had become the Redevelopment Agency's biggest obstacles and most vocal critics. For the RA, UMIS could prove an invaluable tool, one which would be able to "draw a street and property map of a redevelopment area and show the location of families with specific characteristics."[15] Such information would enable the RA to more strategically plan which streets, blocks, and properties to acquire, where dissent would most likely exist, and where it would be most threatening.

UMIS would also allow the RA to revolutionize a practice it had so painstakingly perfected over the years: the production of promotional materials. Using computer data, "various permutations and combinations could be displayed visually until the most meaningful of these displays were determined. These in turn could be produced on hard copy."[16] Manipulation and careful selection of data could yield a particular map, chart, or data set to be used to promote and publicize particular projects. But the applications of such a technology for urban renewal went far beyond the creation of visual aids. As public meeting encounters with Hill activists indicated as early as 1964, the Hill Redevelopment Plan was not going to fall into place as easily as Oak Street had a decade earlier. City Hall routinely underestimated the number of community members who would show up to speak out against the Hill's master plan, and just as often underestimated the opposition's level of understanding about the redevelopment process, ignoring alliances across race, class, and geography in organized resistance and alternative proposals to the RA's plans.

The spectacular powers of assessment and prediction promised by UMIS's design team were, in fact, abilities already prevalent in much less expensive and more user-friendly technologies—community organizing and collective action. "A computer could alert the controller to sudden changes in financial need," boasted the proposal. So, too, could a welfare protest, a delegation of Hill residents sitting in at the mayor's office, or—as the intervening events would demonstrate—civil unrest. The same could be said for the data bank's ability to predict the ramifications of a new roadway or school in a particular location. New Haven had plenty of case studies to examine at that point, and plenty of relocated families and business owners more than willing to testify to the effects of particular roadways.

The IBM/Lee team insisted that UMIS would provide "information not currently available or collected because of cost considerations."[17] Less explicit was the extent to which UMIS could provide a license for the city to collect information previously uncollected because of the right to privacy, or the political costs of explicit surveillance. Offering an interesting take on the process of municipal decision making in the age of "citizen participation," the architects of the UMIS project said that their data bank could provide a "clinical decision support system," which demonstrated "current applications in diagnosing diseases, but they think it could be applied to urban management decision making."[18] Not only would citizens be taken out of the decision-making process, but so too would living, breathing elected officials.

"It is hoped," wrote the task force in its application to Washington, that additional ideas could be developed through "combined efforts of the Hill residents and the various participating agencies."[19] This nod to citizen participation was the only hint of the Hill's role in developing a plan for its own surveillance—and a close reading of the categories of data to be cataloged reveal it very clearly to be just that.

Figure 4.1

Photo-cartoon from the cover of the *AIM Newsletter*, January 15, 1969. Members of the AIM Urban Renewal Committee and the Hill Neighborhood Corporation met with State Highway Department officials in Wethersfield, Connecticut, on December 12, 1968, to argue for a halt to the construction of Route 34 through the Hill and Dwight neighborhoods. State Director of Planning David John is pictured on the left "proclaiming" that computers have determined the need for the highway. At the board, pointing to the map, is architect and activist Harris Stone.

Lee's plans for urban management in a computer-age city garnered the attention of city officials around the world. The mayor of Imola, Italy, addressed a poorly translated correspondence to "Mayor of New Evan (New England)" in which he indicated that he and his staff took "great interest" in New Haven's partnership with IBM, since his own city was developing a plan to make their own municipal operations "automatic."[20] What seemed like a simple lapse in translation was actually a revealing linguistic turn: Lee's plans to ostensibly turn urban decision making into an "automatic" process ran counter to the spirit of citizen participation, and to the demands of increasingly organized poor communities.

The task force's final report claimed that that the computer data bank would eventually be programmed to make decisions in dealing with urban "complexities."[21] The *New Haven Register* reported "opposition" from "various sources" concerning privacy issues, but the task force asserted, "We believe the time is ripe for the joining of forces of two of the most disparate activities of the mid-twentieth century—computer technology and urban management." In retrospect, the city's proposal for a UMIS smacks of 1960s technological utopianism. Like the Cartesian models of the previous decade, the very concept could facilitate both urban renewal and "human renewal" through top-down antipoverty programs. UMIS could technologize the process, making it easier for architects, planners, developers, and city officials to avoid looking at the real neighborhoods, on the ground level, just as the proliferation of maps, blueprints, and scale models had done in the days of Oak Street's clearance.

But as the nation's involvement in the "quagmire" of Vietnam escalated, financial resources and technologies for programs like UMIS would be diverted. And, as the streets of urban America continued to erupt in violent summers—as they would do in New Haven in August of 1967—officials, policy makers, and citizens would be forced to see through the possibilities of a technological utopia, and past the maps, blueprints, and scale models, to the reality of neighborhoods that could not be "managed" in the way Mayor Lee had hoped. This is a lesson that might have been gleaned less destructively from the uninvited testimony that shook the New Haven hearings of the National Commission on Urban Problems. The city sought unquantifiable volumes of quantifiable information about poor communities, while those very communities collectively stormed structured "public" conversations to offer up, free of charge, unobstructed, and unimpeded by clerical and computational processes, firsthand information about these "urban problems" that had become so urgent as to necessitate a national commission.

The Hill Parents' Association

We sensed great local hostility to the program. . . . Unknown to us until the end of our day of hearings there, New Haven Police had been stationed inside and outside the hall in case our hearings got out of hand. We prevented that by welcoming the views of unscheduled as well as scheduled witnesses. In fact, the "walk-in" witnesses talked with a fire and eloquence which the others had not matched.

—Howard Shuman, Housing and Urban Development
Chief of Staff on New Haven's hearings before the
National Commission on Urban Problems[22]

I don't like a lot of talk.

—Fred Harris

The National Commission on Urban Problems visited New Haven in May of 1967 because it was a "showplace" for urban renewal and antipoverty programs. The "model" HUD went to examine was not exactly the one with which it was presented. Not only was the testimony of experts interrupted by direct demands from the black community, but it was also contradicted by similarly excluded (and newly assertive) voices from white New Haven. One expert on the meeting's agenda put forward an alternative plan for solving the city's problems that reflected the needs and demands of the "walk-in witnesses," articulated in the language of experts in cooperation with the grass roots. Criticizing the city's existing antipoverty program, Yale sociology professor Robert Cook (identified for the purpose of the hearing without any mention of his 1966 bid for Congress) charged that the War on Poverty was "not dealing with the fundamental issue of misdistribution of income, which has remained approximately the same since 1900; that is, one-fifth of the American people get 45 to 50% of our income and the poorest people get about 4.6% of our income." Cook suggested that the problems of the city could be most effectively addressed by an increase in the income tax, a redistribution of income, the confiscation of slumlord properties, and a plan to "pay the people in the slums a decent salary to rehabilitate and rebuild their own neighborhood."[23]

"That's quite a program, Mr. Cook," responded Senator Douglas, bringing an abrupt end to the proceedings and dismissing Cook's proposed antipoverty model. That program was essentially what the HPA had been advocating. The HPA was founded in the spring of 1965, which was, according to Fred Harris, before the "whole Black Power thing had even started."[24] At that time, Rose and Fred Harris' two children, Ronda and Madera, were enrolled in the Hill's Prince Street School on Washington Street. Concerned with what they saw as racism in the curriculum and in the classroom, and with the poor physical condition of the building, they united with other Prince Street parents to form the Hill Parents' Association.

"The kids had no toilet paper," Fred Harris recalled. "They had to use hard brown paper. This made Rose furious. She already knew the kids had to share books . . . but I think it was no toilet paper that flipped Rose."[25] The first major public meeting of the HPA took place at one of the neighborhood's other elementary schools in the spring of 1966. Organizers from the HNU joined the Prince Street parents, and by April, the group began going door-to-door throughout the Hill to share their concerns with other parents. Within weeks they had mobilized a group to go to the board of education. Their first direct action was a two-day picket, both outside the school and downtown. The demands were toilet paper for the students' restrooms, paint for the walls, books for the classrooms, and a black principal. The toilet paper, books, and paint arrived the day after the pickets.

Shortly thereafter, they were able to secure a meeting with city officials and members of the board of education, and by the time of that hard-fought meeting on April 28, 1966, the Prince Street School also had a new black principal. More than fifty HPA members showed up to meet with him at the HNU office later that evening. "We secured a partial victory—let's give ourselves a hand," said Harris to the group of gathered parents. "This is an organization of people and as long as we stick together, we'll be strong."[26] The city's plans for the "Hill Project Area" threatened the very physical capacity of Hill families to "stick together" both by placing a multilane highway through the heart of the neighborhood, isolating it further from downtown resources, jobs, and centers of power, and by proposing institutional uses for existing residential spaces, while making little or no provisions for desperately needed affordable housing.

Organizers noted the significance of the fact that the new principal had come to meet the parents "in their territory," rather than in a meeting downtown. The Hill families had demonstrated that they could force the city to respond through door-to-door organizing and direct action. "We basically cared about the people and we cared about what we were doing," said Harris. "We were serious."[27] And people in the neighborhood took Harris very seriously. As John Wilhelm recalled, "You could not walk down Congress Avenue with Fred Harris because every single person would stop him and want to talk about something. Landlord problem, welfare problem."

Fred Harris grew up in New Haven, and his first job, at the age of twelve, was shining shoes outside a local bar. He soon found himself running numbers, racing across town on his bike with policy slips hidden in a hole he cut in the heel of his shoe.[28] His father worked as headwaiter at Yale's elite faculty club, and as soon as Harris was old enough, he was wearing the same waiter's uniform. Donning the white jacket he had seen his father wear each day, he "learned to be invisible" while waiting on people he described as "big shots."[29] As a community leader in the Hill, he would very effectively make a habit of being visible. His assertive dealings with the city's police force were particularly well known. "A lot of these brothers on the streets [had] never seen nobody stand up to white people—especially police men. There were times I took people right out of a squad car who were gonna be arrested. I'd open the door and just tell them to get out. I was nuts. The police would just stand there with their mouths open," he recalled in a 1999 interview.[30]

The HPA was often portrayed in the local media as militant and aggressive. Fred Harris admits that the group understood its place in New Haven politics. "We were the sick-em group—no respect, wild crazy, uneducated— a lot of times, [city hall] would rather deal with the [more conservative] black organizations and ministers. . . . with us, we would go and talk to them and if we couldn't come to no agreement, something would happen in the city."[31] One often-told story, repeated on the floor of Congress by Representative Robert Giaimo, was that the night after a CPI official denied funds to the HPA to run its summer programs in June of 1967, four of the agency's neighborhood offices were firebombed. The next morning, the mayor met with HPA representatives and informed them that OEO funds would cover their needs for the summer.[32] No HPA member was ever accused of the firebombs, nor was there ever any direct evidence to suggest that the organization was responsible.

The fact was that HPA's demands were quite squarely the demands of the Hill community, and the demands of not only poor blacks and Puerto Ricans in New Haven, but also poor people throughout the nation's increasingly crowded and isolated urban ghettos. With the HPA's network of organizing—itself a network of neighbors and families—news of both victories and refusals, like decisions to act or respond, traveled and transpired in ways that could be called neither official nor deliberate. If a group of Hill youth did bomb the CPI offices, they were more likely than not—by virtue of family, friendship, or geography—somehow "connected" to the HPA. That relationship worked both ways, and people in the neighborhood who were not members of the HPA participated in its programs and helped shape the organization's demands. "I wasn't trying to be the radical of the radical," said Harris. "I was trying to get the community changed."[33] The demands for neighborhood control over poverty funds, financial support for summer programs, and a voice in urban renewal struck at the core of the black community's discontent, and of neighborhood sentiments about the relationship between the Hill and "downtown."

Over the course of a few months, Harris developed an acute understanding of what it took to make his friends and neighbors into activists. By his own account, he "didn't like a lot of talk," but he did, by everyone else's account, spend a significant amount of time talking with people in the Hill about their schools, housing, and access to the city's decision-making structures. Nonetheless, he grew impatient with the city's endless supply of talking heads and the lengthy agendas of public meetings, and believed more strongly in the power of action. "Just going down to the mayor's office and kicking in the door, confronting these men at meetings and stuff like that," said Harris. "Brothers from the street had never had the opportunity and had never been involved with stuff like that. Once they got an opportunity to stand up and say what they really felt as men, most of the time they were hooked."[34]

When New Haven's prominence as a model city—and its "unlikely" descent into civil unrest—brought the Hill national media attention, the national press, like New Haven's city hall, preferred to focus on Harris's role as a "militant," rather than on the HPA's community programs. The *New York Times* called him "gentle-mannered," but noted that Harris "goes out of his way to tell white inquirers that 'this is not a nonviolent organization.'" Physical descriptions often focused on the "green fez" he wore, which many associated with Black Muslims, a movement with which Harris had no affiliation. "He has attracted a number of white youngsters, male and female," wrote a *Times* reporter, "who like to use 'black' words like 'soul' and avoid 'white' words like 'Negro.'" Downplaying the HPA's origins as an organization of parents fighting for school improvements, and its focus on family issues such as housing, welfare, and jobs, the *Times* noted that Harris' "followers seem to include more ghetto adolescents than parents."[35]

It seemed that the white establishment didn't know what to make of the HPA. In a time of racial hysteria, civil unrest, and faltering antipoverty programs, Harris' militancy was more legible to the press than his organization's grassroots community programs. Those who lived in the Hill, for whom the HPA meant summer camp, a community park, collective tenant power in the face of slumlords, challenges to the welfare bureaucracy, or a voice for the neighborhood in the redevelopment process, might have agreed with the *Times'* characterization of the organization as "the new militant voice from the ghetto . . . harsh . . . impolite, unpredictable, certainly not always controllable." However, its claims of adolescence and its fixation on violence were incongruous with the grassroots reality of the organization's work, which built not only community programs and vital neighborhood networks, but also cross-racial alliances with activist groups throughout the city.

In 1966, members of the American Independent Movement (AIM), a predominantly white antiwar, anticorporate political organization, approached Fred Harris about running for the Connecticut State Assembly. Sociologist Robert Cook was at the top of the ticket, attempting his first run for U.S. Congress as a peace candidate. Harris joined Cook, and they set up campaign headquarters on Washington Avenue in the Hill. Cook's campaign opened Harris' eyes to the connections between the war in Southeast Asia and the struggles of his friends and neighbors at home. Activism in the Hill was not driven by opposition to the war, but Harris' entrance onto the local political scene sparked a greater interest in both the draft and the diversion of funds from America's poorest communities to support a war in Vietnam. Connections between the two were becoming more prevalent as the 1966 campaign progressed. Yale architectural scholar Vincent Scully asserted, at the time, that "redevelopment and Vietnam were intimately connected, and were indeed the two massive failures of liberalism." Scully argued that they "were alike in the arrogance of their intrinsic, if more or less unconscious, racism."[36] This was an analysis that also resonated with activists at the street level.

The connections between liberalism's failures at home and abroad were not at all lost on Fred Harris and those assisting with his campaign, but neighborhood issues remained the focus on Washington Avenue and its surrounding streets. This enabled Harris' team to focus press attention on the issues in his neighborhood, a previously difficult feat. "The only reason why I ran for state assemblyman was I wanted to use that platform to exploit the media," Harris said in 1999. "A lot of times we'd have press conferences . . . and for some reason . . . it would seem as though what we said was never reported the way we said it. I believed that by running," he explained, "it would give us a chance to try to get the things we were working on, our views, our opinions, out in the media so people could hear without it being chopped up too much."[37]

Although his bid was unsuccessful, his entrance into the political arena gave added weight to the issues and actions of the HPA. When Harris and a handful of other HPA leaders were among more than 300 New Haven residents arrested in front of the state welfare office in Hartford, the organization took on statewide prominence, and the Lee administration—fielding increasingly harsh scrutiny about the lack of citizen involvement in CPI— began to pay much closer attention to the Hill.[38] In 1966, not long after the welfare protests, CPI conducted a survey of the neighborhood in which they concluded that the needs of "inner-city residents" were dominated by "housing and recreation."[39] It was right around this time that the HNU office at 605 Congress Avenue officially became the office of the HPA, an address that would gain widespread notoriety in the months to follow, as civil unrest in the summer of 1967 placed New Haven among the ever-growing list of large and small "riot cities" across the country.

The drama, fire, and rubble of the "riot" as a historical marker tends to mask the less visual and newsworthy struggles—often just as devastating and invigorating—that took place on the ground in neighborhoods like the Hill. These were struggles over political power and urban territories played out in public hearings, meetings, and organized confrontations with local and state officials. The riot could be explained away as violence provoked by "outside Communist agitators," or as it was in other cities as sporadic and depraved acts of hooliganism, but nonviolent and highly organized (yet politically and ideologically aggressive) acts of protest, engagements in legitimate political arenas, and alternative plans for the model city revealed the limits of citizen participation in New Haven and the potential of grassroots alternative models.

If the Model Cities program was President Johnson's official response to the failures of the War on Poverty and the summer riots that devastated black neighborhoods, terrified suburban families, and baffled policy makers in the 1960s, it was also his official response to community organizing and local mobilizations against city governments and police forces in "demonstration cities" throughout the country. Although these local campaigns, like those organized by the HNU and later the HPA, were not coordinated on a national level, they were, in the words of one scholar, "sufficiently threatening or persuasive to precipitate a national urban policy."[40]

Johnson's 1966 Demonstration Cities and Metropolitan Development Act sought to "build not just housing units, but neighborhoods, not just construct schools, but to educate children, not just raise income, but to create beauty and end the poisoning of our environment."[41] Community organizations such as the HPA and the HNU were already working toward these same goals, and with very limited resources. The city's antipoverty agency, CPI, and later its Model Cities governing board, actively sought to dismantle these community organizations, denying them funds, targeting their leaders for harassment and arrest, and defusing their power in the community through the displacements and disruptions of urban renewal.

Bracing for Summer

Even after Newark went down—and Detroit and Spanish Harlem and Hartford and Syracuse and all the rest—many believed (some merely hoped, others even prayed) that it would not happen in New Haven.

—Bernard Asbell, "They Said It Wouldn't Happen in New Haven," *New York Times*, September 3, 1967, p. 151

Between May and July of 1967, incidents of civil unrest were reported in nearly twenty cities, large and small, across the country. As the press reported "race riots" from coast to coast, there was some sense among national policy makers and urban fire watchers that New Haven would be exempt, with its nationally renowned antipoverty initiatives and its highly publicized urban renewal successes. In the McCone Commission Report, charged with investigating the Watts riots of 1965, New Haven was cited as a "model city," where "a great deal ha[d] been done" for poor African Americans.[42] One *New York Times* account proclaimed that the city had "so disproportionately and for so long bagged federal dollars in the cause of remaking itself" that it had become known among bureaucrats as "Fund City," playing on New York's distinction of "Fun City." By 1967, the city had "bagged" more than $120 million for urban renewal programs, breaking down to roughly $800 per man, woman and child. Its closest competitor, Newark, had spent only $286 per person.[43] "Yeah, $800 is my share," said an "angry negro" in front of a "shabby row of tenements," according to one *New York Times* reporter. "But you don't see one dime of it on my block."[44]

Both the RA and CPI had an ambivalent and complicated relationship with the Hill. By the early 1960s, it became clear that the Hill was the city's most promising ticket to antipoverty funds, but in many ways it was, to quote an RA memo, their "most challenging inner-city neighborhood." The challenges posed by the Hill—a high concentration of poor, black, unemployed, and newly organized people—made the mayor's plans for more systematic "urban management" seem increasingly difficult. Not only did the Lee administration expect some kind of urban unrest by the late 1960s, but it actually attempted various forms of intervention over the years, from neighborhood discussions to a proposal for a police intern program that would recruit black youth to work for the police department, patrolling their neighborhoods and informing on potential instigators.

On August 12 and 13, 1966—nearly a year to the day violence would break out in the Hill—a CPI official reported cases of racial unrest between the Puerto Rican and black communities on Washington Avenue. Fighting and "slashing" incidents were alleged by "informed sources" to be the result of "dating and 'molesting' of Negro girls by Puerto Ricans." In a confidential memo to the mayor, one official reported that the police, the Commission on Equal Opportunities, the Prince Street School, the Hill Executive Coordinating Board, and CPI had come together over the course of the week to calm neighborhood tensions. The police had the area around Prince Street School "under close surveillance" by the afternoon of August 15, as rumors circulated that a "rumble" was planned for the evening, and weapons were being "gathered" by area youth. In order to collect more information and ease tensions (goals that sometimes worked in contradiction), CPI staff went door-to-door on what they called a "special visitation project" to every home in the Washington Avenue area.

On these visits, CPI staff asked for any information residents had about plans for more violence, and urged them to stay inside and call the police in the case of any incidents in their neighborhood. They also informed families about a special meeting to be held at CPI's neighborhood Skill Center the following week—Puerto Rican and black residents were invited to two separate meetings in order to avoid a violent outbreak on site. "Some people we talked to think that patrol cars might not be a good idea," a CPI visitation script read. "They think that having foot patrolmen . . . is better. If you agree, it is important for you to be at this meeting to explain this to police."[45] In the four years CPI had been managing antipoverty programs throughout the city, rarely had they gone door-to-door. However, the threat of a riot, like those the nation had witnessed in Watts and Harlem, compelled city officials to take to the streets and elicit the help of many leaders in the black and Puerto Rican communities whom they had previously avoided.

As a CPI advisory committee member explained, they would have to "tour the area's trouble spots to seek information and plead for the cooperation of key persons, especially the well-known Negroes and Puerto Ricans who frequent the bars."[46] As with the city's forays into the Dixwell neighborhood a few years earlier, the CPI chose to turn to the bars, rather than to the HNU/HPA office, in their search for "key persons." (This is a mistake they would not repeat the following summer.) By August 17, rumors of interracial violence had spread to Congress and Legion avenues. Many residents were scared to attend the upcoming meeting to discuss these tensions. Those who did attend—forty-two black residents at one meeting, and twelve Puerto Rican residents at another—informed the police department, CPI, and RA officials that many were also afraid to call police when incidents occurred for fear of being "involved or identified."[47] Nonetheless, the meetings proved to be worth the trouble when one resident revealed that pipes, sticks, knives, and "other weapons" were "stashed away" along Washington Avenue in preparation for another violent clash between Puerto Rican and black youth.

Scattered throughout a CPI employee's account of these meetings is the insistence of all Hill residents—black and Puerto Rican—that they lacked any real police protection, that police consistently failed to respond to their calls, and that they felt they would be in grave danger in the event of a significant outbreak of violence. The confidential report and its various "results" and "findings" failed to address this issue, instead focusing on the extent to which useful information could be acquired through individual and group conversations with residents. This assertion among community members in the summer of 1966 is illuminating when considered alongside the tensions between police and Hill residents that would persist in the summer unrest a year later. Demands for *more* attention from the police went unheeded in a neighborhood that, a year later, would become a police state, despite the call at that time from neighborhood people to calm tensions by lessening the police presence.

CPI's analysis of the "widespread tensions" in the Hill community was limited to its conclusion, based on information from "informed sources," that the fighting arose out of racial conflicts over the treatment of young black girls by Puerto Rican youth. Despite the example offered by the findings of the Warren Commission Report on Civil Disorders, CPI did not consider structural or economic causes and left no evidence of any attempt, in the course of six days of intense discussions, door-to-door visiting, and closed-door interagency meetings, to address issues such as summer youth and jobs programs, unemployment, housing, or redevelopment.

Bracing for the return of summer in 1967 in a city with persistent racial tensions, Mayor Lee was determined not to repeat that mistake. He enlisted directors of the city's Commission on Equal Opportunities (CEO) to attend the National Commission on Community Values and Conflict, sponsored by the city of New York's Commission on Human Rights. CEO Director Richard Belford and Deputy Director John C. Daniels (who would later become New Haven's first African American mayor) attended workshops on summer riots and a handful of other related subjects in early May of 1967. They returned to New Haven and drafted a lengthy memo outlining their commission's recommendations on the subject of "Potential Summer Unrest." "There is general agreement in the field of intergroup relations," wrote CEO officials, "that riots have not been planned, but, rather, have been the end *result* of long-standing unbearable conditions and containment, sparked usually by a specific unplanned incident . . . it is like a spontaneous explosive event in which frustration ripens into aggression."

In May of 1967, they recommended that steps be taken immediately to "ease the tensions and alter the conditions" in the Hill in order to minimize the chances of a riot, but added, "This is not an attempt to deal with the important long range programs to bring about social change, but rather to meet the immediate problems of this summer."[48] Although the commission recognized that tensions in the Hill arose out of a host of identified "social problems," they chose not to focus on these causes. Instead they proposed helpful (but largely cosmetic) solutions such as more streetlights, street cleaning, summer employment, recreation programs, summer camps, and a raise in salary for police officers patrolling the area. The CEO representatives placed significant emphasis on their recommendations for civilian involvement in policing and police involvement in the black and Puerto Rican communities. "Civilians can join individual policemen on patrol on a one to one basis, either walking the beat or riding in the patrol car," the CEO suggested. "The civilian and the police officer would have the chance to see things through each other's eyes, and to get a better understanding of what makes each other tick."

Although it would have been unrealistic to expect the CEO to lay out a plan in May 1967 to address housing and job discrimination, police brutality, citizen access to redevelopment programs, and housing code violations, all in time to ease summer tensions, as the agency charged with protecting "equal opportunity" they might have offered more official recognition of the problems at the root of racial tensions and outlined a long-term plan to begin addressing them. Instead, what they provided was ultimately a blueprint for more invasive and clandestine policing; of all of their recommendations, the one most aggressively pursued by the city was the suggestion to increase police presence in the Hill and find new creative methods of information gathering. This response was very consistent with national trends. Whereas demands the previous year for more police responsiveness and protection received little attention, a proposed "antiriot bill" in Congress—heavily supported by police departments, mayors, and conservative legislators—had begun to refocus the "urban crisis" debate on law and order.

The Anti-Riot Bill (HR 421) would increase police powers and funds for policing while making it illegal to cross state lines or use "the facilities of interstate commerce to incite violence."[49] The bill had its critics. UCLA professor Nathan E. Cohen testified against it, claiming that a two-year study of the Watts riots showed that no significant role was played by either "black power activists" or "outside agitators." Cohen warned that government agencies needed to stop treating the black community "like yo-yos" who get "cool-it-off summer programs" but no comprehensive, long-term solutions to the problems of the ghetto.[50] Commission after commission and study after study echoed the demands of people in Hill and other poor communities across the country: jobs and housing. That was the recommendation of the Urban Coalition, an association of more than 800 leaders from the business, religious, labor, municipal government, and civil rights communities formed in July of 1967. Walter Reuther and Henry Ford II were among them, suggesting the range of unlikely partnerships in the project of solving urban problems. In striking contrast to the responses proposed by the antiriot bill, the coalition's recommendations were reminiscent of Roosevelt's WPA programs, calling for an emergency allocation of funds to create 1 million federally sponsored jobs.[51]

In New Haven, CEO recommendations for more summer camp and employment programs were passed along to the CPI, which immediately cut off funds to HPA's summer camp and employment programs. Meanwhile, the CEO reimagined the role of the police department, proposing that it could "act as a clearinghouse for information about the state of the city." They proposed a program by which the department could "collect, analyze, and present" data on "racial tension" in a confidential report to the mayor on a daily basis. They identified key "tension indicators," including the temperature, as well as "number of personal abuse or mocking of police officers," "number of suspected cases of arson," "number of Negro-white altercations," and "number and size of crowd gatherings." These daily reports, submitted in the form of tally sheets, would also include "arrivals of out-of-town Negroes identified with previous riots," "findings of caches of stones, bricks, and sticks on roof tops," "rumors," "contents of racists literature distributed in the city," "activity of store-front church meetings," and "major community events that will increase crowds."[52]

Although it may be too easy to criticize these programs as surveillance without contextualizing the proposal within the palpable fear of race riots in the summer of 1967, it is also fair to question the extent to which this "Tension Indicators Report" criminalized the exercising of basic democratic rights within the black and Puerto Rican communities. Making fun of a cop, writing fliers or leaflets, gathering for worship in a storefront church (the Hill's black community had virtually no other kind), organizing any form of nonviolent protest, or even moving into town became suspicious acts in the minds of police and city officials, rendered suspect simply by virtue of a combination of race and geography. There was no proposal to conduct such a daily survey in other areas of the city—the aim was simply to keep track of comings and goings in the Hill neighborhood. Considered alongside the concurrent proposal for UMIS's massive computerized database of the Hill Project Area, this was a highly sophisticated plan for surveillance of a small percentage of the city's total land area and population.

In order to gather all of this information, the police needed some on-the-ground help. The CEO proposed "neighborhood police centers" in the Hill, Legion, and Newhallville areas, all primarily poor, black neighborhoods. Like similar programs implemented along Dixwell Avenue a few years earlier, these centers were imagined as community gathering places, which would "have none of the other physical attributes of a police station." The police would use the space to hold "discussions, forums, and panels," and also use it as a base of operations for a proposed Police Aide Program.[53] Under this initiative, the CEO proposed "three groups of neighborhood young men between the ages of 17 and 21 be recruited." These young men would be uniformed, perform clerical and investigative police duties, and "maintain

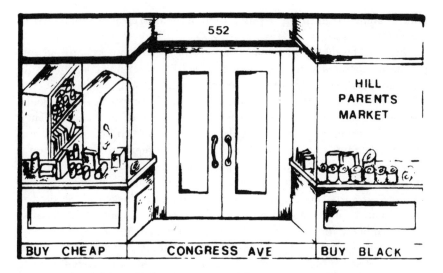

ADVERTISMENT

Figure 4.2

Advertisement for "Hill Parents Market" printed in *Ram and the Sheep*, a publication of the HPA. The articles and images in *Ram and the Sheep*—highly critical of the white establishment and encouraging people in the Hill to "buy black"—could easily have been classified as "racist literature" under the proposed "Tensions Indicator Report." *(Hill Parents' Association,* Ram and the Sheep, *date and edition number unreadable [probably 1966], personal files of David Dickson, on loan to the author.)*

close contact with juveniles in the community." In a gesture that might have sparked some degree of interest among potential "aides," they added, "he might use a radio dispatch scooter to move around the neighborhood."[54] The proposal specifically suggested that these aides assist patrolmen in handling demonstrations, protests, and delinquency problems. Each of these aides would be paid an annual salary of $4,500, an amount that far exceeded the average annual salary in each of the target neighborhoods.

Meanwhile, the HPA was scrambling to gather the necessary resources for all of its summer programs, which included an employment project, a neighborhood park with a performance space, a day camp, and an adult education program. With the price tag of the CEO's policing proposal set at a total of $81,871, and CPI programs and salaries already running the city more than ten times that amount, the HPA struggled to keep its widely used grassroots programs afloat on a last-minute $32,000 grant from the OEO. As the HPA struggled to make ends meet, the Hill Project Office reported that a total of nearly $3.5 million had already been spent on the city's redevelopment plan for the Hill neighborhood, although no direct input from the residents had yet been sought.[55]

The HPA's programs were the initiative of neighborhood people, and grew out of community planning and community labor. The HPA park, located on Congress Avenue across from the HPA office, was just one example. The HPA hoped to keep the park open thirteen hours a day, Monday through Friday, and seven hours a day on the weekends, with fifteen paid employees. The assistant director of the park program, James "Kelly" Graham, was a twenty-three-year-old Hill resident with an eleventh-grade education. After losing his job as a machine operator at Winchester Arms, he threw himself into his community work with HPA, overseeing the volunteer work of community members as they designed and built play equipment, benches, a stage, and tables. As the work progressed on the HPA park, one participant explained in a memo to the mayor's office, "no one has even taken the precaution to lock up the lumber and tools at night—members feel that 'with all the time and labor put into the park, no one in the neighborhood would dare remove one sliver.' "[56] With the volunteer help of a local contractor and the loan of cleaning equipment from CPI, work on the park continued seven days a week, straight through the Fourth of July holiday.

Similarly, HPA's day camp operated on a shoestring and through the inspiration and sweat of neighborhood people. By the beginning of the summer of 1967, more than 150 children had enrolled, and that number was expected to reach 200 by the end of the season. But the camp, which was free to all Hill children and provided transportation to its donated suburban site—as well as two snacks and one hot meal daily—struggled to meet operational costs. The site for the camp, an open space in nearby Hamden, had no means of shelter in case of rain. "Since tents are too expensive, a substitute is being sought—probably some sort of plastic material," explained an HPA memo to the mayor. The original food budget of $1 per child per day had to be revised when enrollment swelled and money became more scarce. Willie Smith and Tyrone Pulley, neighborhood men in charge of the camp's food program, contacted the state purchasing department to inquire about USDA surplus donated food.[57] Pulley, a twenty-seven-year-old father of three, quit a three-day-a-week job to work without salary to set up the food program. He had a diploma from the culinary program at Eli Whitney Technical High School and served as the day-camp chef.

Despite the extent to which HPA's preexisting programs actually fulfilled many of the recommendations proposed by the CEO, and despite the extent to which they employed a significant number of people in the community while doing the work of the antipoverty program on a relative shoestring of antipoverty funds, the HPA office was still regarded by police as a suspicious location. Even before the violence erupted later that summer, patrol cars were a common sight outside the Congress Avenue office, despite the fact that the community had long since made it clear that foot patrols were preferable. At Congress and White Street, at around 10 p.m. one July evening in 1967, New Haven Police patrol car number 9 was "struck on the roof by a bottle" while responding to reports that someone had thrown stones at an ice cream truck. The police sergeant "noticed a large crowd in front of the HPA" and immediately began questioning Fred Harris. Harris said the HPA had nothing to do with the incident, but was cooperative and said he'd try to clear people off the sidewalk. The crowd dispersed, but moments later, another patrol car, also driving nearby, was struck by a bottle. Again, the officer returned to Fred Harris at the HPA office. Harris reiterated that those involved were not connected with the HPA.[58] No damage was sustained by any of the patrol cars in the area, but these acts of aggression on the part of neighborhood youth underscored the persistent and well-known resentment of the community when it came to constant car patrols, and the police response illuminated the extent to which the HPA office was held in suspicion despite the organization's positive community projects.

Despite the veil of suspicion that hung over the Congress Avenue address of the HPA office, it was the first place city officials sought help a few weeks later, when the first reports of "rioting" hit city hall and police department headquarters. When it became clear that the demands of a police state were incongruous with the demands of the HPA—to end curfews, remove barricades, reduce police presence, and put away firearms—the force of an entire metropolitan police force, state police, and National Guard occupied what amounted to a few square miles of the city, targeting activists and their spaces of resistance. The mass arrest and detention of hundreds of Hill residents on minor, nonviolent charges was carried out without regard for what most would consider "law and order." The names and locations of arrestees were withheld, and most were detained without being formally charged. There was cruel irony in this control of information. As the civil disorder erupted, the city was drafting its Model Cities proposal, hoping to win federal dollars for a program that had as a central element the computerized surveillance of the Hill neighborhood.

The Hill remained the last extensive "project area"—a pocket of poverty and physical disorganization—in a model city that faced rising and increasingly effective organized resistance to urban renewal. Wartime surveillance, reconnaissance, and pacification technologies offered the possibility of, to use the words of computer historian Paul Edwards, "a world represented abstractly on a screen, rendered manageable, coherent, and rational through digital calculation and control."[59] Writing of the "closed world" made possible by computer war technologies, Edwards could also have been speaking of the urban renewal process, and the way in which its public modes of representation obscured the true destruction visited upon neighborhoods. The civil disturbances of 1967 exploded the "blips on a screen" or "dots on a map" perception of urban renewal projects, bringing cameras and people into the Hill Redevelopment Project area, where they saw, at ground level, both the rubble of redevelopment and the dire need for real resources and reforms.

5

Renewal, Riot, and Resistance

Reclaiming "Model Cities"

The Riot

Enflamed by the liquor they had looted from about 50 package stores (a liquor industry spokesman said later the loss would reach nearly $1 million), the wild-eyed hooligans whooped it up during a long, hot weekend that lasted until Wednesday. . . . Unless you give each and every resident of a slum neighborhood $1,000 in cash every week (and even THIS might not work), you can expect to be firebombed, looted, and otherwise blackmailed.

—Editorial, *Connecticut Sunday Herald*, August 27, 1967

As police cars screamed by the front entrance to a downtown hotel toward the panicked Hill neighborhood one August afternoon in 1967, the doorman shook his head and stated indignantly, "I thought the city gave the CIA $32,000 so we wouldn't have any riots this summer." Obviously, the city of New Haven was not providing summer funds to the Central Intelligence Agency.[1] The doorman had confused his acronyms. He meant the HPA, which had received a small amount of money from the Office of Economic Opportunity to run its summer camp program and provide other crucial neighborhood resources for the

Hill. Many people downtown saw this infusion of funds as a payoff to make it a quiet summer in the model city, as memories of Harlem and Watts and news of Detroit and Newark heightened fears of summer riots. When the doorman inadvertently confused the HPA with the CIA, he could not possibly have understood the irony. The HPA would be the subject of intense surveillance and policing in the coming months. But in the thick of the chaos that ensued between August 19 and August 22, 1967, the most salient image for Hill residents and HPA leaders was not wiretaps and dossiers, but police rifles trained on their street corners and gathering places. Guns seemed to be everywhere. If only the police would get "all of their rifles out from under [our] noses," Fred Harris said to the press, things would calm down.[2]

At 5:55 p.m. on Saturday evening, August 19, the white owner of Tony's Snack Bar, on Congress Avenue, a man named Ed Thomas, fired his shotgun at his own floor as a warning to a young man who had just hurled a rock through his shop window. Hearing gunfire, a thirty-five-year-old Puerto Rican man named Julio Diaz entered Tony's, brandishing a knife. Thomas shot Diaz in the chest, resulting in a fairly minor injury. Diaz was released by the hospital into police custody later that evening, but by then a crowd had long since gathered, and within a half hour of the first gunshot, shop windows were shattering up and down the street. Before sundown, police had sealed off Congress Avenue, one of the Hill's main thoroughfares. Anger mounted in the stretch of road between the New Haven Police Department's (NHPD) barricades. Some of the anger was directed toward a local market, one that—as Fred Harris explained—"had all the bad practices most supermarkets in ghettos have," including high prices, hostility toward its black and Puerto Rican customers, and total disengagement from the community whose purchases paid its rent.[3]

By 7:30, reports of looting were flooding the police phone lines, and the HPA office was swamped with people, calls, and police. HPA leaders met with law enforcement to assess the disorder and come up with a plan to contain it. As the police erected more barricades and stationed themselves in groups of two, three, and four along Congress Avenue, Fred Harris suggested that the city send in a sanitation truck with 100 brooms so that the youth of the Hill could begin cleaning up their own neighborhood. Meanwhile, a group of about twenty young black men on nearby Washington Street—"unarmed and laughing"—approached a group of New Haven police officers. Without warning, the police dropped seven or eight canisters of tear gas. The street erupted, and shortly thereafter, Mayor Lee put in a call to the state police.[4] By 9:30 that evening, looting and fires had spread to Dixwell, Newhallville, and Fair Haven, prompting the mayor to notify the National Guard. A truck from the sanitation department, carrying 100 brooms for the young men of the Hill, was stopped by barricades of police officers carrying automatic weapons. It was not allowed to pass.

Like the rest of the nation, the people of the Hill saw images of urban riot control on television and in newspapers as civil unrest struck Harlem,

Watts, and—earlier that summer—Newark and Detroit. But New Haven's disturbances marked the first massive deployment of a new technology. The NHPD was the first force to adopt regular use of a chemical irritant manufactured by Smith & Wesson, known as Chemical Mace. The editorial page of the *Connecticut Herald* called the weapon "a little aerosol bomb that is capable of instantaneously quelling the ardor of any rioter if the hooligan is within the range of 20 feet." The paper offered its readers a detailed account of the irritant's effects. "When squirted into the face of a violent person," reported the *Herald*, "Mace quiets him down pronto by reducing his oxygen supply and irritating his eyes in a manner similar to tear gas. Although it sounds brutal," they claimed, "it actually is a humane defense weapon since it obviates the need to shoot rioters dead on the spot."[5] Tear gas, a more common riot-control weapon, was adapted by the New Haven police so that it could be fired from a shotgun grenade, dropped in tear gas bombs, or sprayed from helicopters.

The problem with this, noted one activist, was that—like napalm—it could not possibly be aimed at an individual, but rather, had to be sprayed on everyone in a particular area.[6] The same seemed to be true of the NHPD's patterns of arrest. Men on the street seemed to be guilty by virtue of geography, their proximity to the HPA office flagging them as instigators, and subjecting them to unspecific charges such as loitering and causing a disturbance. "Pacification by force is a last resort that has become standard for the United States both at home and abroad," one activist wrote in the *AIM Newsletter*, in an article revealing the city's plans for a computerized urban management system in the Hill. It was this "pacification by force" that turned the Hill upside down for nearly a week, and initiated a long-term assault on the HPA offices and on Fred Harris and other HPA leaders. They would all ultimately be arrested on an array of charges—from drug possession to an alleged bomb plot—that were, according to one account in the alternative press, "guaranteed to induce hysterical news coverage and prejudice the public against the activities of the HPA and other black militant groups."[7] Within a year of the riots, the only organization that had provided leadership and grassroots community programs for the black people of the Hill was essentially "destroyed."[8]

The importance of Fred Harris and the HPA to the Hill community—and to the power brokers at city hall—was never more evident than the day violence erupted on Congress Avenue. As Harris left the Hill to meet with Mayor Lee downtown, Police Chief Francis McManus drove his car down Congress Avenue ordering people to go home. It was 10:00 p.m., and McManus was "answered with obscenities." As firebombs exploded, and armed police heavily patrolled every corner and side street of the Hill, families began to evacuate. By 11 p.m., the Hill had cooled down, anxiously awaiting Harris' return from the mayor's office, where he was demanding that the police presence be lessened, that the rifles and shotguns be put away, and that the state police and National Guard be called off. Harris returned to the Congress Avenue office with HPA vice president Ronald Johnson late that night, disappointed and angry. Before long, the fires reignited, and the Hill's streets once again filled with people.

HPA leaders spent that first night of unrest in the HPA office.[9] Early Sunday morning, the "wholesale arrest" of people in the Hill commenced. Police in light blue helmets carried shotguns and automatic weapons. Some brandished attack dogs as they, in the words of one contemporary account, "scoured the panicked city for troublemakers." Police trucks on nearly every corner stored extra Mace, tear gas, and ammunition. By 10 a.m., traffic on Congress Avenue was bumper to bumper, a jumble of those trying to get out and those who had come to watch. That afternoon, a meeting attended by Lee, HPA leaders, the RA, and CPI yielded a promise to neighborhood leaders that shotguns and automatic weapons would be put away and the police presence reduced. Additionally, the mayor agreed to dispatch four black policemen to the Hill to work in cooperation with Harris. But as HPA leaders returned to the Hill, the state police arrived. The black cops never materialized, and the guns remained drawn. By the afternoon, Congress Avenue was again crammed with both angry bodies and onlookers. Lee called for the dispatch of 225 state police and declared an 8 p.m. curfew for the entire city.[10]

The people of the Hill worked quickly to set up "emergency centers" and navigate the nightly patrols that interrupted their usual family routines. Their familiar neighborhood took on an otherworldliness as barricades altered the geography, curfews disturbed the schedule, and armed state troopers ran "up and down the street doing little war maneuvers."[11] Two police officers stood permanent guard outside the HPA office, and two more watched with trained rifles from across the street. It was on this out-of-the-ordinary Sunday afternoon—the second day of the riot—that Betsy Gilbertson found herself crouching in the kneehole of a desk in the HPA's storefront window while rooftop snipers in riot gear pointed their rifles at 605 Congress Avenue. Gilbertson had been living and organizing in the Hill for a few years. She had tried her hand at Yale's public health program but had "checked out" the day she heard a prestigious professor lecture to 200 students that it was a "really great thing" for a highway to replace the Sergeant Factory, eliminating hundreds of union jobs in exchange for six high-speed lanes of traffic.[12]

The HPA office was like a second home for many of its members, organizers, and neighbors, but on that afternoon, a loose and scattered collection of police and guardsman suddenly trained their sharpshooters on the office's front window from the adjacent rooftop. In an instant, the office became a bunker. "I was the only white person there," Gilbertson recalled nearly forty years later, "and it dawned on me if something bad happened, I was not going to be in a good situation when I had to leave the HPA office. I was fine in the office because I knew everybody—they considered me a friend, but I would not be considered a friend in the streets in the middle of this." As she hunched beneath the desk, she looked up at the two portraits that hung on the office wall. One was of Faith Whitney, an elderly white woman from the nearby suburb of Hamden who donated the use of her property to the HPA's summer camp, and who—each month—sent whatever small cash donations she could afford to the HPA office. To the members of the Hill community, particularly those who frequented the HNU and HPA offices, she offered an alternative model for the nature of "the suburbs," one by which suburban people could maintain an open and engaged relationship with the city's people and places. When she donated the use of her two-acre property to the summer camp, one HPA member wrote, "She read in the newspaper that we needed land and she volunteered. That's the way the whole world should be."[13] It was less than a month later that the disorder ensued outside the HPA office on Congress Avenue. Faith Whitney's picture—with her calm face and silver hair—hung ear to ear with the portrait of Malcolm X.

Meanwhile, Hill organizer John Wilhelm was downtown at the courthouse, where a different kind of chaos had ensued. While the media and many local authorities in cities across the country took to portraying urban rioting as spontaneous hooliganism, Mayor Lee and his police chief, Francis MacManus, took a slightly different tack. They decided, in Wilhelm's words, "Oh, this is not a spontaneous uprising, this is a conspiracy instigated by those communists out there." Before the riots broke out, the HPA office was a vital neighborhood gathering place, but this role was complicated by the police department's focus on that address in identifying "rioters." "They arrested the key leaders on purpose," said Wilhelm. "They sought to discredit them or intimidate people. And they seemed to have had a significant amount of success in that regard."

The police's tactic, it seemed, was to pick up everyone they could find, put them in jail, and leave them there. "There were hundreds of people—six or seven hundred of them at the peak—who, to the extent they had jobs—were going to lose them on Monday," recalled Wilhelm. "So we decided that one of the things we needed to do was to figure out a way to bail people out." The bails were set unusually high—anywhere from $10,000 to $15,000 per prisoner. Most of the area bail bondsmen, presuming the families of the Hill didn't have that kind of money, effectively bailed out on their usual customer base. "The number of arrests overwhelmed ordinary procedure," wrote one activist, causing the legal process to grind to a halt. As police station holding cells burst at the seams, prisoners were sent off to facilities as far as Fairfield and Hartford, despite the fact that they had yet to be charged. A significant number were either sick or had been injured by the police or other rioters, and had still received no medical attention.

"While everyone else in New Haven put himself on an emergency schedule," recalled AIM member Robert Gelbach, "the court personnel continued on their 9 to 4 business as usual basis." Meanwhile, families scurried from courthouse to jailhouse, from the HPA office to their own blockaded streets, desperately seeking answers.[14] Wilhelm and other AIM and HPA organizers "commandeered" an office in the front of the courthouse building. The humid hallways smelled of sweat and old coffee, and hundreds of voices—from loud halves of arguments made into telephone receivers to the shrill whines of babies—intensified the chaos. "There were families running all over trying to find people, there were cops running around. Everyone was angry. . . . No one had any idea what was going on because . . . New Haven never had 700 people in jail before," said Wilhelm.[15] The police made it clear that they wanted to keep everyone locked up. "Well you can't really do that," the judges told them, but that's exactly what they proceeded to do.[16]

By Sunday evening, the extremely brittle olive branch connecting downtown officials and HPA leaders in some semblance of cooperation had snapped. "Fred Harris and others who had been promised freedom of movement to attempt to restore order were held virtual prisoner in the HPA office," reported an AIM member.[17] On the six o'clock news, Lee declared a state of emergency and called on 250 National Guardsmen to wait at the ready at the city's Fire Department Training Center. City and state police packed patrol cars with four to five men in each and patrolled the city's black neighborhoods in what seemed to residents like the police chief's armed motorcade.

A "War Zone" on Congress Avenue

Agents in blue helmets answer the shriek.
Their function finds a victim, bare-chested in August,
And a force of four lift him limb by limb,
Carry him belly to the ground,
Playing skin the cat under glass.
They blind passing motorists with danger signals.
He screams: HELP ME! HELP ME!
The radio is louder: "Citizens are advised
To remain at home; the police are well-equipped,
And among their anti-riot weapons is 'apathy mist.'"

—Elizabeth Rose, excerpt from untitled poem, *AIM Newsletter,*
Special Riot Edition, August 31, 1967

Gun barrels and rooftop snipers formed a terrifying skyline around the HPA's Congress Avenue office as the sun set on Sunday, August 20. Sometime between 8:30 and 10:00 p.m., as cars were torched and businesses were looted throughout the city, and as New Haven police officers checked into rooms rented for them by the city at the Park Plaza hotel, the HPA's phone lines were cut. The phone company refused to venture beyond police barricades into the "war zone" on Congress Avenue.[18] In a community in which a considerable number of families didn't have private phones, many counted on the HPA office for support during the riot. The central line of communication between an entire neighborhood and the outside world was severed for more than twenty-four hours, as firebombs lit the sky and broken glass blanketed the streets.

Early the next morning, Monday, August 21, HPA leaders requested that Mayor Lee remove the 8 p.m. curfew and the barricades from the Hill community, both of which were fueling neighborhood anger. Their request was denied. Lee claimed to have no control over the state police and told Hill citizens that all of the troopers fell under the purview of the city's police department. Rumors spread that the entire neighborhood would be burned to the ground that evening. Families were terrified, sons and fathers were missing, and fires and violent outbursts continued in what had become twenty urban acres of a police state. Unable to reach the HPA office by phone, many showed up at the door with their children. The AIM and the HPA coordinated the evacuation of hundreds of women and children to nearby suburbs on chartered buses that left from outside 605 Congress Avenue in the shadow of police artillery. Some were housed downtown at the Connecticut Mental Health Center. As it became evident that beds were becoming scarce, Harris called Yale University's housing office to ask if dorm rooms—vacant during the summer recess—could be used to house Hill families. The request was denied.[19] Left with no other options, many families holed up in their homes hoping the chaos would end soon.

By Monday afternoon, as Lee granted interviews to two television networks and rumors spread throughout the city that the entire Hill neighborhood was to be demolished by fire, two problems were evident at the courthouse. First, arrested men continued to flood New Haven's holding cells, and the police and courts refused to release a list of names, charges, and locations at which individuals were being held. Families didn't know whether or not their fathers, sons, and brothers were in jail. Second, bail money was needed for those who sat in the increasingly crowded cells. With the assistance of some very dedicated legal aid attorneys, HPA launched a concerted campaign to lower bail amounts, raise bail money, and obtain detailed information about those who had been arrested. They mined the membership lists of community organizations to find people who were willing to help. Legal assistance lawyers worked to force arraignments since, for the most part, young men were "just sitting around in the jails" without formal charges.[20]

Ultimately, the HPA was able to bond fifty-two men from holding cells throughout the state, and the money came from some surprising places, including individuals who were willing to proffer the deeds of their houses.[21] Wilhelm recalled the generosity of one well-known Yale professor who, having been out vacationing on Fishers Island, must have heard about the arrests on the radio. "I looked up and there's this guy standing there in a yachting outfit," recalled Wilhelm. While there were people of all kinds crowded into the courthouse that day, Professor George Lord certainly stood out. "White pants, a double-breasted blue blazer, and a blue yacht hat. I did a double take," remembered Wilhelm. Lord held in his hand the deed to his St. Ronan Street house, "worth probably as much as all the other houses combined." Other supportive members of the Yale community also came to the aid of the movement, including one law professor who, according to Wilhelm and Gilberston, always kept a significant amount of cash stashed in a book on his library shelf in case someone needed to be bailed out in the middle of the night.

Often left out of the accounts of arrests made during the summer riots of the 1960s is the extent to which mass arrests—many subsequently dismissed—caused significant hardships for the families involved. Not only were the homes and small businesses of the Hill quite literally in the line of fire, the families divided and scattered to flee the violence and the police, and services such as trash collection, and sometimes phone and electricity interrupted, but hundreds were arrested, detained, and held for days—whether or not they were guilty of any crimes. They faced the loss of jobs, along with the accumulation of legal fees in excess of $100–$150, an amount that few Hill families could afford.[22] Groups like AIM, New Haven Legal Assistance, and HPA collected donations to assist the families of those detained, while they aggressively pressed the city to provide information about the hundreds who crowded every available square foot of cell space in the greater New Haven area.

"There are no organized efforts or organized groups behind the disturbances," Mayor Lee told television reporters, yet the police presence was noticeably greater around the HPA office, and the neighborhood leaders who had been trying for the past forty-eight hours to restore peace and order to their community would soon find that the holding cells at the police station were starting to look like the site of an HPA event. By that evening, the Hill had quieted down as fires flared in other New Haven neighborhoods. A citywide curfew was being aggressively enforced only in black and Puerto Rican neighborhoods by police officers working twenty-hour shifts. Before the night was over, the HPA office went dark and the radio fell silent. The electricity had been cut.[23] It was clear that 605 Congress Avenue was under attack, revealing that the mayor and the police understood its symbolic weight as a neighborhood space of resistance, but suggesting that they failed to understand its logistical importance as the Hill's most viable, responsive neighborhood institution.

By Tuesday, August 22, the word on the street was that everything would go back to "normal" in the Hill if only the police left, along with their guns, dogs, tear gas, and Mace. By that afternoon, when it became apparent that this wasn't going to happen, the looting and bombing started early. Police patrols followed suit: by 3 p.m., heavily armed state and city police walked the streets. The city reported an "incalculable" loss of downtown shopping business because, as described by *Progressive Architecture*, the riot areas formed a "ring" around the downtown shopping "Mecca," a ring through which suburban shoppers preferred not to pass.[24] It seemed that the people of the Hill, Dixwell, Fair Haven, and Newhallville (where "rioting" was heaviest) had turned the Ring Road geography on its head, and with the help of an overly aggressive and deliberately visible police presence, had asserted their presence in the master plan of New Haven. A confidential police report issued after the disturbances would, however, reveal a very different story.

With shopping revenues irreparably damaged, suburban neighbors scared out of their wits, and downtown centers of business and government threatened, Mayor Lee and the city's police chief ordered 650 state and city police officers, armed with gas masks, rifles, Mace, tear gas, riot sticks, and riot guns, to "penetrate" all riot areas. Chief McManus issued orders to arrest anyone refusing to "clear the streets." The number of arrests increased that night. The *New Haven Register* reported that by Tuesday there were 350 people in custody, but HPA and AIM accounts asserted that the numbers were much higher. The *Register* also reported that many were charged with "carrying a dangerous weapon," but in grassroots accounts of the events, the guns were in the hands of the police, or in the hands of white vigilantes who rushed into riot areas to "help" the police.[25]

The pacification of the Hill by police force meant not only an aggressive and highly visible armed presence on street corners and rooftops, but also a tight control on the collective voice of the neighborhood, and the flow of information in and out of the barricaded area. A number of Hill residents were arrested early in the morning as they attempted to hang up fliers announcing a mass meeting planned for Wednesday evening. The day after HPA office phone lines were severed, a man was arrested for carrying a bullhorn after curfew.[26] Considering the range of weapons in the hands of hundreds of police officers, this seemed especially ironic to angry Hill residents, who were already incensed by what they saw as draconian enforcement of the curfew. That night, a number of residents stole police department receivers in order to monitor the police and get some account of the events taking place in other parts of the city. This was an act of community resistance—and in some respects, an act of warfare—reclaiming collective voice and reversing the direction of surveillance. People were starved for information about the identity and whereabouts of those who had been arrested, and desperate to see the armed police presence on their streets reduced; one of the first pieces of information that they were able to glean from the stolen radios was that the police had been given permission to sweep all riot areas throughout the city and seal off all streets.

By Tuesday night, the Hill was fairly quiet, but disorder on Dixwell, Grand, and Legion avenues intensified. A firebomb shattered the window of a Legion Avenue bakery, and then another exploded in a house down the street. According to the *Register*, the fire department answered thirty-eight alarms in twelve hours. "All the fires appeared suspicious," said the fire chief. "I can't remember one fire not considered as having been started."[27] The fire chief said firefighters responding to an alarm at a housing authority office on Ashmun Street were "pelted with objects from rooftops." The *Register* reported that police officers were injured by "rocks, bottles, and flying glass."[28] But the account provided by residents told a different story. Tuesday night, police allegedly beat the heads of two young Dixwell men against a brick wall. In the Hill, a young woman was allegedly assaulted by police after calling to them for help. The police told the press that, in the course of the rioting, they had still fired "not a single shot." "Bull!" said a young Dixwell man in response to that claim during an interview with *Progressive Architecture*.[29]

"There is no trust in Lee or the police," Fred Harris told the *Register* on Tuesday. "There's no dialogue between the black community and downtown."[30] The relationship—or rather the distance—between black New Haven and those who made decisions in city hall was defined geographically. It had been for a long time, but the sense of distance and irreconcilability was made tangible by the events of August 19–23, 1967, as Hill community leaders attempted to work with the police and the mayor to calm tensions and restore order. They were subsequently cut out of the process and, in some cases, arrested or antagonized.

By Wednesday afternoon, the courthouse efforts of AIM, HPA, and Legal Assistance were beginning to pay off. Bails were reduced to about one-tenth their original amounts and activists were able to secure a partial list of detainees. Many had already been released, and AIM and HPA sent vans to pick them up at various jails and deliver them home.[31] The curfew remained in effect, and police kept their guns drawn, but there seemed to be less of a visible presence on the street. By eight o'clock Wednesday evening, an air of normalcy fell over the looted and burned skeleton of Congress Avenue as kids played a game of horseshoe in the nearby children's park. On Thursday the curfew was lifted, as was the official state of emergency, which had lasted 111 long summer hours. But it would be a long time before the Hill would recover—socially, economically, and physically. A week after the first arrests were made, many still waited in holding cells, and AIM member Robert Gelbach reported that, still, "no public agency possesses a complete and accurate list of the persons being held. Each day a new name or two reaches us and the process of locating the prisoner and finding bail funds begins again."[32]

The Aftermath

NASA announced a plan for a space mirror
Which could be orbited to light up
Much of South Vietnam at night
And thus curb guerrilla activity.

Law And Order sits before the Looking Glass
Which says: "You are the fairest of them all."
It cracks when you see the whites of their lies.
— Elizabeth Rose, excerpt from untitled poem, *AIM Newsletter,*
Special Riot Edition, August 31, 1967[33]

The August civil disturbances and their aftermath were both trying and revealing; they tested the limits of white liberal New Haven's patience, the strength of leadership in the black community, and the lengths to which the police and city hall were willing to go to protect the image of the "model city." They also revealed the strength of cross-racial alliances, and the ease with which city hall was willing to sell out the indigenous leaders on whom they had depended in the past to keep the Hill under control. HPA was the most glaring example of this sudden reversal. Earlier that month, the organization had received a "Citizen of the Month" award from the *New Haven Register* for its work on developing neighborhood parks and a summer camp for the children of the Hill. After the disturbances ended, the paper essentially blamed the HPA for the rioting.[34] Four days after the disorder had subsided, Fred Harris recalled, "the news people came in anxious to find out why the model city had blown up." Harris and others who had fought for community control over the shape and scope of this "model" but had lamented and attempted to stop the wave of rioting in the city saw its aftermath as an opportunity to directly challenge the notion that New Haven was any kind of model. "New Haven was supposed to be different," he said. "We told them if they had ever stopped and looked past all the fancy words and the downtown buildings, they would know why things happened."[35]

The New Haven Police Department issued a confidential memo just a month later in which they revealed some surprising findings, which—if publicized—would undercut the city's plans for the Hill and debunk common assertions that the HPA and its members were dangerous agitators, responsible for the disturbances. It turned out that most of those who rioted lived not in the Hill but in other areas of New Haven, or in the suburbs. Moreover, when it came to arrests for violent or weapons-related charges, the majority of the alleged offenders were, in fact, white. "The proportion of whites involved rises steadily from the first day . . . reaching equal proportions by the last two days," reported the NHPD.[36] On the fifth day of the disturbance, a majority of those arrested (53 percent) were white, despite the fact that all of the incidents occurred in black neighborhoods, and most of the arrests occurred in the central Hill area.

This meant that "outside agitators" had come into the Hill in large numbers to incite or exacerbate the violence. These were largely men from the suburbs or white areas of the city, not the "outside agitators" ("communist elements") alleged by government officials and the mainstream press to have instigated riots of the 1940s, and thought by many to be responsible for this later round of civil unrest. Although whites accounted for only about a quarter of the more than 550 recorded arrests, they accounted for nearly half of those arrested on weapons charges, and the majority of those individuals came from the suburbs.[37] Furthermore, the New Haven Police Department concluded that the riots were not overwhelmingly "a teen-age disturbance," nor were they "overwhelmingly non-white." Whites "accounted for a larger proportion of teen-agers, as well as a larger number of older men, including many drunks," the NHPD reported.[38] The police report showed that the most violent offenses, such as weapons violations and assaults, were committed not by people from the "trouble areas," but by people from outside who traveled in—often by car—to contribute to the escalation.

A breakdown of arrests by race shows that whites were the only ones arrested for the most violent of crimes, including aggravated assault, assault with intent to kill, and discharging a firearm. Significantly more whites than blacks were charged with "abusing or vilifying police," and nearly equal numbers of black and white individuals were charged with carrying a dangerous weapon, despite the much higher density of blacks in the affected areas. More whites than blacks were charged with criminal motor vehicle violations, as well, suggesting that automobiles were used as an instrument of intimidation by civilians as well as police. By contrast, charges of disorderly conduct—a far more subjective and abusable charge—were levied strictly upon black individuals. Similarly, blacks were arrested on loitering charges at a rate nearly four times greater than whites.[39]

The identities of many of these "loiterers" and disorderly individuals could be found in CPI's "Manpower Databank," which included detailed information on more than 2,000 men who had, at one point or another, sought the assistance of CPI in job placement. The NHPD cross-referenced this data bank with its arrest records to determine some of the characteristics of "rioters." Their focus on these lesser, nonviolent charges inaccurately depicted the disturbances as strictly an incidence of black unrest. Nonetheless, since CPI had gathered such detailed information, the police believed they could compare the profiles of those in the data bank who had been arrested with the profiles of those in the data bank who had not, in order to determine some riot-prone characteristics. They claimed that the CPI sample was "more representative of the hard-core than of the population at large" but was nonetheless useful in exploring reasons for the unrest.[40]

Of the total number arrested, about 25 percent were identified as applicants to CPI's Neighborhood Employment Centers (NECs) where their names and personal information were entered into the Manpower Databank.[41] Table 5.1 from the confidential police report reveals both the categories of analysis considered significant by police and CPI, and the features that distinguished "rioters" from "nonrioters" in this particular subset of 2,000 men.

As the police explained, these general "population" numbers were skewed to the poorer segment of the population (what they called more "hard-core") since they were from data gathered by CPI at their employment centers, but the figures show that, by the CPI's own data, the indicating factors for rioting (or for *being arrested for rioting*) were a previous police record, failure to finish high school, lack of homeownership, and bachelorhood. But the most damaging piece of information revealed in this data set was that an inordinately high number of those arrested were involved in some way with the CPI employment centers, which meant the programs supported by huge sums of federal antipoverty money were basically ineffective. To use the NHPD's words, as stated in this report, these individuals "were never significantly affected by their involvement with CPI."[42]

For all of the information revealed by the report with respect to the racial and geographic breakdown of "rioters," many aspects of its accounting remained problematic. First of all, the police used the terms "those arrested" and "rioters" more or less interchangeably, oversimplifying the dynamic and chaotic nature of civil disorder, which involved a wide spectrum of participation. References made in the press and in internal police and CPI documents about people from outside the Hill "coming to the aid" of police suggests that white "participants" were more likely than black

TABLE 5.1   NHPD 1967 DISTURBANCE ARREST STUDY

CHARACTERISTIC	SAMPLE (ARRESTED)	TOTAL POPULATION (OF NEC APPS)[43]
Mean age	26.5	30.3
Mean family size	4.13	4.03
Mean educational level	9 years	9.7 years
Mean family income	$3,903.41	$4,060.35
Mean wage on most recent job	$74.79/wk	$65.88/wk
% not presently married	76.9%	66.6%
% high school graduates	16.7%	36.7%
% unemployed > 1 month last yr	46.2%	45.5%
% homeowners	7.1%	15.7%
% with previous record	47.7%	16.3%

Richard C. Lee Papers, Box 114, Folder 2032

"participants" to be seen taking the side of law and order, whereas black people—be they bystanders, peacemakers, or looters—were more likely to be seen by police as "rioters." Still, the police reported that although whites accounted for only a quarter of the arrests, they accounted for half of the weapons charges. Additionally, more than 70 percent of those arrests were people from the suburbs, even though suburban offenders made up only about 40 percent of the white people arrested. These numbers are more shocking if considered alongside the probability that blacks were more likely than whites to be subject to excessive arrest rates. The overflow of blacks in the city's holding cells also suggested that they were detained for longer and at greater rates than whites, despite the fact that their charges rarely involved violent acts.

Nevertheless, the report was not publicized at the time nor made available to the public, and the public image of the Hill community as a chaotic and criminal space was only buttressed by mainstream accounts of the events of August 19–23, and by public understandings, in 1967, about the nature of urban rioting. "Connecticut's muddle-headed 'liberals' and free-spenders got a shock this past week when violence erupted in New Haven, the one city in the state where it 'couldn't happen,' " declared the *Connecticut Sunday Herald*. "The 'demands' made on Mayor Lee by the rioters last week were insulting. He was entirely justified in telling them to go to hell."[44] Mayor Lee and the New Haven Police Department made an ongoing project of doing just that. In the months and years to follow, HPA leaders were implicated in every conceivable type of investigation, and by 1968, both Fred Harris and HPA vice president Willie Counsel were in jail. Counsel was released soon after when an investigation into the robbery allegations against him turned up no evidence. Harris was initially arrested following a police raid of his home in the middle of the night, during which police allegedly discovered a stash of heroin under a vase, as well as a "stolen" typewriter. Although Harris openly admitted to past drug use, he maintained that he was long since clean at that time, and that the heroin was planted by police. The typewriter, he maintained, was a gift that had long been in his possession.

Soon after, HNU and HPA leader Ronald Johnson was alleged to have conspired to bomb some government buildings in downtown New Haven. He and his alleged coconspirators were convicted in 1968, but their case was overturned by the Connecticut Supreme Court two years later. Johnson always maintained that he was entrapped by an undercover cop who was subsequently involved in a series of other entrapment cases. Throughout the legal process in all of these cases, the HPA leaders were quickly indicted in the press, even in those cases in which a lack of evidence ultimately reversed convictions. According to architect and activist Harris Stone, it was the relentless legal assault on the HPA that eventually caused the organization's collapse.[45]

But in the tumultuous years between the summer of 1967 and the decade's close, organized protest took the center of many stages. Eclipsed as they were by civil unrest in more than 100 cities following Martin Luther King, Jr.'s, assassination in April 1968, community responses to the failure of antipoverty and civil rights legislation took the form of mass meetings, door-to-door organizing, marches, and pickets. As the HPA effectively dissolved under the weight of police repression, the strategies and spirit of community resistance transformed the streets of Paris in May of 1968, the streets of Chicago at the Democratic National Convention later that summer, and college campuses across the United States as students mobilized against the war in Southeast Asia. As young people worldwide tried to disrupt the social order by converging in large numbers on culturally and politically significant sites, America's poorest streets made headlines and newscasts around the world for race war, chaos, and violence. Meanwhile, in the times and places between the live news reports and visits from photographers, communities organized peacefully but without deference, strengthening alliances across class and race, in a fight for the future of those streets. This was the context of the Hill neighborhood's hard-fought victory in an ill-fated struggle for community control over the urban model.

Whose "Model Cities"?

The board will be selected, according to state officials, to be acceptable to the minority groups whose neighborhoods will be affected. It is expected therefore that there will be at least one Negro or Puerto Rican on the board.

—Description of the board of New York City's
Urban Development Corporation (UDC)[46]

The people of the Hill had been enacting their own version of citizen participation since the HNU rent strikes first inserted the community's voice into the enforcement of housing codes. The Hill Cooperative Housing project, although never followed through to completion, offers an instructive template for the grassroots view of "citizen participation" as one in which individuals and families are included in the initial stages of urban planning, involved in all stages of development, and integral to the day-to-day implementation of a project. Rather than a "master plan" serving as the starting point for urban design, the point of departure became a conversation with the people who would live in a particular space. Their needs, imaginations, and desires would form the basis of the design, if not direct the entire process.

The city's version of citizen participation almost defies comparison because it was predicated on an entirely different necessity. "A program has to involve citizen participation, not so much as a matter of doctrine, but as a matter of simple expediency," Edward Logue, former redevelopment director for New Haven, testified in Boston before the National Commission on Urban Problems. "The success of an enterprise of this kind depends upon elected officials who must believe that it's not only good for the city but that it won't cost them their survival," he explained.[47] Similarly, Lee's RA viewed the citizen participation process as an obstacle rather than a resource and, as a result, sought to fulfill the minimum requirements when it came to public notification of meetings and plans. There was no public participation in design or implementation of design—only a limited and highly controlled public opportunity to comment. At the same time, the need to show evidence of public participation necessitated the types of strategies utilized in the process of Oak Street's redevelopment—even before legal requirements for citizen participation were in place. These strategically designed agendas, expert testimonies, and visual aids worked the first time around, but by the time plans for the Hill and the Ring Road surfaced in 1966 and 1967, organized communities were not willing to swallow them wholesale. The AIM, the HPA, and the HNU were instrumental not only in cultivating neighborhood activists and leaders, but also in putting forth the kind of alternative plans for their community's spaces and programs that made the RA's plans look like a pretty raw deal.

This stark comparison was never more clear than in April of 1968, when the Hill community took over New Haven's Model Cities program, a feat that was as much of a surprise to those who took to the streets day after day to make it happen as it was to the RA director, Melvin Adams, who could do nothing but watch and grimace as his $105,000 federal grant was handed over to the people of the Hill. The public debate was over who would control that pile of federal money, and whether the poor were "capable" of designing and administering their own antipoverty programs, a conversation that would have seemed inconceivable just a few years earlier to the New Left activists and the neighborhood people who had been asserting that the best course of action was to "let the people decide."

The sequence of events that would culminate in the community's monumental (if fleeting) victory in April 1968 was set in motion at Lee High School a few months before the summer violence erupted. More than 250 Hill residents returned to the same auditorium in which they had gathered one summer day in 1965 to hear about the city's plans for the Hill Project Area. At a meeting chaired by Redevelopment Director Melvin Adams and the new head of CPI, Lawrence Spitz, the people of the Hill were informed that "final plans" were not yet being made, but that a "planning grant" was being submitted.[48] Clearly, plans *were* being made, and a boardroom full of IBM executives could have described them in great detail, but the Hill community would not hear about them at that meeting. City officials were taken aback when they were questioned not on the content of the Hill plan, but on the lack of citizen participation in its development. In his book *Workbook of an Unsuccessful Architect,* Harris Stone recalled the central question of that meeting: "Will we be able to decide what happens in our own neighborhood under the Model Cities program, or will someone downtown decide?" It was clear, he asserted, that at this meeting, the people never got an answer.[49]

"HPA people are tired of going to meetings, offering suggestions, then having 'people downtown' decide whether or not those suggestions are worth anything," wrote John Wilhelm in the AIM newsletter following the meeting. "They usually aren't." An Italian immigrant resident of the Hill noted that the city hadn't even sent a stenographer to record the suggestions of those who turned out that day. Confronted with the mounting anger of Hill residents demanding to have their suggestions taken seriously, Spitz grew "annoyed" that people weren't offering "concrete suggestions." Deaf to their assertion that past suggestions were never taken seriously, he suddenly started taking a series of "votes." "How many people are in favor of a comprehensive neighborhood health center?" he asked. About twelve hands hesitantly rose, and many looked around in confusion. "All opposed?" he asked, and nobody responded. At that point, the audience seemed to give up. "Of course we were all in favor of health," wrote John Wilhelm in his account of the meeting. "He had missed the boat completely. He had no idea what people meant when they talked about wanting to be involved in the actual planning and administration of the programs which are going to change their lives." A man in the back of the auditorium drew laughs and applause when he suggested the meeting adjourn for coffee and donuts.[50] That's exactly what they did, still unaware of the fact that IBM and a city task force had already authored a detailed plan for their "demonstration area."

Subsequent meetings about the Hill's Model Cities program would recreate the conversational frame established that day, just months before the outbreak of violence, in which discussion concerned not the particulars of the plan for the Hill, but the question of citizen involvement in its development. Organized opposition to the form (if not the particular content) of the Hill's Model Cities program was highly effective, and the civil unrest that summer would ensure that those who weren't listening in April were certainly listening in August.

Just days before the violence began, on August 15, a group of HPA members attended a meeting of the Hill Executive Coordinating Board, the city agency responsible for overseeing all Model Cities funds. HPA vice president Ronald Johnson reported to HPA and AIM members, "They wanted to just finalize everything and get this Citizen Participation thing over with so that they could send the application in."[51] In response, HPA members proposed the formation of their own committee, which they called the Hill Neighborhood Corporation (HNC), with the explicit intention of "taking over" the Model Cities program in New Haven. The HNC would have twelve seats, six of which would go to HPA members. Six other spots were reserved for people from other city agencies and for clergy. Plans were abruptly interrupted when the Hill devolved into a police state, but as soon as the riot curfew was lifted, the HNC convened formally for the first time and "appointed itself investigating committee" for what it called "the police riot, and for the urban renewal program in New Haven."

"We want to take over urban renewal," Johnson stated. He meant that the community organization planned to win control not just of "the Hill Project," as defined by the RA, but of the form, content, and finances of the city's entire urban renewal program. It was a roadblock unlike any the CPI or the RA had ever faced. A vocal, organized community of poor people demanding control over antipoverty funds in their neighborhood promised to throw a wrench into the Lee administration's plans to use that money, in large part, for slum clearance and surveillance.

In November 1967, the Department of Housing and Urban Development (HUD) provisionally approved New Haven's Model Cities proposal on the condition that it be redesigned to allow for more neighborhood involvement.[52] It was a cloudy, cold Thursday morning when HUD secretary Robert Weaver announced the names of the sixty-three cities—including New Haven—that would receive federal funds through the Demonstration Cities and Metropolitan Development Act. Nearly 300 cities had submitted applications. The victory was celebrated in city hall, but the New Haven Model Cities program was not yet guaranteed the $4 million it could receive over the next five years. An initial grant of $125,000 would be made for the Hill Project, and a second application would have to detail the programs that New Haven's Model Cities agency would establish. "Although there is enough money for all 63 cities," reported the *Register*, "HUD will only approve those cities that have acceptable applications."[53] The success or failure of proposals for the Hill would determine if New Haven would get more substantial funds citywide.

In the months to follow, the city held "a series of meetings with various Hill representatives." The *Register* reported that these representatives could "decide which programs will be chosen and how they would be carried out." A published list of the proposed programs included a neighborhood health center, a library, and housing and employment programs, but no mention was made of the city's joint project with IBM. This "series of meetings" proved contentious, again, not because of their content, but because of their form. A February 1968 meeting of the city-appointed Hill Inter-Agency Council, at which Model Cities was to be discussed, was never announced or opened to the general public.[54] In response, Hill residents formed the Hill Citizens Ad Hoc Steering Committee to plan and organize for a series of neighborhood meetings in the winter and spring of 1968. "The goal was to bring the discussion of Model Cities out into the neighborhood where it belonged," said one organizer. In the coming months, six mass meetings were held throughout the Hill neighborhood. Some were conducted in Spanish for Puerto Rican residents.

As the board of aldermen met "behind closed doors" for four hours to discuss citizen participation in the Hill's Model Cities program ("they reached no decision"), organizers in the Hill went door-to-door to mobilize for a mass bilingual meeting at Lee High School on April 16, 1968, at which the community would officially vote on the formation of the Hill Neighborhood Corporation.[55] "For it to work," wrote one of HNC's founders and board members Ronald Johnson, "people need to come to meetings, organize their neighbors, and become aware of the important issues that will mean life and death for the Hill as an important neighborhood."[56] The community's organized opposition was based on the notion that the HNC would simply forge ahead with its own alternative plan, garnering widespread support, and putting forward its own group as an alternative to the Lee administration's Model Cities board.

By the HNC's charter, any Hill resident age sixteen or older could become a voting member. All decisions would be made at mass meetings, such as the one planned for April 16, and all members could vote. For all the debate and perceived ambiguity over requirements for "citizen participation," HNC had developed a very clear template for it. Theirs was not simply a plan for organized opposition to the Lee Model Cities program, but rather an alternative model for neighborhood planning. "We need to hire architects, workers . . . ," Johnson explained. That is what they would do with the "planning grant" from Washington that Lee planned to spend on an Urban Management Information System.

The HNC drafted a petition to city officials, which also provided an opportunity to demonstrate to Hill residents that the HNC had a clear alternative plan. The petition declared, "We, the undersigned residents of the Hill, believe that a majority of the members of the Model Cities Agency, which controls the Model Cities Program, should be Hill residents selected in a manner approved by the citizens of the Hill." Organizers went door-to-door on every street in the neighborhood. "There is not much left of the Hill," said an article in the *AIM Newsletter*. "Vacant lots appear every day—but the only way it can be saved is if we unite together, from City Point to Legion Ave." Neighborhood canvassing revealed that the people of the Hill—even those who had never been involved in the HNU or the HPA—were becoming increasingly angry. "Children that were five years old in the middle fifties when redevelopment in the Hill started have been forced to move five or six times since then," said one resident, "and now we wonder why they break windows when they are fifteen?"[57] As AIM and HPA organizers educated their neighbors about the structure of the city's Model Cities program, and proposed the possibility of a more participatory model, they found people eager to talk. "We do need 'experts,'" said one Hill resident, "but we must have experts who will plan what we want instead of what the people downtown want." He cited the plan for the state's Route 34 as a key example. The state highway was scheduled to extend right through Legion Avenue, a dense street of residences and small businesses on which the remaining occupants were unanimously and vocally opposed to the Route 34 plan. In just under three weeks, the HNC collected 1,400 petition signatures.[58]

At the April 16 meeting at Lee High School, with nearly 300 Hill residents in attendance, the HNC won unanimous neighborhood approval. "People around Congress Ave. are tired of getting pushed around by the RA, the people in City Point need a recreation area for their children, and families on Vernon St. are worried about having their homes turned into parking lots for the hospital," declared one Hill resident. "I mean, don't these people downtown understand that my family can't sleep on the Oak St. Connector?" added another. Two nights after the mass meeting at Lee High School, the board of aldermen met to consider HNC's proposal in a late-night "special session," just two days before the HUD proposal deadline. RA director Melvin Adams got word that HNC, AIM, and HPA had been working around the clock to lobby for the aldermanic votes, and that they had received considerable support from a few of the board members. "Adams has never believed average people could make intelligent decisions about their neighborhood," wrote an AIM member, "and he wasn't about to give the Hill a chance to try it." As the aldermen deliberated inside their chambers, Adams grew increasingly frantic, pacing up and down the city hall corridor. Inside the chambers, key aldermanic support came from Alderman Alan Lesser, who refused to back down in his support for the HNC's proposal. Finally, the aldermen began to file out of the room. Adams rushed to the chamber door to reason with the officials as they walked past him, on their way to the final vote. "The federal government will never go for it," he said. "We'll lose all the money!" Those present described him as "visibly upset."[59]

The aldermen returned to their seats and the vote was called. Unanimously, by a vote of 27–0, the board of aldermen voted to support the HNC's plan for the Model Cities program. "I think those who feel that the little fellow in the street cannot plan what he needs to have planned and needs others to plan for him are wrong," said Alderman Lesser. "We are going to give the people a chance for them to explore ideas, to develop ideas, and plan. . . . We are going to go all the way with them. There should not be any question."[60] The amendment read that night declared that all federal Model Cities money would go directly to the HNC, rather than the city's Hill Executive Coordinating Board. For the first time in the history of New Haven's urban renewal program, the federal money intended to "renew" the city would not go to the RA or CPI. In response to Adams' threat that such a decision would threaten the city's ability to win the grant, Lesser stated, "Something is very wrong with our federal government if a plan like this is not accepted. People can plan their own program. I am at a loss to see an agency of the government reject a plan because we have given every penny of the planning grant to the people."[61]

The aldermanic hall erupted with applause, in a scene that was repeatedly and for years to come described as "jubilant." Hill residents, many of whom had been sitting nervously for hours, took to their feet all at once, applauding, darting across the room to congratulate one another, or to thank Alderman Lesser. It suddenly became evident that the chamber was packed with families, and that—in a reversal of recent events—the Hill had invaded downtown, and had emerged victorious. It was a victory that had the potential for implications far beyond New Haven. "We can prove to other communities in the [Model Cities] program that grass roots can become effective in model cities planning," said Alderman Bartholomew Guida. Shortly thereafter, both Mayor Lee and the RA signed on to the plan, calling it "a good beginning." They urged the federal government to give its approval, and just as it had been so many times before in its dealings with Mayor Richard Lee, the federal government was happy to oblige.

In New Haven, as in struggles over Model Cities funds in Philadelphia, St. Louis, Boston, Chicago, and Oakland, to name just a few, the epilogue to this story does not see the people's victory that evening through to completion. While the HNC, HPA, and AIM were able—if only temporarily—to change the city's power relationship with the Hill neighborhood, and—if only momentarily—to call into question urban renewal's problematic decision-making process, this all happened just in time for an event that would mark the beginning of the end for citizen-driven programs: the election of Richard M. Nixon. His national "Special Committee on Urban Renewal" mirrored the makeup of Lee's various agencies—one lawyer, four professors, two insurance company presidents, and two finance company presidents would decide the fate of the poor. In January 1969, after three months of studies, the committee called for the "dispersal of low income housing to suburban communities" and warned against putting too much decision-making power in the hands of grassroots organizations like the HNC. "The most satisfactory approach is that of public discussion and hearings before an official body," declared the committee, "with the final discussion left to the regularly elected members of the local group." As New Haven activist and architect David Dickson pointed out, this was the very "formula" used by the city's RA since its conception to push through a program that went against the wishes of the people.[62]

The already watered-down "citizen participation" requirements of the Johnson administration were explicitly eliminated when Nixon took office in January. He kept a strict policy of avoiding the name "Demonstration Cities" in favor of "Model Cities," echoing Strom Thurmond in his assertion that the former carried "too sinister a connotation."[63] Nixon announced that the program would serve as "an administrative device to improve federal services," and his secretary of housing and urban development, George Romney, told the *New York Times* that city hall would have "final control and responsibility over all Model Cities funds." By May 1969,

HUD had an official policy of denying funds to all projects initiated by community groups.[64] In the words of one member of Johnson's original Demonstration Cities Task Force, and author of a book-length study of the program, within months of Nixon's inauguration, "The word was out: deemphasize participation."[65]

New Haven's battle over Demonstration Cities funds was one of many that year played out in courtrooms, city halls, and "project areas" across the country. In some cases, cities fought with the federal government, whereas in others, as in New Haven, local community groups fought with city hall. At the root of these clashes were the vagueness of citizen participation requirements, and the often insufficiently explicit differences between the language of the Economic Opportunity Act of 1964 and the Demonstration Cities and Metropolitan Development Act of 1966. While the Economic Opportunity Act called for programs "developed, conducted, and administered with the maximum feasible participation of residents of the areas and members of the groups served," the Demonstration Cities Act suggested that programs "should foster the development of local and private initiative and widespread participation—especially from the demonstration area—in the planning and execution of the program."[66] A wide variety of programs took shape under the 1966 Demonstration Cities Act, but "citizen participation" was by no means a defining feature. A 1973 study of seventy-seven cities found that fewer than half had any citizens involved in the creation and development of Model Cities programs, and citizen approval of the city's proposals was necessary in only forty-eight cities.[67] Compounding confusions and misunderstandings about legal requirements for citizen involvement was the extent to which both community groups and city officials seized upon their own interpretations of the legislation in a time of both fear and possibility.

Of the 150 cities receiving planning grants totaling more than $290 million, 52 "Demonstration Cities" were still waiting for their money a year later, due to conflicts over citizen participation guidelines. In Philadelphia, a community-elected citizens' group, the Area-Wide Council (AWC), sued HUD for "illegally stripping the board of power." AWC's president, Rev. J. Jerome Cooper, told the *New York Times*, "the community has a right to be involved in decisions and policymaking." The lawsuit was dismissed by the U.S. District Court, but urban renewal programs were suspended in North Philadelphia as the fight continued. Meanwhile, in Boston, 63,000 residents of that city's "demonstration area" elected an eighteen-member board, which proposed a plan for a community development corporation to create neighborhood capital and jobs. HUD refused to recognize the board despite city hall's cooperation, and the mayor supported a delegation of board members in the decision to head to Washington "to protest."

A $5 million HUD grant to St. Louis came with the caveat that the city revise a democratically -ratified ordinance reserving ten out of seventeen seats on the Model Cities Elective Board for project-area residents. The ordinance gave community members veto power over city hall. Nixon officials insisted they had "not moved against citizen participation," but simply that they wanted to recognize the powers and responsibilities of regularly elected officials. "We were sold down the river on citizen participation," said Arthur J. Kennedy, director of the St. Louis Model City Agency. "[The residents] were originally promised a Cadillac, and then a Ford. Now they're being told they have to walk."[68] Many people in "demonstration areas" like New Haven's Hill neighborhood were choosing, instead, to march. Increasingly, those marches were uphill.

Severe cuts to HUD and the reorganization of the Model Cities program delayed the planning process in the Hill, and control of whatever federal money existed went back into the hands of downtown officials. As plans to redevelop the Hill, and later the Newhallville and Fair Haven neighborhoods fell to the wayside, local critics—including a group of former RA employees—charged that the agency wasted time and money on "prestige downtown projects like the Coliseum, the Knights of Columbus Office Building, and the State Street Garage."[69] Downtown certainly was imagined to be the *New* New Haven's economic engine and international showplace, and to the extent that city hall conceded whatever Model Cities plans it had for the Hill, that may simply have been a reflection of the neighborhood's marginality. The Hill neighborhood offered an opportunity to bring in significant antipoverty funds, but as federal support for HUD waned, and the Nixon administration, like Richard Lee, looked to corporate models to solve urban problems, the RA pushed forward with renewed enthusiasm for a plan to remake downtown into a modern showplace.

Its bravado would be checked by an organized and angry group of residents who had a very different vision of what a downtown should be. "Everyone knows throughout the country that there were riots in the Model City, [and] that these riots were caused by frustrations created by the whole urban renewal program," declared a 1969 public statement by an organization called "People Against the Garage," which formed in the thick of a fierce battle to halt the construction of a half-mile-long, six-story-high parking garage on State Street's downtown corridor. "Let's now try to make New Haven known for putting the redevelopment bulldozer into reverse."[70]

6

The City and the Six-Lane Highway

Bread and Roses and Parking Garages

> *It won't be a six-lane highway, but two three-lane roads.*
> —Redevelopment Agency official speaking
> at a 1968 public meeting in defense of a plan
> to widen State Street into a six-lane highway
> and build a half-mile-long parking garage[1]

> *It is clear that such public hearings are a farce. The city does its planning in secret with the corporations, not in public with the people.*
> —Harris Stone, testimony at public hearing on
> State Street Renewal Plan, October 23, 1969

By May of 1967, New Haven's prominence as an urban renewal showplace had long since waned, but the legacy of Lee's unfinished vision persisted in plans for highway ramps, parking garages, and high-speed, six-lane stretches of road through the center of the city. At that time, the *New York Times* reported that "planners and urban experts" across the country had turned their attention to two particular projects—the New Orleans Expressway, which had been "under planning and attack for 10 years," and a 600-foot, $14.6 million "tension bridge" to span Baltimore's Inner Harbor. Both projects were controversial proposals that intensified what the *Times* called the "urban expressway debate," one that had failed to materialize in New Haven when Oak Street was cleared to make way for a highway ramp in the 1950s, but which nonetheless took center stage a decade later.

The Baltimore bridge was seen by some as a potential "trademark for Baltimore in this century," and by others as a sure death sentence for the neighborhoods at either end of the fourteen-lane span. The New Orleans project, like New Haven's master plan, called for six lanes of high-speed traffic to shoot across the edge of the city's historic Vieux Carre, cutting by the corner of Jackson Square, a National Historic Landmark. "Few subjects have stirred more local controversy," wrote *New York Times* architectural critic Ada Louise Huxtable. Citing preservationist and environmental reasons for opposition, Huxtable reported, "Almost every city is split down the middle today between the need for new traffic arteries and the displacement and blight that giant roadways seem to bring in their wake."[2] But New Haven didn't seem to be split anywhere near the middle when plans for a six-lane divided highway and a massive parking garage threatened a low-rent downtown section of the city, home to a dense collection of small businesses, light industry, and cheap apartment buildings. In fact, the State Street Redevelopment and Renewal Plan, which was tied to controversial and covert plans for a six-lane loop highway through the city, was roundly condemned by citizen groups, and significantly revised by a vote of the city's board of aldermen after a series of public hearings attended by hundreds of angry and organized people.

Resistance to the city's plan for State Street mobilized in and around particular neighborhood spaces, while bringing together residents from different neighborhoods and backgrounds to fight for a new urban model. This model took into account the changing regional framework of urban life in which automobile traffic was an unavoidable reality in and out of growing suburbs, but in which a combination of improved public transportation and a system of peripheral parking garages would keep the city accessible to those who lived outside of it, while keeping its interior spaces intact and both economically and geographically accessible to those who wanted to live urban lives. This fight in New Haven unfolded as the ongoing "urban expressway debate" extended its reach beyond dense and decaying downtowns. Even for those who chose the seclusion and quiet of rural and suburban areas over the "street ballet" of the city, and who defined their ideal communities in very different ways, six-lane expressways posed a significant threat. "We love silence," said Mrs. Milton S. Ross, who moved with her husband, a doctor, to suburban Bedford, New York, in 1956. Forty miles north of New York City, the Rosses built a high-ceilinged house on eight acres of land, nestled between two wildlife sanctuaries. Before too long, six concrete lanes of Interstate 87, a thirty-one-mile highway built with nearly $50 million in federal aid, took out the houses of three of their neighbors, then gobbled up six acres of the Rosses' own land. "And now [the silence] is gone," said Mrs. Ross. "When I drive home, it's not home anymore. We're not a neighborhood anymore."[3]

Bedford's residents tried to stop the expressway, taking the State Highway Commission all the way to the Federal District Court. The judge told them it was too late, and the town of Bedford was cut in half by six high-speed lanes. "Bulldozers at work on the roadbed groaned and clanked," reported the *Times*. "You just couldn't do anything to stop it," said Mrs. Ross. The visual and auditory trope of the bulldozer, common in accounts of urban renewal, made its way into the backyards of those who thought they had moved up and out of the urban morass. In the 1960s, with federal money pouring into the project of completing an interstate highway system by

1973, "the people versus the highway" became a familiar refrain. From center city to wildlife sanctuary, people fought six-lane highways in their backyards. As the story (and its realities) reached beyond pockets of the urban poor, the parking garages and multilane highways that had, a decade earlier, signaled progress and modernity began to fall quickly out of public favor.

By 1969, Huxtable would declare parenthetically, as if it wasn't even necessary to declare, "(The cases of inner-city destruction by expressway are too numerous and well-known to recount. Almost every one is a demonstrated environmental catastrophe.)"[4] She was speaking specifically of the Lower Manhattan Expressway, a project that was nearly three decades in the making. Along its route, where construction would never actually begin, the "social and physical fabric of the city" had been deteriorating. "This is the blight that comes from being fingered for an expressway route," she wrote, "where the uncertain future of the area is its only certainty." This is exactly what happened along the State Street corridor in New Haven, which—in the conjecture of Redevelopment Agency (RA) blueprints and maps—was a downtown nexus of highway ramps aligned with six-lane roadways and massive parking garages. It was a section of the city that lived, for years, in fear of its future.

The State Street Redevelopment and Renewal Plan sought to transform more than 100 acres of the central business district into a modern downtown retail and parking complex with a cultural center and government facilities, aimed at providing "a more attractive downtown, improv[ing] shopper access and convenience, [and] assur[ing] better utilization of land."[5] The original plan included a new city hall, police station, library, and art center, all made accessible by the transformation of State Street, a two-lane, one-way road, into a six-lane thruway divided by a half-mile-long, six-story parking garage.

While the city sought to remove "blighted industrial uses," it left this classification open to interpretation. The plans stated a commitment to "stimulating existing" businesses in the area but made no provisions for ensuring that new retail spaces would be affordable for small-business owners. They offered displaced tenants the "opportunity" to relocate into the new retail spaces on the ground floor of the proposed garage but offered no subsidies to make the new spaces affordable, and no provisions for the interim demolition and construction period during which these businesses—most of which existed on the day-to-day business of area residents—would lose economic viability.

About three-quarters of the residential, commercial, industrial, and public buildings in the project were declared "substandard" by the city's survey teams.[6] The RA counted thirty-four families and 162 individuals who would be displaced by the project but stated that "available housing resources" were "within reasonable distance of the area from which families and individuals are displaced." This "reasonable distance" was actually five miles.

Figure 6.1

"Artist's Conception—State Street Project." The proposed parking garage is pictured on the left side of the drawing. Three of the six lanes of traffic are visible—the other three lanes of State Street would be on the other side of the garage. *(New Haven Redevelopment Agency, Annual Report, 1966, New Haven Free Public Library, Local History Room, Redevelopment Agency collection.)*

Those who had walked to work downtown would no longer be able to do so after their relocation.[7] Of the families to be displaced, 68 percent were eligible for low-rent housing, of which the city had built (and planned to build) very little. Although this total number is small compared to those of other project areas, the proposal came at a time when the issue of an inadequate affordable housing supply was making headlines, yet proposals for new housing developments tended toward the "moderate-income" or "luxury" variety, such as University and Madison Towers, or the new housing cooperatives in the University Park Dixwell development.

The price tag for the State Street Project was $48 million, and the proposed transformation—particularly the image of this enormous parking garage imposed both graphically and imaginatively on the city's existing State Street—ignited a wave of grassroots organizing that would alter the city's physical and political landscape. The day of State Street's first public hearing, hundreds packed the aldermanic chambers and the stairways that led to the overstuffed hearing room. More than a thousand residents from the neighboring Wooster Square neighborhood signed a petition denouncing the 5,000-car garage and the street widening that would pollute their air with car exhaust and threaten State Street's low-rent, small-business, and mixed-use landscape. "We suggest that State St. could be rehabilitated and planned by the people in the area," a spokesperson for the American Independent Movement (AIM), a local activist organization, told the board of Aldermen in the spring of 1968. "It could be maintained as a shopping street and low-rent area for the small businesses that are being squeezed out of New Haven."[8] The board of aldermen decided, by a vote of 18 to 9, to reduce the length of the parking garage from eight blocks down to two blocks, and the State Street Redevelopment and Renewal Plan was approved by a vote of 16 to 11.[9]

The reduction of the garage's footprint marked a significant moment in New Haven politics, at which the board of aldermen, in response to an organized and angry public, went against the will of the Lee administration. The reduction of the garage plan would, in fact, save six city blocks. It would spare the Artists Audio Studio, Brown A. Clothing Manufacturers, Frank

Figure 6.2

Sam's Smoke Shop and W.B. Saw Shop, two of the small businesses that would potentially be spared by the six-block reduction of the proposed State Street Garage. *(Photograph by New Haven Redevelopment Agency, August 1967. Courtesy of New Haven Museum and Historical Society.)*

Brothers' Paint Shop, J&N Fruit and Vegetable Market, Alois Beauty Salon, Royal Eyeglasses, Sam's Smoke Shop, and Gambardella Brothers' Produce, just to name a few.[10] It would also spare Chef's Corner Restaurant, described by one organizer as a popular hangout for local activists.[11] But that particular aldermanic decision was just the beginning of the battle between organized people and the six-lane highway in New Haven.

Bread and Roses

Near the northern end of the half-mile that the city hoped would one day be a parking garage was 536 State Street, bordered by a jumble of shops, low-rent apartments, and vacant properties. At the time of this writing, 536 State Street is the home of LaborReady, a temporary employment agency. A sign on the window reads, "All Skills Needed." It's an ironic tenant for an address that was once home to a movement-run coffeehouse, where strikers came for free coffee to take a break from their fights for fair contracts with job security.

When the Coffeehouse Committee of the American Independent Movement first visited that block of State Street in the spring of 1969, they found two connected storefronts looking out onto one of the city's busy but endangered thoroughfares. One storefront was to be the new offices of the Draft Action Group (DAG), an antiwar organization that educated city residents about the draft and assisted in draft resistance. The other side was most recently a restaurant called La Mina de Oro, which, the Coffeehouse Committee reported, had a kitchen and a bathroom, both necessary for the day-to-day operations of the new "movement center" they hoped to build. It was in one of the last remaining sections of downtown still untouched by urban renewal, which meant low rent, a necessity for an organization with a total annual budget of less than $4,000, with its own operational costs and office rent to pay a few blocks away.

AIM emerged out of a coalition of Yale-affiliated New Left organizations and a collection of socialist and Marxist discussion and reading groups that came together to consider an effective means of opposition to the Vietnam War. As the conflict escalated, AIM's numbers tripled and its membership expanded beyond university circles. An undated document entitled "Possible Short Platform" makes legible the somewhat scattered constellation of ideas, activities, and politics of the organization, which would evolve over time and—primarily through its comprehensive assault on the RA—become a significant political force in the city.

"A Possible Short Platform"

1. End the war in Vietnam—bring the troops home.
2. End poverty and discrimination NOW.

3. Let the people decide.
4. Organize a new and independent political force dedicated to these ends.[12]

This platform draft, from sometime in 1965, illuminates the connections between AIM and New Left organizing efforts in the Hill, and similar projects across the country. It illustrates the extent to which the organization grew out of the fight to define both citizen participation and the War on Poverty in a segregated and economically stratified city. However, it was opposition to the Vietnam War that animated the group's formation and its initial foray into platform item 4, which would take the form of a campaign to win an antiwar congressional seat for one of AIM's founding members, Robert Cook, a young ex-Marine and Yale sociology professor.[13] The thirty-two-year-old professor would face popular four-term Democratic incumbent Robert N. Giaimo.

In the summer of 1966, the *New York Times* reported that Cook had won support among "trade union groups and in New Haven's substantial Negro community" by his many visits to picket lines, and through "protest marches he staged" after the shooting of civil rights activist James H. Meredith in Mississippi.[14] In fact, Cook's popularity in New Haven's black community was more directly a result of his alliance with Fred Harris and the HPA, and AIM's involvement in fights in the Hill and Dixwell neighborhoods for better housing, better schools, and more say in the redevelopment process. One *New York Times* reporter predicted, in the days leading up to the election, that had Cook confined himself to criticisms of the Johnson administration's war in Vietnam, he might have had a chance. "But in recent weeks," wrote a *Times* reporter, "he has combined his anti-war campaign with bitter criticism of New Haven's popular Mayor, Richard Lee, on such issues as civil rights, education, and urban renewal."[15]

Cook's 1966 bid for Congress was unsuccessful, as the *Times* had predicted, but he won as much as 25 percent of the vote in some wards, and AIM quickly became one of the city's most radical voices for change. Although it was often misidentified as a Yale group, AIM members had a variety of affiliations and backgrounds, from artists to urban planners. Cook's unsuccessful bid for Congress would be repeated in 1968, by which time AIM's concerted assaults on the RA's plans for New Haven had made the organization a much more prominent local voice. During his 1968 campaign, Cook urged people to organize to gain "control over their society" and said he supported what the *Times* called "militant tactics," such as sit-ins, demonstrations, and marches. When the reporter asked what he would "substitute" for the current form of government, and the current economic system, Cook responded, "We don't have a blueprint, but programs will emerge out of the struggle."[16] Cook's rejection of a "blueprint" was a rejection of both the form and the content of urban renewal programs, and of the city's existing mechanisms for citizen involvement.

AIM's structure, and its activist work, similarly rejected the notion of a blueprint. Committees formed around emerging issues, such as urban renewal, labor, education, the environment, and women's liberation. Through research, collective action, and local politics, AIM generated not only fights against the RA, but also draft resistance, challenges to Yale University's tax-exempt status, and public condemnation of employers for scaling back job sites in Connecticut and expanding operations in the nonunion South.[17] The organization held weekly meetings of a coordinating committee, met in both large and small groups, and attempted, in the spirit of the New Left, to maintain a decentralized form of leadership in which responsibilities rotated, and in which individual strengths and expertise could be put to good use. It became a growing, often rotating, and somewhat scattered affiliation of local people—artists, planners, scholars, and some students—all of whom participated to varying degrees. A core of committed activists worked in the organization's downtown office on Orange Street, wrote and published the newsletter, and served as contact people for various committees and campaigns. Since many of the activists were involved in other organizations around the city, personal alliances often became organizational alliances.

AIM's Urban Renewal Committee saw highway opposition as "an opportunity for active opposition i.e. sitting in front of bulldozers" and understood that participation in direct action was a crucial component to building a viable movement. A 1969 internal campaign proposal stated, "This is clearly an issue that can involve a large number of persons. Its diversity would make it an ideal educational issue for both AIM and the community . . . it is also a good door-to-door campaign issue."[18] But AIM organizers also admitted that the strengths of highway opposition as a community campaign were also its weaknesses—it demanded cross-neighborhood alliances, which were particularly difficult to cultivate. Although individual issue campaigns among different groups and communities generated exciting momentum and some clear victories against city agencies, the committee noted that "different neighborhoods in the city are concerned with local issues and don't see the relevance of understanding and helping those in other neighborhoods grappling with similar, related, or different issues." The interrelated nature of highway, parking, luxury-housing, and downtown revitalization plans necessitated a comprehensive plan to "fight city hall." "The feeling that you can't fight city hall is prevalent," wrote a member of the AIM Urban Renewal Committee. "A vehicle is needed which will collect all these various aspect[s] of the renewal/highway program and present them as parts of a single issue; that of changing the political structure."

Part of the challenge to building and sustaining such a movement was the extent to which people in the city were increasingly segregated and compartmentalized by class, educational level, race, and occupation. Organizers noted that even people who worked for the same factory or went to the same school often had no place to interact casually or politically. "One of the worst things that happens these days is that people who really have a lot in common are isolated from each other," said an AIM organizer. "They soon begin to distrust each other . . . even though [they] are concerned about many of the same things (the draft, drugs, school, the future) and are being screwed up by the same forces."[19]

As opposition to the war intensified, and opposition to urban renewal in the city began to demand more comprehensive and far-reaching alliances, both AIM and DAG sought a way of bringing the antiwar movement into a "broader political action project" and attracting new people who were "not yet aware of their potential as political activists." A coffeehouse, organizers proposed, could reach a broader public, attract even "non-political" people, and create the kind of comfortable atmosphere in which people could "explore political possibilities" and become involved at their own pace.[20] The Coffeehouse Committee reported that similar places had been established by "soldiers in Army towns" to give GIs and antiwar students a place to meet and discuss the war, and to "think of a way to change things."[21] New Haven draft counselors needed a "neutral place" to talk with people from the community, and both AIM and DAG sought a way to reach out to "young working people" in the city—high school and community college students, in particular. They sought a clearly defined movement space, welcoming and accountable to the broader public, to counteract the increasingly compartmentalized social geography of the city.

The coffeehouse would operate at cost, and a full-time AIM or DAG representative would always be on hand to "answer questions and initiate discussions." They envisioned a reading corner, a movement bookstore, and a system by which volunteers would stop by to "sing, plan programs, and wash dishes." Organizers proposed a number of formal programs, including speakers, films, and discussions, as well as weekend entertainment such as concerts, parties, dramatic performances, and even a regular Sunday "family get-together." One organizer suggested having babysitters on hand so the women's liberation group could meet with neighborhood women. Although planning a coffeehouse was a much different undertaking than planning a city, the ideology and the physical design of the shop's interior were in great contrast to the proposals set out by RA in the State Street Redevelopment and Renewal Plan, combining spaces of work with spaces of play, and accounting for the importance of both industrial and reproductive labor.

The Coffeehouse Committee met with the property's neighbors—all small stores and low-rent tenants. Storeowners felt the coffeehouse would be good for business, and tenants seemed "welcoming." "Prices will be just enough to keep the place going," they decided, and a local restaurant helped outline a simple low-preparation menu while artists and architects started to work on the interior design concepts. Over the summer of 1969, the committee began transforming the vacant storefront into a movement space. Activist Harriet Cohen recalled an afternoon spent shellacking newsprint onto the tops of old tables, around which she would later sit for meetings of the AIM Urban Renewal Committee and the Anti–Route 34 Coalition. Over tabletops covered with onetime current events, organizers wrote press releases and strategized about ways to push their fights into the morning papers. Architect Harris Stone was one of many AIM members who spent long hours designing, constructing, and decorating the shop's interior. Stone had left his job at the RA in 1966 to protest such plans as the one for the State Street Garage, so his work on the movement space that would sit in its path took on added significance.

The coffeehouse, organizers hoped, would be many things—an "educational experiment," a site for the distribution of movement literature, a meeting place for AIM and other community groups, as well as "a platform for speakers and a rallying point for marches and demonstrations."

A close analysis of the plans, proposals, and underlying vision for this storefront space, read alongside concurrent plans to turn that same stretch of road into a highway and a parking garage, reveals the importance of a collective space to political movements, and the importance of such a movement to the creation of collective spaces in the redeveloped city. Facing a dramatically altered urban landscape, organizers sought a way not only to build their movement, but to provide a downtown space for culture and exchange in a city newly designed around shopping and driving. The moment

Figure 6.3

Architect Harris Stone works on the coffeehouse's interior. *(Photograph by Virginia Blaisdell, 1969.)*

at which the coffeehouse was proposed, discussed, and conceived was a time of transition for the State Street corridor, a short moment during which such a space could potentially redefine the terrain in the battle between the people and the highway. By the summer of 1969, they had decided upon the name Bread and Roses, a phrase made famous by a 1911 poem by James Oppenheim, later set to music, proclaiming, "Hearts starve as well as bodies; give us bread, but give us roses!"[22] As a State Street storefront, the name offered a living reminder of the city's cultural and social needs in the face of increasingly alarmist demands for more parking spaces and more efficient roadways.

"It quickly became a meeting place for all radicals," recalled Rick Wolff, an AIM organizer and Bread and Roses volunteer. "Local folks [were] drawn to the relaxed, friendly atmosphere, and this was a political plus for us." Besides offering a convenient and welcoming place for meetings and interactions, Wolff (now a professor of economics) asserts that the coffeehouse also demonstrated the movement's "ability to operate a small business—and the complex benefits" that entailed. As a locally grown, volunteer- and donation-supported small business run at cost, and open to even the "local poor" and "drug addicts" who found themselves unwelcome elsewhere, Bread and Roses flourished (albeit briefly) at a time when the large corporate retail model was beginning its long-term and aggressive takeover. The coffeehouse, in Wolff's words, "concretized" the movement's presence in the community.[23]

Despite the best intentions of AIM's Coffeehouse Committee, Bread and Roses never became the popular hangout for the "working people" they had hoped. While non-AIM people did frequent the space—John Wilhelm recalls, in particular, a group of elderly men with whom he often played pinochle at its newsprint-covered tables—it was not successful at bringing "workers" into an organization that was dominated by radical or left-leaning professionals, intellectuals, artists, and students. One member described the organization as more "workerist" than "of the workers" in that its programs, campaigns, and spaces attempted to draw factory workers, community college students, and other kinds of non-university-type "regular people." Bread and Roses was conceived, in part, in an unsuccessful attempt to do just that. However, its gestures to labor, in both name and action, reflected the same ideologies that guided AIM's alternative plans for State Street: the city and its spaces should take into account the needs and desires of working people.

In July of 1969, 3,000 employees of Olin Mathieson's Winchester-Western division walked off the job, halting production of sporting firearms and ammunition at the company's New Haven plant. Bread and Roses offered "free coffee for Olin strikers" between noon and midnight. Twelve weeks into the protracted strike, which would last into November, the coffeehouse hosted a screening of Harold Mayer's 1964 documentary, *The Inheritance,* to raise money for the IAM Lodge 609 strike fund.[24] As the city imagined a move toward computer-generated assessments and models, which would predict the need for more parking spaces and widened roadways, one striking Olin worker, in the last days of the strike, declared, "We will show mighty Olin that we are people and not just clock numbers."[25] His words were published in the *Olin Strike News*, a publication compiled and distributed by AIM, copies of which were circulated in three places: on the picket line, in the *AIM Newsletter*, and on the literature table at Bread and Roses.

AIM member and coffeehouse regular Nina Adams said spaces like Bread and Roses were key sites for interaction and cultural exchange between different movements. The coffeehouse provided a venue for the literature, performance, and artwork of the antiwar, labor, civil rights, and women's liberation movements, which, in Adams' words, "put the 'social' in 'social movement.'" By locating this site in the heart of a neighborhood facing redevelopment, an area presumed to lack cultural value and a viable economic life, AIM asserted the coffeehouse's own economic model (operating at cost rather than for profit) and management design (a cooperative community model) in opposition to the one put forth by the city, big businesses, and the RA—a master plan designed around efficiency, profit, and middle-class assumptions about family and work structures. Adams saw the physical site of the coffeehouse as a form of resistance in that it sat, quite literally, in the path of what would prove to be the Lee administration's most controversial redevelopment plan.[26] State Street's proposed widening would be the "first leg" of the "Ring Road," which AIM revealed to the public a year before Bread and Roses opened.[27] The RA entered a particularly rough period of public criticism that was exacerbated if not initiated by AIM's public disclosure of the Ring Road plan, which the city had intended to keep under strict cover.

Unmasking the Ring Road

Throughout the late 1960s, urban renewal programs across the country were beginning to encounter mounting resistance. In November of 1967, the federal Department of Transportation, the agency responsible for the allocation of 90 percent of highway construction funds, issued an official warning "against planning which ignores esthetic, economic, and social considerations." A *New Haven Register* editorial suggested that the department add "common sense" to that list of considerations. The *Register* observed, "Citizen opposition has already stopped some planning dead in the route—such as the State Highway Department plan to run a connector between I-91 and Whitney Ave. through East Rock Park."[28] Although the editorial was ultimately preservationist at heart, reacting to the threats highways posed to middle-class residential areas, "valuable parklands, historic sites, and landmarks older than the nation," it marked an important cultural moment, in which this thing called a highway was understood in opposition to this thing called a city.

The RA consistently denied the existence of plans for a Ring Road, in part because of mounting resistance—on a national scale—to urban highway plans. However, to educated and practiced urban planners and architects like Harris and Joan Stone, Harriet Cohen, and David Dickson, it was not too difficult to infer from existing projects and proposed designs— viewed alongside the 1953 master plan—that this was what the city had in mind. Since many of those active in AIM's Urban Renewal Committee had worked for the RA in recent years, such inferences weren't even necessary. A member of the redevelopment staff leaked the Ring Road plan AIM's Urban Renewal Committee, which immediately began crafting the drawings, explanations, and strategies necessary to get that plan out to the broader public. Through a series of maps and close neighborhood-by-neighborhood analysis of the effects such a roadway would have on the city, AIM's urban experts were able to translate the city's complicated and covert urban renewal plans into images and explanations that were accessible to the public.

After gaining widespread publicity in the city's daily papers, this Ring Road map was a compelling tool for those who had—for years—been trying to figure out what the RA was doing, and where their own homes, businesses, and daily lives fit into those plans.

At a community meeting in January of 1968, more than 100 New Haven residents showed up to confront Melvin Adams, the city's redevelopment director, carrying copies of AIM's Ring Road map in their hands. Adams adamantly denied that the city had plans for such a road, stating that there were no "city, state, or federal funds available" for such a project. He did admit that the city had been acquiring properties, but that those plans had been "temporarily abandoned" pending "a study." The crowd did not appear to be convinced by Adams' responses to what the *Register* called a "barrage of questions," but the redevelopment director did offer them one clear certainty. The State Street Project, "unlike the Ring Road," he said, was "a reality."[29]

A few weeks after the federal Department of Transportation issued its warning to redevelopment agencies across the country, U.S. Representative Robert Giaimo, a Democrat representing Connecticut's third congressional district after defeating AIM candidate Bob Cook, called for an "open study" of the New Haven Redevelopment Agency. The demand was at the request of an employee in the Hill Project office, Charles Ashe, who said he was calling for the inquiry not as an RA employee, but as a citizen of the city. His concerns involved the ways in which the RA addressed (or failed to address) the needs of New Haven's poor. He called for an investigation into the use of federal money for what he called "partisan political propaganda under the guise of Public Information," and questioned the primary motives of the RA, suggesting they were first and foremost concerned not with improving the city or providing housing for the poor, but with keeping the mayor in power. Ashe "unofficially estimated" that more than 30 RA staff were paid annual

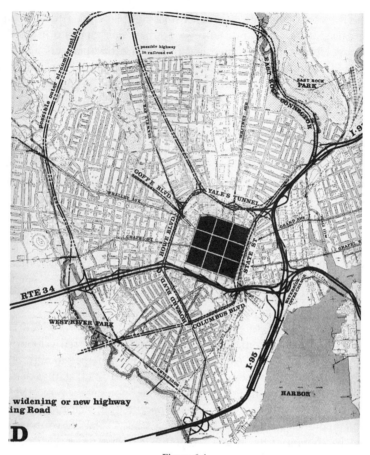

Figure 6.4

First published in *AIM Newsletter*, Vol. 2, No. 8, November 25, 1967,
p. 3, this map of the proposed Ring Road was drawn and circulated by
the AIM Urban Renewal Committee and published not only in the *AIM
Newsletter* but also in the local mainstream press. The *New Haven
Register* printed AIM's map on the top fold of the front page. *(Francis J.
Whalen, "AIM Charts and Condemns 'Ring Road,'" New Haven Register, January 16,
1968, p. 1.)*

salaries of between $10,000 and $19,000 in neighborhoods in which residents earned, on average, around $4,000 a year, and that only four of these
employees were black.[30] This was a potential lightning rod in a city with a
redevelopment program that affected primarily low-income people of color.

Although AIM and other community organizations had been openly criticizing the RA for a number of years, it was not until AIM's intervention—
the translation of often complicated, confounding, and convoluted plans,
maps, and proposals to everyday images and language—that people in New

Haven's project areas could envision the lived repercussions of these proposals, and begin to assert their own alternatives. Public dissatisfaction with urban renewal was both implicated in and facilitated by summer rioting, which in New Haven not only affected African American and Puerto Rican neighborhoods in the Hill, Dixwell, and Newhallville, but also frightened downtown into an 8 p.m. curfew and led to the deployment of Connecticut National Guardsmen throughout the city.

By the spring of 1968, much had been hypothesized, presumed, and argued about the causes of New Haven's summer violence. Calling for a complete "abolition" of the RA and the resignation of director Melvin Adams, HPA's new president Willie Counsel called the agency the "greatest enemy of the black man. The people are going to take it to the streets this summer," he warned, "and it won't be on Congress Avenue or Dixwell Avenue, it will be out here in your lily-white community." He issued this warning at an April 1968 meeting of the Coalition of Concerned Citizens, a predominantly white group, which formed to challenge the New Haven Police Department's harassment of HPA leaders following the 1967 riots. The Coalition of Concerned Citizens criticized the RA for "failing to provide replacement housing for low-income families displaced by redevelopment and highway programs." They alleged that the agency had provided only twelve new low-income units in the entire city after demolishing more than 6,000.[31]

While community organizations waged war on the RA, Melvin Adams and his staff attempted to push through their master plan for the State Street Redevelopment and Renewal Project, which they hoped would overshadow the agency's new public relations problems. The RA approved a $48 million plan for the State Street area after its January 30, 1968, hearing, despite repeated and intense objections to the plan on the grounds that it was "part of a ring road plan linking I-91 to Rt. 34." With Ring Road accusations still lingering, the agency set out to win the necessary aldermanic approval.[32]

This was not so easily done considering the community opposition and the adamant position of a few members of the board, most notably Democratic Ward 1 Alderman William H. H. Rees. Citing recent acquisition actions of the agency, Rees claimed it was clear that, despite their assertions to the contrary, the RA was still planning a Ring Road, and sought approval for the State Street plan as one key stretch of that loop. He charged that the RA had purchased land in the path of the proposed loop highway, and refused to place it on the open market despite the fact that housing was desperately needed. He also noted that the agency refused to plant trees and initiate beautification efforts on another street, also along the Ring Road route, creating a slum "similar to Legion Avenue" (where demolition was already under way) for the purpose of later justifying clearance and the construction of the widened highway route.[33]

The mayor's office and the RA continued to fend off charges that a plan for a loop highway was still covertly in the works. In September of 1968, a coalition of community groups, including the Hill Neighborhood Corporation, the Dwight Area Association, the New Haven Preservation Trust, the Save the (East Rock) Park Committee, and a number of state officials, requested a meeting with Mayor Lee to discuss what they saw as evidence that the city was still pursuing a Ring Road plan. The request came after a group of citizens met with state assembly members to discuss plans for Route 34, and were surprised to learn that planning in the Dwight area had been based "upon the assumption of a six-lane Howe St," which was consistent with a Ring Road scheme. Michael A. McConnell, president of the Dwight Area Association, wrote to Lee, "It has long been at least my personal understanding that planning for an inner circumferential (ring) road would be undertaken only after studies by the State Highway Department and not at the initiative of the city, and that therefore the Ring Road was being dropped from Redevelopment plans. Yesterday, however, we learned that the State's planning was entirely dependent on the 'operational plan' of the City of New Haven—a plan that none of those present knew of, and that this 'operational plan' had nothing to do with the advice or consent of the Board of Aldermen, State Legislators, or the residents of the affected areas."[34] The mayor responded four days later suggesting a meeting be held in Melvin Adams' office, a space that would presumably limit the amount of community turnout possible and minimize public attention.

Route 34: "Like Blowing into a Hurricane"

Connecticut's Route 34—like many highway plans in the 1960s—was supposed to be a high-speed, multilane artery connecting other larger high-speed, multilane arteries to a new, modern highway network. As early as the 1940s, the city developed a proposal, submitted to the State Highway Commission, to extend a widened Route 34 through New Haven's neighborhoods, eventually connecting the downtown to points further west, reducing travel time in and out of the city. The Oak Street Connector was actually the first of a two-part plan for the construction of Route 34. The second part would not avoid public scrutiny quite so easily.

Although Route 34 was part of the "Short Approach" plan approved by the City Plan Commission in 1953, Mayor Lee was unable to secure state funds to build the extension of the state highway until 1965, when the state legislature authorized $20 million to fund the first section. Still, the state refused to provide funds for a second stretch until the city provided a clear relocation plan for the estimated 608 families that would be displaced by the highway extension. The RA claimed that the city had an "ample supply" of affordable housing and that the RA would pay moving expenses of up to $250 per family. In August of 1966, that relocation plan was approved, and it seemed the city was on track to finally win approval and funding from the state for their Route 34 plan.[35] Things would change dramatically a few months later, when AIM exposed the city's Ring Road plan, which to that point had been discussed only behind closed doors. "Rt. 34 was to be the main spoke in the Ring Road wheel, connecting the downtown hub to the inner and outer circumferential roads," an AIM document explained, citing a letter from the state's highway commissioner.[36] Finally, the pieces of the city's many redevelopment schemes seemed to fit together, and AIM's analysis was compelling for many citizens fearing, recovering from, or in the throws of displacement.

With public criticism of a Ring Road scheme mounting, public awareness of and resistance to the Route 34 plan also grew, and an increasingly large and powerful number of community organizations lent their voices to the opposition, which came to be known as the Anti–Route 34 Coalition. Since Route 34 was a state highway, organized opposition to its construction was aimed at the state level as well as at the city officials responsible for the master plan. One clergy member, criticizing the state's plans for Route 34, said, "The State's devotion to highway building is a prime example of the kind of mixed-up priorities which assume that a car is more important than a home."[37] These "mixed-up" priorities were what drove urban planner Harriet Cohen out of the conventional "planning" world and into the movement.

As a graduate student in Yale's architecture school, Cohen once got into an argument with a professor over an assignment about "land use." She was asked to identify a New Haven site appropriate for "elderly housing." It was the only assignment for which she was actually asked to venture into the city. "When we studied housing, we studied about Latin America," she recalled. Cohen set out in search of a vacant space near transportation, health care, and shopping. She couldn't find any. Puzzled, she returned to speak with the professor about the situation. "*That* is the perfect site," she asserted, pointing out the downtown York Street window of his Architecture School office. The professor disagreed because the spot was "already in use." What about the things elderly people needed to have near their homes? "You don't have to worry about that," he told her.[38]

Cohen wrote her master's thesis on the alternative plan for Cooper Square, a redevelopment area on New York's Lower East Side. The plan was created by a community organization called the Cooper Square Committee, which started in 1959 to oppose Robert Moses' slum clearance plans. Through demonstrations, mass meetings, and public hearings, the committee came up with its "Alternate Plan," with three basic governing principles: "Displacement must be minimized, Development must be carried out in stages," and "site tenants must have first priority for the housing that is developed."[39] While these proposals spoke directly to the people living in New Haven's redevelopment areas, Cohen knew very little about what was happening near Yale's campus at that time. After graduation, she took a job as an urban planner in Philadelphia. As some in the New Haven Redevelopment Agency had done, she resigned her position in protest, and took a job with a group organizing to defeat the city's plans for a crosstown expressway. They organized Philadelphia residents and business owners around an alternative highway plan, agitating through pickets, petitions, and public hearings. It was during this time that Cohen learned about what was happening back in New Haven by reading biweekly copies of the *AIM Newsletter*.

"AIM raised consciousness that people should have a say, and that the community has rights and expertise," said Cohen in a 2005 interview recalling her decision to return to New Haven. As she had done in Philadelphia, Cohen joined Stone, Dickson, and other experts in both educating and advocating for people who were affected by the city's plans. "We could talk the language," she said. Cohen was a leading voice in both AIM's Urban Renewal Committee and the Anti–Route 34 Coalition. Reviewing the state's highway plans for multilane "speedways" with multiple "connector-distributor systems" and frontage roads, she suggested—translating the language of urban planning into the language of community agitation—that "perhaps these excessive standards are appealing because they permit the city to cut the widest possible swathe through neighborhoods they find inconvenient."[40] As the Cooper Square Committee had done in New York, and as a coalition of architects and organizers had done in Philadelphia, the Anti–Route 34 Coalition drafted an alternate plan.

By taking their analysis to the street level, and articulating it in the language, images, and experiences of everyday life, leaders of the Anti–Route 34 Coalition redefined the notion of "expertise" and engaged, educated, and mobilized a diverse group of activists. In an *AIM Newsletter* article by a coalition member entitled "An Expert Speaks," the "expert" was Barnard School PTA president Mrs. Charles Flannigan, offering testimony to state highway officials in January of 1969 about the impact that an extended Route 34 would have on her family, and all of the students at Barnard School. A set of maps demonstrated the "proposed destruction of the community," the extension of the highway. "Note, also, the route Mrs. Flannigan's children would have to take to school," read the caption, "including walking along several large streets."[41]

In community meetings, before the board of aldermen, and in its correspondence with state officials, the Anti–Route 34 Coalition pushed its alternative design, calling for a narrowing of the roadway to a total of six lanes, depression and slight reorientation of the highway to minimize the loss of residential and commercial land, and a system of peripheral parking in contrast to the State Street's plan for a massive downtown parking garage. As AIM had done with the Ring Road plan, members of the coalition articulated and illustrated their proposal alongside the state's highway plan, articulating the possibility of a completely different outcome for the neighborhoods in the highway's path.

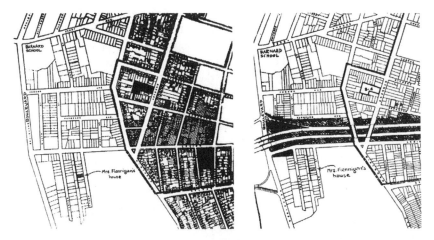

Figure 6.5

Map supporting the expert testimony of PTA president Mrs. Charles Flannigan about the impact that an extended highway would have on her children's route to school. *(John Bancroft, "An Expert Speaks," AIM Newsletter, January 15, 1969, p. 5.)*

"The experts who plan our environment do not have to listen to the people," said David Dickson of AIM's Urban Renewal Committee, testifying before the State Highway Commission during hearings on the extension of Route 34. "They are required to hold hearings like this one but they are not bound by the opinions expressed here."[42] Nonetheless, Dickson called on the commission to reconsider its plan for a sixteen-lane speedway that would "cut through the heart of the [residential] Dwight neighborhood, intensify the geographical isolation of the Hill neighborhood from the rest of the city, and exacerbate the antagonisms between [the Hill] and other areas."[43] The coalition's alternative proposal, explained Dickson, called for the construction of two divided three-lane roads in place of the sixteen lanes proposed by the state. This would free up thirty-five more acres for "community use," which Dickson estimated could accommodate 1,000 housing units, a school, a park, and a health center. The alternative plan would save most of the twelve side streets that connected the Hill community to the Dwight community, whereas the state's plan would eliminate nine of these roads and "create a canyon of concrete fumes" between the two neighborhoods. The coalition's plan would also preserve the West River Memorial Park, the only open-air space adjacent to the Hill, which would be eliminated by the state's highway plan.

The second part of the coalition's alternate plan for Route 34 spoke directly to the debate over the State Street Parking Garage. Coalition planners pointed to the Department of Traffic and Parking's own report, "Transportation in Connecticut 2020," which called for seven peripheral parking garages to be built to serve downtown New Haven between 1970 and 1980. Noting that the city was already behind on its own plan where that was concerned, the coalition recommended the construction of peripheral parking garages located just off of the Connecticut Turnpike, Route 34, and Route 1, connected by public transportation to the local city streets.

This alternative parking plan would help curb downtown traffic congestion and support the development of more accessible mass transit. "We are at a turning point," the coalition asserted. "We can plunge deeper into the morass of highways, parking garages, and suburbanization, or we can turn around and plan for a new age." For organizers and community supporters of this alternate plan, "progress" meant transcending the auto-centered city and forging a new type of transportation network, designed to serve both suburban commuters *and* city dwellers, rather than putting them at odds with each other. The Anti–Route 34 Coalition, and its team of urban planners, architects, and educated citizens backed by hundreds of grassroots activists, redirected the urban renewal debate when they refined the definition of "progress" to demand considerations of community, environment, and public transit in an era challenged by a shortage of housing, parking, and clean air.[44]

As the alternate plan demonstrated, the "radicals" were actually not all that radical in their proposals. Although AIM was not shy about its organizational critique of capitalism, its criticism of the political system, and its alliances with "radical black nationalist" groups, as the mainstream press called them, its proposals for urban renewal and highway construction called for neither a halt to development nor a massive redistribution of wealth and power. They simply proposed alternatives that would limit the destruction of housing, low-rent retail, and recreational space, and reduce the reliance on private automobiles.

The Anti–Route 34 Coalition secured a meeting between community members and state highway officials at the State Highway Department headquarters in Wethersfield, Connecticut, about thirty-five miles northeast of New Haven, straight up the newly completed I-91. On December 12, 1968, as Hill activists fought for control of Model Cities programs, members of the Anti–Route 34 Coalition presented their alternative plan to the State Highway Commission. Later that month, the coalition received a written response from Assistant State Highway Commissioner Ralph Hagar in which he reiterated that "studies show" the necessity for the highway plan. Despite repeated requests for copies of these studies, the coalition never received any response. "If such studies exist," said Cohen, "they are merely traffic counts and computer runs that do not include the probable effects of building mass transit facilities or alternative routes."

Commissioner Hagar offered another reason for the road's construction, citing that the state legislature had already appropriated money for the project. Furthermore, Hagar stated, the coalition's alternative proposal was "impractical" because "it would take longer for the automobile driver to reach downtown that way." In subsequent meetings with community members, state officials did admit that living conditions were becoming "intolerable" for families in relocation areas. But overall, Anti–Route 34 organizers found dealings with state and city officials to be frustrating. Harriet Cohen recalled her experience presenting the group's alternative plan to state and city agencies in December 1968. "It is like blowing into a hurricane: what we say never reaches the eye but adds to the volume of nonsense blowing out of it." Cohen called on New Haven activists to "mobilize as many witnesses as possible" to testify at upcoming hearings to be held by the state's Joint Legislative Committee on Roads and Bridges. The plan for Route 34 had to be opposed virulently, or else authorities would be "encouraged" in their "dream of making the city merely, in the Mayor's words, 'the nexus of a unique set of highways and highway interchanges.'"

The Language of Agitation

With opposition to Route 34, as with opposition to the Ring Road, detailed maps and sketches of the city's plans and proposed alternatives helped to translate the RA's formerly indecipherable language and maps into words and images that community people could understand. This enabled a newly educated and agitated public to see where they were in the RA's plans. These informational and agitational materials were not always in the form of maps. Creative use of photography and collage enabled organizers to make imaginatively visible the proposals of the RA, as in the case of a composite image of the State Street Garage, created by David Dickson by pasting an image of the six-story Crown Street Garage across a photo of a busy, snow-covered, two-lane State Street.

Often the movement's use of such images mirrored or parodied the RA's watercolors, sketches, renderings, and photographs. Both Dickson and the RA painstakingly documented every storefront on State Street in photographic form, but while one was a testimonial of history, occupancy, and street life, the other sought to prove blight and inefficiency, and facilitate the acquisition and redevelopment of a half mile of storefronts and residences. The city was selective about which images it published. AIM strung the State Street storefront photos together in a film reel on top of its map of the Ring Road's effect on that area, suggesting the storefronts' inseparability and their collective meaning.

The publicly accessible depictions, photos, and maps published by AIM and its allies reached an audience that far exceeded the organizational reaches of these groups. In early April of 1969, a downtown property owner named M. L. McAviney ("of Woodbridge, CT and Ft. Lauderdale, FL") wrote to Mayor Lee to say that a "good paying tenant" in his building was planning to vacate after receiving information from the RA that the property

Figure 6.6

This composite image of State Street and the Crown Street Garage was used in the *AIM Newsletter* and in fliers and posters for the fight against the State Street Garage. Compared to the RA's 1966 rendering of the proposed garage, its use of the real photographed street and garage offer a commentary on the difference between the lived city and the "proposed city": AIM's composite image shows State Street as though it is jailed by the six-story structure, and gives a sobering sense of the destructive scale of the garage. *(AIM published a redrawing of the sketch in AIM Newsletter, Vol. 2, No. 8 [November 25, 1967], p. 7.)*

he occupied, which McAviney owned, was about to be acquired by the city because it was in the path of a redevelopment plan. The acquisition evidently did not happen, and McAviney set out to find a new tenant. Although there was interest from a few parties, none would take the space because, according to McAviney, "a circular . . . came out . . . showing our property to be taken. . . . It puts me in a hell of a fix, Dick," he said to the mayor, "to meet my obligations, taxes, and maintenance of that property." The circular to which he referred was one of AIM's widely circulated maps showing the properties to be eventually taken in service of a Ring Road plan. "Why don't they stop this racket," McAviney asked, "which undoubtedly is costing the government tremendous money?"[45]

Organized resistance to the Route 34 plan continued at the state and local levels as the coalition pressured city hall, and sympathetic state legislators pro-

Figure 6.7

AIM photo collage of State Street storefronts using photographs taken by David Dickson. *(Published in the* AIM Newsletter, *Vol. 2, No. 11 [February 12, 1968].)*

posed bills to block the highway. At a community meeting at the Troupe School (held for those who couldn't travel to Hartford to attend the meeting of the state legislature at which the highway was considered), critiques of Route 34 came from a broader cross section of the public than ever before. PTA representatives, clergy, a city planner, an architect, and individuals from neighborhood corporations all testified about the destruction the sixteen-lane state highway would cause to New Haven's neighborhoods, from the danger posed to children, to the disruption of the local urban fabric. One state senator in attendance pointed out that the State Highway Department was ignoring an October 1968 resolution passed by the board of aldermen in opposition to the extension of Route 34. On the agenda to speak in favor of the highway were officials from the New Haven Department of Parking and Traffic, and the city chamber of commerce legislative affairs director. The latter was so moved by the testimony from residents that he stood up to say he could not bring himself to "espouse the chamber's position in favor of the highway."[46]

In an apparent effort to divert criticism, Mayor Lee unveiled his proposal for a "platform city," in which housing, businesses, and services could be constructed on top of massive parking garages, which coalition members were not alone in asserting was "uneconomic and unlivable." By the fall of 1969, when the State Street controversy began to dominate the headlines of both the mainstream and alternative press, Mayor Lee was on his way out of office, and mounting opposition, along with limited funds, prompted the state to significantly reduce funding for Route 34.

The fight over these two pieces of the Ring Road puzzle, State Street and Route 34, animated the 1969 mayoral race. Mayor Lee was leaving a sixteen-year legacy of highway building, and he was vacating the mayor's office with many plans still in limbo. In a special issue of the *AIM Newsletter*, devoted to "The Race for Mayor," the editors asserted, "Construction of these highways has been accompanied by the massive disruption of working-class neighborhoods and the loss of hundreds of houses and apartment buildings." Bringing together the two most recent and most controversial redevelopment proposals, they explained what they saw as the self-justifying and destructive cycle of highway and garage construction in New Haven, in which "the policy of road and garage building . . . brings in an apparent need to build still more highways and garages." AIM called for state and city funds to support the development of mass transit, rather than the construction of more of these highways and garages.[47]

In what had emerged as a political and cultural battle between highway and neighborhood, residents and organizers seemed to be gaining ground, but much of that ground had already been cleared of desperately needed housing, small business, and recreational facilities for sixteen lanes of imaginary traffic. The New Haven Housing Consortium, a housing advocacy group, announced that it would use the cleared land for elderly housing and would investigate whether the families displaced by highway clearance had a basis for a lawsuit over the conditions of their relocation. According to the Anti–Route 34 Coalition, "The city's own figures showed that highway relocation had greatly increased the racial segregation of neighborhoods inside and outside the city."[48] Amid waves of criticism at the local level, two prominent New Haven redevelopment officials resigned and published a revealing report calling Route 34 "the most destructive highway development yet."

This was the context in which the reemergence of the plan for the half-mile State Street Garage took shape. In the spring of 1968, intense organized opposition to the garage had prompted a board of aldermen vote in favor of restricting the proposed half-mile garage to two blocks between Fair and Chapel streets. Eighteen months later, in a hurry to gain approval from a soon-to-be-replaced Lee-dominated board, RA chairman Mathew Ruoppolo sent a letter to the board asking for an amendment to the State Street Redevelopment and Renewal Plan that would reextend the garage to its original half-mile length. The letter cited an agreement between the city and the New Haven Savings Bank that required the city to provide "sufficient parking facilities within reasonable, convenient walking distance of the new Savings Bank building."[49] The city had privately agreed to this provision in its negotiations with the bank during the relocation process.

Public Rehearings

At the public hearing on October 23, 1969, twenty individuals signed up to testify against the RA's plan in front of a crowd of more than 400 people. Henry Tamarin, whose "last known address" had been demolished by the

RA a week before the hearing, spoke on behalf of Bread and Roses, which he described as the "only new business on State Street." Bread and Roses customer and volunteer Rick Alper testified that there were many "people who live and work downtown who want a place to go." He asserted that places like Bread and Roses, the Draft Action Group, and the offices of another radical publication, *View from the Bottom*—all located along that same stretch of State Street, in the potential shadow of the proposed parking garage, and in the way of a widened State Street—represented the "kind of renewal which will better serve the needs of the people than a half-mile long, six story 5000 car" place to park.[50]

Another witness, Jack Gabriel of Artisan Street, referenced the summer of 1967 when he implored the board to "listen now so you don't have to call 'law and order' when these hearings don't work." Harriet Cohen testified for the Anti–Route 34 Coalition, asserting that not only should the garage be stopped, but so should the expansion of Route 34, the East Rock Connector, the widening of Howe Street, and a number of other interconnected highway plans that only exacerbated the traffic problems of the city, the need for more parking, and the shortage of affordable housing.[51] Harris Stone testified on behalf of AIM, calling the garage "a parking monster which will form a wall between downtown and all the neighborhoods in the eastern half of the city." Relating resistance to the State Street Garage to the waves of organized opposition that had risen over the past few years, Stone explained, "Residents and small businessmen displaced by I-91 and the Oak St. Connector and now the extension of the Connector to the Boulevard have protested over and over again; the board of alderman have passed resolutions and made amendments to Renewal plans demanding more housing—not more highways—be built."

Stone outlined the deal the city had brokered with the New Haven Savings Bank, and the extent to which the wishes of one powerful institution were attempting to overturn a decision that reflected the will of the public. "The people have said 'No garage,' and the Aldermen have said 'No garage" . . . but the New Haven Savings Bank says that it wants a garage," he testified. "Approval of the amendment [to allow the 5,000-car garage]" would mean that "the single voice of the New Haven Savings Bank carries more weight than the combined voices of all the people in this room and all the people they represent." Stone stated that the bank owners were among a "handful of people" who seemed to have "the power to manipulate the Urban Renewal Program," a group that also, he argued, included the owners of Macy's and Malley's department stores, who had influenced the city's decisions and plans for the Crown Street Parking Garage.[52]

The RA formally presented its amendments with what one person at the hearing described as a "slick brochure and a zappy slide show" designed to demonstrate the ways in which the 5,000-car garage was necessary in order to generate businesses, jobs, and tax revenue. Five individuals testified before the board in favor of the RA's expanded parking garage plan. A "Mrs. Robinson," representing the Council for the Arts, testified that "people from 50 miles around" needed to be able to park their cars in downtown New Haven to enjoy its cultural offerings. Joseph Pellegrino of the North Haven Chamber of Commerce also testified to the need for downtown parking, as did Arthur Horowitz of suburban Woodbridge. The owner of a downtown beauty salon, located at Orange and Court streets, testified to the dire parking needs that were crucial to his business's success, and one other New Haven resident impressed upon the board that the agency's plans for a parking garage could "not be delayed any further," so desperate was the need for him to have a place to park his own car downtown.[53] AIM's alternative proposal never challenged the legitimacy of parking needs. In fact, the inclusion of peripheral parking garages in the alternate plan demonstrates that the AIM Urban Renewal Committee understood that the need for more parking spaces was an unavoidable reality. But AIM attacked what it saw as the root of the problem: lack of good, efficient, accessible public transit.

Most accounts of the public hearing on Thursday evening, October 23, 1969, agree on the fact that, in the words of a *New Haven Register* reporter, "the Redevelopment Agency was roundly condemned." "The will of the constituency was apparently being challenged," the article reported, noting that many citizens appeared angry that they had to come and testify again about an issue they had gathered in the same room to discuss a year before. Both the public and the board of aldermen had considered it a settled issue.[54] The *Register*'s analysis reflected an understanding of the two sides that had taken shape when it reported that, of the hundreds gathered, only "nine persons, including one from the RA, two from other city agencies, and two persons living outside the city, supported the [agency's expanded garage] proposal."

It wasn't until weeks after a heated public hearing, after repeated delays, as the public awaited word from the RA, that the *Journal-Courier* broke the story of a break in the agency's ranks. Stanley Rogers was the newest member of the RA, appointed to a five-year term in December of 1968. He was president of UAW Local 979, and the agency's first African American member. Rogers shocked and outraged more seasoned agency officials when he distributed a two page "fact sheet" at one RA meeting, outlining his reasons for opposing the garage plan, which included air pollution, the need for housing and jobs (rather than garages), and an interest in promoting the development of more public transportation. He asked why the New Haven Savings Bank had not testified at the public hearing on October 23, and why the agency had never "interested itself" in any of the alternative plans that had been presented. "It just shouldn't be built," Rogers asserted, officially proposing that the plan for the garage be tabled. At that point the other officials "went up in arms," and began what was described as a "heated argument" for about a half hour, until another member, Bishop Joseph F. Donnelly, seconded Rogers' proposal. "This marks the first time in memory that the agency has had less than unanimity from its board members on any of its proposals," reported the *Journal-Courier*.[55]

RA officials worked swiftly to rectify this publicly embarrassing episode. After receiving what he described as a "memo" from Charles Shannon, Executive Director of Operations for the Redevelopment Agency, explaining the State Street Garage would mean the creation of 2,000 jobs and $250,000 annually in property taxes, Rogers made an "about face." This enabled the RA to approve the State Street plan unanimously on Monday, November 17.[56] "Mr. Shannon says there will be 2000 jobs in the New Haven Savings Bank and the Federal Building," Rogers told the *New Haven Register*, referring, in part, to the controversial agreement the city had made with the bank to provide parking for its facilities in the proposed State Street Garage. "Black people will have a chance at these jobs. And I know these jobs will go somewhere else if these buildings are not built here."[57]

With the RA and the City Plan Commission officially on board, and only aldermanic approvals standing in the way, the board of aldermen's Urban Development Committee announced it would hold another public hearing on November 26, 1969, the night before Thanksgiving. The meeting was announced in time for AIM organizers to insert a flier into the November 15 issue of their newsletter. In block letters across the top, it read, "URGENT URGENT URGENT!" and noted that the "lame duck Board" was the last opportunity for the RA to pass its 5,000-car garage plan, since expectations were that a newly elected board, more independent and bipartisan, and elected in the context of increasing opposition, would refuse to pass it.[58] In meetings with their friends, neighbors, and sometimes strangers, AIM members talked about the possibility of an alternative to the current plan for New Haven. They explained in great detail their proposal for peripheral parking and mass transit. This meant "high-speed buses, more routes, more frequent runs and cheaper rates," rather than the existing privately run fleet operated "for its own profit and at great expense to the rider." In order to create a more effective system of mass transit, AIM asserted, the city had to stop "RIGHT THIS MINUTE any and all plans that have to do with highways and parking garages."

Two days before the hearing, AIM organizers met at Bread and Roses to prepare public statements, draft a press release, and account for any loose ends. One organizer suggested that it was important to remind the public and the board, at every opportunity, of the number of times they had testified on this garage issue. Another, doubting the city's data, suggested that they look into the administration's claims about the number of jobs that would be created by the project. Harris Stone volunteered to do a survey of the project area and add up the number of employees in all of the businesses that were to be displaced, then prepare a brief report.[59] Having fully investigated the city's Operational Traffic Plan, Dickson and the other Urban Renewal Committee members concluded that it was designed around "maximum convenience for automobile movement and parking to the exclusion of any other considerations." Citing the fact that building downtown parking and more highways only leads to more downtown traffic, Dickson called this the "domino theory of highway construction." "Well," members of the Urban Renewal Committee concluded in their press release, "we all wish you'd take your dominoes and go home."[60]

The night before Thanksgiving 1969, the board of aldermen convened, once again, to hear testimony relating to the State Street Redevelopment and Renewal Plan. The results of Harris Stone's last-minute investigative work revealed that by the time the State Street plan was finished, more than 330 businesses would be displaced, almost 100 of those on the half-mile site of the proposed State Street Garage. "The [Redevelopment] Agency is trying to use the need for 'new jobs' in New Haven to justify the very kind of redevelopment project that has helped create the serious job shortage here in the first place," argued AIM's written statement. They asserted that the RA's intention was not to create jobs for New Haven, but to create "more office and parking space downtown" for people who lived in the suburbs. Outlining an alternative proposal for the State Street Project area, AIM's Urban Renewal Committee called for the construction of low-rent commercial and industrial space and low-cost housing. On the issue of the agreement made between the RA and the New Haven Savings Bank, AIM suggested that the bank should feel free to go ahead and build any parking garage it wanted—at its own expense, on its own property.[61]

The tenor of the debate had intensified. Exchanges between the two sides became more personal and aggressive. When Harriet Cohen testified to the need for improvements in mass transit, the city's director of traffic and parking, John Cavalerro, responded by reporting to the board that she "was seen driving downtown in an automobile." David Dickson concluded his testimony by charging that the RA had created a secret "dossier" to keep track of those who publicly opposed the garage. "Last week I visited the Redevelopment Agency for some information," Dickson told the board, the public, and the press, "and I accidentally discovered one of the things they spend their time on over there, instead of planning the city." Dickson claimed he saw a list of names, addresses, occupations, spouses, and political affiliations for all of the witnesses speaking against the State Street plan. RA director Charles Shannon admitted to a reporter from the *New Haven Journal-Courier* that he had, in fact, ordered that a list be made of everyone attending the hearing, but later told the same reporter, "As far as I'm concerned, that's a non-existent list."[62] By the time the meeting ended, it was 12:15 a.m., and only four people, besides the RA members, had lasted to the bitter end. The four-person board of aldermen Urban Affairs Committee rendered a split vote on the garage issue, two voting to expand the plan to the 5,000-car garage plan, and two voting to approve the plan at a 1,200-car limit.[63]

With just weeks remaining in his term, Mayor Lee called two special aldermanic sessions in hopes of getting the RA's expanded garage proposal passed before a new board took office. The seven Republicans who would take office after the final session of the year stood in opposition to the garage, and one group of incoming Republican aldermen said the garage issue was "too vital to be rammed through the board of aldermen in a lame duck session."[64]

People Against the Garage

With the State Street Redevelopment and Renewal Plan still being volleyed around the aldermanic chambers, a number of disparate organizations and individuals formed a nonpartisan organization they called People Against the Garage (PAG). Among their ranks were Yale professors, nurses, and representatives of area nonprofits such as the New Haven Preservation Trust, the Puerto Rican Human Resources Foundation, and a housing development in Wooster Square called Friendship Houses. The new organization also included many members of AIM and the Anti–Route 34 Coalition. It was a "last ditch effort," after the RA had ignored public opposition and evidence presented at public hearings, and disregarded an aldermanic decision in opposition to the garage plan. PAG suggested that the $20 million estimated cost of the parking garage could be used to develop public transportation, affordable housing, or low-rent retail space.[65]

On January 14, 1970, PAG spokesman David Ertman told reporters, "The garage is part of a plan to have a six-lane ring road around New Haven which will destroy small businesses, worsen air pollution, and cut into existing neighborhoods. . . . yet none of these neighborhoods has been consulted about the project." Ertman announced that a rally would be held on January 24 at noon, on the corner of State and George streets, the corner of the proposed site for the garage.[66] PAG members canvased their neighborhoods, offices, and community spaces with fliers announcing the "Rally Against the State Street Garage" and articulating the demands for responsive government, clean air, and "people facilities for New Haven, not free commuter facilities for suburbia."[67] Once again, the artist's image of the massive parking garage circulated at community meetings, in kitchens and on buses. A last-minute insert in the *AIM Newsletter*, printed on long, narrow strips of colored paper, read "LINE UP ALONG THE EIGHT BLOCK LENGTH OF THE PROPOSED MONSTER. LAST STAND BEFORE ITS FINAL RECONSIDERATION BY THE BD. OF ALDERMAN . . . ASSEMBLE AT STATE & GEORGE NOON SAT. JAN. 24."[68]

Saturday was one of the coldest days of the year. The crowd gathered slowly. Parking meters stuck out of the dirty snowbanks that lined State Street, and as friends greeted one another with visible breath, a crowd of onlookers began to assemble on the other side of the street, in front of the Zenith Furniture Company. By the time the march began, more than 300

Figure 6.8

People Against the Garage march in the snow. *(Cover of the* AIM Newsletter, *Vol. 5, No. 2 [February 1, 1970]; photo by John Moulder.)*

people had gathered, despite the "sub-zero temperatures." There were children, dogs on leashes, whole families with their hands in their pockets, taking turns holding the signs they had made. "Does REDEVELOPMENT run this town?" asked one. It was a peculiar parade. In the January chill, hundreds marched down State Street with bandannas covering their faces to protest the project's potential air pollution, and maybe also to keep their noses warm. They marched a half mile—a short distance as marches go, but an astonishingly long stretch in that it marked the full length of the garage.[69] A short speaking program featured two unsuccessful mayoral candidates who had consistently fought the State Street Project, Paul C. Capra and Henry Parker. PAG spokesman David Entmar also addressed the crowd, explaining that the proposed garage would serve "an average of 1.2 persons per six-passenger car at a cost of $4000 a car space," which he called "a very inefficient way of handling downtown visitors." After the speaking program, the gathered crowd—having increased in size—once again removed their frozen hands from their pockets and picked up their signs. They marched back the length of the proposed garage, another full half mile, made by most accounts to seem significantly longer because of the weather.[70]

With the board of aldermen scheduled to debate the garage plan yet again on February 2, and public opposition making itself more visible, public defense of the parking garage also surfaced. The day after the PAG rally, the *New Haven Register* ran an editorial in support of the garage plan. "One

Need But Look to See the Need for State Street Garage," proclaimed the headline, referring to a map of downtown with dark circles drawn around new developments like the site of the New Haven Savings Bank, a concert hall, and the new federal building. While citing other new development to justify *this* new development, the paper dismissed claims that a half-mile-long garage and six-lane roadway would divide the city, stating that the existing "railroad cut" already did so. The *Register* claimed that those who opposed the garage were disregarding "the marginal nature of the site," and again citing redevelopment plans as justification for more redevelopment, the paper asserted that widening State Street to six lanes "would even further reduce its desirability for other uses." The editorial concluded with a pronouncement that the "economic health" of the city was above all other concerns, including considerations like low-income housing and jobs. Beside the text was a cartoon showing cars being stacked, one on top of the other, by a crane bearing the name "City Parking," as an alderman looked on. "Hurry up and decide," read the caption, "before we end up like this!"[71]

In a meeting that the local press described as "the rowdiest session ever held by the 1968–1969 board of aldermen," the garage plan ultimately passed by one vote.[72] However, by this time, after repeated delays, the state funding sources had become skeptical. A new mayoral administration proved not as adept as Lee's in securing state and federal money, most likely a combination of rising public resistance and a changing national agenda that siphoned money away from urban programs. The RA continued pushing for both the State Street Garage and its similarly controversial plans for the extension of Route 34, but five months after the final aldermanic vote, the State Street Garage plan was effectively dead.[73]

"You Can't Argue with Concrete"

Amendments to the language of the State Street Redevelopment and Renewal Plan reflect the extent to which organized resistance intervened in the original design. In Section 603 of the plan, which prescribed the widening of the roadway, the wording was changed from its original "widening of State Street to a 6-lane divided roadway" to "widening of State Street to a two way divided roadway," indicating that the number of lanes was still a point of debate, and suggesting some resistance to the idea of lining up multiple six-lane legs of what many still believed was a Ring Road scheme. By the time of the December 23 hearing, the qualifier "six-lane" seems to have become synonymous with "Ring Road," in that this was the prescribed width of the widened roadways and bridges of each section. Also omitted was mention of the completion of I-91 and highway interchanges at Humphrey and Trumbull streets, both of which were also associated with the Ring Road plan. In the December 1969 revision of the redevelopment plan, there was a clear attempt by even the Lee-friendly lame-duck board to dissociate the State Street Garage from the broader highway schemes in place (or under review), so as to distance the Ring Road and highway-related criticisms from the proposed garage plan.[74]

Also evident in the amended plan was organized public pressure on the issue of mass transit. Although no substantial effort was made to implement any peripheral parking or extensive mass-transit system, language that had formerly been dismissive of public transit, stating, "Public transportation is available on every major street in the project area. No changes in the pattern of public transportation are contemplated under this plan," was changed to "Public transit stops will be provided along the length of new State Street to serve bus passengers." The revision also noted that the reconstruction of State Street as a two-way artery would benefit public transportation by "allowing sufficient northbound and southbound bus service." Organized public intervention not only prevented more sweeping and significant changes in accordance with the RA's vision, but also asserted and inserted a small part of the alternative vision into the master plan.

While they may not have directly succeeded in reversing the bulldozer, AIM, People Against the Garage, and the Anti–Route 34 Coalition did ultimately succeed in jamming up its works until funding and political support at the state and national levels had disintegrated. And although RA officials maintained to the end that there was no longer an intention to build a Ring Road, their individual six-lane designs for a series of connected roadways were transparent to any involved citizen. Anyone with access to a map of the city—such as those designed and distributed by AIM—could see that plans to widen State Street to six lanes, build a ramp from State Street to the Oak Street Connector, and construct a six-lane bridge at Howe Street, in combination with a widened and extended Route 34, and the shape of property acquisitions and new construction setbacks along the route of that ghost "ring," constituted undeniable proof that, regardless of what redevelopment officials claimed, this Ring Road was looming. To use Mayor Dick Lee's own famous words, "You can't argue with concrete." In ultimately defeating the State Street plan, which included the widened six-lane roadway, and smothering the master plan for an extended Route 34, organized citizens succeeded in defeating the Ring Road plan for the city of New Haven.

"The highway lobby has lost some battles and some momentum since its heyday, but the reports of its death are greatly exaggerated," reported the *New York Times* in the spring of 1971.[75] It did look as though resistance on the ground was delaying or killing plans to plot multilane highways through many urban neighborhoods. The six-lane highway that threatened New Orleans' French Quarter was rerouted by order of the secretary of transportation, John Volpe. Plans for a ten-lane "Lower Manhattan Expressway," looming for nearly three decades, were laid to rest, and an Inner Belt Expressway slated to cut through residential neighborhoods and parks in Cambridge and Boston was, according to the *Times*, "studied to death."

Nonetheless, the 1970 Highway Act secured the financial future of multilane road building, increasing the federal share of highway construction costs, and increasing the total cost of the Interstate Highway System to $70 billion. "Highway construction has always been a function of auto production and use," reported the *Times*, so as car ownership climbs, "so will the asphalt continue to spread." The federal budget for 1970 allocated only $400 million for urban mass transit, while putting aside $9 billion for the construction of highways. "A visitor from outer space might read the budget," proposed an editorial in the *New York Times*, "and conclude that ours is still a rural society."[76] Where organized resistance was possible, local mobilizations succeeded in pushing back local proposals, rerouting highway routes, and confounding the state highway departments, redevelopment agencies, and chambers of commerce that constituted the bulk of urban highway advocates. But just as the AIM Urban Renewal Committee predicted the difficulties of mounting a coherent and sustainable fight across geographical and social boundaries, of articulating the political and economic connections among different highway plans, and of convincing people on a large scale that, yes, you could "fight city hall," the lack of a unified

Figure 6.9

One night in December of 1970, bullets shattered the storefront window of Bread and Roses. Many attributed the incident to police. *(Photograph by Virginia Blaisdell, 1970.)*

national movement for mass transit and affordable housing prevented any significant changes on a national level.

On a local level, the movement faced significant challenges, not only by shifting national priorities, but also by "law and order." Like the offices of the Hill Parents' Association at 605 Congress Avenue, Bread and Roses was believed by many of its volunteers and regulars to be the target of police harassment. Late at night on Saturday, December 5, 1970, Bread and Roses was "riddled with bullet holes." The shop was closed and empty at the time, so nobody was injured, but, in the words of Richard Wolff, "The police were so disinterested in any serious investigation or follow-up that suspicions arose about their role."[77] The alternative press reported that the shop had been attacked "several times coinciding with political events in the city."[78]

Bread and Roses closed for a month while volunteers repaired the damaged window and interior. It reopened for a few months, but then closed permanently, two years after its initial opening.

While Bread and Roses never became the model for new development along State Street, the massive garage and six-lane speedway never did materialize. One must look outside the conventional political structures and the most obvious historical narrative to see the ways in which those who organized in New Haven for an alternative vision of the city actually redefined "citizen participation" as a grassroots struggle, rather than a legislated mechanism. AIM, the Anti–Route 34 Coalition, and PAG understood that control over the city's landscape and character had to be taken by organized force, just as the children of the Hill understood that a playground came not through urban planning but through protest.

7

Downtown Lives and Palaces

From "A Space of Freedom" to
"A Space of Exclusion"

> *We can not rely on the city for our 'bread and roses.'*
> —Resident of the Hotel Strand before its demolition,
> speaking at a meeting with redevelopment officials

> *Most of us would rather live at the Strand than the new [Park]*
> *Plaza [Hotel].*
> —Harry Cornwall, fifteen-year Hotel Strand resident, May 1969

The city said they all had to be out by May 1, 1969. But it was more than a year later when Rose Conte, the Strand Hotel's final holdout tenant, decided at the last minute to lock the door to her room and refuse to leave. Behind her door in the century-old five-story building at 184 Orange Street, she had one room with a bed, a closet, a mirror, a chair, and a bathtub. She had her radio, her books, and a few magazines. Although others around her had packed up their belongings and resigned themselves to nursing homes, extra bedrooms in the suburbs, new elderly-housing developments, or tenements elsewhere in the city, Conte clung to her independent, unobtrusive, downtown life until she was forcibly removed a few hours later by police, the last remaining tenant in a downtown residency hotel that was one of the last of its kind in New Haven.

This eviction scene marks not just an act of resistance, played out in residency motels across the country in the 1960s and 1970s, but also a moment of transition, in which the downtown was transformed from one type of space into another. This transformation—and resistance to it—was most famously played out in a residency hotel in what became known as the "Wall Street of the West," San Francisco's Manilatown. This thriving Filipino community once covered ten blocks between Chinatown and the financial district, and was home to about 10,000 Asian immigrant laborers. By the late 1960s, after urban renewal had destroyed more than 4,000 low-income housing units, and four out of five residential hotels, the last remaining trace of Manilatown was the International Hotel (I-Hotel), a low-rent residency hotel built after the 1906 earthquake, and home since the 1920s to Asian laborers. In March of 1968, the hotel was purchased by a private developer who planned to turn it into a parking garage. In October, eviction notices were sent to 196 tenants. They had until the first of the year to vacate.

Eight years later, in January of 1977, more than 350 protesters from community and student organizations formed a "human chain" around the building to prevent police from posting their ninth eviction notice, drawing national attention to the struggle. The following week, after notice was posted, 5,000 people formed a barricade around the block, arms linked, to prevent the police from forcibly removing tenants. They won a stay of eviction, and in August the fight resumed. More than 400 police in riot gear were greeted by a 3,000-person barricade protecting the fifty remaining tenants, who, like Rose Conte, had locked themselves in their rooms. The police chief forced his way through the human chain and broke through the tenants' doors with a sledgehammer. As Larry Solomon describes in his book *Roots of Justice*, which contains a detailed account of the I-Hotel fight, "The pictures of old immigrant tenants being forced out into the street were shown on newscasts across the country."[1] It was a nine-year battle that galvanized the tenant movement and crystallized, for many, the human and cultural costs of downtown redevelopment.

This was an intricately engineered transformation of downtown—to borrow some phrases from Manuel Castells—from a "space of freedom" into a "space of exclusion," from an overlapping patchwork of residential and commercial spaces into a highly compartmentalized and controlled urban system, from a place where poor and working-class people could live into a place from which their residences were excluded. It took shape under the camouflage of exciting downtown developments that promised a new and modern city, such as New Haven's shopping "mecca," or San Francisco's "Wall Street of the West." Places previously inhabited by the poor and working class would become clean, vibrant, commercially viable spaces.[2] In New Haven, this new urban center never quite materialized according to plan, but the transformation of the downtown from mixed living, working, and commercial center to prescribed and economically enforced government, arts, parking, and shopping units directly circumscribed the kinds of living choices available to the city's working class.[3]

Ultimately, the battle between Rose Conte and the Redevelopment Agency (RA)—like the more famous fight between riot police and the elderly tenants at the I-Hotel—ended as one might expect: Rose was removed from her room and relocated into another rooming house where, at last report, she was "living unhappily." Rose Conte was the last of a strong, close-knit group of twenty residents who stood their ground more than a year after the final eviction deadline at the Strand Hotel, determined to keep their unique community together, even though it didn't fit into the city's master plan. When the city's eviction orders were first issued in March of 1969, the Strand was home to more than fifty middle-aged and elderly residents, but by the time of the city's final "blitz," as one newspaper called it, in June of 1970, many had given up and moved, or had died fighting.[4]

The Strand Hotel

The Strand Hotel occupied a five-story property at 184 Orange Street for a generation, between Lou's novelty shop—a popular spot for Strand residents—and a fur store owned by the Strand's landlord. In 1965, the RA first unveiled its plans for a new government center, which—after a series of amendments and negotiations—would include a library, city hall, a federal office building, and a 300-car garage. By 1969, the design called for a government center police station wing to take the place of the Strand Hotel. Residents could see the transformation of downtown outside their windows, and they had already witnessed the disappearance of nearly twenty other downtown residency hotels in New Haven.

Many of the Strand's tenants had been active in other recent fights with the RA to save the small businesses and storefronts on State Street and Legion Avenue where they walked to work or did their shopping. They had

Figure 7.1

The Strand Hotel at 184 Orange Street. *(Photograph by Virginia Blaisdell, 1970.)*

been among the hundreds who packed the aldermanic chambers and lined a half-mile snow-covered stretch of road in opposition to the State Street Garage. They were not strangers to the tactics and strategies of the RA, nor were they unfamiliar with organized resistance to the city's plans. So even before their landlord received an official notice of eviction from the city, Strand residents drafted a petition demanding that, if the Strand was torn down, the city agree to provide decent housing for all of the tenants together in an acceptable location. "If they [would] build replacements for all the hotels and houses they tear down, it wouldn't be so bad," said Harry Cornwall, a New Haven native and fifteen-year Strand resident who eagerly signed the petition, "but they build restaurants or parking lots or let the land stay vacant. I think the city delights in breaking up communities. They have no feeling for the people."[5]

Cornwall and many of the other residents could recall a time when the city had more than twenty hotels like the Strand where people of "modest income" could live, walk to jobs downtown, and rely on neighbors as a kind of family. In his book-length study of hotel life, historian Paul Groth explains that, for the residency hotel tenant, "home" was a place that was "scattered up and down the street."[6] People ate, lived, and interacted in public spaces, and often saw their neighbors as an extension of family, just as they saw the street, lobby, lunch counter, and corner store as an extension of home.

Hotel living became a highly visible and necessary reality in New Haven, and in other large and small cities nationwide, following the Second World War, when a severe shortage in housing pushed both low- and middle-income renters into the hotel market. In New Haven in 1945, hundreds of veterans were on waiting lists for permanent hotel accommodations in the city's eleven hotels. The *New Haven Register* reported that the city had a total of 1,370 hotel rooms. "But try and find one," they challenged their readers. "Never before in the city's history have hotels been so crowded."[7] The paper reported that turnover in these hotels was "slight." New Haven's second-largest hotel, the Hotel Garde, had 250 rooms and they all seemed to be permanently full. "It's terrible," said the manager. "We have people sleeping in the lobby waiting for rooms to be vacated." The largest New Haven hotel, the Taft, had 25 percent of its 450 rooms allocated for permanent residents, but manager Craig LeVin said he was sure he could rent "every room" as a permanent residence if he chose to do so.

At that time, thirty-eight of the Strand's sixty-five rooms were occupied by permanent tenants, and the rest of the rooms were rented on a first-come, first-served basis. The manager said he couldn't take reservations because he didn't want to "tie up rooms and then have people fail to show up. It isn't fair." Between 1930 and 1950, thirty-eight new hotels opened in the Elm City, largely to meet these residency needs. By 1970, after redevelopment had intervened, all of them were gone. Large luxury and chain hotels, like the Park Plaza and the Holiday Inn, along with suburban motor lodges, took their place.[8] These new hotels met the needs of travelers but didn't fill the housing vacuum left by the demolition of residency hotels and other low-rent units.

The Park Plaza

Just as the Strand's residents began to uneasily witness the slow extinction of residency hotels throughout the city, the Park Plaza, a nineteen-floor "glittering new hotel," took over the New Haven skyline. At a VIP reception celebrating the hotel's grand opening in October of 1966, Yale president Kingman Brewster and his wife accompanied Mayor Lee and Redevelopment Director Melvin Adams on a special tour of the new facilities, including the Trianon Cocktail Lounge, an 1,100-seat ballroom, a coffee shop, a gourmet restaurant, and 310 state-of-the-art guestrooms. The rooms boasted picture windows, "direct-dial phones," televisions, radios, and soundproofing for "restful privacy." They were accessed by "high-speed elevators" and "decorator-designed in the Modern manner."[9] A rooftop heated pool and sundeck and the Top of the Park restaurant and lounge finished off

Figure 7.2

Artist's rendering of the Park Plaza's rooftop sundeck and heated pool. *(From a brochure titled "The Park Plaza Hotel in Chapel Square, New Haven, Connecticut," New Haven Free Public Library, Local History Room.)*

the VIP tour with expansive views of both the Long Island Sound and Yale's campus. Brewster called the hotel "superb." Lee called it "magnificent."

The *Register* called the Park Plaza one of Mayor Lee's "pet projects." He announced plans to build the hotel in June of 1957, and nine and a half years and $7 million later, a team of more than 500 staff worked all day to prepare for the grand opening.[10] Crowds watched from a distance as Pinkerton guards kept all unauthorized personnel away from the building. Many onlookers were skeptical of the hotel's plans to open that night, since they had seen no furniture enter the building in the course of the preparations. What they didn't know was that an underground tunnel originating at South Orange Street had been constructed to hide the construction and other unsightly day-to-day operations of the luxury hotel. Furniture had been moved in under the city's streets and sidewalks while crowds watched the front entrance. As the first guests, Mr. and Mrs. John Graham, checked into their luxurious room, with its television, radio, and high-speed elevator access, photographers for the local papers captured them at the reception desk, completing the modern consumer city tableaux that had been conceptualized, mapped out, and constructed over the last decade in the "*New New Haven.*"

The opening of the Park Plaza marked the completion of what developers, urban planners, and the local press saw as a key stage in New Haven's transformation from urban problem to urban model. The *Register* called the hotel the "new center of activity in the redeveloped downtown." It was the city's first large luxury hotel in fifty years, and with its construction came the final redefinition of downtown as a place of "comfort," "elegance," and "convenience." At the Park Plaza, this meant "the comfort of excellent overnight accommodations, the elegance of quality dining, and the convenience of in-hotel parking." The hotel unified all key elements of Mayor Lee's redeveloped vision for downtown. Guests could walk from their soundproof rooms to a parking garage, a "connected and enclosed shopping center," or a "glass- walled rooftop rendezvous" at a restaurant and lounge with "panoramic views over the Yale campus and Long Island Sound." The Park Plaza was what Groth categorized as a "palace hotel," a particular breed of public space that was public only to the upper and middle classes, one in which the worlds of production and consumption were kept strictly separated.[11]

The Park Plaza was depicted as safe, clean, insulated, and exclusive—a foil to contemporary definitions of "blight"—and everyone was spared the sight of any raw materials or manual labor by the construction of the underground delivery tunnel. Perhaps the VIP tour of the new Park Plaza, and the effectiveness of its underground entrance ramp, was what inspired Kingman Brewster—just a year later—to push for a multimillion-dollar underground passage of the proposed Ring Road to avoid disruption or unsightly traffic on Yale's campus. Or perhaps both tunnel concepts simply reflect a common impulse among the power brokers of the urban landscape to conceal the necessary baggage of the modern city—the traffic, the deliveries, the rubble, the work, and the workers—while celebrating its riches. In any event, the Strand residents were counted among that rubble, and while they fought for their simple rooms, their rich if unconventional community, and their near-extinct form of hotel living, the Park Plaza announced to them, in a full-page advertisement in the daily paper that they shared in their lobby, at the nearby Minute Lunch lunch counter, or from room to room, that "an urbane renewal of elegance in all aspects of contemporary hotel living has just come to downtown New Haven."[12]

The construction of the new Park Plaza Hotel, like the impending demolition of the Strand, was intricately linked to the city's comprehensive redevelopment plans. As distressed urban areas nationwide struggled to redefine themselves, major hotel chains seized the opportunity for an industrywide explosion of downtown luxury hotels. In 1961, the *New York Times* called it a "new trend," noting that "leading hotel chains have either given impetus to, or become a key facet in, the redevelopment and revitalizing of rundown areas."[13] Redevelopment projects from Pittsburgh to San Francisco were anchored by massive hotels. The Sheraton Corporation was about to celebrate the opening of its sixth new luxury hotel in Chicago, an 1,100-room development that was part of a $149 million redevelopment project. Its $16 million Philadelphia Sheraton Hotel, built in 1957, facilitated the redevelopment of the Penn Center site and served as a "model for other cities." A new Hilton hotel was the centerpiece for Pittsburgh's Golden Triangle Redevelopment Area, and the Hotel Corporation of America planned a 250-room hotel in Constitution Plaza in the heart of Hartford's twelve-acre redevelopment area, as well as a 1,000-room, $26 million hotel in the middle of Boston's Prudential Center redevelopment plan. "Good-looking modern hotel buildings," asserted the *Times*, were regarded as a "pillar or fountainhead of a community," and created a "favorable public attitude," enabling a city to attract new business.

The plans for the Park Plaza, as well as the redevelopment venture calling for the demolition of the Strand Hotel, were both part of a nationally publicized $85 million plan to clear "96 blighted acres," announced by Mayor Lee in early summer of 1957. *Time* magazine brought the story of this renewal plan to its readers around the world, calling New Haven "foremost among New England cities in striking at the illnesses that plague all U.S. municipalities,"—suburban flight, the spread of slums, and the decline of downtown.[14] The language of infectious diseases had become common in the vocabulary of urban problems. The *New York Times* described Boston's urban crisis as "a hardening of the commuter arteries, with the deterioration of mass transportation and population anemia brought on by flight to the suburbs." The city's "ills," explained the *Times* reporter, had been "diagnosed by a hundred municipal pill dispensers over the years."[15] General sentiment surrounding urban blight, to quote historian Howard Gillette, was that "we must cut out the whole cancer and not leave any diseased tissue."[16]

Reflecting on redevelopment initiatives over the past year, Lee told New Haven's board of aldermen in November of 1960, "Our goal is a slumless city—the first in the nation. In the past five years we have made substantial and significant strides towards this goal. . . . In the twelve months which have passed since I last stood before this honorable body, the face of our city has changed substantially." He went on to describe the revolutionary medical procedure that had taken place. "Massive surgery undertaken in Oak Street and in parts of Church Street . . . has begun to rid the city of its depressing slums—slums which we, not only as legislators and administrators, but as thoughtful and responsible citizens, would not accept as part of normal urban living."[17] This correlation between a "slumless city" and "normal urban living" raised questions about the subjective nature of the many structural, cultural, social, and even architectural decisions made throughout the process of urban renewal. By equating "slumlessness" with normality, Lee and other urban movers and shakers of his time equated "abnormality" with blight. Although hotel living certainly fell outside of conventional definitions of normalcy in the 1960s, it did not necessarily mean slum living.

Defining Home

When the Strand's demolition plans were set in 1969 to clear the site for a new government building, only one other residential hotel remained in New Haven. The National Hotel on Crown Street was already turning people away every day, and many of those unable to find hotel accommodations wound up sleeping on the street. But the Strand was not simply a "last resort"—it was the housing of choice for its residents, who appreciated the community atmosphere, proximity to downtown, and the desk clerk, Don, who would run the elevator, deliver messages, and sometimes just call up residents to talk. According to one fourteen-year resident who moved to the Strand from another downtown residential hotel after it closed down, Don would call her room if she didn't come down the stairs by noon to find out if something was wrong or if she needed anything.

The Strand was always nearly filled to capacity. Its rooms were small but contained all the necessary elements, including a "large bed, mirror, cabinet, and closet."[18] Not long before the eviction notice was issued, the hotel had also added baths to the rooms. The New Haven Register, in an article covering the February 1969 petition, called the building "dark and dingy," which sent some residents into a rage. "It's not the most beautiful hotel in the world, but we like it and we're satisfied," insisted Mr. Cornwall. "So why does the city come and tell us it would be better if we moved?" Addressing the Register's coverage of the Strand petition, AIM members charged that the RA was using the local press to construct a narrative of blight, asserting,

"By focusing on superficial appearances, the Register reporter . . . played into standard redevelopment procedures of labeling what they wish to demolish as a 'blighting influence.'"[19] In reality, the lives lived within the Strand's walls were generally as productive (or unproductive), unobtrusive (or obtrusive), and mainstream (or unconventional) as those contained within the bricks and mortar of most other New Haven apartment buildings. Most residents had radios, and many also had televisions. "Books and magazines are present in every room," reported the *AIM Newsletter*, noting these important markings of culture inside a structure that was presumed to contain only the marginal, the blighted, and the socially disposable.

The Strand residents were a diverse group, a significant number of whom had been displaced repeatedly, in some cases from other resident hotels throughout the city that fell to the RA without any discernable resistance. Many were around retirement age or older, but half of the residents still worked, some full-time, some part-time. Of those who worked, nearly all walked to jobs downtown, and few said they made enough money to afford bus or taxi fare, so living in the heart of downtown was a necessity. Despite common perceptions of hotel residents, almost all were permanent tenants of the Strand, some reporting that address for more than fifteen years.

Outlining what he calls the "culture of hotel life," housing historian Paul Groth writes that hotel residents are unbound by the "social contacts and tacit supervision" of traditional house or apartment living. He cites residents' individualized pattern of life and day-to-day schedule, and calls hotel living "not just urban, but urbane" in that it offers a twenty-four-hour lifestyle and a mix of people. Hotel residents, he argues, are freer from material possessions and more mobile.[20] Groth seeks to "expand the notion of 'home'" and explicate the unique cultural elements of hotel housing, not as an aberration—as it so often has been framed—but as a viable alternative and an important form of community.

Groth argues that "the built environment is not merely a result or background for human action, but a participant, a player in collective human life."[21] He asserts that the destruction of residency motels across the country has been based on underlying misconceptions about who lives in hotels and why. Not all hotel tenants are poor, he argues, and according to one study of hotels in San Diego, more than half of hotel residents were "independent, self-reliant individuals" who were not and had never been on public aid. His studies reveal that although residency hotels did fill significant housing gaps and offer affordable shelter for the jobless, indigent, and recently institutionalized, the majority of hotel tenants were workers who chose to live in the unique flexible environment of residency motels, or whose unstable or insufficient incomes necessitated these week-by-week, low-rent residencies. Among elderly tenants in Groth's San Diego study, the average length of employment at their longest-held job was twenty-one years, indicating, contrary to popular misconceptions, that their work was consistent and long-term. He also cites a Chicago study that shows "a small prosperous minority, a majority barely earning enough to make ends meet, and a large majority of impoverished workers." Hotel residents in New Haven, as in the cities reported in Groth's study, were not generally transients or indigents (although hotels did provide an option for those who had no other housing choices); they were most accurately described as working people.

In New Haven, as in many other cities, residency hotels were used as emergency shelters through organizations such as the welfare department, travelers' aid, and the Red Cross. This is one reason for the hotels' reputation for transience and marginality, but the vast majority of tenants in the fifteen or twenty residency hotels in New Haven in the interwar and immediate postwar period were permanent tenants. For example, the National Hotel—one of the last New Haven hotels to fall—had a total of forty-five rooms, thirty-seven of which were occupied by long-term residents.[22] As one National Hotel employee explained in the wake of news that the one other remaining downtown hotel, the Strand, would be torn down, "Most of the people in this hotel work in the downtown area. Every day we turn away people and I know that the Strand does the same thing. We used to be able to send to the Yale Hope Mission, but that was closed down, too. I really don't know where all these people go when we turn them away." The employee, Elizabeth Pieraccini, knew firsthand about what the RA had in store for the Strand, and probably the National, as well. She had worked at another downtown hotel, the Milner, which had been torn down just a few years before to build a new fire station.

By eliminating an entire style of living from the urban repertoire, the RA erased one significant form of working-class life. The other available forms of housing for New Haven's working people included home ownership in the deteriorating areas of the inner city or in the more affordable of the immediately adjacent suburbs, such as Hamden and East Haven, a quickly diminishing supply of low-income rentals, and low-rent public housing, of which there was very little, and for which there were extensive waiting lists. The ideal, of course, was a move into a house in the suburbs, where a younger generation of working-class families with the means and the desire had started new lives with new cars. They could travel to a downtown parking garage and walk through a windowed corridor above the street into the Park Plaza Hotel if they desired a taste of urban life. For the working-class men and women who had lived, often by choice, for ten or twenty years in residential hotels, the RA envisioned a more appropriate system by which they would move into newly constructed elderly-housing units.

But the Strand's tenants preferred the accommodations they had, and the community they had built, to the new subsidized elderly-housing developments scattered throughout the city. When Carl Reichbart, the Strand's owner, received an eviction notice in March of 1969, the hotel's lease wasn't due to expire until 1971. Nonetheless, the city informed Reichbart that his Strand tenants had to be out by May 1, 1969. The tenants formed a committee right away, and John Donovan, a three-year resident and founder of the Police Athletic League, wrote up a petition. Donovan met with AIM organizers, who agreed to help the Strand tenants come up with a plan to fight the RA. "We are willing to move if the city will build another structure for us—one that will hold elderly people and be in the downtown area," said Donovan. The tenants set up a folding table in the Strand's front lobby and taped a sign to it that read, "Be Aware—Care. Help us save our home! Sign the petition to save the Strand." Within a few days, fifty-four tenants had signed on.[23]

With the new petition drafted, two Strand tenants walked over to AIM's Orange Street office, just a few blocks away, understanding both the organization and its downtown office to be the key site of resistance to the city's redevelopment plans. The Strand residents' relationship with AIM, and the pedestrian link between 184 Orange Street and 241 Orange Street, illustrate one small section of a map of organized resistance in this small city, demonstrating the extent to which discrete fights over seemingly unconnected spaces—like the site of a parking garage on State Street and the site of a residency hotel on Orange Street—constitute a unified narrative of resistance.

"Clear a Space": Fighting for a Different Downtown

The fight of Strand Residents, Hill and Dixwell families, and the professional planners, intellectuals, artists, and activists in AIM was uniquely collective in very concrete ways. AIM's alliance with Strand residents grew not only out of sympathy and political allegiances, but also out of a common fight for physical space in the changing city. As redevelopment plans mapped out a new downtown, in which art and culture had its designated spaces, and low-rent commercial areas faced extinction, a dancer (and also a former redevelopment employee, Yale-educated urban planner, and AIM member), Joan Stone, was about to be displaced from her studio, "one of the last remaining warehouses on State St."[24] In the lobby at the Strand, where residents and supporters had gathered to protest the building's demolition, Stone performed a solo dance she called "When the landlord left, I did the only thing a poor soul could do, I walked around the room and scratched my head." She choreographed the piece not long after completing her master's thesis for Yale's urban studies program on relocation. The piece was based on an experience narrated to her by a Hill Parents' Association (HPA) member named Oscar. As the story went, a man was home sick one day when the police barged into his apartment. Soon after, a housing inspector came in, followed by an employee of the city's antipoverty program, who wanted to ask him some questions. The next knock at the door was a student who wanted to "collect material for a sociology paper." Finally, he was visited by the landlord, who told him that the building had been sold to the RA, so he would have to move.[25]

This piece was one of four solo political dances Stone had choreographed and performed in community spaces throughout the city since 1967. These performances required Stone and her audiences—at least for a brief period—to literally claim space in the city. "We painted about two dozen coffee cans bright red," explained Stone, "filled them with rocks, and set them up wherever we went to define a rectangular playing area." This was more difficult in some places than in others. Downtown areas proved to be the most difficult, explained Stone, "because all streets in New Haven are highways and you have to have a good reason to obstruct a highway." A performance on the New Haven Green drew the attention of "local, state, or federal agents," Stone claimed, and when she attempted to perform at a shopping center, she was told that "shopping centers were strictly for shoppers and shopping."

Stone performed her pieces up close to her audience, at street level rather than on a stage, and was able to interact with, observe, and "learn from" those who watched her performances. "I was clinging to that space like the people who came to see the dance," said Stone. Often they were followed not only by discussions, but by notes, suggestions, and sometimes even spontaneous forms of participation from her audience. Because her pieces were silent, and she wore only street clothes, the performance itself could be a spontaneous act. That's what happened in the lobby of the Strand Hotel, where Stone—moved by the tenants' protest—told them, "Clear a space and I'll dance."[26] Before long, the audience, captivated by the story, began telling their own. One of the tenants spoke of his time working as a clown in Ringling Bros. and Barnum & Bailey circus. Two others described their experiences at the Battle of the Bulge. Another handed Stone a handwritten note. "I am glad that you came and showed us your play. Did you ever see that man they put out on the street? Was he old or young? Some people that I know got relocated. We don't want to be relocated. The foot taps you did were good and nobody can do them like you. My sister and I wanted to learn steps like that. Everyone was glad that you came. Will you come back again?"[27] The request and its context offered a disquieting view of the attack on collective spaces like the Strand's lobby, and the stories, relationships, exchanges, and actions that their extinction would preclude.

Such exchanges were facilitated by the fact that Stone's choreography placed her on a level with the people watching her pieces. "I've been able to observe, react to, and learn from my audience," she wrote in 1969.[28] She often revised her choreography in response to what she saw, heard, or was explicitly told by those for whom she performed. In choreographing *Landlord*, she had trouble creating the appropriate space until her husband, architect

Harris Stone, arranged some chairs into the form of a house. The audience would become the walls, situating the performer (and choreographer) in close contact and interaction with the people. This form—down to its altitude—spoke to the distinction between the city's master plans and the street-level planning that Stone and AIM's other urban experts employed in their development of alternative plans. "I don't perform on the proscenium, but right up close to the people," wrote Stone, articulating the compositional difference between RA aerial photos and the images, accounts, and experiences of neighborhood spaces emphasized by Harris Stone, David Dickson, Harriet Cohen, and other activist architects and planners in AIM's Urban Renewal Committee and the Anti–Route 34 Coalition.

Some AIM members were skeptical of Stone's political dances. "Some only wanted to live from the neck up and were suspicious of art," she recalled in a 2005 interview. "They were very unhappy when I went off and danced. They wanted me to be working on the newsletter, things like that." But she had many supporters within AIM who understood the potential of her work to "make people uncomfortable." It was this ability to cause discomfort, says Stone, referencing Bertolt Brecht, that made AIM as successful as it was.[29] In the spring of 1969, the RA was far too comfortable in its plans to evict the residents of the Strand Hotel, even as it uneasily fielded AIM's challenges to and allegations about its plans for State Street and the Ring Road in the press, in hearing rooms, and in the streets.

The relationship between the Strand tenants and AIM dated back to a 1967 petition for the Save Our Stores (SOS) campaign, which was aimed at protecting the shops and small businesses along State Street at which many of the Strand's residents shopped and worked. One seven-year Strand resident, Louis Abington, had lived at another residency hotel, the Hotel Garde, for fourteen years, until it was torn down by the RA. Abington, like other Strand residents, attended many public RA hearings and became very critical of urban renewal and the city's proposal to tear down shops and small businesses on State Street, a few blocks from the Strand, to build a half-mile-long parking garage. As AIM organizers explained, if the garage was built, "most of the stores we have now will be gone. Instead, there will be fancy, expensive shops for suburbanites."[30]

Some residents also signed a Save Our Stores petition initiated by Wooster Square residents demanding "clear and definite guarantees that we will not be deprived of conveniently located grocery, meat, and fruit markets." More than 5,000 people signed the document in less than three weeks, asserting that "a prime reason for living in this area has been its nearness to stores of high quality and genuine individuality. We do not see why we should now be forced to shop by car, nor do we see in particular why the elderly, those with children, and those who do not have cars should have their daily lives so drastically altered by the plans of the Redevelopment Agency."[31] Strand resident Louis Abington signed the petition when it was circulated at a local store that would be affected by the city's proposed plan. Another resident, whom AIM organizers encountered at a petition table near another small grocery store, illuminated the ways in which the power struggle underlying the Save Our Stores petition hit home, quite literally, for many older and low-income residents. "I can buy food, but I got to find a place to cook it," he said. "They tear down all the rooms and hotels."

"We don't want to be separated," Abington said in 1969. "I have a family who would take me, but I don't want to go. I feel free here and I have my own friends. I don't want to depend on my family. What about the other people here? They have no place to go and the thought of having to move is frightening for them." The community about which Abington spoke was not only a family, but also an organizing committee. For Abington and many others, the RA was a familiar opponent, just as other opponents of urban renewal, such as AIM, were familiar allies.

It quickly became clear to the members of the RA that they would have to pay attention to the tenants at 184 Orange Street. In response to the Strand tenants' petition, redevelopment officials made their first mistake by scheduling a meeting with residents for 11 a.m., when many had to be at work. "They didn't even consult us," said Donovan. "They just said it was at 11:00. They could have scheduled it for the evening when most of the people would have been available." The residents decided to decline that invitation and call their own meeting for 8 p.m. on Tuesday, April 8, 1969. They invited redevelopment officials to join them. By the time everyone had filtered in, thirty-five residents were present, along with representatives from social service agencies, the Strand's landlord, and five officials from the RA. Donovan spoke first on behalf of the tenants, echoing their petition in declaring that they had no intention of moving unless the city gave them an acceptable alternative. Another resident, Rich Moore, who had lived at the Strand for two years, listed a number of other hotels that had recently been torn down. "We can not rely on the city for our 'bread and roses,' " he declared.

RA officials, sensing the situation would be harder to diffuse than they had originally expected, tried to placate the angry crowd. The director of family relocation, Ray Call, spoke about the agency's "perfect intentions" despite an "imperfect relocation record." Mike Catania, director of operations for family relocation, repeatedly and nervously stated that he would "not put anyone out on the street." Growing increasingly defensive, Catania claimed that the tenants had been told about the May 1 move-out deadline as early as August of 1968. The room became animated with shouts, and shaking heads. In an attempt to calm heightening tensions, city officials introduced Ed Grant of the Union of Indigent Peoples, who attended the meeting through the organization's affiliation with CPI. This elicited an even more virulent response—working tenants were offended at the suggestion that they were "indigent peoples."

Desperate to win over some of the residents, RA officials spoke of plans to offer free furniture to Strand tenants who were relocated into apartment housing, but the tenants had no desire to own their own furniture. A fundamental misunderstanding was evident as city officials spoke at length of newly constructed or planned apartments scattered throughout the city. In a move that one tenant referred to as "divide and conquer," RA officials had visited tenants one at a time to persuade them to give in, and to make additional offers of new furniture, more privacy, and more living space.[32] But in those private meetings, as at this more public one in April, the Strand's tenants were unconvinced. "To us, the Strand is home," said tenant Harry Cornwall. "There is a warm feeling among the people here that I haven't seen in apartment buildings or convalescent homes or old-age homes. I guess it's because we all care about each other."[33]

Cornwall had lived at the Strand for fifteen years and had worked at other area residency hotels, including the nearby Tresmond and the Rip Van Winkle motels. He noted that ten or fifteen people stopped by the Strand each day, and all had to be turned away for lack of vacancy. Contemplating the Strand's impending demolition, and the fate of other such buildings in the area, he told a local reporter, "The Strand and the National are the only two hotels left where a person can get a room for three or four dollars a day. And there is a need for this kind of hotel. We are not young, but that is no reason for the city to treat us in such a fashion," said Cornwall. "Most of us would rather live at the Strand than the new [Park] Plaza [Hotel]." Preferring the low-rent downtown residency hotel he called home to the "urbane renewal of elegance" that was the new Park Plaza was an unpopular cultural notion at a time when correlations had been clearly drawn between "normal urban living" and the new "slumless city."

The Strand's tenants, along with their supporters, fought desperately for their vision of the ideal city to be understood and respected, just as they had done in their fight to keep the small groceries and pedestrian accesses along State Street. But what they were up against was a complete top-down overhaul of what "downtown" was supposed to mean—one that was mired in millions of dollars in federal grants, a new and developing interstate highway system, and the promise of a seemingly infinite bankroll in shopping revenues and corporate tax money.

"Pulling Power, Buying Power, Growing Power"

The RA imagined New Haven to be "New England's Newest City," conceptually erasing a long, rich urban history and replacing that with what it called "Pulling Power, Buying Power, Growing Power."[34] This was the title of a promotional publication the RA released in 1960, the cover of which displayed a watercolor of the incipient Macy's department store. Its edifice stretched out along a straight length of highway, with cars zooming by in the foreground. The city itself formed a dim, hazy background, in great contrast to the Macy's building, which seemed illuminated in its whiteness. The parking garage for this Macy's, and for the nearby Malley's department store, would be connected by protected walkways to the new Park Plaza Hotel.

The document was aimed at business and industry leaders—it boasted the promise of New Haven's "pulling power" through its "ultramodern downtown," expressways, "9850 Parking Spaces," "two great stores" and, more generally, "the ultimate in customer convenience." This convenience would be laid in concrete and glass in the heart of the city. "Both the [Park Plaza] hotel and the office building will be built on a two-story retail area, which will cover the entire downtown and overlook the historic New Haven Green," the RA explained, imagining a city built, quite literally, on a shopping mall, using retail as both its material and economic foundation. From this elevated city on a mall, shoppers and hotel guests could see the historic New Haven Green—history visible from behind the glass, and elevated above the city streets.

The vision for the new downtown could be distilled down to the "protected promenade," an elevated walkway described in the RA's brochure, leading "directly from Malley's, Macy's, and the garage to the quality shops, hotel, and office tower." Protected from what, exactly, the brochure did not specify, but the RA assured its readers that, whatever might be happening on the street below, or in distant pockets of urban blight, the "shopper" (the publication's key protagonist) would be "protected from the elements wherever she may walk within New Haven Center." The emphasis was on safety and insulation, because those who would use the walkway, the garage, and the stores in the "*New* New Haven" were, as depicted in a cartoon map of the state of Connecticut, armies of identical, white, blond-haired suburban housewives carrying shopping bags and purses.

In this depiction, the city identified its target audience and clarified many gendered valences inherent in the redeveloped city. New downtown centers—such as the Park Plaza and its connected garages and shops—were protected and sometimes fortressed against a host of urban problems, most of them racially coded. The great white walls of Macy's would protect the suburban housewife from the city's dangerous elements so that she could spend her husband's money in comfort and convenience. The RA called this "the pulling power of a $2 billion market," citing that the state ranked first or second in per family income in twenty-seven of the last thirty years. An eye-catching chart revealed "drive times" (a phrase that would eventually take hold) from all suburban points to this "New Haven Center" (a name that never really would) of just a few minutes. From these points, wealthy families could easily access New Haven on new highways, park in new parking garages, and spend their amassed wealth at the city's retail offerings.

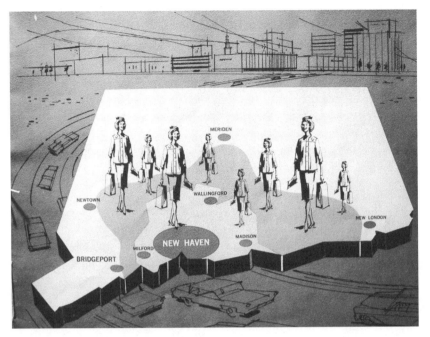

Figure 7.3

"Buying Power," as depicted by the RA in 1960. *(New Haven Redevelopment Agency,* New Haven: New England's Newest City—Pulling Power, Buying Power, Growing Power, *1960, New Haven Free Public Library, Local History Room.)*

Interestingly, the RA offered a motley grouping when they listed the suburbs from which shoppers with "buying power" would be drawn, including Ansonia, Derby, and East Haven—all less affluent, more working-class areas—along with Hamden, Guilford, and Branford—all of which did have pockets (or entire zip codes) of considerable wealth. This suggested the promise of a new kind of regional perspective on the growth of suburban settlement and affluence, one that—like most literature on suburban sprawl during the time—ignored the complicated suburban picture, in which explicit and carefully constructed exclusion from the central city of particular kinds of working-class living (including residency motels, public housing, and affordable single-family homes) made for many economically (if not racially) heterogeneous suburban communities, formed not always by choice, but sometimes by necessity.[35]

In his 2003 study of public spaces and social justice, geographer Don Mitchell argues that inherent in spaces like the new downtown "shopping mecca" is the "perceived need for order, surveillance, and control over the behavior of the public."[36] The primary aim of corporate planners, like those who planned New Haven's new downtown shopping, parking, and hotel

center, argued Mitchell, was to impose "limits and controls on spatial interaction." In this way, public spaces such as malls, shopping centers, and redeveloped downtowns become what Mitchell calls "spaces of controlled
spectacle." But Mitchell also asserts that such spaces have *never* actually
been inclusive, even in their most basic early forms—such as the forum of
ancient Rome or the colonial town square. It was only through what he calls
"concerted social protest and conflict" that they were opened up. "Spaces
were only public," he asserts, "to the degree that they were *taken* and made
public." The increased control, surveillance, and insulation, as orchestrated
by the particular design of the Park Plaza, its connected and covered parking
garage, and the closed and protected shopping outlets that visitors accessed
by new "protected promenades," significantly diminished such opportunities
for taking public space.

One crucial component to the success of this downtown shopping
mecca was "The BUYING power of a revitalized city . . . $143,529,500 in
redevelopment construction." The RA boasted that New Haven had completed more redevelopment projects than any other New England city, asserting, "Entire neighborhoods have been transformed from blighted,
deteriorated areas into high-quality residential sections." In other words,
part of the city's new buying power would come from people moving from
nearby suburbs back into the downtown, into new luxury and moderate-
income housing throughout the city, much of which replaced the "slums" in
which low-income renters and homeowners had once lived. The footprints
of demolition crews and the broad dark lines drawn into redevelopment
plans marked the contours of how the "slum" was defined, often coming to
mean anything that lacked "pulling power" and "buying power," such as
small, low-rent residency motels.

This, of course (as many scholars and critics of urban renewal have
noted), was counterproductive to solving one of the city's biggest on-the-
ground problems: the shortage of affordable housing. Often unseen, un-
counted, and to this point undisturbed, the number of individuals living in
small residency hotels throughout the city climbed steadily. Between 1954
and 1962, 993 new hotel and motel rooms of all kinds were added to the
city's total accommodations. By the date of that count in April of 1962, the
New Haven Register reported that another 478 were in the planning
stages.[37] In a fascinating and prescient piece of conjecture, an artist's rendering for the newspaper answered the question of "How Area's New Motel
Rooms Would Look as a Hotel." The question was a natural one, as the RA
had been clear on its intentions to build a luxurious, high-rise downtown hotel, and the trend toward the large, new, and luxurious, and away from the
small, old, and scattered (Macy's and Malley's department stores instead of
small downtown storefront businesses) did beg the basic efficiency question
of why the city had all of these scattered, small, not-very-luxurious hotels
and motels.

The artist drew a vision of this sleek, towering edifice—exemplifying the "flow of architectural lines" promised by the RA in its "Pulling Power" promotional brochure—shooting upward out of the corner of Church and Chapel streets, generally considered the heart of the downtown. On the sidewalk below, dwarfed by the building, the miniature figures of pedestrians scurried about.

In the image, the massive hotel building dominates both the street and the skyline, forms a seemingly infinite vertical barricade along the sidewalk, and constitutes a city "block," which based on a reading of the unscientific scale, would be—for most—unwalkable. But this was the vision of the "renewed" downtown; the word was an odd choice to describe the transformation of downtown that the city had in store. Central to dictionary meanings of "renew" is the idea of restoring something to its original form. Central to the vision of what lay ahead in 1962 was the sense that everything had to be brand-new. This didn't bode well for old tenants in old residency hotels.

The drive to rebuild and remake the city in response to urban blight and suburban flight only intensified with the civil unrest that hit American cities in the summers that followed. In New Haven in August of 1967, coverage in the mainstream press was disproportionately concerned with the effects that the "disturbances," as they were commonly called, had on downtown shopping. The *New Haven Register* reported that Macy's, Malleys, and the downtown Chapel Square Mall closed early on the fourth day of rioting to obey the newly instituted 8 p.m. curfew, as did Hamden's "Magic Mile," a suburban string of shopping centers a few miles north of downtown New Haven. The paper noted recent fears that "the disorder might spill into the suburbs," and while nearly all of the vandalism and looting was concentrated in the black neighborhoods of Dixwell, Newhallville, and the Hill, fears of the effects on downtown shopping and the potential of spreading "disorder" into the suburbs led the front-page coverage.[38]

Just as reports suggested it was finally growing quieter in the "most troublesome [black] areas" of Dixwell, Legion, Grand, and Congress, the press began reporting incidents of looting downtown, on Chapel and Whitney. Police and bystanders were being injured by "rocks, bottles, or flying glass."[39] The city rented fifty rooms in the Park Plaza Hotel, with its "protected promenade," to house police officers working extended shifts to patrol downtown. The events of the 1967 riots—with police housed in a magnificent downtown fortress—brought irony to the notion of a "protected promenade." Another irony was that the Park Plaza represented precisely the priorities of redevelopment spending that provoked anger in sections of the city where those resources were sorely needed for improvements, but more often allocated for clearance.

Disorder erupted in New Haven and other cities around the country just as many were conceiving of new structures and landscapes. In his 1973 book *Revolutionaries*, historian Eric Hobsbawm argues that the rebuilding and reorganization of cities is one of three strategies employed by the state to counter urban insurrections (the other two being the development of police forces and "systematic arrangements for deploying troops," both of which were also part of New Haven's master plan).[40] As cities become bigger in size, Hobsbawm argues, they become less residential and serve more as centers for government and commerce, making revolt less likely. Certainly, in the case of New Haven, the master plan for the "*New* New Haven" reflected a desire to eliminate concentrations of low-income (and nonwhite) people in the downtown area, the people most likely to revolt. Insurrections were less likely in developed Western cities, Hobsbawm argues, because of the increased segregation of classes and of residential and business areas. The plans for New Haven's new downtown would not only limit the overlap of business and residential uses, but also intensify the preexisting geographical class and racial divisions in the city.

In his study of hotel living, Groth notes that hotels, as the home of many working-class individuals without traditional family entanglements, have historically been "fertile ground for union activists and liberal and radical political workers."[41] He characterizes the urban renewal period as one of "hotel resident removal," just as the period has been called one of "Negro removal" by many scholars and politicians (all of whom were actually quoting comedian Dick Gregory). Just as many erroneously understood race as a cause of blight, rather than understanding racism as an underlying factor contributing to the perpetuation of poverty, "rooms to rent" signs hanging on hotel entrances, front doors of homes, and rooming houses came to be seen as a cause of blight, rather than an effect of the labor market, migration, real estate speculation, or urban renewal.

New Haven's RA officials, like their counterparts in other cities, understood that to eliminate low-income residential communities in the city's center required the elimination of all residential hotels, and the prohibition of the construction of any new forms of "transient housing." This was reflected in revised redevelopment plans.[42] By 1970, nearly all of the city's single-room occupancy units were destroyed.[43] A photo of the Strand's demolition appeared in the November 15, 1970, issue of *Modern Times*, the biweekly newspaper that grew out of AIM's organizational newsletter. Commemorating the residents' long "fight against the Redevelopment Agency to keep their homes," the use of the image offered a bitter contrast to the appearance of similar demolition images scattered throughout the city's mainstream press in the 1950s. The captions for those pictures celebrated the elimination of blight and the birth of a new city, yet the visual vocabulary remained the same in the image of the Strand's demolition: the wrecking ball, the crooked rubble, and the cars and passersby that indicated the city would proceed without pause. Nonetheless, the Strand photo's caption pointed not to the raw materials of construction and demolition or the promise of a slumless city, but to the immediate human cost of downtown's transformation, when it reported, "Some of the former residents may be sleeping in doorways."[44]

Despite this challenge to conventional representations of the wrecking ball, and despite the shift in public sentiment surrounding urban renewal that took shape between the 1950s and the time of the Strand's demolition, the revision of downtown's identity still relied heavily on the power of image-making. Architect and activist Harris Stone said of downtown New Haven, "The image of the renewed area was similar to the image of the new buildings: clean, impersonal, and rich."[45] As much as urban renewal was falling politically and intellectually out of vogue by the late 1960s, the possibility of a cleaner, wealthier, more easily managed downtown seemed an irresistible premise in the wake of a decade of urban disorder.

Harris Stone saw New Haven's transformation as directly "in line with national objectives," which included enticing the rich to move back to revitalized urban areas, getting suburban housewives to shop in the city, and encouraging increased use of private automobiles. In his cultural and economic analysis of urban renewal, Stone tied these objectives directly to the country's most prominent corporate engines. "Of the giant corporations which currently dominate the American economy," he wrote in 1974, "eight of the top ten are car manufacturers and oil companies." He also noted the prominence of the rubber and steel industry. "Inner city areas can, for the most part, be rehabilitated by small contractors and individual craftsmen," he asserted. "Renewal projects which call for totally new construction, however, require the organization and expensive equipment of large heavily financed corporations, as do highways and parking garages."

The notion that redevelopment plans were significantly influenced by the desire to provide lucrative contracts for America's top corporations was not a widely accepted one, but at the intersection of these structural, economic, and political forces, Stone located a particularly oppressive culture of compartmentalization, enforced by these newly redesigned urban landscapes. "People were not to walk, meet, investigate alternatives, but rather to drive on limited-access highways to fixed destinations," he wrote in his *Workbook of an Unsuccessful Architect*. "Mother would be at home, father at work in an industrial park, children at school in an educational park, old people in senior citizen centers, artists in cultural centers, government officials in government centers, shoppers in shopping centers—all traveling to and from their assigned destinations in individual automobiles. Very neat. Very predictable. Very easily managed—even capable of being programmed for a computer."[46] A brochure advertising Dixwell's Florence Virtue townhouses depicted family members literally placed in boxes in which they could carry out gender-, race-, and class-appropriate activities in prescribed private spaces. It was precisely in this manner that the lives and homes of the Strand's residents failed to conform to the master plan. They defied the roles and compartmentalizations of mother, father, child, shopper, artist, and senior citizen. They lacked "assigned destinations," to use Stone's terminology, and their lives lacked the efficiency inherent in regular commuter routes and schedules. They refused to confine their participation in culture to a cultural center, or to organized forms, such as the symphony or the theater, and they refused to shop at efficient shopping malls and shopping centers, instead preferring the small shops and groceries that the city had already earmarked for extinction.

The market-driven reconfiguration of the downtown landscape circumscribed individuals' right to choose how and where to live. The "slumless city" came to mean not just a city without tenements or condemned buildings, but also a city without residency hotels—a downtown built around a luxury hotel to the exclusion of a working-class residential one. Downtown redevelopment plans not only mandated the eviction and dispersal of coherent working-class residential communities like the one at the Strand, but also explicitly and deliberately transformed downtown from one kind of space to another: from a collection of densely populated residential and business spaces with a variety of shapes, sizes, and characters, to megablocks compartmentalized into units of highly controlled, large-scale commercial, tourist, and municipal uses.

What was lost in this transaction was much more than the physical spaces—the housing units, the lunch counters, the small grocery stores, and the light-manufacturing firms. The social costs of urban renewal have been—to quote the *New York Times*—"studied to death," but less often studied is the political and cultural importance of access to low-rent commercial and residential space in the heart of the city.

Between the Strand and the Plaza

I love the highways
And I love to watch when the man
puts sixteen lanes right through my door.
And our anger hasn't let up
—won't be long before we're fed up
and the town will see us GET UP
and we'll change the way they treat us in New Haven.
— David Kaetz, "Model City Blues," final verse,
in *AIM Newsletter*, Vol. 4, No. 8, April 1, 1969

In March of 1969, as the Strand tenants gathered in the hotel lobby to watch Joan Stone dance out their protest, a woman named Adele Grady was about to have sixteen lanes put right through her door. Grady worked for the city in the assessor's office and was the widow of a New Haven firefighter. She'd lived for twenty-seven years at 27 Dwight Street, where the city and the state seemed to think Connecticut Route 34 should be located. "Living in this area means a great deal to me," she wrote in a personal letter to Mayor Lee. Grady requested an apartment in a new labor-sponsored, nonprofit housing cooperative that had just been built at 65 Dwight Street.[47] The new development, Trade Union Plaza (TUP), consisted of nine brick buildings arranged around two courtyards. With rent subsidies through the federal government's new 221(d)(3) housing program, no tenant would have to pay more than 25 percent of his or her income for rent. Bounded by Dwight, Howe, and George streets, and North Frontage Road (the projected extension of Route 34 and access point from the west to what would be the Ring Road), the project's location ensured that many of its residents would be able to walk to their jobs downtown, at Yale University, and at nearby manufacturers, at a time when the city's master plan—and many redevelopment projects—encouraged reliance on automobiles and parking garages. The project was also within blocks of the hospital, Lee High School, and "Protestant, Ukrainian, and Catholic churches, as well as a Jewish synagogue."[48] Location and design considerations were economically fundamental to providing housing at low cost, and logistically fundamental to making that housing available to the city's workforce.

Like the 1966 Hill Cooperative Housing proposal, TUP emerged and operated out of a more comprehensive understanding of the connections that linked work, wages, family structures, and housing. As the testimony of many of the original tenants demonstrates, those who would move into the first apartments were part of the project's planning from the earliest stages. Charlotte Edwards, one of the original tenants, was "one of the first people to sit in and look at the blueprints."[49] In this way, TUP effectively shattered the tableau (if not the reality) of white men in suits hunched over blueprints inside boardrooms. Edwards went on to serve as president of the tenant association for a decade. "I had the keys to each person's house in case they got locked out," she recalled in 2001. By the early 1970s, New Haven had fourteen nonprofit cooperative housing developments that provided nearly 1,200 new units of low- and moderate-income housing. In reality, the number of slots reserved for low-income people—the most heavily subsidized—were vastly insufficient to meet the needs of all of the families and individuals displaced by demolitions throughout the city, but TUP offered (for a time, and for a handful of families) an alternative model for housing working people in the city.

As Adele Grady penned her written request to the mayor, TUP's first families arrived from New Haven's public housing, from the rubble of its slums and tenements, and from the temporary shelter of "relocation areas." As a project of the city's Central Labor Council, supported in large part by the Building Trades Unions, TUP was, in many respects, built by New Haven's rebuilding. Contrary to understandings at the time of how the government should help supply housing—with separate pockets of "middle-income" and "low-income" developments—the subsidy program allowed low-income families to live and participate equally in nonprofit cooperatives alongside moderate-income families, with no means of distinguishing the former from the latter. It was by no means a utopian space or a solution to the city's housing crisis, but it did offer an alternative model—something between the Strand and the Park Plaza—by which working people would live in the heart of the city in a space that was part collective, part private, and designed (as TUP's motto described) "for working families, by working families."

The first people to move into TUP in 1969 were twin sisters, Ovella Watts and Lovella Moore. Both women worked at the Park Plaza Hotel, and they were living together with their six children in one three-room flat on Henry Street when Vincent Sirabella, the president of their hotel workers' union, HERE Local 217, offered them an opportunity to live in the new housing cooperative. Sirabella was also the president of the New Haven Central Labor Council and an original TUP board member. Many of the original tenants of the seventy-seven-unit project came from the membership rolls of the unions at the Park Plaza, the phone company, the electric company, and the school system. "A lot of union families lived here," Ovella Watts recalled. "We all enjoyed that unity."[50] Like the tenants at the Strand Hotel, who saw their neighbors and doorman as an extended family, Ovella Watts recalled that, at TUP, "Everybody looked out for everybody. It was a clean, pleasant place to live. If some families ran low on food in the middle of the week, we'd cook up some food and bring it to them and all eat together. We'd sit down late at night, laughing and talking."[51]

Although the Strand Hotel was spared demolition until the fall of 1970, and more than twenty tenants were still living in their rooms until that summer, it was clear that—although they would not go quietly—they would, in fact, have to go. As the city bickered over the designs for the government center, some of the Strand tenants searched for other spaces in the city to rebuild their lives. In August of 1969, the mayor received a letter marked "special delivery" in the unsteady script of an aging hand. It was from Mrs. Jeanne Bay, a resident at the Strand, who identified herself as "disabled," and informed the mayor that she had written to him a number of times, awaiting response. She, too, was demanding an apartment in TUP. She said she'd seen a story in *Reader's Digest* about New Haven's wonderful urban renewal projects, and warned that she would go to the press and expose the truth about the city's redevelopment programs unless she was given a suitable apartment in the new labor-sponsored cooperative. "I'm being given the runaround," she wrote.[52] She wasn't the only one.

Charlotte Simms also fought her way into TUP, and nearly forty years later was still fighting to stay there. Simms first moved to New Haven in 1952, and by the 1960s, she and her six children were living in the Dixwell neighborhood. Her youngest son was terrified by the bulldozers that ushered in the construction of Florence Virtue, the middle-income development that would soon displace the family. "He was scared to go out—I would take the kids to the Freddie Fixer parade . . . and he was just petrified because they had these big bulldozers. There was so much construction going on." It wasn't long before her home was designated a "relocation area." The family was moved to a house on Day Street in the Dwight neighborhood, but nine months after they moved in, Simms was informed that they would have to move again. "Day St. became a relocation area, and I flipped because I told them I was not gonna be moving all over the city going from one relocation area to the other with a family."

The house into which Simms' family had been moved was actually owned by the State Highway Department. She hand-delivered her rent each month to a "little building" on nearby Linwood Street that served as the state highway office for the neighborhood. "I said this is ridiculous—of course they had it on paper [that] it was going to become a relocation area but they didn't tell us that." As it turned out, like Adele Grady's home, Simms' house was in the path of sixteen proposed lanes of State Highway 34. She and her neighbors were furious. They formed a committee. "We went downtown to the mayor, and we told *him*. We picketed city hall. We had signs and we made slogans. . . . First they said 'you people are not voters!' and we said 'we *are* voters.' " Eventually they were granted a meeting with state highway officials. "We told them exactly what they were doing," she recalled. "We said, 'You're just moving these people from one neighborhood to another neighborhood, you know, moving them all over town.' " They were angry and organized. "I just *wasn't* going to *move* anymore," she told the highway officials. "I said 'if you're gonna *build* in this neighborhood, then I'm gonna *live* in this neighborhood.' " She criticized the highway department and the city for flooding the local papers with stories about all of their new projects. Like Grady, she liked the Dwight neighborhood and was determined to stay there. "When we got finished with them I was *guaranteed* a place," she recalled. "We were all guaranteed places. They had it on paper . . . that's how I got in Trade Union Plaza."

As with the other original residents of TUP—union and community activists for a generation disrupted by both redevelopment and deindustrialization—it has proven to be difficult to get Charlotte Simms *out*. She was an active member of HPA, a familiar face in picket lines at city hall, a passenger on chartered buses to Washington, DC, to protest the war in Vietnam, and a member and leader of many neighborhood organizations. She has had her phone tapped by the FBI, her family—six children— displaced three times by the RA, and by 2001, her home of thirty-five years was threatened by TUP's conversion to "luxury apartments." A new owner bought TUP in 2001 for $4.1 million with plans to market it to students, professors, and those who worked in the biomedical field at the nearby hospital and drug corporations.[53] The new owner decided not to renew the project-based subsidy that enabled low-income families to have their rents subsidized, opting instead to charge more than $900 monthly for a one-bedroom apartment, doubling and in some cases tripling the rents. She told a local reporter that she needed the money for repairs, and even toyed with the idea of changing the name to "University Village."[54] But the problem with this plan was that, at the time she purchased the property, seventeen of TUP's original families still lived there, and they weren't willing to quietly surrender the character, nature, and use of this square block of urban space.[55]

Seeing their rents rise and the demographics of their community change in the hands of new ownership, the original residents strengthened a long-standing tie to the city's labor community in a fight not just to keep their homes, but to keep TUP a project-based Section 8 site. This distinction is important. The sixty-seven Section 8 families living in TUP as of August of 2002 may well have advocated simply to keep their own subsidies in order to stay in their own apartments. Instead they chose to fight to maintain a working community so that TUP could remain a housing option for low-income families for years to come. Ovella Watts, a hotel cook and union organizer for more than thirty years, explained to a local reporter the type of fight that the new owner of "University Village" was up against. "She bought it. It's hers," Watts said, conceding the realities of the for-profit real estate market. "But she's got to think about the families here. We're a bunch of fighting people. We know how to organize."[56] TUP, and other urban communities of working people, like the Strand—or spaces such as the Bread and Roses Coffeehouse and the Hill Neighborhood Union—not only required considerable organizing to build and preserve, but have also proven to be necessary spaces for a movement culture to survive.

Political scientist Gordon Lafer pointed out that redevelopment has many potential outcomes. "Depending on the interests of those driving the strategy," he argues in his study of Yale University's land and labor policies through the 1990s, redevelopment "may aim primarily at expanding the tax base for local governments, raising real estate values, or in the case of a progressive leadership or an influential labor movement, creating jobs for working class residents."[57] For people to assert, from the grass roots, a different strategy for redeveloping cities along an alternative set of community-centered priorities, they need to be able to organize. They need the right alliances (with labor, for example, as Lafer suggested), sufficient resources (for educating community members and running campaigns), and easy access to existing development plans, as well as engaged experts who can help navigate both the technical and the political. Otherwise they surrender all spaces and plans to a set of actors with very different interests.

Those who organized against the city's master plan in the 1960s did so not as radicals or preservationists, but as neighborhood people and trained experts demanding alternative strategies and visions for the spaces in which they lived and worked. They challenged the existing interests with heavily researched alternative plans that often differed from the city's master plans not in scope, feasibility, or effectiveness, but in interest. The best example of this was the fight against the State Street Garage. Although the State Department of Transportation had called for more investment in public transit and the construction of peripheral parking, the city had developed a plan for a massive 5,000-car parking garage because of the influence of Macy's and Malley's department stores, the desire for suburban shoppers to be able to travel easily into the city, and a secret deal brokered between the city and a private bank.

It is not surprising that many people who lived and worked in New Haven didn't want to see a half-mile of downtown demolished for a giant garage. But those who protested the garage plan did so not as defenders of a particular status quo—their activism was not conservative in that sense. They acted out of a sense that the area should be redeveloped along a different set of priorities. They proposed an alternative plan in which the underlying interest was not only saving neighborhood spaces and affordable housing, but also reducing the number of cars flooding the downtown and improving public transportation. Their proposal for peripheral parking and a shuttle service was not dissimilar to plans advocated by the state's own research report. They were not resisting development or impeding "progress"— they were redefining both.

Conclusion

The "After"

It's just not credible they can come in, invest $10 million in our neighborhood, and then be coy and say they can't tell us what their plans are! We've had so many homeowners displaced already. Something is wrong here.
— Hill Alderwoman Jackie James speaking at New Haven City Planning Commission meeting, June 20, 2007[1]

There are only six houses left on Sylvan Avenue. Who's to say if we go through with this, you might not come to us and say, 'We have two and a half acres, now we would like the rest—Sell us your house.'"
— Hill resident Marisol Rosario speaking at New Haven City Planning Commission meeting, June 20, 2007

Look, a lot of these people said they were not informed, they were not involved. But just by being here they are involved.
— Will Smith, vice president of Boston-based Intercontinental Real Estate Corporation, responding to demands from Hill residents for more say in the redevelopment of a site along Route 34, June 20, 2007

To stand on just about any corner in New Haven's "revitalized" downtown is to be reminded of the persistent and often aggressive newness of American cities, where progress is also eviction, improvement is also exclusion, and one person's on-ramp was once someone else's front porch. This is true of every developed and developing space because it is the nature of development. The pavement on which you park your car was probably once someone's living room. The highway you take to work cuts through what was once an elementary school, four apartment buildings, a corner store, and a dry cleaner. Even an analysis free of judgments about the uses and reuses of particular spaces (which this is not) would have to concede that the transformation of these spaces—for better or for worse, for progress or for profit—has some unquantifiable costs and some irreversible effects. As the displaced tenants, homeowners, and businesspeople who once made their lives on what are now highway extensions and convention centers pass away, so do their histories. Without the anchor of a physical space—albeit in disrepair, out of date, or in the way—these histories become the personal and separate properties of people who move away.

Such unquantifiable losses lead to the dangerous assumption that the form and content of these urban transformations are inevitable—that the biggest speed bump along the way is the work of the wrecking ball, and that the most important changes taking place are physical. In fact, there is nothing inevitable about turning low-rent apartments into parking spaces. It is the deliberate choice of one model over another, and in many cases, that transformation does not come easily. It faces significant organized opposition, the voices, faces, and forms of which are too often lost in the landscaping, paving, concrete, and steel of newly developed city spaces.

This account has focused on the ways in which people organized around alternative plans for their city—be they architectural, institutional (as in an alternative design for antipoverty or Model Cities programs), or socioeconomic (in the case of a movement-run coffeehouse, designs for cooperative housing, or programs run by a neighborhood union). These alternative proposals were created and promoted by coalitions of neighborhood people and a collection of educated professionals who were driven not by corporate alliances or financial possibilities, but by their own sense of what a "demonstration city" should demonstrate, what a "model city" should model. This could too easily be narrated as a story about the problems and failures of urban renewal. That story has been told many times over. The question is not whether cities should be revitalized or redesigned—anyone who has visited, lived, or worked in an urban area could probably draw up a to-do list. The question is who controls the strategy, process, and model for such a transformation, and what are the criteria for deciding on the importance, use, or fate of a particular space.

The preceding stories, threaded together along a highway that was never quite built, suggest the ways in which people can act collectively to shape the future of their cities. Although the results had limitations, there are instructive lessons written into the street patterns, high-rises, and empty lots of this still-struggling city. Through coalitions across race and class, the development of viable and sophisticated alternative plans, and intense grassroots organizing around street-level concerns, people in New Haven—like their counterparts in Chicago, Philadelphia, Boston, St. Louis, Cleveland, and many other cities in the mid- to late 1960s—defined "citizen participation" and urban democracy in broad and powerful terms through their struggles over particular urban spaces and forms. Coming as they did just as policy makers at the federal and local levels embarked on a model of "urban management," these grassroots campaigns affirmed the logistical and political impossibility of more repressive modes of managing the city.

In New Haven, the fight against the Lee, Johnson, and Nixon administrations' version of a model city offers particularly salient lessons in the relationship between urban space and social movements, the nature of urban democracy, and the legacy and future of urban development. New Haven is a small city with a historically vibrant network of activists; its history between Oak Street's demolition and the Ring Road's conceptual disappearance reveals the ways in which social movements are grounded in particular community spaces, which in turn are often threatened by master plans for redevelopment. The loss of these spaces makes it harder to fight back the urban models and imagined maps that threaten their existence. At the level of the street, movements like those for civil rights, war opposition, and black power—their national political and ideological frameworks notwithstanding—mobilized on the ground around demands for citizen control over, or representation in, both urban renewal and antipoverty programs.

These campaigns revealed the importance of door-to-door, face-to-face organizing. Conversations on street corners, in neighborhood union offices, and at dining room tables formed the basis of the movement's alternative model for the city. The vulnerability of the city's model, as the New Haven hearings of the National Commission on Urban Problems revealed in 1967, was that it was based on ideological and sometimes even computer-generated notions of what a city should be. Fred Harris' assertion that the elected officials should go out and talk to more people was not a challenge or a potshot—it was a reasonable suggestion. Accounts of that hearing in the summer of 1967, and others like it in New Haven and other cities across the country, offer instructive lessons about the nature of urban democracy. Given in context, they reveal that behind history's most visible moments of organized protest are thousands of other moments—often invisible and unquantifiable—of conversation, research, debate, and movement building. A "public hearing," the conventional mechanism for citizen involvement and urban democracy, can be a misleading beast. As these events demonstrate, one must ask what is really being heard, and by whom. What are the power relationships and structures at play as witnesses, experts, and community members offer up their statements, watch and listen from the gallery, or live their lives blocks or miles away?

How does the historian read or interpret the voices of those who had to be at work, had to leave early to care for the family, were afraid to speak in public, or just sat in the back, speaking their piece later that evening in more familiar spaces with more familiar people? How does the policy maker or urban planner draw from the protest songs, activist poetry, or stick-figure drawings of neighborhood children? The answer is that they don't unless the mandates quite explicitly articulated in the everyday conversations, expositions, and compositions of poor communities are amplified by mass movements, trained experts, and powerful political allies. Yet these movements and coalitions are, themselves, threatened by the increasing racial and economic segregation of metropolitan areas, and by shifts in development and employment that widen existing geographical, social, and cultural gaps.

The centrality of good jobs to both strong communities and vigorous citizen participation is evident from this historical study, but it demands more comprehensive, quantitative study. When the lives of potential community leaders are necessarily consumed by more minimum-wage hours and additional low-wage jobs, how can they effectively organize their neighborhoods? How can people effectively organize unions to secure good wages and benefits if urban housing prices and the migration of jobs demand that they live far from work—or work two or three jobs to pay rent? If their jobs don't provide the securities, protections, and living wages of a good union contract, how do they achieve the "collective self confidence" and the "high level of personal political self-respect" that Goodwin argues are necessary prerequisites of movement building? In the 1960s, programs aimed at solving the problems of poverty, and redevelopment schemes intended to reverse the decay of the inner city, failed to comprehensively address the disappearance of good manufacturing jobs or improve the wages, benefits, or security of the service-sector jobs that remained.

John Wilhelm came to realize this in the 1960s as he tried to organize for better housing, services, and a say in redevelopment for the Hill neighborhood. "An antipoverty program didn't make any sense if you weren't addressing the fact that people were poor," said Wilhelm, who took a job as an organizer with the New Haven local of the union of Hotel Employees and Restaurant Employees (HERE) following his organizing work in the Hill. "It seemed to me that unions would have a better opportunity, a better possibility, of addressing the fact that people were poor . . . that's why I became interested in the labor movement."[2] Wilhelm later became the president of the hospitality industry sector of UNITE-HERE, an international union for the hotel, restaurant, apparel, and textile industries representing nearly a million workers and retirees throughout North America. The labor movement continues to be interested in the Hill, as many residents—employees at Yale–New Haven Hospital—fight a virulent antiunion campaign to turn their jobs into good union jobs, which would not only improve wages and benefits at one workplace, but also revitalize a persistently poor neighborhood.

The Hill neighborhood—like the nine brick buildings of Trade Union Plaza—remains a contested terrain. Over the years, many streets in the Hill have become buildings and parking lots for Yale–New Haven Hospital, but plans to reorganize and redevelop the space in one massive redevelopment project were stalled over the years—executed in fits and starts—because of the unwillingness of the Hill community to go without a fight. In the summer of 2004, after the hospital announced its plans to build a new fourteen-story, 497,000-square-foot cancer research and treatment center, a group of Hill residents called Community Organized for Responsible Development (CORD) went door-to-door to identify the top concerns of people in the neighborhood. After surveying more than 700 households, they authored a proposed "community benefits agreement" (CBA), demanding good jobs, more affordable housing, youth programs, and environmental standards in exchange for new developments such as the one the hospital had in mind.[3] At four o'clock in the morning on Monday, March 22, 2006, after not only forty-eight hours of "intense closed-door negotiating," but also two years of intense neighborhood organizing, New Haven mayor John DeStefano, Jr., stepped out onto the second-floor atrium of city hall, where Charlotte Simms had sat a generation earlier, and announced that the hospital and the community had reached an agreement.

This CBA included not only the terms of design and land acquisition, but also a fair process for union recognition for Yale–New Haven's hospital workers and a number of programs and payments to the surrounding community.[4] (By the fall of that year, YNHH had violated the fair union election clause of the agreement, as well as federal labor law, and the union election was called off.) In the meantime, the hospital was given the green light to build its cancer center. The height was a point of contention, with city officials and neighborhood groups asserting that it was too tall for the neighborhood's scale. With the signing of the agreement, Yale–New Haven Hospital got all fourteen of its floors, and the city agreed to sell two parcels of land for a 1,300-space parking garage and offices along Route 34, yards from the street-facing porches of Trade Union Plaza.[5] There are many competing plans for this stretch of road, which is often referred to in the press or in public meetings as "the highway that goes nowhere." The city's Office of Economic Development unveiled plans in 2006 to build a "residential and retail, biomedical and garage development" along Route 34, where Oak Street's masses once lived and worked. It is what one reporter called a "still-open wound from Urban Renewal failures of the '50s, '60s, and '70s."[6]

Residents packed the community room at the Timothy Dwight School in February of 2006, some handing out fliers that read "People First! Cars Second!" as a team from city hall offered a slide presentation of their "drawn plans" for Route 34. True to the legacy of alternative proposals in New Haven, one former neighborhood organization president was—in the words of a local reporter—"Reputed to carry around his own group's ten-year-old plans for the corridor zone, now beat up nearly beyond legibility." The activist told the reporter that the city's plan was about "big-box buildings, and bringing people in from the outside," while his organization's plan was about " 'blending with community fabric' and creating jobs for people from the neighborhood." It was a familiar refrain from a half-century-long fight song. It's a fight that hadn't really been won by community organizers, but hadn't yet been lost either, as the unfinished highway waited for an answer.

More than a year later, in June of 2007, fifty Hill neighborhood residents packed into a City Planning Commission meeting after hearing that a Boston developer planned to seek a zoning change for the two-and-a-half-acre parcel it had just purchased along Route 34, adjacent to the hospital. Many of those present, one paper reported, lived within fifty feet of the site, and nobody had "even knocked on their doors."[7] The developer, Intercontinental Real Estate Corporation, offered few details, asserting that the proposals were in line with the city's master plan. It was clear that the site would primarily be used for parking, and that some of the parcel would be tax-exempt. There was also talk of low-income and elderly housing, but no clear plans and no guarantees. One community leader, Maurice Blest Peters, asked Intercontinental if they would be willing to sign a community benefits agreement. A lawyer for the developer said he would advise against it. "Look," said Peters, "we live here. We have no place to go." In fact, Intercontinental already owned every parcel on the block except one. The William Rowe Apartments on Howard Avenue were owned by the New Haven Housing Authority, and Cameron Davis Taylor lived there, along with the other eighty-five people he spoke for at that meeting. "We may not have a lot of money," said Taylor, "but we count because we're here."

"Why aren't you talking to us, for example, about job training programs in our neighborhood?" asked Peters. "Why aren't you talking to us about having, as part of your development, a 24-hour daycare so our women can go to work? Yes, there's poverty out there, and poverty breeds violence. This development will not just happen any old way. We've seen too much of this. If necessary, this will be taken to the streets." The story of resistance to the city's master plans a generation ago, and the repeated assertions of alternative plans, models, and visions by organized neighborhood people, informs this ongoing debate while illuminating the complex meanings of yet another stretch of road in a still-contested city.

In a June 2005 decision by the U.S. Supreme Court concerning the power of eminent domain, the court ruled 5–4 that the government can seize private property not only for the purpose of constructing public resources like highways and schools, as it has historically been used, but also for the purpose of private development. In her dissenting opinion, Justice Sandra Day O'Connor wrote, "Under the banner of economic development, all private property is now vulnerable to being taken and transferred to another private owner, so long as it might be upgraded." She asked, "Who among us can say she already makes the most productive or attractive use of her property?" She noted that the decision would place a greater burden on the powerless and poor, stating, "The government now has license to transfer property from those with fewer resources to those with more."[8] A few months later, Charlotte Simms sat in a meeting room at the New Haven People's Center, where Trade Union Plaza's tenants' organization met each week to share ideas and support. As the new owner continued renovations on the newly vacant units right across the street, Simms shook her head. "It's the same thing over and over again," she said. "I'm 75—why should I be worried about housing today? I have to fight the same fight now that I had to fight in 1965, and it should not be that way."[9]

Today the Strand is gone—in its place is the corner of a massive, gray, concrete federal building that cannot, by law, be photographed.[10] The Park Plaza is now the Omni New Haven Hotel at Yale, a union hotel hosting parents during graduation weekend and prestigious speakers during their engagements. Although the roof deck pool is gone, it has a fabulous view of the Long Island Sound and Yale University from the bar and restaurant on the nineteenth floor, just as advertised at the time of the Park Plaza's grand opening. Trade Union Plaza, where many of the hotel's employees have lived over the years, looks the same (with the exception of some wear and tear), but its tenants are slowly being replaced by students and scientists, as the new owner planned. The few original tenants who stayed and fought have been given lifetime rights to their apartments at subsidized rates. On Dixwell Avenue, plans for a new University Park Dixwell faded quickly, and although Elm Haven was replaced with an attractive, mixed-income, new urbanist development called Monterey Place that houses far fewer poor people, the Monterey, a once-famous jazz club a few blocks down the street where every big name once played to packed houses, never reopened.

Florence Virtue never became the destination of choice for white middle-class families, the Dixwell footbridge never materialized, and the suburban-style shopping plaza is now anchored on one end by a new low-end grocery store that sat vacant for more than a decade, and on the other end by a church. Dixwell is still a busy, vibrant street, and the Freddy Fixer Parade still draws thousands to its sidewalks and corners each spring, but contrary to the predictions of the Redevelopment Agency forty years ago, it is still relatively poor, still predominantly black, and still isolated from the university that has inched its way farther up the avenue in the intervening years, expanding expensive boutiques and restaurants onto blocks that were once part of the "town" rather than the "gown."

On State Street, where the "monster" garage was drawn and planned, is a new and somewhat underutilized train station, a massive, high-fenced, narrow-windowed FBI headquarters, and a scattering of old storefronts, once connected, but now separated by vacant spaces and parking lots. Overlooking the town green, where the Progress Pavilion was erected one fall day by an army of eager volunteers, there was—for a brief time—a shopping mall, where the city's first escalator drew excited crowds. The mall was vacant for more than a decade, and luxury apartments have since moved in as part of the city's most recent downtown revitalization. The long-quiet carcasses of Macy's and Malley's have been resurrected as expensive coffee shops, upscale restaurants, and trendy bars. Across the street, the marquis of a new art cinema lights the windows of vacant luxury lofts up and down Temple Street. It is hard to argue with the before and after images. The people who lived and worked on these downtown streets were "cleared" half a century ago, so the most recent transformation could hardly have been controversial.

Writing about La Casita Salvación, an important contested site of Puerto Rican culture and social life in New York City, Juan Flores recounts the community's struggle to keep that space intact in the face of gentrification. "The purpose . . . was to show, by sheer human presence and activity, that the space is not at all vacant and is already being put to valid use," he explains. "The best way to keep the authorities at bay is to celebrate the blatant fact of collective occupancy."[11] Or, to borrow a phrase from Hill resident Cameron Davis Taylor, "We count because we're here." The pressure to prove "valid use" and blatantly occupy a community space speaks to the importance of control over redevelopment strategy, and the need for cultures and spaces of organizing. Organized struggles for an alternative plan, such as those described in the preceding chapters, were the ultimate assertions of occupancy in that they claimed not only the existence of living bodies in a particular space, but also the insistence of those bodies to collectively control both the physical and ideological shape of their city.

Historical accounts of urban transformations too often do "leave out the citizens," as sociologist and urban theorist Manuel Castells has argued, rendering spaces uncontested and promoting a narrative of inevitability.[12] There is nothing inevitable about uprooting and replacing a cultural space like Flores' La Casita. These spaces are, in Flores' words, "already being put to valid use." These uses are challenged only because of the perceived "undesirability" of the inhabitants, or the potential profitability of alternative uses. Urban renewal (or redevelopment, or gentrification, or revitalization) is not simply a natural, progressive process by which particular areas are renewed and improved. It is a conscious choice of one kind of space over another, and often more to the point, one kind of people over another.

The intrusion of the present tense into this historical account underscores the fact that this "urban renewal" period is not a twenty-year moment in the past. It is not something that was executed, reconsidered, and condemned around 1962 when Herbert Gans published his critique of the redevelopment of Boston's West End. Cities continue to struggle, and in devising new solutions and models, the interests of people living in poor and working-class neighborhoods continue to conflict with the interests of those in power—in New Haven and across the country. Plans for urban redevelopment cannot be separated (then or now) from the constraints and effects of persistent segregation, economic and educational inequality, and the ever-growing social, cultural, and geographic gap between rich and poor. How we define "urban problems" often determines the range of imaginable solutions. Problems such as crime and blight have very different solutions than problems such as poverty, segregation, lack of affordable housing, and lack of good jobs. For whom and to what end is a city "renewed"? Who should be asked, who should be told, and who should be moved? These are politically and culturally difficult questions, but there is untapped lived expertise among people in struggling neighborhoods and their allies.

Across the country, communities are forced to organize and assert their occupancy in contested urban spaces, as rising housing costs and the disappearance of good jobs bare the human cost of this persistent urban model. The poor, working, and middle classes are all being squeezed out of cities, as a very deliberate transformation—not unlike the one that pitted the Strand against the Park Plaza forty years ago—turns one kind of space into another. By 2005 in Scottsdale, Arizona—a city similar in size to New Haven—low-rent apartments were scarce, and one-bedroom condominiums were selling for as much as a half million dollars. "Every day, Scottsdale's working-class south moves a bit closer to resembling the moneyed north," wrote reporters for the *Arizona Republic*. "Small ranch homes built for Motorola workers now fetch luxury prices." As in New Haven, a large university (in this case, Arizona State) worked with developers to plan a high-tech research park, the $340 million ASU Scottsdale Center for New Technology and Innovation, in hopes of attracting workers from the "knowledge economy" to some 4,000 high-paying technology jobs. But "teachers, firefighters, and regular people" would no longer be able to live in Scottsdale, the *Republic* reported. When WestStone Properties attempted to redevelop the Wheel Inn Trailer Ranch, a plan that would displace elderly renters on fixed incomes to build new luxury condos, residents fought back. The developer withdrew the proposal after considerable public opposition, but that was only one of many plans to remake Scottsdale into a different place for different people.[13]

In Hartford, Connecticut's capital city, downtown luxury apartments advertise monthly rents in excess of $3,000, and condominiums in the city's center have begun to sell for more than $400,000. This is an entirely new vision for what has traditionally been a city of poor people. A recent nationwide study of "socioeconomic stress" ranked Hartford the nation's most "stressed" city based on factors that included poverty, unemployment, education, and housing. It beat out both Newark and Buffalo for the title.[14] Since 1970, the Rockefeller Institute has released a similar "urban hardship index," and Hartford always seems to find its way to the top. Its suburban neighbors, however, have always ranked among the nation's most affluent, making Hartford's metropolitan area the most segregated in the nation, according to a 2004 study published by the Brookings Institution.[15] Struggling with all this "socioeconomic stress" and "urban hardship," the city has adopted a strategy of attracting suburban affluence to solve urban problems, a very popular model of urban revitalization most commonly called gentrification.

"Gentrification was once a dirty word in American urban politics," wrote Mike Swift of the *Hartford Courant,* but Hartford's political leaders are now openly staking this very poor city's future on redesigning downtown to suit the demands of the affluent. Hartford mayor Eddie A. Perez told the *Courant* that it wouldn't actually be "gentrification" if they could attract an influx of wealthy people without displacing poor people. This might actually be possible in downtown Hartford, where—as in New Haven—housing for poor people was more or less removed from the center of the city decades ago. An urban model that caters to the wealthy—a plan for renewing a city of poor people that is rooted in attracting the rich, rather than, say, good jobs—constitutes a distinct cultural and political assertion of what a city actually is. It is a threatening assertion to poor, working-, and middle-class people who choose to live an urban life.

Two time zones away, low- and middle-income tenants in Los Angeles also experienced that threatening assertion firsthand. In LA's Koreatown, in a tableau of resistance familiar to urban neighborhoods across the country, residents of one apartment building slated for demolition hung a sign from their windows that read, "Save our neighborhood. Your building could be next." In the summer of 2006, the landlord announced that the historic building was to be replaced by a six-story luxury condominium complex. "It's not just having to pick up and find another apartment, which will be smaller and more expensive," one twenty-year tenant told *LA Weekly*. "It's also breaking the ties to the community that we've had for 20 years now. We've been to various neighborhood parties. We've hosted neighborhood parties. We've patronized the local businesses here. It's total upheaval." Urban reinvestment initiatives throughout Los Angeles have longtime residents worried. The elimination of graffiti, the construction of new playgrounds, police stations, light rail lines, and library branches, all seem to fuel or signal new interest by the region's affluent in previously ignored areas. Community organizations have begun to march at the first sign of development, understanding that improvements and investments in poor neighborhoods are tied to real estate and not to people.[16]

When improvements signal imminent eviction for the not-so-rich, as they did in Dixwell in the 1960s, San Francisco in the 1990s, or Koreantown in more recent years, it becomes all the more urgent to reexamine the notion of a model city, the priorities set by the power brokers of urban development, the role of communities in deciding the fate of troubled urban spaces, and the blueprint for an urban future. Never in recent memory has this urgency been more clear than in the aftermath of Hurricane Katrina, which has forced a renewed discussion about the question of how, for whom, and on what model a city should be rebuilt. The problems at the nexus of poverty, segregation, and urban design that the storm washed ashore were only illuminated—and not caused—by Katrina, and they exist in every struggling city, but the sudden slum clearance and fast-forward demolition of an entire urban space and system required both a new reckoning with the concept of a model city and the notion of citizen participation. "We all know that the prevailing model for urban development is to get rid of poor people," wrote commentator Glen Ford in September 2005, shortly after the storm subsided, in an article subtitled "Will the New New Orleans Be Black?" "The disaster provides an opportunity to deploy this model in New Orleans on a citywide scale, under the guise of rebuilding the city and its infrastructure," he wrote in his online journal, *Black Commentator*. "The question that we must pose, repeatedly and in the strongest terms, is: Through whose vision, and in whose interest, will New Orleans rise again."[17]

Many believe, hope, or fear that New Orleans will rise in the vision of Disneyland and in the interest of the Hiltons, Marriotts, and Trumps of the world. Few disagree (whether happily or unhappily) with predictions that the new New Orleans will have an economy dominated by tourism and entertainment. Developers are salivating over that idea as they draft proposals for new luxury hotels, condominiums, and high-end restaurants. In a post-Katrina interview, Loyola University law professor Bill Quigley noted the political and economic landscape left in the storm's wake. "The people in charge in the federal government, in cooperation with some private developers in the areas, have actually seen Katrina as an opportunity to get rid of the lowest-income people in the community and to, in a sense, start over without the participation of people who used to live here," he told Amy Goodman of the TV and radio program *Democracy Now*. "This is really a pitched battle for who gets to come back to New Orleans and who is going to participate in the rebuilding."[18] Questions of citizen participation in the new New Orleans, like those confronting the new New Haven a generation earlier, are challenging cities across the country as they struggle to revitalize and redefine themselves in a competitive and relatively placeless global marketplace, where service jobs can't pay urban rents, the real estate market discourages affordable housing, and the erosion of both housing subsidies and labor rights at the federal level have absolved the government of any responsibility.

For all the debate that erupted and then quickly fizzled in the late 1960s, the legislative definition of "maximum feasible citizen participation" was ultimately irrelevant. The grass roots defined it through community demands and collective action. While it is true, as Frederick Douglass said in 1857, that power concedes nothing without a demand, the transformation of urban geographies and economies has made it even harder than it was in the 1960s to build the movements necessary to make those demands. The burden for articulating those demands could not then, nor can it now, be placed entirely on the community. Every attempt from the grass roots starts at a financial, organizational, and historical disadvantage. In order to fairly determine democratic models and visions for the city, people in disadvantaged communities need the resources for civic education, access to information, and mobilization for proposing alternatives on a more level playing field. Governments, businesses, and institutions must account and correct for this imbalance of power.

There is not much money to be made in housing poor people. Perhaps this could change if economists, planners, architects, developers, corporations, and governments cooperate creatively with that goal in mind, but for the time being, the reality is that those who live in the city must fight to stay there. To make matters more difficult for working families, there happens to be a lot of money to be made in taking housing *away* from poor people. Luxury apartments, upscale retail, biotech, and high-rent office spaces can make money for the city, for developers, and for investors without offering any of the housing or jobs that low-income people need. That is why citizen participation has to be more than a democratic ideal—it has to be a real working and enforced mechanism, like a Community Benefits Agreement (CBA), in which development is subject to rules, guidelines, and stipulations made by community groups seeking more affordable housing, access to public transportation, day care, environmental protections, organizing rights, good jobs, and control over the physical shape of their neighborhoods.

For a community to win these kinds of agreements, it has to define itself broadly and organize aggressively. Experts and academics can work in partnership with low-income families as equal partners contributing different strengths to the comprehensive process of reshaping the city. In a less segregated world, they would in fact be (and sometimes are) neighbors. In building their models, they should start door-to-door, on front steps, and in union halls, because the model they need must demarcate not only an urban form and content, but also a viable social movement to make it happen. This is, perhaps, the greatest lesson to be learned from those who fought for a different urban model in New Haven's model city. Through collective action, they staked a claim on particular city spaces, and in doing so, enacted—if only for a brief time—their alternative vision for an urban future. While their blueprint never became the master plan, it challenged the dominant definition of "progress" and the prevailing cultural trajectory for cities, transforming a demonstration area into a contested space.

Notes

INTRODUCTION

1. For more on redlining, see Gregory D. Squires and Charis E. Kubrin's *Privileged Places: Race, Residence, and the Structure of Opportunity* (Boulder, CO: Lynne Rienner Publishers, 2006).

2. Neil Smith, *New Urban Frontier—Gentrification and the Revanchist City* (New York: Routledge, 1996), p. 27; see also Mike Davis, *City of Quartz: Excavating the Future in Los Angeles* (New York: Verso, 1990).

3. See Robert A. Dahl, *Who Governs: Democracy and Power in an American City* (New Haven: Yale University Press, 1961); William G. Domhoff, *Who Really Rules: New Haven and Community Power Reexamined* (New Brunswick, NJ: Transaction Books, 1978); William Lee Miller, *The Fifteenth Ward and the Great Society* (Boston: Houghton Mifflin, 1966); Nelson W. Poslby, *Community Power and Political Theory* (New Haven: Yale University Press, 1963, 2nd ed. 1980); Douglas Rae, *City: Urbanism and Its End* (New Haven, Yale University Press, 2003); and Allan R. Talbot, *The Mayor's Game: Richard Lee of New Haven and the Politics of Change* (New York: Praeger, 1967).

4. On Boston, see Herbert Gans, *The Urban Villagers: Group and Class in the Life of Italian-Americans* (New York: Free Press of Glencoe, 1962); and Thomas H. O'Connor, *Building a New Boston: Politics and Urban Renewal, 1950–1970* (Boston: Northeastern University Press, 1993). On New York, see Joel Schwartz, *The New York Approach: Robert Moses, Urban Liberals, and Redevelopment of the Inner City* (Columbus: Ohio State University Press, 1993); and Robert A. Caro, *The Power Broker: Robert Moses and the Fall of New York* (New York: Knopf, 1974).

5. Arthur Krock, "In the Nation: It Must Have Been Christmas or Something." *New York Times,* December 25, 1952. Document ID: 84382321, from ProQuest Historical Newspapers, *New York Times* 1851–2004 database, retrieved October 21, 2007. The plumber was Labor Secretary Martin Durkin, president of the Plumbers Union, who resigned in October of 1953, less than a year after his appointment.

6. Brian Akre, "Misquote of the Century: What's Good for GM." General Motors Global Corporate News Department, http://fyigmblogs.com/2006/05/misquote_of_the_century_whats.html (accessed October 21, 2007).

7. Morris Dickstein, "From the Thirties to the Sixties: The New York World's Fair in Its Own Time," in *Remembering the Future: The New York World's Fair from 1939 to 1964,* ed. Robert Rosenblum (New York: Queens Museum, 1989), p. 28.

8. This 1937 clash became known as "The Battle of the Overpass." Ford had constructed an overpass across a busy street so that shift changes at the plant wouldn't interfere with traffic. Reuther, along with about fifty other union activists, attempted to distribute fliers to workers informing them of their rights under the Wagner Act. Ford's private security guards repeatedly kicked Reuther in the face and stomach before tossing him down the stairs of the overpass. See John Barnard, *Walter Reuther and the Rise of the Auto Workers* (Boston: Little, Brown & Co., 1987).

9. Walter Reuther, memo to President Lyndon B. Johnson, May 15, 1965, published in Charles M. Haar, *Between the Ideal and the Reality: A Study of the Fate, Origin, and Legacy of the Model Cities Program* (Boston: Little, Brown & Co., 1975), appendix.

10. Haar, *Between the Ideal and the Reality,* p. 48.

11. Ibid., p. 56.

12. Ibid., p. 144.

13. Robert T. Chase, "Class Resurrection: The Poor People's Campaign of 1968 and Resurrection City," *Essays in History* 40 (1998), http://etext.virginia.edu/journals/EH/ (accessed November 20, 2006).

14. The historians never seemed to see it that way. As the home of a major research university with a world-renowned history department, New Haven and its sidewalks, coffee shops, and restaurants have long been the haunts of historians in the process of writing their books, so although few academic histories have been written *on* the Elm City, thousands have been written *in* it. So much for the old historians' adage "Dig where you stand." The city's *local* historians, however, particularly those who were at their most prolific before the widespread use of electricity, have been fascinated with the city's origins, railroads, and clock, corset, and carriage factories, but beyond the realm of local history, a search yields few published texts. Again, this is not to discount the existing social scientific scholarship on New Haven, much of which has been, since the 1960s, in response to Robert Dahl's *Who Governs? Democracy and Power in an American City* (1961). Dahl's pluralism theory (derived from a case study of New Haven politics) would be a springboard for many future studies, including William Domhoff's *Who Really Rules? New Haven and Community Power Reexamined* (1978). Responding directly to Dahl, Domhoff documents a link between New Haven's local power structure and what he argues is a national ruling class. Domhoff reexamines Dahl's data and challenges him for failing to consider the national context for political decisions made in New Haven. Domhoff claims to have relied at first on "the work of political activists who published the alternative newspaper *Modern Times*" (p. xi). This publication started as

the *AIM Newsletter* on which I rely heavily for this account. The most recent and prominent of New Haven's social scientific legacy is Douglas Rae's *City: Urbanism and Its End* (2003), in which he argues that the end of urbanism—defined by very centralized localism: neighborhood grocers, schools, workplaces, and a mixed-income urban geography—came around 1917 with the convergence of automobility, the electric grid, and the growth of big business. As a political scientist, Rae is interested in the political and sociological patterns that chart the contours of what he sees as this city's "rise and fall." When he says "786 votes" were "wasted on socialism" (p. 183) in the 1910 mayoral election, a historian interested in movements for change cannot help but think of 786 socialists in a factory town. By the end of Rae's account, New Haven has become a dot on a regional map of New York City. He laments the passing of local sidewalk culture and small businesses, while seemingly accepting the inevitability of these transformations and eagerly anticipating a time when better regional transportation networks will allow all New Haveners to get more quickly to high-paying jobs in New York. By this model, sidewalk culture will be revived by more of the city's residents walking from their downtown luxury homes and apartments to the few operational and overpriced small groceries instead of driving to big chain supermarkets.

15. See Gordon Lafer, "Land and Labor in the Post-Industrial University Town: Remaking Social Geography," *Political Geography* 22 (January 2003): 89–117.

16. Fred Powledge, *Model City: A Test of American Liberalism; One Town's Efforts to Rebuild Itself* (New York: Simon & Schuster, 1970), p. 17.

17. "Forward Look in Connecticut," *Time*, June 24, 1957, p. 28.

18. Harris Stone, *Workbook of an Unsuccessful Architect* (New York: Monthly Review Press, 1974), p. 21. Stone was part of a national movement of progressive architects. See also Robert Goodman, *After the Planners* (New York: Simon & Schuster, 1971).

19. Stone, *Workbook*, p. 21.

20. Because this project is organized around the path of the Ring Road, neighborhoods not directly in that path are somewhat neglected in this account. The most notable and regrettable absences are Fair Haven, the heart of the city's Latino community, and Wooster Square, New Haven's Little Italy. Both deserve significant scholarly attention as studies of race, class, ethnicity, urban development, politics, and neighborhood organizing, both past and present.

21. Richard Wolff, interview by the author, November 11, 2004, New York.

22. Douglas Rae et al., "Urban Renewal Figures, New Haven 1950s–1960s," Historical New Haven Digital Collection, Yale University Library, http://www.library.yale.edu/newhavenhistory/documentlist.html (accessed April 10, 2005).

23. Rae, *City*, p. 340.

24. Rae et al., "Urban Renewal Figures, New Haven 1950s–1960s."

25. U.S. Census of Population and Housing, *Summary Population and Housing Characteristics: Connecticut* (Washington, DC: U.S. Government Printing Office, 1960).

26. Robert Cook, untitled document on the Hill neighborhood, n.d., personal files of Robert Cook, on loan to the author.

27. Information about State Street's occupants comes from Price & Lee's *New Haven* (New Haven, CT: Price & Lee, 1968, 1972). Additional information is from Joan Stone, interview by the author, July 18, 2005, New Haven, CT.

28. Elizabeth Mills Brown, *New Haven: A Guide to Architecture and Urban Design* (New Haven, CT: Yale University Press, 1976), p. 117.

29. *New Haven* (New Haven, CT: Price & Lee), 1972.

30. Lawrence Goodwyn, *The Populist Moment: A Short History of Agrarian Revolt in America* (New York: Oxford University Press, 1978).

31. Quoted in Nancy A. Naples, ed., *Community Activism and Feminist Politics: Organizing Across Race, Class, and Gender* (New York: Routledge, 1998), p. 261.

CHAPTER 1

1. Victoria Thomas, letter to Mayor Richard C. Lee, November 2, 1955, Edward J. Logue Papers, Yale Manuscripts and Archives, Yale University Library, box 41, folder 183.

2. "Troubled and Troublesome Families," *Journal of Housing* (April 1957). The phrase came from a 1956 study by the Baltimore Housing Authority, which found that such "problem families" tended to be long-term public housing residents, and often fatherless. The study explicitly responds to an understanding on the part of the housing authority that it must house all low-income families, and not just what it called "model" families. Problem families were defined by the Baltimore study as "every family you consider to be a problem . . . those who have difficulties they cannot handle; require continuing assistance in obtaining services from social and welfare agencies . . . become involved in difficulties with other tenants; or for any other reason require more than their share of time and effort on the part of agency staff " (p. 118). By this definition, those who agitated or organized for better social services and living conditions would be deemed "problem families." The Baltimore study reported between 5 and 10 percent of the families in their housing projects to be "problems." These families were disproportionately white, which the study attributed to the fact that white families in public housing tended to come from lower income groups than black tenants.

3. Charles M. Haar, *Between the Ideal and the Reality: A Study of the Fate, Origin, and Legacy of the Model Cities Program* (Boston: Little, Brown & Co., 1975) , p. 7. For more on the "urban crisis," see Thomas J. Sugrue, *Origins of the Urban Crisis: Race and Inequality in Postwar Detroit* (Princeton, NJ: Princeton University Press, 1996). For earlier accounts, see James Q. Wilson, ed., *The Metropolitan Enigma: Inquiries into the Nature and Dimensions of America's Urban Crisis* (Cambridge, MA: Harvard University Press, 1968); and Richard A. Cloward and Frances Fox Piven, *The Politics of Turmoil: Essays on Poverty, Race, and the Urban Crisis* (New York: Pantheon Books, 1974).

4. Mayor Richard C. Lee, letter to Commissioner G. Albert Hill of the Connecticut State Highway Department, April 9, 1954, p. 8. Edward J. Logue Papers, Manuscripts and Archives, Yale University Library, box 39, folder 144. Even the city planning department's new logo emphasized this commitment to a suburban vision. A black-and-white rendering of the three trademark churches on the New Haven Green sat below the exclamation "Tomorrow is here!" Over this, in blue ink, the city's nine squares were superimposed and a web of highways and railroad tracks stretched out in all directions, pointing to those suburban neighbors. The very agency charged with the reorganization of urban space infused its own letterhead with a vi-

sion of the city as a place intended to serve its suburban neighbors. The birth of the RA was contemporaneous with New Haven's innovations in the burgeoning field of highway design ("Tomorrow" was, in fact, "here" in New Haven, as the slogan suggested), and from the earliest plans for Dixwell, the Hill, State Street, and downtown, notions of highway design shaped visions for those neighborhood blocks. In the words of the planning director Norris Andrews, "The very nature of the city's highway proposal . . . is so complex and involves advanced planning considerations which are novel in the field of highway design." Norris Andrews, New Haven City Planning Director, letter to Samuel Speilvogel, Director of New Haven Redevelopment Agency, July 16, 1953, Edward J. Logue Papers, Manuscripts and Archives, Yale University Library, box 39, folder 138.

5. Daniel Solomon, *Global City Blues* (Washington, DC: Island Press, 2003), p. 9.

6. "Development Chief Explains Oak St. Connector," *New Haven Journal-Courier*, October 7, 1955, Edward J. Logue Papers, Manuscripts and Archives, Yale University Library, newspaper clipping file.

7. *New Haven Journal-Courier*, August 12, 1953, Edward J. Logue Papers, Manuscripts and Archives, Yale University Library, newspaper clipping file.

8. Undated, untitled typed document on the origins of the New Haven Redevelopment Agency, Edward J. Logue Papers, Manuscripts and Archives, Yale University Library, 1955 file, series V, box 35, folder 92.

9. "Factors Pushing New Haven," undated typed memo, 1955 file, Edward J. Logue Papers, Manuscripts and Archives, Yale University Library, series V, box 35, folder 92.

10. Internal RA memo, November 12, 1953, Edward J. Logue Papers, Manuscripts and Archives, Yale University Library, box 39, folder 138.

11. Mrs. Robert L. Smith, New Haven Human Relations Council Housing Committee Chair, letter to Everett Dirkson, Senate Appropriations Committee, May 1, 1955, Edward J. Logue Papers, Manuscripts and Archives, Yale University Library, box 41, folder 171.

12. "Land and Finance in Urban Redevelopment in the Interest of the Municipality: A memorandum submitted in October 1945 to the Mayor and the City Council as part of a report on the Groundwork and Inventory for The Master Plan of Pittsburgh," p. 7, Edward J. Logue Papers, Manuscripts and Archives, Yale University Library, box 39, folder 139. This term, "economic rent," really translated into the higher rents intended for redeveloped areas, a key factor in making them more desirable.

13. S. Spielvogel, NHRA, letter to Arthur Van Buskirk of T. Mellon & Sons, Pittsburgh, PA, February 15, 1954, Edward J. Logue Papers, Manuscripts and Archives, Yale University Library.

14. *Berman et al., Executors v. Parker et al.*, 348 U.S. 26 (1954). The case involved the redevelopment of a low-rent area of Washington, D.C. The court stated that "redevelopment of an entire area under a balanced integrated plan so as to include not only new homes but also schools, churches, parks, streets, and shopping centers is plainly relevant to the maintenance of the desired housing standards and therefore within congressional power" (pp. 34–35).

15. Mayor Lee, draft of letter to Connecticut Highway Commissioner G. Albert Hill, May 1954, p. 3, Edward J. Logue Papers, Manuscripts and Archives, Yale University Library, box 39, folder 144.

16. HHFA was the Housing and Home Finance Agency that existed between 1947 and 1965. Ed Logue, memo to Ralph Taylor, RA Executive Director, December 21, 1955, Edward J. Logue Papers, Manuscripts and Archives, Yale University Library, box 35, folder 91.

17. Undated, unlabeled newspaper clipping, "Oak Street Connector," New Haven Free Public Library, Local History Room, clipping file.

18. Redevelopment Agency notice of public hearing, November 1955, Edward J. Logue Papers, Manuscripts and Archives, Yale University Library, box 41, folder 180.

19. *New Haven CAC Annual Report and Development Guide of 1959*, p. 26, Edward J. Logue Papers, Manuscripts and Archives, Yale University Library, box 92, folder 885.

20. Ibid., p. 33. This phrase was used to describe the "University Towers skyscraper," pictured in the guide in a photograph that contained no signs of any "living" at all—only the buildings themselves, free of not only blight, but also people.

21. Jacob Riis was a turn-of-the-century photojournalist whose published 1890 tract, *How the Other Half Lives*, documented the living conditions of New York City's poorest inhabitants. The most recent publication to date is Jacob A. Riis, *How the Other Half Lives: Studies Among the Tenements of New York* (New York: Penguin Books, 1997).

22. This redevelopment-era use of photographic proof is part of a larger tradition of documentary photography in the United States, particularly the documentary tradition of the 1930s and 1940s, which included the Farm Security Administration's images documenting rural poverty. See William Stott, *Documentary Tradition and Thirties America* (New York: Oxford University Press, 1973).

23. New Haven CAC Annual Report and Development Guide of 1959, p. 47.

24. New Haven Democratic Town Committee, *Promises Made . . . Promises Kept* (New Haven, CT: City of New Haven, 1962), p. 1.

25. Allan R. Talbot, *The Mayor's Game: Richard Lee of New Haven and the Politics of Change* (New York: Harper & Row, 1967), p. 90.

26. New Haven Redevelopment Agency, letter to Charles McQueeney, Managing Editor of *New Haven Register*, July 29, 1955, Edward J. Logue Papers, Manuscripts and Archives, Yale University Library, box 35, folder 19.

27. According to the 1959 *New Haven CAC Annual Report and Development Guide*, "Only photographs and memories remain of the 42-acre Oak St. area which three years ago was Connecticut's worst slum. . . . New Haven's most modern, well-planned area has replaced the squalor in which 886 families confronted a hopeless, miserable way of life" (p. 31).

28. Undated press clipping from the *New Haven Register*, Edward J. Logue Papers, Manuscripts and Archives, Yale University Library, clipping file: "1955," box 41, folder 176.

29. "Data on Residential Occupancy Concerning the Relocation of Route 34, Brewery to Howe St.," October 13, 1955, Edward J. Logue Papers, Manuscripts and Archives, Yale University Library, box 41, folder 176. These data concerned the block bounded by Oak, Spruce, George, and Park.

30. U.S. Census Bureau, Table H-1, 1940, "Occupancy and Structural Characteristics of Housing Units by Census Tract."

31. *General Statutes of Connecticut* (Bristol, CT: Hildreth Press, 1959), Chapter 55.

32. CAC press release, 1955, Edward J. Logue Papers, Manuscripts and Archives, Yale University Library, box 41, folder 180.

33. Undated article, "State Ready to Acquire Oak Street Connector Land," Edward J. Logue Papers, Manuscripts and Archives, Yale University Library, local clipping file, box 41, folder 176; Mayor Lee, memo to Ed Logue and other staff, October 3, 1955, "As far as we are concerned, this is a State meeting and not a city meeting," Edward J. Logue Papers, Manuscripts and Archives, Yale University Library, box 41, folder 180.

34. Mayor Richard Lee, memo to Ed Logue, October 17, 1955, Edward J. Logue Papers, Manuscripts and Archives, Yale University Library, box 41, folder 176; Statement by Newman E. Agraves at public meeting, October 5, 1955, Hall of Records, Edward J. Logue Papers, Manuscripts and Archives, Yale University Library, box 41, folder 180.

35. Ralph Taylor, memo to Ed Logue, November 14, 1955, Edward J. Logue Papers, Manuscripts and Archives, Yale University Library, series V, box 41, folder 175. A typed agenda for the December 1 meeting, prepared in advance of the event, noted that if one minute of transition time was allowed for every two speakers on the city's roster, "the presentation . . . [would] consume almost two hours." ("NHRA Public Hearing on Redevelopment Plan for the Oak St. Connector" Edward J. Logue Papers, Manuscripts and Archives, Yale University Library, series V, box 41, folder 175).

36. Ed Logue, memo to Mayor Lee, November 1, 1955, Edward J. Logue Papers, Manuscripts and Archives, Yale University Library, box 41, folder 180.

37. Ralph Taylor, memo to Ed Logue, November 14, 1955, Edward J. Logue Papers, Manuscripts and Archives, Yale University Library, box 41, folder 180, p. 3.

38. Typed testimonies from public hearing, December 1, 1955, Edward J. Logue Papers, Manuscripts and Archives, Yale University Library, series V, box 41, folder 175.

39. Ralph Taylor, Executive Director of Redevelopment Agency, letter to Mr. Charles J. Horan, Regional Director of Region 1, Urban Renewal Administration, HHFA, New York, Edward J. Logue Papers, Manuscripts and Archives, Yale University Library, box 41, folder 180.

40. Ralph Taylor, Executive Director of New Haven Redevelopment Agency, letter to Mr. Charles J. Horan, Regional Director, Region 1, Urban Renewal Administration, HHFA, New York, December 6, 1955, Edward J. Logue Papers, Manuscripts and Archives, Yale University Library, box 41, folder 180.

41. Edward Logue, personal handwritten notes from public hearing, December 1, 1955, Edward J. Logue Papers, Manuscripts and Archives, Yale University Library, series V, box 41, folder 175.

42. Mayor Lee, draft of letter to State Highway Commissioner G. Albert Hill, May 1954, Edward J. Logue Papers, box 39, folder 144, Yale Manuscripts and Archives, Yale University Library.

43. Mayor Lee, letter to State Highway Commissioner Hill, June 18, 1954, Edward J. Logue Papers, Manuscripts and Archives, Yale University Library, box 39, folder 144, p. 1.

44. "Flares, Balloons, Talks Greet Oak St. Connector," *New Haven Journal-Courier*, October 27, 1959, p. 1.

45. *Catalyst*, CAC newsletter, January 24, 1959, Edward J. Logue Papers, Manuscripts and Archives, Yale University Library, box 92, folder 885.

46. *New Haven CAC Annual Report and Development Guide 1959*, p. 26, Edward J. Logue Papers, Manuscripts and Archives, Yale University Library, box 92, folder 885.

47. "Making a Business of Being Destructive," *New Haven Register*, August 5, 1956, p. 1.

48. *Annual Report of the Citizens Action Commission's Public Relations Coordinating Committee*, John W. Ghoreyeb, Chair, 1960, Edward J. Logue Papers, Manuscripts and Archives, Yale University Library, box 111, folder 1141.

49. "Ceremony Marks Dedication of City's 'Progress Pavilion,'" *New Haven Register*, July 8, 1960, New Haven Free Public Library, Local History Room, clipping file: "Housing."

50. See extensive coverage in the *New York Times*, including Fred Powledge, "Civil Rights Groups to March on Fair in Its Opening Days," April 9, 1964, p. 1; Robert Alden, "CORE Maps Tie-up on Roads to Fair," April 10, 1964, p. 1; Walter Carlson, "South's Exhibits Await Picketing," April 15, 1964, p. 24. The 1964 World's Fair was a significant site of protest because it was an explicit and self-conscious celebration of 1950s corporate culture and suburban sprawl in the context of an increasingly militant civil rights movement. Whereas demonstrations for nondiscriminatory hiring practices took place at factories and corporate headquarters all over the country throughout the mid-1960s, the fair offered an unparalleled convergence of corporate giants, all very publicly celebrating their corporate identities and cultures, many of which included discriminatory employment practices. By blocking access to the GM Pavilion, for example, while storming the bar at the Schaeffer Beer exhibit, Congress of Racial Equality (CORE) protesters were able to wage a simultaneous, highly coordinated, and highly visible assault on discriminatory employment practices around the country.

51. Richard C. Lee Papers, Manuscripts and Archives, Yale University Library, series I, box 32, folder 688.

52. Al Jepson, letter, September 28, 1960, Richard C. Lee Papers, Manuscripts and Archives, Yale University Library, series I, box 32, folder 688.

53. "Opening Set for Pavilion of Progress—Guests to Witness Friday Dedication," *New Haven Journal-Courier*, July 6, 1960, New Haven Free Public Library, Local History Room, clipping file: "Housing."

54. RA photograph label, New Haven Colony Historical Society, Photography Archive, Redevelopment Agency General File.

55. Norris Andrews, memo to Barry Passett, August 16, 1960, Richard C. Lee Papers, Manuscripts and Archives, Yale University Library, series I, box 32, folder 688.

56. New Haven Redevelopment Agency, *Dixwell Redevelopment and Renewal Plan*, August 1967.

57. Report of Anita Palmer to the Mayor, October 1960, Richard C. Lee Papers, Manuscripts and Archives, Yale University Library, series I, box 32, folder 688.

58. Mayor Lee, memo to Anita Palmer, October 12, 1960, Richard C. Lee Papers, Manuscripts and Archives, Yale University Library, series I, box 32, folder 688.

59. Anita Palmer, memo to Mayor Lee, December 19, 1960, Richard C. Lee Papers, Manuscripts and Archives, Yale University Library, series I, box 32, folder 688.

60. Anita Palmer, memo to Mayor Lee, October 10, 1960, Richard C. Lee Papers, Manuscripts and Archives, Yale University Library, series I, box 32, folder 688.

61. Mayor Lee, memo to Anita Palmer, November 22, 1960, Richard C. Lee Papers, Manuscripts and Archives, Yale University Library, series I, box 32, folder 688.

62. Anita Palmer, memo to Mayor Richard C. Lee, November 28, 1960, Richard C. Lee Papers, Manuscripts and Archives, Yale University Library, series I, box 32, folder 688.

63. Alan Jepson and Norris Andrews, "Report on Progress Pavilion," October 4, 1960, Richard C. Lee Papers, Manuscripts and Archives, Yale University Library, series I, box 32, folder 688.

64. Al Jepson, memo to Thomas Appleby and Mayor Richard C. Lee, September 14, 1961, Richard C. Lee Papers, Manuscripts and Archives, Yale University Library, series I, box 41, folder 873.

65. Mayor Richard Lee, letter to James Gibbs, June 21, 1961, Richard C. Lee Papers, Manuscripts and Archives, Yale University Library, series II, box 113, folder 2016.

66. Mayor Richard Lee, letter to James Gibbs, August 11, 1961, Richard C. Lee Papers, Manuscripts and Archives, Yale University Library, series II, box 113, folder 2016.

67. Ron Buford, "Doc Edmonds: 'God Gets You from Strange Angles,'" United Church of Christ, June 2003, http://www.ucc.org/ucnews/jun03/profiles.htm.

68. Letter from Barry Passett to Mayor Richard Lee, September 27, 1961, Richard C. Lee Papers, Manuscripts and Archives, Yale University Library, series II, box 113, folder 2016.

69. The title Citizens Action Commission was a particularly misleading one, especially where the word "action" was concerned. Mayor Lee and his redevelopment staff established the CAC for the purpose of rhetorically engaging the public (particularly the business community) in the project of urban renewal, and communicating its benefits and challenges to the wider public. The commission was never intended to—nor did it ever—"act," nor did it ever call for any "action."

70. Script for Mayor Lee's statement, Housing Exhibit, Progress Pavilion, September 1961, Richard C. Lee Papers, Manuscripts and Archives, Yale University Library, series I, box 41, folder 873.

71. Citizens Action Commission, New *New Haven: Progress Pavilion*, 1962, New Haven Free Public Library, Local History Collection.

CHAPTER 2

1. "Sit-outs Proposed in Slum Streets," *New York Times*, July 30, 1960, p. 40.

2. New Haven Redevelopment Agency, *New Haven Development Guide 1961* (Published jointly by the RA, Mayor's office, City Plan Commission, and Citizens Action Commission, 1961).

3. "Mayor Lee and 'Sit-Outs,'" *Hartford Times*, August 1, 1960, p. 24.

4. George E. Sokolsky, "The Mayor and His 'Sit-Outs,'" publication unidentified, n.d., Richard C. Lee Papers, Manuscripts and Archives, Yale University Library, clipping file, series II, box 114, folder 2040.

5. A handful of letters from the civil rights and activist community also expressed wholehearted support for the mayor's "proposal," taking it as seriously as those who wrote to criticize the idea of a sit-out.

6. " 'Mosque' Dedicated by 'Black Muslims,' " *New Haven Journal-Courier*, July 14, 1961, New Haven Free Public Library, Local History file: "New Haven Negroes."

7. Charles Shannon, "Dixwell Project Summary," February 2, 1960, Edward J. Logue Papers, Manuscripts and Archives, Yale University Library, box 110, folder 1114.

8. Maurice E. H. Rotival and Associates, Planning Consultants, *Dixwell Redevelopment and Renewal Plan* (New Haven, CT: New Haven Redevelopment Agency), August 1960, p. iii.

9. Charles Shannon, memo to Mayor Lee, "Lake Place—Dixwell Renewal Project," August 2, 1960, Richard C. Lee Papers, Manuscripts and Archives, Yale University Library, box 36, folder 791.

10. Whit Smith and Tom Harmon, "Dixwell Renewal: A Critique and Alternative," *AIM Newsletter*, Vol. 2, No. 3 (July 5, 1967): 4–5.

11. New Haven Redevelopment Agency, *Florence Virtue Co-operative Town Houses, University Park Dixwell*, c. 1960, New Haven Free Public Library, Local History Room, City Planning file.

12. Lula Parker, letter to Mayor Richard C. Lee, June 2, 1969, Richard C. Lee Papers, Manuscripts and Archives, Yale University Library, box 103, folder 1863.

13. Mary Hommann, "Symbolic Bells in Dixwell," *Architectural Forum*, July–August 1966.

14. "GOP Negro Candidates to Lead 'Housing' March," *New Haven Journal-Courier*, August 8, 1961, New Haven Free Public Library, Local History Room, clipping file: "Civil Rights."

15. "Council Lists Proposals on Fair Housing," *New Haven Register*, March 14, 1962, p. 1.

16. Dick Dowdy, Human Relations Advisor, memo to Mayor Lee, October 31, 1960, Richard C. Lee Papers, Manuscripts and Archives, Yale University Library, box 36, folder 791.

17. Richard C. Lee, remarks at the Dixwell Neighborhood Renewal Committee Meeting, Winchester School, August 10, 1960, Richard C. Lee Papers, Manuscripts and Archives, Yale University Library, series II, box 114, folder 2040.

18. Ibid., p. 7.

19. "Praise, Some Warnings, Mark Dixwell Hearing," *New Haven Journal-Courier*, August 23, 1960, New Haven Free Public Library, Local History Room, clipping file: "City Planning."

20. Charles Shannon, Redevelopment Director, letter to Mayor Lee, August 23, 1960, Richard C. Lee Papers, Manuscripts and Archives, Yale University Library, box 36, folder 791. Consider this comment alongside previously explored analysis of such phrases as "Watch the picture change" and Ed Logue's suggestion that photos could "do the trick" when it came to justifying the Oak Street demolition.

21. Sherman Drutman, letter to the Mayor and the *New Haven Register*, August 6, 1960, Richard C. Lee Papers, Manuscripts and Archives, Yale University Library, box 36, folder 791.

22. *New Haven Redevelopment Guide*, New Haven Redevelopment Agency, 1960, p. 21.

23. Mayor Richard C. Lee, letter to Jackie Robinson, March 8, 1962, Richard C. Lee Papers, Manuscripts and Archives, Yale University Library, box 53, folder 1076.

24. "Mosque Dedicated by 'Black Muslims,'" *New Haven Journal-Courier*, July 14, 1961, New Haven Free Public Library, Local History Room, clipping file: "New Haven Negroes."

25. Don Rubin, "Leader Says Muslim Mosque Here Thriving: Defends Aims," *New Haven Register*, February 23, 1965, p. 1.

26. This model was also by no means a perfect one—for example, it reinforced prescribed gender roles, instructing women in "running the home and cooking" while teaching men to "hold together their families."

27. "NAACP Head to Propose Housing Sit-Out Here," *New Haven Journal-Courier*, September 18, 1961, New Haven Free Public Library, Local History Room, clipping file: "Civil Rights."

28. "City Opening New Exhibit on Housing—Results of Survey to Be Exhibited at Progress Pavilion," *New Haven Register*, September 17, 1961, New Haven Free Public Library, Local History Room, clipping file: "Housing." It did not go unnoticed by the local press that, "ironically, it was Mayor Lee who had urged in a speech last summer that Negroes draw attention to otherwise unheeded complaints by 'sitting out' in the city streets."

29. "Three New Haven CORE Leaders Jailed in Baltimore in Sit-in Drive," *New Haven Journal-Courier*, December 4, 1961, New Haven Free Public Library, Local History Room, clipping file: "New Haven Negroes."

30. Yohuru Williams, *Black Politics / White Power: Civil Rights, Black Power, and the Black Panthers in New Haven* (St. James, NY: Brandywine Press, 2000), p. 16.

31. For a complete account of the NAACP and other civil rights organizations in New Haven during this time, see Williams, *Black Politics / White Power*, particularly pp. 20–27.

32. Williams, *Black Politics / White Power*, pp. 27–29.

33. "Threat to Charter Kills NAACP Talk of Sit-Out," *New Haven Journal-Courier*, September 21, 1961, New Haven Free Public Library, Local History Room, clipping file: "New Haven Negroes."

34. "City NAACP Acts Tonight on 'Sit-Outs'—Gibbs Refuses to Heed Warning from Group Headquarters," *New Haven Register*, October 1, 1961, pp. 1–2.

35. "Outspoken Negro Leader Is Shot in New Haven," *Hartford Courant*, April 3, 1962, New Haven Free Public Library, Local History Room, clipping file: "African-Americans Biography."

36. "CORE Pickets Stage March at City Hall—Daily Noon-Hour Demonstrations Held at Sit-Out Prelude," *New Haven Register*, October 9, 1961, New Haven Free Public Library, Local History Room, clipping file: "New Haven Negroes."

37. "CORE to Picket 'Pavilion' to Protest Housing," *New Haven Journal-Courier*, October 11, 1961. New Haven Free Public Library, Local History Room, clipping file: "New Haven Negroes." There is some confusion in the chronology of this paper trail. The *New York Times* account reports that the Dixwell sit-outs occurred on October 6, 1961. The *New Haven Journal-Courier* account, five days later, reports that the previous weekend's proposed action had been canceled due to rain and that the protest would take place the following Saturday. Efforts by the author to locate a participant in the action or otherwise clear up this ambiguity proved fruitless, so an attempt has been made here to construct a useful chronology.

38. "CORE to Picket 'Pavilion' to Protest Housing."

39. "Sit-out in New Haven: 100 Negroes Stage Protest Against Discrimination," *New York Times*, October 7, 1961, p. 11.

40. Jane Jacobs, *The Death and Life of Great American Cities* (New York: Vintage, 1961), p. 73.

41. In fact, it was the modern-day interpretation and application of Howard's model that Jacobs opposed. His original designs, although indeed isolating or reorienting urban life away from the street, called for the same mixed-use design that Jacobs advocated. See Robert Fishman, *Urban Utopias in the Twentieth Century: Ebenezer Howard, Frank Lloyd Wright, and Le Corbusier* (Cambridge, MA: MIT Press, 1982).

42. As one of the country's most prominent urbanists of the time, Jane Jacobs was a woman in a male-dominated field who claimed and celebrated 'the street,' which itself had conventionally been considered a male domain, considered either contaminated by the sexual presence of women, or a dangerous space from which respectable women had to be protected. Jacobs' notion of a "street ballet" redefined the gendered identity of the street, casting it in a newly feminized and more respectably feminine light—one that suggested strength, movement, and music, rather than venereal disease, prostitution, a proliferation of children, or the clutter of clotheslines. Jacobs had no formal training in the field of urban planning; she made observations of her own urban environment. She was both a writer and an activist. See Alice Sparberg Alexiou, *Jane Jacobs: Urban Visionary* (New Brunswick, NJ: Rutgers University Press), 2006; Jane Jacobs, "Downtown Is for People," *Fortune*, April 1958; "Jacobs Is Arrested at Expressway Hearing," *New York Times*, April 11, 1968.

43. Robert Cook, untitled document on Hill Cooperative Housing, 1966, personal files of Robert Cook, pp. 4–5.

44. Alphonso Tindall, Executive Director of Dixwell Community House, letter to Mayor Lee, September 6, 1960, Richard C. Lee Papers, Manuscripts and Archives, Yale University Library, box 36, folder 791.

45. "Valenti Raps Dixwell Area Demolition," *New Haven Journal-Courier*, May 25, 1961, Richard C. Lee Papers, Manuscripts and Archives, Yale University Library, clipping file: "Dixwell Redevelopment," box 36, folder 791.

46. "Dixwell Groups to Study Valenti's Petition Claim," *New Haven Journal-Courier*, July 17, 1961, Richard C. Lee Papers, Manuscripts and Archives, Yale University Library, clipping file: "Dixwell Redevelopment," box 36, folder 791.

47. "Sen. Bush Raps Redevelopment in New Haven," Associated Press, sent to Mayor Richard C. Lee, October 27, 1961, Richard C. Lee Papers, Manuscripts and Archives, Yale University Library, series I, box 3, folder 60.

48. Herbert Gans, *The Urban Villagers: Group and Class in the Lives of Italian-Americans* (New York: Free Press, 1962); and Martin Anderson, *The Federal Bulldozer: A Critical Analysis of Urban Renewal, 1949–1962* (Cambridge, MA: MIT Press, 1962).

49. "Belford Urges Sweeping Changes in Policy of Redevelopment Agency," *New Haven Journal-Courier*, June 27, 1962.

50. "Lee Names Advisory Group for Dixwell Renewal Plan," *New Haven Register*, August 6, 1961.

51. Charles Twyman, interview by Tamar Rubin, New Haven Oral History Project, March 26, 2004, "Life in the Model City," transcript lent to author by curator, online exhibit, http://www.yale.edu/nhohp/modelcity.

52. "Malcolm X Outdebates Integration Leader," *Open Gate News*, 13th ed., May 18, 1962, p. 9. See also Rubin, "Leader Says Muslim Mosque Here Thriving," p. 1.

53. Within a year, the RA would announce significant raises for the project director's salaries, bringing Lloyd Davis' annual earnings to $14,500 in a neighborhood with an annual salary of around $3,100. "Sweeping Salary Raises for Staff Approved by Redevelopment Agency," *New Haven Journal-Courier*, December 12, 1963, p. 1.

54. New Haven Redevelopment Agency, *Dixwell Renewal News*, Vol. 1, No. 1, December 1962, p. 2.

55. The name was alternatively spelled "Freddie" and "Freddy"—in the end it seems the latter won out, but early suggestions of the character and early proposals and announcements of events used the former.

56. "Freddy Fixer to Fix Community," *Open Gate News*, November 2–November 15, 1962, p. 8.

57. The indoctrination of the neighborhood's youth through Freddy Fixer Clubs contrasts strikingly with the involvement of youth through the Hill Neighborhood Union and the Hill Freedom School, discussed in Chapter 3.

58. "Freddy Fixer to Fix Community," *Open Gate News*, November 2–November 15, 1962, p. 8.

59. Twyman interview.

60. "Mitchell Invites All," *Open Gate News*, 30th ed., January 18–February 1, 1963, p. 4.

61. "NAACP Official Lashes Dixwell 'Peace Corps,' " *New Haven Register*, December 10, 1962, New Haven Free Public Library, Local History Room, clipping file: "New Haven Negroes."

62. Lloyd Davis, memo to Mayor Richard Lee, "Re: Williams Incident," December 14, 1962, Richard C. Lee Papers, Manuscripts and Archives, Yale University Library, box 54, folder 1080.

63. "Dixwell's First Annual Freddy Fixer Parade," *Open Gate News*, 37th ed., May 3–16, 1963; and "Dixwell Neighborhood Improvement Efforts," *Open Gate News*, 39th ed., June 7–20, 1963, p. 8. The first chairman of the parade was Dr. Frederick Smith, who some say was the basis for the name "Freddy Fixer." Smith was born in Jersey City, New Jersey, in 1903—the son of a railroad porter and a domestic worker. He attended Columbia University, and then Howard Medical School, and came to Connecticut in 1930 to work for a Hartford doctor. The Hartford doctor passed away before Smith arrived, so he decided to settle in New Haven, where he set up a home and medical practice at 82 Dixwell Avenue. By the end of World War II, he was one of only four doctors in the Dixwell neighborhood. He was also an active church leader, a cofounder of the urban league, and the city's police commissioner from 1962 to 1965. In 1964, Smith would oversee the building of twenty-five housing units in "Dixwell Plaza"—a housing development that would take his name. Both Mayor Lee and Ed Grant, director of Freddy Fixer, Inc., which has run the parade for the past four decades, agree that the connections between the name of the fabled character and the community leader are simply coincidental. William H. Banks, Jr., "In Search of Freddy Fixer," *New Haven Independent*, February 16, 1989.

64. U.S. Census, Table P-1, General Characteristics of the Population:1960, p. 16. Even by the most liberal measurements, families in 1960 were expected to spend no more than 35 percent of their total income on housing. A rent of $100–200 per month would constitute between 40 and 80 percent of the average black Dixwell family's income, which would not leave enough for other basic necessities.

65. "City Promoting Dixwell Housing," *New Haven Journal-Courier*, August 27, 1964, New Haven Free Public Library, Local History Room, clipping file: "Housing."

66. "Legal Opinion Sought on State Renewal Aid—Yale Role in Dixwell Project Involved—Attitude on Future Programs at Issue," *New Haven Register*, November 6, 1962, New Haven Free Public Library, Local History Room, clipping file: "Housing."

67. Haar, *Between the Ideal and the Reality*, p. 7.

68. Howard Zinn, *A People's History of the United States* (New York: Harper & Row, 1980), p. 458.

69. Daniel P. Moynihan, *Maximum Feasible Misunderstanding: Community Action in the War on Poverty* (New York: Free Press, 1969), p. 79.

70. Rubin, "Leader Says Muslim Mosque Here Thriving," p. 1.

CHAPTER 3

1. Calvin West, Jr., "Why I Like Freedom School," *ERAP Newsletter*, July 31, 1965, p. 14. Calvin's poem was published in a July 1965 issue of the newsletter for ERAP, Students for a Democratic Society's (SDS) Economic and Research Action Project, which was established in 1962 through a grant from the UAW to support activists living in poor communities to organize for improvements and a voice in local government. Although New Haven did not have an official ERAP project site, organizing projects in the Hill at that time closely resembled the projects established by SDS in other cities, and the New Haven Project would remain financially and administratively independent from ERAP while keeping a close line of communication with ERAP projects around the country, even at one time compiling and publishing the national project's newsletter.

2. Daniel Solomon, *Global City Blues* (Washington DC: Island Press, 2003), p. 8.

3. Office of Economic Opportunity, "The War on Poverty: A Hometown Fight," 1964.

4. Ibid.

5. Economic Opportunity Act of 1964, Title II, Part A, Section 202(a), "Community Action Programs."

6. James Ralph, *Northern Protest: Martin Luther King, Chicago, and the Civil Rights Movement* (Cambridge: Harvard University Press, 1993). The outcome of this campaign demonstrated how decline in white support for civil rights was not simply about the black power agenda, but more about expanding civil rights demands into the realms of private life, housing, and neighborhoods. Ralph argues that these marches "first exposed the limits of civil rights consensus" (p. 6).

7. For more on the top-down nature of the city's antipoverty agency, Community Progress Incorporated, see Douglas Rae, *City: Urbanism and Its End* (New Haven, CT: Yale University Press, 2003).

8. Betsy Gilbertson, interview by the author, January 28, 2006, Guilford, CT.

9. Robert Cook, "Neighborhood Organization Workers," 1965, personal files of Robert Cook, on loan to the author.

10. John Wilhelm and Betsy Gilbertson, interview by the author, January 28, 2006; and Robert Cook, interview by the author, July 16, 2005.

11. Robert Cook, "NOW in New Haven: February Through July, 1965," personal files of Robert Cook, on loan to the author.

12. Whereas four "neighborhood men" were hired and paid by the HNU to do organizing work, it was the personal and political networks of many neighborhood women that made this organizing possible. Feminist social movement scholarship has interrogated the ways in which women's community organizing work has been marginalized, the gendered distinctions between "spokesmen" and grassroots organizers, and the ways in which the political nature of women's community networks is often overlooked. See Nancy A. Naples, ed., *Community Activism and Feminist Politics: Organizing Across Race, Class, and Gender* (New York: Routledge, 1998); and Susan Stall and Randy Stoecker, "Community Organizing or Organizing the Community: Gender and the Crafts of Empowerment," *Gender and Society*, Vol. 12, No. 6 (December 1998): 729–756.

13. Rae, *City*, p. 349.

14. For a thorough account of CPI, see Rae, *City*. The *Hill Union News'* assertion about the makeup of CPI was essentially correct: of the nine seats on the CPI board, three were directly appointed by the mayor, one was appointed by the Redevelopment Agency (RA), one by the Citizens Action Commission (CAC), and one by the board of education. An additional three members were appointed by some combination of Yale University, the United Way, and other dominant local institutions and agencies. As Rae shows, Mayor Lee appointed his own "loyalists" to nearly every seat.

15. "C.P.I. Must Listen to Us," *Hill Union News*, Issue 2, July 27, 1965, p. 2.

16. "On HNU," *Hill Union News*, Issue 1, July 2, 1965, p. 1.

17. One scholar of New Haven's redevelopment period called *Opening Opportunities* a "revolutionary document" for its time in that it dealt with "human renewal" as well as the renewal of physical spaces. Fred Powledge, *Model City: A Test of American Liberalism; One Town's Efforts to Rebuild Itself* (New York: Simon & Schuster, 1970), p. 52.

18. Community Progress, Inc. *Opening Opportunities: New Haven's Comprehensive Program for Community Progress* (New Haven, CT: City of New Haven, 1962).

19. Vicki Mittlefehldt (NOW), Ronald Johnson (HNU), and Mrs. Ruth T.I. Emerson, *Monthly Report of Neighborhood Organization Workers (NOW)*, April 30, 1966, personal files of Robert Cook, on loan to author.

20. "Mr. Durham" and Eddie Smith, "What's Going to Happen in the Hill—We Want to Know!" *Hill Union News*, Issue 3, July 31, 1965, p. 1.

21. Some individuals, like Mr. Durham, are identified here only by their last names because the author was unable—through interviews, city directories, or other printed sources—to find or confirm their first names. This difficulty points to a key impediment to doing research on grassroots subjects: the printed record is often sparse, and the poor—particularly—were often displaced, or simply moved very often, making it hard to pin down names and addresses.

22. See Stall and Stoecker, "Community Organizing," p. 747.

23. Durham and Smith, "What's Going to Happen in the Hill," p. 1.

24. Ibid., p. 2.

25. Robert Fisher, *Let the People Decide: Neighborhood Organizing in America* (New York: Twayne Publishers, 1994).

26. For a detailed account of the Harlem rent strikes of 1964–1965, see Mandi Isaacs Jackson, "Harlem's Rent Strike and Rat War: Representation, Housing Access, and Tenant Resistance in New York, 1958–1964," *American Studies* (Spring 2006): 5–29.

27. Mrs. Preston, "Conditions in My House," *Hill Union News*, July 2, 1965, p. 2.

28. Preston, "Tenant's Council Formed at 29 Ann Street," *Hill Union News*, July 27, 1965, p. 1.

29. Eddie Smith, "Rent Strike," *Hill Union News*, August 3, 1965, p. 1.

30. Eufizine Bethea, "From New Haven's *Hill Union News*—Rent Strike on Liberty St.," *ERAP Newsletter*, August 14, 1965, p. 3.

31. "The Hill Neighborhood Union," *Hill Union News*, Issue 1, July 2, 1965, p. 1.

32. See Douglas McAdam, *Freedom Summer* (New York: Oxford University Press, 1988).

33. Jake Blum, "New Haven's Freedom School: Personal Relationships and Social Action," *ERAP Newsletter*, July 31, 1965, p. 14.

34. "Poochie" and "Roy," "A Trip to Washington," *Hill Union News*, Issue 1, July 2, 1965, p. 3.

35. Douglas Rae, *City*, p. 357.

36. "Proposal for a Neighborhood Park in the Hill," personal files of Robert Cook, undated document (probably 1965).

37. Ruth Green, "The Demonstration at the Park," *Hill Union News*, July 2, 1965, p. 4.

38. John Dawson and Duncan McDuffie, "Getting a Better Park," *Hill Union News*, Issue 1, July 2, 1965, p. 4.

39. Iva Pearce, "Cleveland Community News: Playground," *ERAP Newsletter*, July 17, 1965.

40. Leona Wilcox, "Children Playing in the Street," *ERAP Newsletter*, August 21, 1965, p. 7.

41. Letter from James E. Coogan to Dennis Rezendes, "Meeting of Park Supervisors with 'Hill Neighborhood Union,'" July 8, 1965, Richard C. Lee Papers, Manuscripts and Archives, Yale University Library, box 110, folder 1972.

42. Mayor Richard C. Lee, letter to New Haven FBI Director Charles Weeks, July 26, 1965, Richard C. Lee Papers, Manuscripts and Archives, Yale University Library, box 110, folder 1972.

43. Mayor Richard C. Lee, letter to Paul Ylvisaker, Ford Foundation, July 26, 1965, Richard C. Lee Papers, Manuscripts and Archives, Yale University Library, box 110, folder 1972.

44. "Information on Norman Fund," Richard C. Lee Papers, Manuscripts and Archives, Yale University Library, box 110, folder 1972.

45. Robert Cook, letter to Deborah M. Cole, the Norman Fund, Inc., December 3, 1965, personal files of Robert Cook, on loan to author.

46. Harris Stone and Robert Cook, "Hill Cooperative Housing," 1966, p. 2, Robert Cook personal files of Robert Cook, on loan to author. See also Herbert Gans, "Toward a Human Architecture: A Sociologist's View of the Profession," in "Research on the Profession," special issue, *Journal of Architectural Education*, Vol. 31, No. 2 (November 1977): 26–31.

47. Stone and Cook, "Hill Cooperative Housing"; and Harris Stone, *Workbook of an Unsuccessful Architect* (New York: Monthly Review Press, 1974), p. 43.

48. Stone and Cook, "Hill Cooperative Housing," p. 5.

49. Ibid., p. 6.

50. Ibid., p. 7.

51. Ibid., p. 11.

52. Stone, *Workbook*, p. 43.

53. New Haven Redevelopment Agency, "The Hill: A Neighborhood Plans for the Future," 1966, New Haven Free Public Library, Local History Files.

54. City of New Haven, *Ideas for the Hill Model Neighborhood Program*, April 1967, p. 2 (obtained from New Haven Free Public Library, Local History Room); and International Business Machines Corporation, *Concepts of an Urban Management Information System: A Report to the City of New Haven, Connecticut*, p. 37 (obtained from New Haven Free Public Library, Local History Room).

55. Robert Cook, "Too Many People Are a Blighting Influence . . . or the President's National Commission on Urban Problems Comes to New Haven," *AIM Newsletter*, Vol. 2, No. 2, June 11, 1967.

56. Richard Balzer, *Street Time* (New York: Grossman, 1972), p. 32.

57. Balzer, *Street Time*, p. 33.

58. National Commission on Urban Problems, *Hearings Before the National Commission on Urban Problems*, May–June 1967, vol. 1, *Baltimore, New Haven, Boston, Pittsburgh* (Washington, DC: U.S. Government Printing Office, 1968), p. 111.

59. Ibid., p. 153. Woodbridge, originally part of New Haven, was by 1967 a wealthy neighboring suburb.

60. Ibid., p. 149.

61. Ibid., p. 179.

62. Cook, "Too Many People," p. 7.

CHAPTER 4

1. Bernard Asbell, "They Said It Wouldn't Happen in New Haven," *New York Times*, September 3, 1967, p. 151.

2. Howard Hallman, memo to Ed Logue, March 16, 1959, Edward J. Logue Papers, Manuscripts and Archives, Yale University Library, box 106, folder 1066.

3. Charles M. Haar, *Between the Ideal and the Reality: A Study of the Fate, Origin, and Legacy of the Model Cities Program* (Boston: Little, Brown & Co., 1975), p. 19.

4. Quoted in Haar, *Between the Ideal and the Reality*, p. 14.

5. Henry Tamarin, "Pacification of Our Cities," *AIM Newsletter*, Vol. 2, No. 12 (March 5, 1968): 5.

6. Sherry R. Arnstein, "A Ladder of Citizen Participation," *Journal of the American Institute of Planners*, Vol. 35, No. 4 (July 1969): 216–224. See also: Lillian B.

Rubin, "Maximum Feasible Participation: The Origins, Implications, and Present Status," *Annals of the American Academy of Political and Social Science*, Vol. 385, No. 1 (1969): 14–29.

7. Mayor Richard C. Lee, "Personal and Confidential," notes by Mayor Lee, December 1965, Richard C. Lee Papers, Manuscripts and Archives, Yale University Library, box 114, folder 2033.

8. International Business Machines Corporation (IBM), *Concepts of an Urban Management Information System: A Report to the City of New Haven, Connecticut*, n.d., New Haven Free Public Library, Local History Room, p. 10.

9. IBM, *Concepts*, p. 11.

10. Lawrence E. Davies, "Personal 'Dossier' Plan Stirs Fears of Privacy Invasion," *New York Times*, August 1, 1966, p. 27.

11. John Leo, "An End of Privacy by 2000 Predicted," *New York Times*, August 13, 1967, p. 30.

12. Fred P. Graham, "Expert Says Computers Pose a Growing Menace to Privacy," *New York Times*, September 18, 1967, p. 24.

13. IBM, *Concepts*, p. 30.

14. *Ideas for the Hill Model Neighborhood Program*, City of New Haven, April, 1967 (New Haven Free Public Library, Local History Room files), p. O1.

15. IBM, *Concepts*, p. 37.

16. Ibid., p. 37.

17. Ibid., p. 7.

18. Ibid., p. 43.

19. *Ideas*, front cover.

20. Mr. A. Ruggi, Mayor of Imola, Italy, letter to "Mayor of New Evan, New England," October 18, 1968, Richard C. Lee Papers, Manuscripts and Archives, Yale University Library, box 101, folder 1816.

21. Francis J. Whalen, "City Urged to Create Office on Computer Application," *New Haven Register*, attached to memo dated June 16, 1969, clipping in Richard C. Lee Papers, Manuscripts and Archives, Yale University Library, box 101, folder 1816.

22. Quoted in Douglas Rae, *City: Urbanism and Its End* (New Haven, CT: Yale University Press, 2003), p. 350.

23. National Commission on Urban Problems, *Hearings Before the National Commission on Urban Problems*, May–June 1967, vol. 1, *Baltimore, New Haven, Boston, Pittsburgh* (Washington, DC: U.S. Government Printing Office, 1968), p. 185.

24. Richard Balzer, *Street Time* (New York: Grossman, 1972), p. 11.

25. Balzer, *Street Time*, p. 11.

26. Neighborhood Organization Workers, "Monthly Report: March & April, 1966," p. 1, personal files of Robert Cook, on loan to the author.

27. Fred Harris, interview by Yohuru Williams, April 11, 1999, Detroit, Michigan.

28. Balzer, *Street Time*, p. 99.

29. Ibid., p. 87.

30. Fred Harris interview.

31. Ibid.

32. "Investigation into the Operations of Community Progress, Inc.," testimony of Rep. Robert Giaimo, 90th Cong., 2nd sess., *Congressional Record*, 114 (January 18, 1968), p. 167.

33. Fred Harris interview.

34. Ibid.

35. Bernard Asbell, "They Said It Wouldn't Happen in New Haven," *New York Times*, September 3, 1967, p. 151.

36. Recounted in Vincent Scully, "Model City," *New York Times*, January 24, 1971, p. BR8.

37. Fred Harris interview.

38. Balzer, *Street Time*, p. 17.

39. Fred Powledge, *Model City: A Test of American Liberalism; One Town's Efforts to Rebuild Itself* (New York: Simon & Schuster, 1970), p. 82.

40. Susan Fainstein, "Local Mobilization and Economic Discontent," in *Restructuring the City*, ed. M. Smith (New York: Longman, 1987), p. 328.

41. Demonstration Cities and Metropolitan Development Act of 1966, p. 351, quoted in Powledge, *Model City*, p. 149.

42. John Herbers, "McCone Says US Could be Ruined by Racial Strife," *New York Times*, August 23, 1967, p. 1.

43. Asbell, "They Said It Wouldn't Happen."

44. William Borders, "Riot in a Model City," *New York Times*, August 27, 1967, p. E4.

45. "Suggested Statement for Use in Special Home Visitation Project in Washington Avenue Section of the Hill Neighborhood," attachment to confidential memo by Frank Corbett, CPI, August 17, 1966, Richard C. Lee Papers, Manuscripts and Archives, Yale University Library, box 114, folder 2031. Police Chief Francis McManus was, in fact, informed by CPI that "foot patrolmen in the area seemed to have a better calming effect on the residents than motorized patrols." Nonetheless, when violence broke out a year later, he flooded the neighborhood with police vehicles.

46. Frank Corbett, "Review of Activities to Deal with Intergroup Tension in the Washington Avenue Area of the Hill Neighborhood," confidential memo to Mayor Richard C. Lee, August 17, 1966, Richard C. Lee Papers, Yale Manuscripts and Archives, Yale University Library, box 114, folder 2031, p. 4.

47. Ibid., p. 6.

48. Rev. Sidney Lovett, Chairman; Richard Belford, Executive Director; and John C. Daniels, Deputy Director, New Haven Commission on Equal Opportunities, "Potential Summer Unrest," recommendations to Mayor Richard C. Lee, May 12, 1967, Richard C. Lee Papers, Manuscripts and Archives, Yale University Library, box 114, folder 2032, p. 2.

49. John Herbers, "M'Cone Says US Could Be Ruined by Racial Strife," *New York Times*, August 23, 1967, p. 1.

50. William V. Shannon, "Violence and the Cities: The Search for a Pattern Goes On," *New York Times*, August 27, 1967, p. E4.

51. Robert B. Semple, "Conflicting Pressures in Congress," *New York Times*, August 27, 1967, p. E4.

52. New Haven Commission on Equal Opportunities, "A Daily Report of Tension Indicators," May 1967, Richard C. Lee Papers, Manuscripts and Archives, Yale University Library, box 114, folder 2032.

53. More recent developments around Yale University bring to mind the police substation and community police intern proposals of the 1960s. The Rose Center, which houses both the Yale Police and a community and learning center, opened in 2006 in the section of the Dixwell neighborhood closest to Yale's campus. The center

has been well received by the neighborhood, former site of the Elm Haven housing project, which was very recently redeveloped as a mixed-income community. See Melinda Tuhus, "A Rose Blooms in Dixwell," *New Haven Independent*, May 31, 2006, http://www.newhavenindependent.org/archives/2006/05/rose_center_ded.php, for more about the opening of the Rose Center.

54. New Haven Commission on Equal Opportunities, "Establish a Neighborhood Police Aide Program," in "A Daily Report of Tension Indicators," May 1967, Richard C. Lee Papers, Manuscripts and Archives, Yale University Library, box 114, folder 2032.

55. "Mayor's Agenda: Hill Project Office," 1967, Richard C. Lee Papers, Manuscripts and Archives, Yale University Library, box 114, folder 2032.

56. Charles Louis, "Hill Parents Association Summer Project," July 10, 1967, p. 2, Richard C. Lee Papers, Manuscripts and Archives, Yale University Library, box 114, folder 2032.

57. Ibid., p. 4.

58. Sergent S. Tiddei, "Inter-Office Communications Form," New Haven Police Department, Precinct 1, July 19, 1967, Richard C. Lee Papers, Manuscripts and Archives, Yale University Library, box 114, folder 2032.

59. Paul Edwards, The Closed World: Computers and the Politics of Discourse in Cold War America (Cambridge, MA: MIT Press, 1996), p. 104.

CHAPTER 5

1. Robert Gelbach, "Wheels of Justice Turn on Accused," *AIM Newsletter Special Edition* (August 31, 1967): 4.

2. "Harris Says City Needs a Commitment," *New Haven Register*, August 22, 1967, p. 1.

3. Richard Balzer, *Street Time* (New York: Grossman, 1972), p. 34.

4. Ruth H. Cheney and Peter M. Green, "Urban Planning and Urban Revolt: A Case Study," *Progressive Architecture* (January 1968): 136.

5. "A Lesson in Ingratitude," *Connecticut Sunday Herald*, August 27, 1967, editorial page.

6. Henry Tamarin, "Pacification of Our Cities," *AIM Newsletter*, Vol. 2, No. 12 (March 5, 1968): 5.

7. Elizabeth Henderson and Harry Henderson, "How City Hall Tried to Break the Hill Parents' Association," *Modern Times*, September 1, 1970, p. 2.

8. Harris Stone, *Workbook of an Unsuccessful Architect* (New York: Monthly Review Press, 1974), p. 44.

9. Balzer, *Street Time*, p. 34.

10. Cheney and Green, "Urban Planning and Urban Revolt," p. 137.

11. Balzer, *Street Time*, p. 36.

12. Betsy Gilbertson, interview by the author, January 28, 2006, Guilford, CT.

13. Ron Pressley and Tom Battle, "150 Kids Trade City for Camp," *AIM Newsletter*, Vol. 2, No. 4 (July 28, 1967): 5.

14. Gelbach, "Wheels of Justice," p. 5.

15. The police department reported the total number of arrests as 707 by the end of the disturbances, but noted that this number included, in many cases, more than one arrest per person. An account written by Douglas Rae in *City: Urbanism and Its End* (New Haven, CT: Yale University Press, 2003), cites the number of ar-

rests as 225 (p. 352). Movement accounts of the event, through interviews and newsletters, consistently reported much higher numbers.

16. John Wilhelm, interview by the author, January 28, 2006, Guilford, CT.

17. Gelbach, "Wheels of Justice," p. 4.

18. Balzer, *Street Time*, p. 34.

19. Cheney and Green, "Urban Planning and Urban Revolt," p. 138.

20. John Wilhelm, interview by the author, January 28, 2006, Guilford, CT.

21. Tamarin, "Pacification of Our Cities," p. 5.

22. Gelbach, "Wheels of Justice," p. 4.

23. Cheney and Green, "Urban Planning and Urban Revolt," p. 138.

24. Ibid., p. 139.

25. Charles J. Hines, "Arrests Mount in City Disorders; Lee, Police Meeting on Violence; Trouble Continues After Third Night," *New Haven Register*, August 22, 1967, p. 1.

26. Cheney and Green, "Urban Planning and Urban Revolt," p. 139.

27. Hines, "Arrests Mount," p. 1.

28. Ibid., p. 2.

29. Cheney and Green, "Urban Planning and Urban Revolt," p. 137.

30. "Harris Says City Needs a Commitment," *New Haven Register*, August 22, 1967, p. 1.

31. Gelbach, "Wheels of Justice," p. 4.

32. Ibid., p. 5.

33. Elizabeth Rose, untitled poem, *AIM Newsletter, Special Riot Edition* (August 31, 1967.)

34. Balzer, *Street Time*, p. 37.

35. Ibid.

36. New Haven Police Department (NHPD), "New Haven Disturbance Arrest Study—Confidential—Not For Release," September 20, 1967, Richard C. Lee Papers, Manuscripts and Archives, Yale University Library, box 114, folder 2032, p. 1.

37. Ibid., p. 6.

38. Ibid., p. 13.

39. Ibid., p. 7.

40. Ibid., p. 8.

41. The police noted that the computer records on which this data was based dated back only to 1965, so it could be that a much higher percentage of those arrested were involved at some point in the CPI program.

42. Ibid., p. 12.

43. NHPD, "New Haven Disturbance Arrest Study," p. 10.

44. "A Lesson in Ingratitude," *Connecticut Sunday Herald*, August 27, 1967, editorial page.

45. Henderson and Henderson, "How City Hall"; and Stone, *Workbook*, p. 44.

46. Governor Rockefeller recruited Ed Logue, former New Haven redevelopment director, to head up the $6 billion program in 1968. Sydney H. Schanberg, "State's Urban Agency to be Led by Logue, Who Spurned City Job," *New York Times*, April 27, 1968, p. 1.

47. National Commission on Urban Problems, *Hearings Before the National Commission on Urban Problems*, May–June 1967, vol. 1, *Baltimore, New Haven, Boston, Pittsburgh* (Washington, DC: U.S. Government Printing Office, 1968), p. 190.

48. John Wilhelm, "News from the HPA," *AIM Newsletter*, Vol. 1, No. 20 (August 27, 1967): 4.

49. Stone, *Workbook*, p. 52.

50. John Wilhelm, "Model Cities Meeting at Lee High School," *AIM Newsletter* (April 27, 1967): 5.

51. Ronald Johnson, "On the Model Cities Program for the Hill," *AIM Newsletter*, Vol. 2, No. 5.

52. Stone, *Workbook*, p. 53.

53. "New Haven Chosen in Model Cities Plan," *New Haven Register*, November 16, 1967, p. 1.

54. Stone, *Workbook*, p. 53.

55. "Alderman Mull Renewal Plan," *New Haven Register*, March 4, 1968, clipping file, personal files of David Dickson, on loan to author.

56. "Hill Model Cities Neighborhood Corporation," *Special Issue for the Hill of: The Bulletin of the American Independent Movement*, n.d., p. 1.

57. "The Story of Model Cities in the Hill," *Special Issue for the Hill of: The Bulletin of the American Independent Movement,* n.d., p. 3.

58. Ibid., p. 2.

59. Ibid., p. 6.

60. Stone, *Workbook*, p. 57.

61. Ibid., p. 57.

62. David Dickson, "The Housing Crisis: Part III," *Modern Times*, Vol. 1, No. 10 (June 1, 1970): 10.

63. Charles M. Haar, *Between the Ideal and the Reality: A Study of the Fate, Origin, and Legacy of the Model Cities Program* (Boston: Little, Brown & Co., 1975), p. 89.

64. Ibid., p. 176.

65. Ibid., p. 177.

66. President Lyndon B. Johnson, "Special Message to the Congress Recommending a Program for Cities and Metropolitan Areas," January 26, 1966, University of California Santa Barbara, "The American Presidency Project" http://www.presidency.ucsb.edu/ws/index.php?pid=27682, accessed October 25, 2007.

67. Bennett Harrison, "The Participation of Ghetto Residents in the Model Cities Program," *Journal of the American Institute of Planners*, Vol. 39 (January 1973): 4.

68. John Herbers, "Power Struggle Hampers Program for Model Cities," *New York Times*, December 15, 1969, p. 1.

69. Dickson, "Housing Crisis," p. 10.

70. People Against the Garage, draft of public statement, 1969, personal files of David Dickson, on loan to the author.

CHAPTER 6

1. Harris Stone, *Workbook of an Unsuccessful Architect* (New York: Monthly Review Press, 1974), p. 48.

2. Ada Louise Huxtable, "The Expressway Debate: Progress of Destruction?" *New York Times*, May 1, 1967, p. 40.

3. Joseph Novitski, "Roads Bring City Problems to Suburbs," *New York Times*, November 19, 1968, p. 49.

4. Ada Louise Huxtable, "Where It Goes Nobody Knows," *New York Times*, February 2, 1969, p. D29.

5. New Haven Redevelopment Agency (NRHA), *State Street Redevelopment and Renewal Plan*, April 15, 1968, preface, New Haven Free Public Library, Local History Room.

6. Ibid., p. 36. Sixty-eight out of 98 dwellings, 201 out of 292 commercial, 21 out of 26 industrial, and 9 out of 16 public or semipublic buildings were declared substandard.

7. Ibid., p. 37. In the 1968 version of the plan, these numbers are incorrect—there is a typographical error that reports numbers that do not add up to the total reported. The data cited here are taken from the 1969 revision of the plan, in which these numbers are corrected.

8. Stone, *Workbook*, p. 48.

9. Ibid., p. 49.

10. Price & Lee, *New Haven City Directory* (New Haven, CT: Price & Lee, 1968).

11. Joan Stone, telephone interview by the author, July 18, 2005.

12. "Proposed Short Platform," undated and unattributed, files of Robert Cook, on loan to the author.

13. Richard Wolff, interview by the author, November 11, 2004, New York City.

14. William Borders, "2 Morse Disciples Seek House Seats," *New York Times*, July 24, 1966, p. 35.

15. Henry Raymont, "Rep. Giaimo Involved in 3-Way Race in 3rd District," *New York Times*, October 14, 1966, p. 39.

16. Val Adams, "3rd District in Rerun of 3-Way House Race of 1966," *New York Times*, October 16, 1968, p. 28.

17. "Olin Strike News," insert in *AIM Newsletter*, Vol. 4, No. 19 (November 1, 1969).

18. AIM Urban Renewal Committee, "AIM Campaign Proposal Route 34," n.d., personal files of Robert Cook, on loan to the author.

19. AIM Coffeehouse Committee, "Coffeehouse," *AIM Newsletter*, Vol. 4, No. 10 (May 15, 1969): 6.

20. "The AIM/DAG Coffeehouse Prospectus," undated, unattributed notes, personal files of Robert Cook, on loan to the author.

21. AIM Coffeehouse Committee, "Coffeehouse," p. 6.

22. Although Oppenheim's poem is commonly associated with the 1912 strike of textile workers in Lawrence, Massachusetts, a strike often referred to as the "Bread and Roses" strike, the work was first published a month earlier, in December of 1911, in *The American Magazine*. One scholar's inquiries suggest that the slogan originated with the Chicago branch of the National Women's Trade Union League during the fight for the eight-hour wage, and cites an anecdote about a visit to Chicago by British trade unionist Mary MacArthur. In a speech before a group of Chicago women trade unionists, MacArthur summed up her remarks with a quote she attributed to the Koran: "If thou hast two loaves of bread, sell one and buy flowers, for bread is food for the body, but flowers are food for the mind." Jim Zwick, "Behind the Song: Bread and Roses," *Sing Out!* Vol. 46 (Winter 2003): 92–93.

23. Richard Wolff interview.

24. The film chronicled the struggle of immigrants and working people in America from the Civil War through the 1960s, including newsreel footage of the "Memorial Day Massacre" at Chicago's Republic Steel.

25. *Olin Strike News*, published by AIM, n.d., personal files of David Dickson, on loan to author.

26. Nina Adams, interview by the author, New York City, March 10, 2005.

27. Stone, *Workbook*, p. 46.

28. "Highway Planners Told to Listen to Citizens," *New Haven Register*, November 20, 1967, p. 14.

29. Robert A. Jordan, " 'Ring Road' Plans Uncertain, Group Assured by Adams," *New Haven Register*, January 19, 1968, p. 1.

30. "Giaimo Requested to Open Study of Renewal Agency," *New Haven Journal-Courier*, January 30, 1968, p. 1.

31. William J. Jecusco, "CCC Demands Abolition of Redevelopment Agency," *New Haven Journal-Courier*, April 1, 1968, p. 1.

32. "State Street Plan Gets New Airing," *New Haven Journal-Courier*, March 4, 1968, p. 4.

33. "Rees Charges Agency Staff 'Fixing' Road," *New Haven Journal-Courier*, March 22, 1968, p. 6.

34. Michael A. McConnell, Pres. Dwight Area Association, letter to Mayor Richard C. Lee, September 20, 1968, Richard C. Lee Papers, Manuscripts and Archives, Yale University Library, box 96, folder 1717.

35. American Independent Movement (AIM), "A Background Paper on Rt. 34, Presented to the Connecticut State Highway Department," p. 3, unpublished document, personal files of David Dickson, on loan to the author.

36. Ibid., p. 1.

37. Reverend Siggins of Christian Community Action, quoted in *Modern Times*, Vol. 1, No. 13 (November 15, 1970): 5.

38. Harriet Cohen, interview by the author, February 19, 2005, New York.

39. In February of 1970, the Cooper Square Committee succeeded in pushing the board of estimate to vote on its Alternate Plan, and it was adopted as the city's official plan for the Cooper Square area. See "About," Cooper Square Committee, http://www.coopersquare.org/about.html (accessed December 18, 2006).

40. Harriet Johnson (Cohen), "Rt. 34: The Official Nonsense," *AIM Newsletter* (March 1, 1969): 11.

41. John Bancroft, "An Expert Speaks," *AIM Newsletter* (January 15, 1969): 5.

42. AIM, "A Background Paper," p. 2.

43. The distinction between "Dwight" and "the Hill" is itself a product of urban renewal. The experience of residents was that of a single community, as pedestrian crossings between the two areas were common, and families often lived in both. It was only through the identities imposed by these RA "project areas" that the distinction between the two neighborhoods became so strictly drawn, and the plan for a highway between the two solidified the city's intention of severing the connections between them.

44. Johnson (Cohen), "Rt. 34," p. 11.

45. M. L. McAviney, letter to Mayor Richard C. Lee, April 4, 1969, Richard C. Lee Papers, Manuscripts and Archives, Yale University Library, box 103, folder 1846.

46. AIM, "Background Paper, p. 2.

47. "The Race for Mayor," *AIM Newsletter*, special issue (September 7, 1969).

48. AIM, "Background Paper," p. 3.

49. Mathew Ruoppolo, Chairman of Redevelopment Agency, letter to New Haven Board of Alderman, copy in personal files of David Dickson, on loan to author.

50. David Dickson, "State Street Renewal: Round Two," *AIM Newsletter* (November 1, 1969): 13.

51. Notes from public hearing, October 23, 1969, personal files of David Dickson, on loan to author.

52. Typed testimony of Harris Stone, AIM Urban Renewal Committee, labeled "Board of Alderman State Street Renewal Plan Public Hearing Thursday, October 23, 1969," personal files of David Dickson, on loan to author.

53. Notes from public hearing, October 23, 1969.

54. Sam Negri, "State Street Hearing: Revival of Garage Plan Assailed," *New Haven Register*, October 24, 1969, p. 3.

55. Howard Abramson, "Renewal Board 'First': Member Knocks Garage," *New Haven Journal-Courier*, November 11, 1969, p. 1.

56. Andrew L. Houlding, "Renewal Unit Okays Garage Plan," *New Haven Journal-Courier*, November 18, 1969, p. 1.

57. "Rogers Explains Reversal in Voting for Garage Plan," *New Haven Register*, November 24, 1969, clipping file, personal files of David Dickson, on loan to author.

58. Insert in *AIM Newsletter*, Vol. 4, No. 20 (November 15, 1969).

59. Personal notes from AIM Urban Renewal Committee meeting, November 24, 1969, Bread and Roses Coffeehouse, personal files of David Dickson, on loan to author.

60. Draft of public statement for Board of Alderman public hearing, November 26, 1969, David Dickson personal files, on loan to author.

61. AIM Urban Renewal Committee, press release, November 26, 1969, personal files of David Dickson, on loan to author.

62. AIM Environment Committee, "The Redevelopment Game," *AIM Newsletter*, Vol. 4, No. 23 (December 15, 1969): 3; Sam Negri, "Garage Plan is Approved by Aldermen," *New Haven Register*, December 24, 1969, p.1.

63. "Aldermanic Session Lists Major Issues," *New Haven Register*, December 22, 1969, clipping file, personal files of David Dickson, on loan to author.

64. "Lee Calls 2 Special Aldermanic Sessions—Garage Plan to Be Pushed," *New Haven Register*, December 10, 1969, clipping file, personal files of David Dickson, on loan to author.

65. People Against the Garage, "Rally Against the State Street Garage," flier, personal files of David Dickson, on loan to author.

66. "Group Organized to Fight Garage: Rally Is Planned," unlabeled newspaper clipping, January 14, 1970, clipping file, personal files of David Dickson, on loan to author.

67. People Against the Garage, "Rally."

68. Insert in *AIM Newsletter*, Vol. 5, No. 1 (January 15, 1970).

69. "Bodies on the Line," *AIM Newsletter*, Vol. 5, No. 2 (February 1, 1970): 3.

70. Damian Formisano, "300 Protest State Street Garage," *New Haven Register*, January 25, 1970, p. 13B.

71. "One Need But Look to See the Need for State Street Garage," editorial, *New Haven Register*, January 25, 1970.

72. In the days that followed, the conflicting headlines in the city's two daily papers reflected the continuing confusion: one read "Garage Plan Approval Not Altered by Board" while the other read "State St. Plan Stalled: New Aldermanic Vote Will Delay Garage." Both carried an account of the same meeting, and neither could conclusively tell State Street's residents and business owners if they were staying or going.

73. Stone, *Workbook*, p. 50.

74. NRHA, *State Street Redevelopment and Renewal Plan*, adopted amendments, December 23, 1969, p. 31.

75. Christopher Lydon, "Battle over Highway Policy Intensifies," *New York Times*, April 4, 1971, p. A24.

76. "Unbalanced Budget Priorities," *New York Times*, editorial, January 16, 1969, p. 40.

77. Richard Wolff interview.

78. "Bread and Roses Hit by Night Gunman," *Modern Times*, Vol. 1, No. 16 (December 15–31, 1970): 2.

CHAPTER 7

1. Larry S. Solomon. *Roots of Justice: Stories of Organizing in Communities of Color* (New York: Jossey-Bass, 1998). See also *The Fall of the I-Hotel*, documentary film , directed by Curtis Choy, Chonk Moonhunter Productions, (1983).

2. Manuel Castells, *The City and the Grassroots: A Cross-Cultural Theory of Urban Social Movements* (Berkeley: University of California Press, 1983), p. 67.

3. Some would argue that center is finally taking shape today, as upscale coffee shops, restaurants, and luxury apartments reoccupy the long-vacant buildings along Chapel, Crown, Temple, and College streets. The rapid gentrification of this area over the past few years has happened quietly and without resistance, primarily since the necessary evictions and dislocations happened a generation ago.

4. Art Fleischner, "City Scatters Strand Community," *Modern Times*, Vol. 1, No. 5 (July 1, 1970): 4.

5. Ibid.

6. Paul Groth, *Living Downtown: The History of Residential Hotels in the United States* (Berkeley: University of California Press, 1994), p. 126.

7. "Shortage of Hotel Rooms Hits City; No Relief in Sight, Say Managers," *New Haven Register*, December 17, 1945, New Haven Free Public Library, Local History Clipping File.

8. Douglas Rae et al., "Hotels, New Haven 1913–Present, by Address and Continuation," Historical New Haven Digital Collection, http://www.library.yale.edu/newhavenhistory/documentlist.html (accessed December 3, 2006).

9. Walter Dudar, "Glittering New Hotel Opens," *New Haven Register*, October 1, 1966.

10. "Park Plaza Brightens New Downtown," *New Haven Register*, October 3, 1966.

11. Groth, *Living Downtown*, p. 54.

12. Full-page advertisement for Park Plaza Hotel, *New Haven Register*, October 11, 1966.

13. Alexander R. Hammer, "Hotels Get Role in City Renewal," *New York Times*, May 21, 1961, p. F9.

14. "Forward Look in Connecticut," *Time*, June 24, 1957, p. 28.

15. John H. Fenton, "Boston Survives a Renewal Crisis," *New York Times*, March 5, 1961, p. 74.

16. Howard Gillette, quoted in Robert Halpern, *Rebuilding the City: A History of Neighborhood Initiatives to Address Poverty in the United States* (New York: Columbia University Press, 1995), p. 67.

17. Mayor Richard C. Lee, speech to the New Haven Board of Aldermen, November 11, 1960, quoted in Fred Powledge, *Model City: A Test of American Liberalism; One Town's Efforts to Rebuild Itself* (New York: Simon & Schuster, 1970), p. 42.

18. Art Fleischner and Liz Rose, "The Strand Community," *AIM Newsletter*, Vol. 4, No. 9 (May 1, 1969): 5.

19. Ibid., p. 6.

20. Groth, *Living Downtown*, p. 7.

21. Ibid., p. 295. See also: Mandi Isaacs Jackson, "New Haven's Trade Union Plaza: 'For Working People, By Working People,'" in *Race and Labor Matters in the New U.S. Economy*, ed. Joseph Wilson and Immanuel Ness (New York: Rowman & Littlefield, 2006).

22. Fleischner and Rose, "The Strand Community," p. 5.

23. AIM Urban Renewal Committee, "Save State Street," *AIM Newsletter*, Vol. 2, No. 8 (November 25, 1967): 2; Karin Cook and Peter Rose, "Citizens' Petition Brings Action, *AIM Newsletter*, Vol. 2, No. 8 (November 25, 1967): 4.

24. Harris Stone, *Monuments and Main Streets: Messages from Architecture* (New York: Monthly Review Press, 1984), p. 235.

25. Joan Stone, "Dance & Politics," *AIM Newsletter*, Vol. 4, No. 6 (March 17, 1969): 8.

26. Joan Stone, interview by the author, July 18, 2005. *Clear a Space and I'll Dance* is also the title of one of Joan Stone's pieces, a dance about Rosa Luxemburg.

27. Stone, *Monuments and Main Streets*, p. 236.

28. Stone, "Dance & Politics," p. 9.

29. Stone interview.

30. Fleischner and Rose, "The Strand Community," p. 7.

31. AIM Urban Renewal Committee, "Save State Street," p. 2.

32. Fleischner and Rose, "The Strand Community," p.6.

33. Ibid., p. 6.

34. New Haven Redevelopment Agency (NHRA), *New Haven: New England's Newest City—Pulling Power, Buying Power, Growing Power*, 1960, New Haven Free Public Library, Local History Room.

35. A recent study by the Brookings Institution reveals that, for the first time in history, more poor people live in America's suburbs than in all of American cities combined. Since 2000, suburban poverty nationwide has increased—in some areas by as much as 33 percent. See Eyal Press, "The New Suburban Poverty," *The Nation*, April 23, 2007, http://www.thenation.com/doc/20070423/press (accessed May 29, 2007). According to the Brookings study, the reason for this reversal in the conventional migration narrative (from the poverty of the city to the affluence of the suburbs) is the confluence of gentrification, which raises urban housing costs out of reach of the poor, and the growing pool of low-wage jobs in suburban areas. New immigrants are chief among these new poor suburbanites, filling landscaping, child-care, domestic, retail, and other service jobs for very low pay in the birthplace

of American affluence. See David Brooks, *On Paradise Drive: How We Live Now (and Always Have) in the Future Tense* (New York: Simon & Schuster, 2004). For the few scattered units of rental housing that exist in suburban areas, rents are lower than those in the city, but affordable housing is scarce. "The suburbs were created, after all, precisely to erect spatial barriers between rich and poor," wrote *The Nation*'s Eyal Press. "This is surely part of the reason new ones keep springing up in ever more remote areas, away from the crime and squalor (read: poor brown and black folk) in urban locales." The suburban poor usually lack public transportation, social services, and organized communities.

36. Don Mitchell, *The Right to the City: Social Justice and the Fight for Public Space* (New York: Guilford Press, 2003), p. 138.

37. "How Area's New Motel Rooms Would Look as a Hotel," *New Haven Register*, April 23, 1962, p. 36.

38. Walter Dudar, "Economic Loss in the Millions Here," *New Haven Register*, August 22, 1967, p. 1.

39. Charles J. Hines, "Arrests Mount in City Disorders, Lee, Police Meeting on Violence, Trouble Continues After Third Night," *New Haven Register*, August 22, 1967, p. 1.

40. Eric Hobsbawm, *Revolutionaries: Contemporary Essays* (New York: Pantheon Books, 1973).

41. Groth, *Living Downtown*, p. 194.

42. New Haven Redevelopment Agency, *Dixwell Redevelopment and Renewal Plan*, published jointly by the Redevelopment Agency, the Office of the Mayor, New Haven City Plan Commission, and the Citizens' Action Commission, 1960, New Haven Free Public Library, Local History Room.

43. Douglas Rae, *City: Urbanism and its End* (New Haven: Yale University Press, 2003), p. 345.

44. Virginia Blaisdell, "Strand Sees Its Final Hour," *Modern Times*, Vol. 1. No. 14 (November 15, 1970): 7.

45. Harris Stone, *Workbook of an Unsuccessful Architect* (New York: Monthly Review Press, 1974), p. 29.

46. Ibid., p. 31.

47. Adele Grady, letter to Mayor Lee, March 17, 1969, Richard C. Lee Papers, Manuscripts and Archives, Yale University Library, box 103, folder 1063.

48. Trade Union Cooperative of New Haven and Federal Housing Administration, *Model Form of Information Bulletin*, February 28, 1969, p. 3, unpublished document, New Haven Free Public Library, Local History Room.

49. TUP Tenants' Council, Families of 65 Dwight Street: Commemorative Booklet, unpublished document (2002).

50. Ibid.

51. Ibid.

52. Jeanne Bay, letter to Mayor Richard Lee, August 15, 1969, Edward J. Logue Papers, Manuscripts and Archives, Yale University Library, box 103, folder 1863.

53. In a 2002 feature on the fight for affordable housing in New Haven, *Advocate* reporter Paul Bass described what happened to TUP in 1986. "The unions ran out of money. The government took control of it and turned it over to a private owner, who shortened the name to Union Plaza," Bass explained. "Blue collar families stayed there. They still paid rents they could afford. Government money made up the

rest." In other words, when the gap between tenants' income and the cost of maintaining the cooperative became too great, and when the project's sponsor—the city's labor unions—became too weak, the project fell into disrepair and eventually into private ownership. Paul Bass, "The Fight for Union Plaza, and for a Home in the 'Livable City,'" *New Haven Advocate*, August 8, 2002.

54. Ibid., p. 17.

55. For a more complete account of the case of TUP, see Jackson, "Trade Union Plaza," p. 125.

56. Bass, "The Fight for Union Plaza," p. 17.

57. Gordon Lafer, "Land and Labor in the Post-Industrial University Town: Remaking Social Geography," *Political Geography* 22 (2003): 114.

CONCLUSION

1. Allan Appel, "Hill to Howard Ave. Builders: Talk to Us!" *New Haven Independent*, June 21, 2007, http://www.newhavenindependent.org/archives/2007/06/hill _to_interco.php (accessed June 26, 2007).

2. John Wilhelm, interview by the author, January 28, 2006, Guilford, CT.

3. For more information on CBAs and community-labor alliances, see David B. Reynolds, *Partnering for Change: Unions and Community Groups Build Coalitions for Economic Justice* (Armonk, NY: M.E. Sharpe, 2004). For a more detailed account of CCNE, FHUE, and the 1996 and 2003 New Haven campaigns, see Chris Rhomberg and Louise Simmons, "Race, Labor, and Urban Community: Negotiating a 'New Social Contract' in New Haven," in *Race and Labor Matters in the New U.S. Economy*, ed. Joseph Wilson and Immanuel Ness (New York: Rowman & Littlefield, 2006), pp. 145–164; and Sumanth Gopinath, "Breaking Down the Ivory Tower: The University in the Creation of Another World," Paper presented at the World Social Forum, Porto Alegre, Brazil, January 2005.

4. City of New Haven Public Information Office, John DeStefano, Jr., Mayor, "City, YNH, and Union Announce Cancer Center Agreement," press release, March 22, 2006. On YNHH's violation of the fair election clause, see Mary E. O'Leary, "Mayor Rips into Y-NH Hospital," *New Haven Register,* March 11, 2007, http:// www. nhregister.com (accessed June 28, 2007); and "Mistakes Were Made," *New Haven Independent,* March 12, 2007, http://www.newhavenindependent.org (accessed June 28, 2007).

5 See the following press coverage of the CBA and the cancer center: Kim Martineau, "Cancer Center a Go in New Haven," *Hartford Courant,* March 23, 2006; Mary O'Leary, "Deal on Cancer Center: Pact Covers Labor, Traffic, Aid, Housing," *New Haven Register,* March 23, 2006; Paul Bass, "Deal Struck on Cancer Center," *New Haven Independent,* March 22, 2006. See also Yale–New Haven Hospital, "The Planned Cancer Hospital at Yale-New Haven," http://www.ynhh.org/cancer/why_ynhh/cancer_center.html (accessed November 2, 2006).

6. Tess Wheelwright, "They're Skeptical," *New Haven Independent,* February 8, 2006, http://www.newhavenindependent.org (accessed November 2, 2006).

7. Appel, "Hill to Howard Ave. Builders."

8. Linda Greenhouse, "U.S. Justices Uphold Taking Property for Development," *New York Times,* June 24, 2005.

9. Charlotte Simms, interview by the author, New Haven People's Center, September 23, 2005.

10. I tried. A security guard yelled at me, unmoved by my assertion that I was photographing what *used to* be there. I do have the photograph, and wonder what might have happened if I published it here.

11. Juan Flores, *From Bomba to Hip-Hop: Puerto Rican Culture and Latino Identity* (New York: Columbia University Press, 2000), p. 65.

12. Manuel Castells, *The City and the Grassroots: A Cross-Cultural Theory of Urban Social Movements* (Los Angeles: University of California Press, 1983), p. 3.

13. Lesley Wright and Casey Newton, "Scottsdale's South Mirroring Pricier North: Changes May Force Out Residents," *Arizona Republic*, September 28, 2005, http://www.azcentral.com (accessed June 26, 2007).

14. "Hartford Carries the Heaviest Economic Stress of Any Large City," *Bizdemographics*, February 14, 2005, http://www.bizjournals.com (accessed June 14, 2007).

15. Todd Swanstrom, Colleen Casey, Robert Flack, and Peter Dreier, "Pulling Apart: Economic Segregation Among Suburbs and Central Cities in Major Metropolitan Areas," Brookings Institution, October 2004, http://www.brookings.edu/metro/pubs/20041018_econsegregation.htm (accessed April 1, 2007).

16. David Zahniser, "Welcome to Gentrification City," *LA Weekly*, August 23, 2006, http://www.laweekly.com (accessed May 30, 2007).

17. Glen Ford, "The Politics of Displacement: Will the New New Orleans Be Black?" *Counterpunch*, http://www.counterpunch.org/ford09022005.html (accessed May 28, 2007).

18. "As Police Arrest Public Housing Activists in New Orleans, Federal Officials Try to Silence Leading Attorney for Low-Income Residents," *Democracy Now*, January 31, 2007, http://www.democracynow.org (June 14, 2007).

Works Cited

BOOKS, MAGAZINE ARTICLES, AND JOURNAL ARTICLES

Alexiou, Alice Sparberg. 2006. *Jane Jacobs: Urban Visionary.* New Brunswick, NJ: Rutgers University Press.

Anderson, Martin. 1962. *The Federal Bulldozer: A Critical Analysis of Urban Renewal, 1949–1962.* Cambridge, MA: MIT Press.

Arnstein, Sherry R. 1969. "A Ladder of Citizen Participation." *Journal of the American Institute of Planners* 35, no. 4: 216–24.

Balzer, Richard. 1972. *Street Time.* New York: Grossman.

Barnard, John. 1987. *Walter Reuther and the Rise of the Auto Workers.* Boston: Little, Brown & Co.

Brooks, David. 2004. *On Paradise Drive: How We Live Now (and Always Have) in the Future Tense.* New York: Simon & Schuster.

Brown, Elizabeth Mills. 1976. *New Haven: A Guide to Architecture and Urban Design.* New Haven: Yale University Press.

Buford, Ron. 2003. "Doc Edmonds: 'God Gets You from Strange Angles.'" United Church of Christ. http://www.ucc.org. Accessed December 10, 2006.

Caro, Robert A. 1974. *The Power Broker: Robert Moses and the Fall of New York.* New York: Knopf.

Castells, Manuel. 1983. *The City and the Grassroots: A Cross-Cultural Theory of Urban Social Movements.* Los Angeles: University of California Press.

Chase, Robert T. 1998. "Class Resurrection: The Poor People's Campaign of 1968 and Resurrection City." *Essays in History* 40. http://etext.virginia.edu/journals/EH/. Accessed November 20, 2006.

Cheney, Ruth H., and Peter M. Green. 1968. "Urban Planning and Urban Revolt: A Case Study." *Progressive Architecture* (January): 134–56.

Choy, Curtis. 1983. *The Fall of the I-Hotel* by Curtis Choy.

Cloward, Richard A., and Frances Fox Piven. 1974. *The Politics of Turmoil: Essays on Poverty, Race, and the Urban Crisis.* New York: Pantheon Books.

Dahl, Robert A. 1961. *Who Governs? Democracy and Power in an American City.* New Haven: Yale University Press.

Davis, Mike. 1990. *City of Quartz: Excavating the Future in Los Angeles.* New York: Verso.

Dickstein, Morris. 1989. "From the Thirties to the Sixties: The New York World's Fair in its own Time." In Robert Rosenblum, *Remembering the Future: The New York World's Fair from 1939 to 1964.* New York: The Queens Museum.

Domhoff, William G. 1978. *Who Really Rules? New Haven and Community Power Reexamined.* New Brunswick, NJ: Transaction Books.

Edwards, Paul. 1996. *The Closed World: Computers and the Politics of Discourse in Cold War America.* Cambridge, MA: MIT Press.

Fainstein, Susan. 1987. "Local Mobilization and Economic Discontent." In *Restructuring the City.* Ed. M. Smith. New York: Longman.

Fisher, Robert. 1994. *Let the People Decide: Neighborhood Organizing in America.* New York: Twayne Publishers.

Fishman, Robert. 1982. *Urban Utopias in the Twentieth Century: Ebenezer Howard, Frank Lloyd Wright, and Le Corbusier.* Cambridge, MA: MIT Press.

Flores, Juan. 2000. *From Bomba to Hip-Hop: Puerto Rican Culture and Latino Identity.* New York: Columbia University Press.

"Forward Look in Connecticut." 1957. *Time* (June 24): 28.

Gans, Herbert. 1962. *The Urban Villagers: Group and Class in the Lives of Italian-Americans.* New York: Free Press of Glencoe.

Goodman, Robert. 1971. *After the Planners.* New York: Simon & Schuster.

Goodwyn, Lawrence. 1978. *The Populist Moment: A Short History of Agrarian Revolt in America.* New York: Oxford University Press.

Gopinath, Sumanth. 2005. "Breaking Down the Ivory Tower: The University in the Creation of Another World." World Social Forum, Porto Alegre, Brazil.

Groth, Paul. 1994. *Living Downtown: The History of Residential Hotels in the United States.* Berkeley: University of California Press.

Haar, Charles M. 1975. *Between the Ideal and the Reality: A Study of the Fate, Origin, and Legacy of the Model Cities Program.* Boston: Little, Brown & Co.

Halpern, Robert. 1995. *Rebuilding the City: A History of Neighborhood Initiatives to Address Poverty in the United States.* New York: Columbia University Press.

Harrison, Bennett. 1973. "The Participation of Ghetto Residents in the Model Cities Program." *Journal of the American Institute of Planners* 39 (January).

Hobsbawm, Eric. 1973. *Revolutionaries: Contemporary Essays.* New York: Pantheon Books.

Hommann, Mary. 1966. "Symbolic Bells in Dixwell." *Architectural Forum* (July–August).

Jackson, Mandi Isaacs. 2006. "Harlem's Rent Strike and Rat War: Representation, Housing Access, and Tenant Resistance in New York, 1958–1964." *American Studies* (Spring).

Jackson, Mandi Isaacs. 2006. "New Haven's Trade Union Plaza: 'For Working People, By Working People." In *Race and Labor Matters in the New U.S. Economy*. Ed. Joseph Wilson and Immanuel Ness. New York: Rowman & Littlefield.

Jacobs, Jane. 1958. "Downtown Is for People." *Fortune* (April).

Jacobs, Jane. 1961. *The Death and Life of Great American Cities*. New York: Vintage.

Lafer, Gordon. 2003. "Land and Labor in the Post-Industrial University Town: Remaking Social Geography." *Political Geography* 22.

McAdam, Douglas. 1988. *Freedom Summer*. New York: Oxford University Press.

Mitchell, Don. 2003. *The Right to the City: Social Justice and the Fight for Public Space*. New York: Guilford Press.

Miller, William Lee. 1966. *The Fifteenth Ward and the Great Society*. Boston: Houghton Mifflin.

Moynihan, Daniel P. 1969. *Maximum Feasible Misunderstanding: Community Action in the War on Poverty*. New York: Free Press.

Naples, Nancy A., ed. 1998. *Community Activism and Feminist Politics: Organizing Across Race, Class, and Gender*. New York: Routledge.

O'Connor, Thomas H. 1993. *Building a New Boston: Politics and Urban Renewal, 1950–1970*. Boston: Northeastern University Press.

Poslby, Nelson W. 1963. *Community Power and Political Theory*. New Haven: Yale University Press.

Powledge, Fred. 1970. *Model City: A Test of American Liberalism; One Town's Efforts to Rebuild Itself*. New York: Simon & Schuster.

Press, Eyal. 2007. "The New Suburban Poverty." *The Nation* (April 23). http://www.thenation.com/doc/20070423/press. Accessed May 29, 2007.

Price & Lee. 1968–1972. *New Haven City Directory*. New Haven, CT: Price & Lee.

Rae, Douglas. 2003. *City: Urbanism and its End*. New Haven: Yale University Press.

Ralph, James R., Jr. 1993. *Northern Protest: Martin Luther King, Jr., Chicago, and the Civil Rights Movement*. Cambridge, MA: Harvard University Press.

Reynolds, David B. 2004. *Partnering for Change: Unions and Community Groups Build Coalitions for Economic Justice*. Armonk, NY: M. E. Sharpe.

Rhomberg, Chris, and Louise Simmons. 2006. "Race, Labor, and Urban Community: Negotiating a 'New Social Contract' in New Haven." In *Race and Labor Matters in the New U.S. Economy*, Ed. Joseph Wilson and Immanuel Ness. New York: Rowman & Littlefield.

Rubin, Lillian B. 1969. "Maximum Feasible Participation: The Origins, Implications, and Present Status." *Annals of the American Academy of Political and Social Science* 385, no. 1: 14–29.

Schwartz, Joel. 1993. *The New York Approach: Robert Moses, Urban Liberals, and Redevelopment of the Inner City*. Columbus: Ohio State University Press.

Smith, Neil. 1996. *New Urban Frontier—Gentrification and the Revanchist City*. New York: Routledge.

Solomon, Daniel. 2003. *Global City Blues*. Washington, DC: Island Press.

Solomon, Larry S. 1998. *Roots of Justice: Stories of Organizing in Communities of Color*. New York: Jossey-Bass.

Squires, Gregory D., and Charis E. Kubrin. 2006. *Privileged Places: Race, Residence, and the Structure of Opportunity*. Boulder, CO: Lynne Rienner.

Stall, Susan, and Randy Stoecker. 1998. "Community Organizing or Organizing the Community: Gender and the Crafts of Empowerment." *Gender and Society* 12, no. 6 (December): 729–56.

Stone, Harris. 1974. *Workbook of an Unsuccessful Architect*. New York: Monthly Review Press.

Stone, Harris. 1984. *Monuments and Main Streets: Messages from Architecture*. New York: Monthly Review Press.

Stott, William. 1973. *Documentary Tradition and Thirties America*. New York: Oxford University Press.

Sugrue, Thomas J. 1996. *Origins of the Urban Crisis: Race and Inequality in Postwar Detroit*. Princeton, NJ: Princeton University Press.

Talbot, Allan R. 1967. *The Mayor's Game: Richard Lee of New Haven and the Politics of Change*. New York: Harper & Row.

Tamarin, Henry. 1968. "Pacification of Our Cities." *AIM Newsletter* 2, no. 12 (March 5): 5.

"Troubled and Troublesome Families." 1957. *Journal of Housing* (April).

Williams, Yohuru. 2000. *Black Politics / White Power: Civil Rights, Black Power, and the Black Panthers in New Haven*. St. James, NY: Brandywine Press.

Wilson, James Q., ed. 1968. *The Metropolitan Enigma: Inquiries into the Nature and Dimensions of America's Urban Crisis*. Cambridge, MA: Harvard University Press.

Zinn, Howard. 1980. *A People's History of the United States*. New York: Harper & Row.

NEWSPAPERS AND ORGANIZATIONAL NEWSLETTERS

American Independent Movement (AIM). 1967–1971. *AIM Newsletter*. New Haven, CT.

Arizona Republic. Phoenix, AZ.

Connecticut Sunday Herald. Hartford, CT.

Democracy Now. Democracynow.org. New York.

Hartford Courant. Hartford, CT.

Hartford Times. Hartford, CT.

Hill Neighborhood Union. 1965. *Hill Union News*. New Haven, CT.

LA Weekly. Los Angeles, CA.

Modern Times. 1971. New Haven, CT.

New Haven Advocate. New Haven, CT.

New Haven Independent. New Haven, CT.

New Haven Journal-Courier. New Haven, CT.

New Haven Register. New Haven, CT.

New York Times. New York.

Open Gate News. New Haven, CT.

Students for a Democratic Society. 1964–1964. *ERAP Newsletter*. New Haven, CT.

INTERVIEWS

Adams, Nina. Interview by the author. New Haven, CT. March 10, 2005.

Cohen, Harriet. Interview by the author. New York. February 19, 2005.

Cook, Robert. Interview by the author. Worthington, MA. July 16, 2005.

Gilbertson, Betsy. Interview by the author. Guilford, CT. January 28, 2006.

Harris, Fred. Recorded interview by Yohuru Williams. April 11, 1999.

Stone, Joan. Interview by the author. New Haven, CT. July 18, 2005.

Twyman, Charles. Interview by Tamar Rubin. March 26, 2004. New Haven Oral History Project. Transcript lent to author by curator, "Life in the Model City." Online exhibit at http://www.yale.edu/nhohp/modelcity.

Wilhelm, John. Interview by the author. Guilford, CT. January 28, 2006.

Wolff, Richard. Interview by the author. New York. November 11, 2004.

ARCHIVES, UNPUBLISHED DOCUMENTS, AND PAPERS

American Independent Movement. 1970. *A Background Paper on Rt. 34, Presented to the Connecticut State Highway Department*. Unpublished document. Personal files of David Dickson. On loan to the author.

Cook, Robert. 1964–1966. Personal files. On loan to the author.

Dickson, David. 1968–1971. Personal files. On loan to the author.

International Business Machines Corporation (IBM). 1967. *Concepts of an Urban Management Information System: A Report to the City of New Haven, Connecticut*. N.d. New Haven Free Public Library, Local History Room.

Richard Charles Lee Papers. Manuscripts and Archives, Yale University Library.

Edward J. Logue Papers. Manuscripts and Archives, Yale University Library.

New Haven Free Public Library, Local History Room, Clipping Files: "City Planning," "Hotels," "Housing," "New Haven Negroes."

Rae, Douglas, et al. "Hotels, New Haven 1913–Present, by Address and Continuation." Historical New Haven Digital Collection. http://www.library.yale.edu/newhavenhistory/documentlist.html. Accessed December 3, 2006.

Rae, Douglas, et al. "Urban Renewal Figures New Haven, 1950s–1960s," Historical New Haven Digital Collection. Yale University Library. http://www.library.yale.edu/newhavenhistory/documentlist.html. Accessed October 4, 2006.

GOVERNMENT DOCUMENTS AND PUBLICATIONS

Community Progress, Inc. 1962. *Opening Opportunities: New Haven's Comprehensive Program for Community Progress*. New Haven, CT: City of New Haven.

Johnson, President Lyndon B. 1966. "Special Message to the Congress Recommending a Program for Cities and Metropolitan Areas." January 26. American Presidency Project. University of California Santa Barbara. http://www.americanpresidency.org. Accessed December 10, 2006.

National Commission on Urban Problems. 1968. *Hearings Before the National Commission on Urban Problems, May-June 1967*. Vol. 1, *Baltimore, New Haven, Boston, Pittsburgh*. Washington, DC: U.S. Government Printing Office.

New Haven Citizens Action Commission. 1959. *CAC Annual Report and Development Guide of 1959*.

New Haven Democratic Town Committee. 1962. *Promises Made . . . Promises Kept*. New Haven, CT: City of New Haven.

New Haven Redevelopment Agency. 1961. *New Haven Development Guide 1961*. New Haven, CT: City of New Haven.

New Haven Redevelopment Agency. 1962. *Dixwell Renewal News* 1, No. 1 (December).

New Haven Redevelopment Agency. 1967. *Dixwell Redevelopment and Renewal Plan* (August).

New Haven Redevelopment Agency. 1968. *State Street Redevelopment and Renewal Plan.* April 15. New Haven, CT: City of New Haven.

Office of Equal Opportunity. 1964. *The War on Poverty: A Hometown Fight.*

State of Connecticut. 1959. *General Statutes of Connecticut.* Bristol, CT: Hildreth Press.

U.S. Census Bureau. 1940. Table H-1. *Occupancy and Structural Characteristics of Housing Units by Census Tract.* Washington, DC: U.S. Government Printing Office.

U.S. Census of Population and Housing. 1960. *Summary Population and Housing Characteristics: Connecticut.* Washington, DC: U.S. Government Printing Office.

Index

Note: *Page numbers in italics indicate illustrations.*

Mandy Issacs Jackson is a writer and researcher who teaches urban history and social movements. She received her Ph.D. in American Studies from Yale University.